WALKING WITH A LIMP

Walking
with a Limp

Chasing the Truth
a Day at a Time

NEB HAYDEN

McFarland Publishing

Walking with a Limp: Chasing the Truth a Day at a Time
© 2019 Neb Hayden
All rights reserved
ISBN-13: 978-164669440-2
McFarland Publishing, North Carolina

TO SUSAN

*whose encouragement and persistence energized me to
write from my heart and express
my most deeply held beliefs.*

*Your confidence in me never wavered.
Your determination to chase the truth with me, shoulder
to shoulder, has made all the difference.*

Contents

*The author suggests that you pause wherever you are reading
two weeks before Christmas and Easter and read these daily
devotionals leading up to these cherished events.*

With Appreciation

Were it not for the wonderful folks listed below, I would have very little to say in this book. The substance of *Walking with a Limp* emerged over many years of exposure to some of God's most faithful people. There have been many, but the following people have made a very significant deposit in my life—

Josh, **Jonathan**, and **David**, my three amazing sons that I love more than life and who have taught their dad time and time again since they were little boys.

Mal McSwain, the Young Life Area Director who drew me in as a rebellious teenager and, by his persistent friendship, "won the right to be heard." God started my journey through Mal's influence and tenacity for the past fifty-five years.

Doug Coe, a man unlike any I have ever known, who mentored me and taught me to think differently and to embrace and love everything and everyone God loves.

Dick Halverson, former Chaplain of the United States Senate, with whom I met weekly for many years. His love for the Scriptures and profound teaching motivated my love for them as well.

Tom Skinner, a prolific thinker and speaker who fought his way from Harlem to have a prophetic voice in this country. Tom showed me the radical Jesus who loved the poor and marginalized and to always ask the hard questions.

Nell Watt, a woman everyone calls "Elvis," has been like a second mother to me since my sophomore year in college. Her constant encouragement, counsel, and extravagant love have saved my life many times over.

There have been many more—like John Bradford, Tom Harris, Jim Hiskey, Kent Hoteling, John Staggers, Steve Sloan, Bill Milliken, and so many others—who have paved the way for these truths that have developed in me over many years. My thanks to all of you.

Introduction

If you are a person who seldom struggles and finds living by faith a relatively easy lifestyle, this book is not for you. On the other hand, if you have wrestled with God and have come away with a limp, these daily biblical reflections will challenge and encourage you. They may cause you to think differently about matters you may have taken for granted. Each day's thoughts are practical, down to earth principles written in a conversational and personal manner from my heart to yours. They will take three minutes to read but will impact your day and your journey ahead. These daily expressions of truth are for those who have grown weary of mindless platitudes and clichés of faith that hold us hostage, rather than set us free. Maybe you have wrestled with God, as Jacob did, and are beginning to realize that in this battle you only win by losing. Your limp is evidence of spiritual growth and serves as a constant reminder of who you are and who He is.

If you desire to walk with God as His friend and companion but have no interest in becoming religious, this book has got your name on it. These short, powerful and practical daily insights are my attempt to give away the most important principles I have learned over many years of trying to help men and women grow and thrive in their walk with God. They are my attempt to separate the Jesus of the Scriptures from the *Christianity* the religious have created. Unscrambling truth from myth provides a glimpse of the adventure of experiencing and personalizing the grace of God.

I have spent over forty-five years teaching, discipling and walking alongside people from every kind of background. I have had the privilege to know and spend time with some of the finest mentors and teachers and have learned much by sitting at their feet. I have labored alongside men and women whose character, during the unguarded moments when there was no one around to impress, always remains consistent. They "walk with a limp."

This is not a typical daily devotional of only comforting thoughts. It is more of a wake-up call that addresses everyday issues with which we all struggle. It is designed to nudge your mind and heart into gear; to encourage and challenge those of us who sometimes stumble along the path of faith but continue onward. Some of these daily missives will fly in the face of the cultural rhetoric to which we have all been exposed. I have sought to be vulnerable and honest in my own journey and to neither romanticize an authentic walk of faith nor pepper it with legalism.

My hope is that you will be motivated toward further exploration of the majesty and adventure of the Scriptures. Most of all, that you will fall hopelessly in love with its Author.

Walking with a Limp

"So Jacob named the place Peniel, for he said, 'I have seen God face to face, yet my life has been preserved.' Now the sun rose upon him as he crossed Peniel and he was limping on his thigh." Genesis 32:30–32

After the Patriarch Abraham died his son Isaac, and his daughter-in-law Rebekah, had two twin boys. Esau was the eldest by mere minutes ahead of Jacob. Esau was the favorite of his father because of his hunting expertise. He was burly and rugged while Jacob, the favorite of Rebekah, was quiet and starkly different from his brother. But Jacob was cunning and manipulative. When Esau was desperately hungry one day, Jacob traded him a bowl of stew in exchange for his birthright as the elder son. The eldest son always received a double portion of the inheritance after the father's death. As Isaac became old and almost completely blind, Jacob tricked him by posing as Esau and receiving the blessing which rightfully belonged to Esau.

Jacob separated himself from Esau, married twice, and years later had an encounter with an angel of God. They wrestled through the night until the break of dawn, and finally, the angel told Jacob to release him. Jacob agreed but demanded that God bless him. The angel gave him a new name. Jacob means rogue, deceiver, cheat. His new name would be *Israel*, meaning *Prince of God*. In the scuffle, Jacob's hip was thrown out of joint and for the rest of his life he walked with a limp, but he lived with a new identity and purpose.

Despite Jacob's unheroic early life, after wrestling with the angel of God, the angel asks him *who he is*. His father had asked him the same question and he lied, claiming he was Esau. This time he responded honestly. "Jacob," he says, *I am a deceiver, a man who plotted and manipulated to get my way.* God forgave Jacob because of his confession and used him as a great leader of the country that still bears his new name, *Israel*.

People wrestle with God every day. Some even believe they can eventually win. But some of us have come to realize that in this wrestling match you can only win by losing. As a reminder of the struggle, Jacob walked with a limp from that day forward. Many of us have had a similar experience. Our *limp* reminds us who we are, who God is, and never to get the two confused. A man or woman who walks with a limp is one who has the potential to be a mighty instrument in the hands of God. Limp on …

Your Time: What's it Worth?

"There is a way that appears to be right, but in the end, it leads to death."
Proverbs 16:25 (NIV)

When I was a few years out of college, I met a man from Washington, D.C., named Doug Coe who would become a lifelong mentor. One of the first things he told me was that the biggest decision I would ever make going forward was the stewardship of my time. How will I spend it? *I can waste it, I can sell it to the highest bidder, or I can give it away.*

Those words marked me for life and have driven my decisions through the years. Many will look back over their life and realize, often too late, that they have *wasted* a precious gift. It may have seemed right at the time but ended badly. If time is our greatest commodity, then wasting it is an extravagance we cannot afford.

Many *sell their skills* and their time to the highest bidder. They envision a lifestyle they crave and then give themselves to the career path which will pay for it. Years later, tired of the treadmill, they become restless and want out, but find nothing that will afford them the lifestyle they have created. They're stuck! Some live productive lives, but many come to the realization that they have sold out.

Then there are some who choose the path of *giving themselves away* to others. It's not an easy path and not one that should be applauded or extolled more than any other. At its core, it is a calling, not simply a choice. It can be realized through *any* profession. It is a way of thinking about life, about people, and things that matter.

Giving yourself away is risky. You will be misunderstood, often resented, and occasionally considered arrogant and prideful. When you focus on the good of others, many will assume that you have a hidden agenda. After all, in today's world, who gives their life away for the good of another?

It is a life that witnesses changes in a human heart, where people go from death to life before your eyes. A light comes on that we never saw there before. It is also a life that witnesses disappointment and often failure. Sometimes that light that shone so brightly begins to dim, and one for whom you had such high hopes is sucked away by the lure of the world. But I have come to believe that failure has a far greater value than becoming successful in all the things that don't matter.

Serving When it's Inconvenient

"God is not unjust; he will not forget your work and the love you have shown him as you have helped his people and continue to help them." Hebrews 6:10 (NIV)

Jesus came to serve ... we all know this, but like so many important things, it can become a cliché. Seldom do we define authentic servant leadership. What does it look like, other than offering to help rake the neighbor's leaves, taking dinner to someone who is ill, or trying to help someone find a job? These random acts of kindness are wonderful, and I have seen and been the recipient of many over the years. What I have learned about myself is that it easy to do many of those things when I have time, but I have failed miserably when I am rushed or when it is inconvenient.

Many years ago, I read a book that had a great impact on me. It was written by a businessman who loved God, was extremely talented, but who chose *not* to go into a full-time ministry. He believed he could better serve God in the grocery business than in being a minister. The book was called "The Velvet-Covered Brick" by Howard Butt. His father started what would become the largest grocery store chain in Texas, with 80,000 employees. "Sure," you might say. "Why wouldn't he feel *led* to serve God as a multimillionaire rather than as a ministry guy living month to month?" But until his death several years ago, Howard Butt was possibly the most prolific layman who ever set foot on this planet.

I heard he was coming to speak at a conference in Chicago. I wanted to go, but I couldn't afford the fee. So I called the sponsoring organization and asked if I could pay my way for the weekend by working in some manner. They agreed, and I was assigned to be a dishwasher. Mr. Butt was to speak Saturday night and Sunday morning, and I was excited to hear him. I was only able to get a seat in the back on Friday night and Saturday morning for the sessions because of all the dirty dishes, so I was determined to get a good seat Saturday night. After dinner, I washed dishes like a man possessed, and another worker strapped on an apron and pitched in. We washed dishes and talked until I mentioned how anxious I was to get a good seat. As the time drew near, he suggested I run on to the conference hall and he would finish up. I thanked him, rushed away and got a seat near the front. Soon the master of ceremonies introduced Howard Butt. A thunderous ovation followed, and to my chagrin, the man who had willingly stayed to wash dishes so I could get a good seat stepped to the microphone.

Self-Disappointment

"The Lord makes firm the steps of the one who delights in him; though he may stumble, he will not fall, for the Lord upholds him with his hand."
Psalm 37:23–24 (NIV)

Have you ever been thoroughly disgusted with yourself? Do you remorsefully remember something you said in haste? Do you shudder thinking of how you acted in the heat of the moment and regret it deeply? I can't imagine anyone who hasn't felt that kind of self-disappointment many times over. I sure have. I expect more of myself than that. I feel that I am better than that, and I just can't figure out *what got into me.*

I remember confessing something to my good friend, Bob Warren, a while back. I had made a fool of myself as in a regrettable confrontation with a surly florist who had been rude to my wife. He smiled lovingly but firmly and said, *"Neb, if you're disappointed in yourself, it means you think you could have done it right in the first place."* He asked me if I spoke first or reacted first. The answer was obvious; it was all about my emotions and my defense of my wife. James says a believer should be quick to listen, slow to speak, and slow to anger.[1]

Bob went on to say that God is never surprised when we mess up. He knows that being in control is a harsh mistress and when the heat is on, that desire to win can overrule that which we believe. When you allow God to control your emotions, a thoughtful response and a calm manner will say volumes about the person you are and can actually temper the response of the other person.

My friend's counsel has stuck with me over the years and I am grateful for it. If you are surprised at your actions you really don't understand yourself as well as you think. Other than God's Spirit working through us, we are capable of doing and saying almost anything. I still regret the brain-dead things I sometimes do and say, but I'm not surprised. They remind me to back off, take a deep breath, and allow God to operate.

If I could shape my own life and destiny, I wouldn't need Jesus. I would just need a rule book and a road map. That is what the Pharisees of Jesus' day thought. They knew the rules, and it was up to them to follow those rules. Every religion is built on that premise; they strive to perform and please God, but never know until they die if they measured up. But by a simple act of trust, anyone can know God and know their destiny right now!

---

[1] James 1:19–20

Are You Fun to Be With?

"When he had said these things, he knelt down and prayed with them all. And they began to weep aloud and embraced Paul, and repeatedly kissed him."
Acts 20:36–38

We often focus so much on the divinity of Jesus that His humanity gets lost in the shuffle. Yet, it is His humanity that makes Him so approachable. It is the humanness of Jesus that first attracted me as a teenager. I learned that He was tempted "in all things;"[1] He became angry at religious frauds,[2] was moved to tears over Israel's unbelief,[3] became frustrated by His disciple's thickness,[4] and was elated when He saw them growing in faith.[5] These were emotions I could identify with. As my faith began to come alive, I couldn't read the gospels without feeling certain that Jesus was a fun person to be with.

These twelve young would-be disciples left everything to follow this fascinating Rabbi because they were captivated by His magnetism, likability, and even playfulness. If you don't *like* someone, the possibility of being enticed to join them on a virtual three-year camping trip is inconceivable. When a rabbi called a Jewish boy to "follow" Him, it literally meant, *"I see in you the potential to be like me."* He might want to learn what the rabbi knows, but the thought of an extended road trip with someone you did not enjoy being with would be unthinkable.

The twelve were mesmerized by His intimacy with God and His "new" perspective on faith and grace. But something about His humanness and His warm, genial manner captured their imagination. It caused them to want to be like this man who could turn a simple walk between cities into an adventure. The same is true of Paul. The people's affection for him was undeniable.

There are many wise, articulate teachers, preachers, and spiritual leaders in the world. Many have great insight and excellent communication skills. How many are fun to be with? I have had the opportunity to be around some of those people when the lights dim and the microphones are off, and there are few with whom I would enjoy being with on a road trip. People follow people to Christ. If you like being around someone, their knowledge alone will not be what brings you back time and again. You will always wonder why the God of whom they speak so profoundly hasn't made them more likable.

When you fall in love with Jesus, you begin to love everything He loves as well. Ask God to make you into the kind of person who is fun to be with, and when the people come allow them to see the affable, likable, vulnerable Christ who resides in you.

---

[1]Heb. 4:15   [2]Matt. 23:33   [3]Luke 19:41   [4]Mark 9:40–41   [5]Luke 10:21

The Character of Greatness

"Truly I say to you, among those born of women there has not arisen anyone greater than John the Baptist!" Matthew 11:11

When we think of the heroes of the Bible we generally think of people like Moses, Abraham, David, the Apostle Paul, and Mary the mother of Jesus. Seldom do people mention John the Baptist. He seems to be taken for granted for some reason, and yet Jesus said that John was the greatest man ever born of women.[1] John was the last and greatest of all the Old Testament prophets.

A look at his character will explain why Jesus would make such an astounding statement and will challenge us in the process. John was born to Zacharias and Elizabeth, parents who were elderly, and had given up on ever having a child. John is the "Dayspring" or "Morning Star" that announces a new day.[2] John, or Yohanan in Hebrew, means "God is gracious;" He will introduce the "Son of Righteousness" to the world, and the entrance of *grace* into the human equation.[3] He was the *herald* who began his ministry in the desert and people came from everywhere. Why? Five hundred years earlier Isaiah had said the Messiah would first appear in the wilderness of the desert.[4]

As the news spread the Jewish Sanhedrin began an investigation to determine if John posed a threat to their power base. The educated thought John was an ignorant savage. Nothing could be further from the truth. John was intelligent, well-spoken, and extremely focused. The Pharisees came pretending to be interested in his message of repentance, but John would not be intimidated. He was unafraid of these people. They resented him because he took the spotlight away from them and because he had Jewish credentials but was not one of them. They were the establishment: prestige conscious, wed to their traditions, and regimented by rules. John was unpretentious and unfazed by symbols of success. He was authentic and spoke from the heart ... a free spirit who understood liberty and grace. The Jewish leaders just couldn't handle it!

The most important thing we can learn from this man is humility. John's life shouts, "It's not about me ... it's about Him!" He was beloved by the people and had his own disciples, yet he gladly turned them over to Jesus. One of the great statements of all time was about His relationship with this One whom he preceded: "He must increase, but I must decrease."[5] John was truly the greatest! He stands as a symbol of true leadership and a rebuke to those who seek leadership out of pride and arrogance.

---

[1]Matt. 11:11 [2]Luke 1:78 [3]Mal. 4:2 [4]Isa. 40:3 [5]John 3:30

Measuring Value

"But the Lord said to Samuel, 'Do not consider his appearance or his height . . .
The Lord does not look at the things people look at. People look at the outward
appearance, but the Lord looks at the heart.'" 1 Samuel 16:7 (NIV)

We measure everything! Who is the best receiver, best golfer, smartest in the class, most successful business-person? Almost everything in our lives is measured so we can try to validate ourselves. After a lifetime of consider-ing our worth, as well as the worth of others, by these measurable results is it any wonder why we feel such stress and instability? If what I do, or what I produce in life defines me, then I am on a treadmill where my only possi-bility of contentment is to run faster than you so I can get a better rating. If what I do is who I am, peace and con-tentment are out the window. If I lack internal harmony, everyone I know better clear the deck because I will be like a time bomb that can take down every relationship around me.

Consider the short three-plus years Jesus had to train the twelve to lead this great revolution of love to the world. What characteristics would you list as the three most important that he wanted to develop in them? Whatever three you list will all have one thing in common; they cannot be measured. Someone says, "Betty is a real woman of prayer." I'll take your word for it, but how do you know that? Is it based on how long she prays, how fervent she sounds when she prays, or how many "yes" answers she gets? "Ben loves God more than anyone I know," I'm glad that encourages you, but how in the world can anyone know that ... even Ben? How do you measure matters of the heart? Why make Betty and Ben the standard? Assessing their prayer life and love of God can never be anything but subjective.

Maybe one reason God made the purpose of life to love Him, instead of doing things for Him, is that you can't measure who is in the lead. You can't keep any statistics to one-up each other. I believe the reason we go for the tangible evidence of spirituality is because of a deep sense of insecurity. We have been taught to compete and to gain our spiritual worth based on measurable results. We are desperate to know how we're doing ... how we match up against the pack. I can think of nothing that could incapacitate a believer more. It's not like the old joke about the bear chasing both of us and I just have to outrun you rather than the bear! Jesus never pitted one disciple against another. When they argued about who was the greatest among them, he said the one who is the servant of all. How will they mea-sure that?

DAY 8
The Work of God

"Then they said to Him, 'What must we do to be doing the works of God?' Jesus answered them, 'This is the work of God, that you believe in Him whom He has sent.'" John 6:28–29 (ESV)

When I was first asked that question as a young man, I gave answers, not unlike hundreds of people to whom I have asked the same question over the years. The word "work" evokes blood, sweat, and tears. It conjures up images of strenuous exertion, diligent struggle, and breathless attention to performance in doing good. *Work* in any culture means, "get busy and do something."

The context of the statement is just after Jesus feeds the five thousand. The multitudes think they have hit the mother lode in terms of social welfare. They like Him because of His miracles, and not because of who He is. They believe He is from God and naturally want to know what actions they can take to get on board so that the free food will keep coming. Yet, to their surprise, Jesus tells them that the work of God is *to believe in the One who God has sent.* In other words, running errands for God, coming home exhausted and bloody after a grueling day of working on His behalf, is to miss the whole point.

That which we refer to as the *Protestant Work Ethic* causes much confusion when we hear the words "work ethic." It is defined as *the view that a person's duty is to achieve success through hard work and thrift, such success being a sign that one is saved.*

Baloney! Salvation is by faith and faith alone. Our lifestyle, and the changes that come from our faith, simply validate that dependence on God. We're not talking about being passive. Walking with God and trusting Him is the hardest work you will ever do. Let's say, you have a sixteen-year-old; he or she is out with friends driving around on Saturday night. You know what kind of morons are out there driving the same highways. Curfew time comes and goes, and your frantic calls to her cell phone go unanswered. Trusting God for your child's protection is the hardest work you will ever encounter. There is nothing passive about it.

Why is *faith* the "work of God?" It is the essence of everything! It is something we can't brag about, prove to others that we did, or take credit for. You can never say that you have more faith than someone else because you can never know. No one will ever introduce you as a man or woman who trusts God. They can say the words, but they have absolutely no idea if you do or don't. They could just as easily say, "He's the luckiest guy I know." Only God knows, and that's the way He wants to keep it. So, go out today and do the *work!* Trust the One who God sent!

Prepared to Stay . . . Prepared to Go

"Be dressed in readiness and keep your lamps lit. Be like men who are waiting for their master when he returns from the wedding feast, so that they may immediately open the door to him when he comes and knocks." Luke 12:35–38

A study done years ago found that people's greatest fear is public speaking. Death was number two. As Jerry Seinfeld famously said, "That means that at a funeral you would rather be in the casket than giving the eulogy." You never invite people over to your house for a steak dinner and a conversation about death. However, Doug Holladay, a friend of mine in D.C., teaches a class at Georgetown University where he has his students write their own obituary. It forces them to think more deeply, re-align their priorities, and consider what's really important in life.

Alfred Nobel, the inventor of dynamite, awoke one morning to his own obituary in the morning paper. His brother had died, and the newspaper had mistaken the two. The obituary was entitled, "The Merchant of Death is Dead." One of the lines said, "Dr. Alfred Nobel, who became rich by finding ways to kill more people faster than ever before, died yesterday." Noble was shocked and distressed that this is how the world would see his legacy. It was due to this jarring wakeup call that he bequeathed most of his fortune to The Noble Foundation which awards the annual coveted Prize for scientific and cultural contribution. Today he is remembered not as a "Merchant of Death," but as a great humanitarian; all because the reality of death caused him to take a serious look at his life and legacy.

In 1999, I lost a dear friend. Robert Fraley was an attorney who represented professional athletes and coaches. One of those was Payne Stewart, who had just won the US Open. They and three others died in a horrible plane crash. The moment I heard, I was on a plane to Orlando to be with Dixie, his dear wife. The shock reverberated across the country. That night, Dixie asked Orel Hershiser, another of Robert's clients, and me to go through Roberts office and try to find any unpaid bills, appointments, and matters that might be left hanging. We searched for over an hour and just stared at each other in disbelief. Everything was in perfect order ... No debts, no unpaid bills, no unanswered letters ... nothing! I later walked in a workout room where Robert and Dixie exercised each morning and understood why. Written across one wall were the words, *Take care of your body as if you were going to live forever and take care of your soul as if you were going to die tomorrow."—St. Augustine.* Robert was 46 years old but understood what most never get in a lifetime ... that we must be prepared to *stay* but also we must be prepared to *go.*

Our Jewish Roots

"A shoot will come up from the stump of Jesse; from his roots a Branch will bear fruit." Isaiah 11:1 (ESV)

"In our Wednesday prayer group, we are praying that our Jewish friend Marsha will become a Christian." This is the prayer of many well-meaning believers concerning Jews. As caring as the intent may be, this is *not* God's desire if you believe the Scriptures. When a Jew acknowledges, in faith, that Jesus is the true Messiah, he does not become a Christian, he becomes a *completed Jew.* Nowhere in the New Testament is a Jew, who comes to faith in Christ, ever encouraged to become a Christian. He or she is now a *follower, a disciple, a believer, a saint, a friend or a brother of Jesus, the Christ.*

Do you know that your roots are Jewish? Consider this: An *olive tree* is symbolic for Israel. God carefully tended and pruned the tree (Israel), but she disobeyed and, over time, was taken into captivity. But God would not give up on her and promised that He would again plant and build.[1] For many years, the olive tree was just a stump, but Isaiah spoke of a time when the stump would again grow.[2] When Jesus was born in Bethlehem,

He was the "shoot" from the "stump" of Jesse who was David's father. Jesus is not a separate "Christian Tree." He is the *shoot that grew out of the Jewish stump.* How do the Gentiles fit into this picture? God grafts us into the *shoot* (Jesus) as we receive Him in faith. For any Jew who understands his own heritage, it is offensive to ask him to become a Christian. To show him Jesus as his true Messiah is another matter. When we receive Jesus, we become *true Jews*.

The apostle Paul never rejected his Jewishness when he met Jesus. He never once uttered the term "Christian." In fact, there is no longer Jew or Gentile, slave or free, male and female; we are all one when we know Jesus.[3] If you care about Jews, Muslims, Buddhists, and others, don't wave Christian or Christianity in their face; it will distract from the real issue. Speak personally about Jesus; put aside the hot button issues that will only cause distraction and tell them His story and your story.

---

[1] Jer. 31:28   [2] Isa. 11:1   [3] Gal. 3:28

"I Want You Back!"

"I have wiped out your transgressions like a thick cloud, and your sins like a heavy mist. Return to me, for I have redeemed you." Isaiah 44:22

Imagine a child leaving a loving home, wandering aimlessly and living unfaithfully for years. A caring father wants him back and pays the ultimate price to do so. This is the story of the Bible.

Abraham and Sarah were desert nomads who had a great love for God. They lived in a patriarchal society where the central idea was that of "redemption." A patriarch lived with an extended family of siblings, children and other relatives. He was responsible for all their needs. He protected them from their enemies, providing clothing and food. It was up to the patriarch to restore to the family anything lost or stolen. This is redemption; God rescues lost children and restores them to His house.

In a patriarchal society, when the father dies, the eldest son gets a double portion of the resources. In our culture, we would not tolerate this, but *they* would have been overjoyed because it meant that the older brother will now take care of all their needs.

Who was God's firstborn? Not Jesus. It was Israel. In Exodus, we read that God wanted Israel to bring back the lost children into His house. Sometimes they were faithful but often stumbled so God brought forth another firstborn ... the only begotten Son. Jesus came with all the resources of God and paid off a huge debt to bring the children back in the Father's house.

The story of Ruth and Naomi reflects this idea. Because of a famine, Ruth, her husband, and two sons emigrated from Bethlehem to Moab. Her husband died, her sons married and some ten years later they died too. One of her daughters-in-law, Naomi, stayed with Ruth. Naomi was marginalized. The family property was gone, the patriarch was dead, and Naomi was on the outside. She met a man named Boaz and he bought back the property she once owned and gave it to Naomi and to Ruth. This cost him a fortune, but he retrieved it with no strings attached. This is true redemption. God loves His children without conditions; no hoops to jump through, no tests to take, and nothing to validate or prove ourselves. He bought us back, and His gift to us is free.[1]

---

[1] Ruth 1—4

"I Want You Back!" (2)

"O Jerusalem, Jerusalem, you that kill the prophets, and stone them which are sent to you, how often would I have gathered your children together, even as a hen gathers her chickens under her wings, and you would not!"
Matthew 23:37 (NIV)

The story of Hosea is a powerful expression of redemption. He lived in a small town of about two to three hundred residents, some seven hundred and sixty years before Jesus was born. It was a time of great prosperity in the Northern Kingdom, and as is often the case it was accompanied by moral and spiritual decline. More than anything God was grieved about rampant idolatry.[1] Since God viewed Israel as His wife, her worship of other gods was spiritual adultery.

God's first words to Hosea the Prophet must have blown his sandals off. God tells him to go down to the local whorehouse, pick out one and marry her. He finds Gomer, a woman who is marginalized and locked out of society. He takes her home amid the gossip and chagrin of his neighbors. Gomer is now restored to a family and bears Hosea three children, at least one of which he feels certain is not his son. Eventually, Gomer decides she likes her former life better than her present one and returns to prostitution. If you didn't know the story, you might think that because of her hard heart, God had to let her go.

However, God comes to Hosea again and says, "Go get her and bring her back." By now, she had really bottomed out. She has even offered herself up for sale into slavery. God tells Hosea to pay the price for her and he stands among the people of his community bidding on a woman who slid back into her former life. But this is the way God thinks and feels about His beloved creation. We look at the world and see some of the most degenerate things imaginable and feel nothing but disgust. God, on the other hand, sees the worst of the worst as children who are in deep trouble and need to be redeemed. Shamed in front of his community, Hosea looks at his family and says, "Will you help me bring back my lost children?"

How do you respond to the outsider, the homeless, the pervert, or the slick-talking salesman who wants to bilk you out of everything you have? God sees them as desperate children who need the touch of His redemptive hand. We often judge without any knowledge of the circumstances that led to their demise. God leaps at the chance to draw them in with his arms wide open. His voice thunders with compassion as He tells them, "I want you back!

---

[1] Hosea 2:3–4

Self-Deception

"Woe to those who are wise in their own eyes and clever in their own sight!"
Isaiah 5:21

It is a common practice to deceive others; it's done all the time. Advertising and marketing are built on the idea of getting you to believe that if you buy the car, the beautiful blond in the commercial comes with it. Vitamins and dietary supplements are not under the control of the FDA so they can claim anything, and most do. All of us say and do deceptive things. It has become more common for people to lie in a conversation than tell the truth.

Self-deception is another matter altogether. Most of us are aware of people who have lied so much that they have come to believe their own lies. Why would anyone do that? Deception can become a comfortable way to avoid either potential embarrassment or to achieve some personal gain that might otherwise be lost. When it works it becomes easier, and soon a habit is formed. The problem is that in addition to the dishonesty of the act itself the deception becomes so natural that you can't remember what you have said to whom, and the sheer volume can cause you to begin to believe your own stories. James tells us not to simply hear God's Word, but to practice it. Otherwise, we are deceiving ourselves.[1] To simply read and memorize the Scriptures, listen to sermons, read books, and think you are magically maturing in your faith is self-deception.

We all remember when the Tiger Woods incident broke on the national news and led to the revelations of his many infidelities.

When he was finally ready to face it publicly, a journalist asked him how he could lie to so many for so long. He answered, "Because I first lied to myself." The baseline deception of all lies is believing that we can violate the boundaries that God has set for our good and still find peace and fulfillment. One of my favorite quotes is from G. K. Chesterton, a prolific early 20th Century writer. He says, "Meaninglessness does not come from being weary of pain, but from being weary of pleasure."

Self-deception is convincing yourself that if you can keep up the charade and the false perceptions just a little longer, you will be happy. But the time always comes when the deception you have created wears you down because it did not deliver what you expected. It's a hollow victory because it violates who you were created to be. There is a way that appears to be right, but in the end, leads to death.[2]

---

[1] James 1:22   [2] Prov. 14:12

The Uninspired Moments

"So, whether you eat or drink or whatever you do, do it all for the glory of God."
1 Corinthians 10:31

It has been said that our lives are five percent joy, five percent pain, and ninety percent the mundane and ordinary. Things like cutting the grass, walking the dog, cleaning the house, and hundreds of other routine activities in which we engage each day make up seventy-two years of an eighty-year life. Wow!

Consider the time and energy we put into the *ten percent*. On the joy side, we fantasize about winning the lottery, our next vacation, a new car, etc. Conversely, we wring our hands over health issues, death, finances, and a variety of stressful subjects.

But how do I deal with the uninspired, hum-drum-moments that make up that ninety percent? I can find reams of material about having a better marriage, being a better father, or lowering my golf handicap, but how do I honor God when the dog pees on the new carpet or the septic system backs up? Jesus honored the Father in all He did, and it was not by being religious; He hated religion! Paul's statement would surprise the religious do-gooder, as he says that even in something as mundane as eating and drinking, we do even that to the glory of God.[1]

It took me many years to grasp this perspective about the way we view life, people, and circumstances. Taking a shower, shaving, and getting dressed for the day are not great spiritual acts, but the residue of those functions has everything to do with honoring God. Putting down the toilet seat is a spiritual act because it serves my wife (I didn't always do that.) Leaving the shower better than when I came or the bedroom in an orderly manner is an act of love. When you unload the dishwasher or have a kind word for the checkout lady you are honoring God. If we develop a mindset that everything matters to God, picking up the newspaper on the sidewalk and tossing it on my neighbor's porch is a simple act of honor.[2] It's not something to get legalistic about, just a way to love God by loving people.

Paul "Bear" Bryant, my coach in college, would always stress to us the importance of what he called the "big-little things." It was the secret to his great success. It was those things that seemed minor or insignificant to other teams but to Coach Bryant, they were the critical things we worked on for hours. Those "big-little things" turned out to be the difference in winning or losing.

---

[1] 1 Cor. 10:31   [2] Col. 3:17 (see also 1 Pet. 4:11)

A Bad Trade

"You make known to me the path of life; in your presence, there is fullness of joy; at your right hand are pleasures forevermore." Psalm 16:11 (ESV)

Some of the most expressive and moving song lyrics came in the 70s from prolific songwriters like Kris Kristofferson. His lyrics came from real life and a place of brokenness. If you listen closely, you will nod your head in identification at some point. One phrase in his huge hit, *The Pilgrim,* describes someone who is "a walking contradiction, partly truth, and partly fiction, taking every wrong direction on his lonely way back home." And, in this framework of brokenness, Kristofferson writes a phrase that captures the quiet desperation of many of the walking wounded with the lyric, "He's traded in tomorrow for today." That's a bad trade but it could be a fitting description of our culture.

From the kids who party their way through college but somehow graduate knowing very little, to the politician who makes promises to get elected then suddenly realizes he never really had a plan; they have *traded in tomorrow for today*. The young couple who want a storybook family but never considers the hard work, patience, and sacrifice over many years that it will take. They've *traded in tomorrow for today*. The man whose obsession to be financially set and who tricks himself by vowing that when he makes it, he'll be a better husband and father has *traded in tomorrow for today*.

There is this natural undertow in our flesh that pulls us toward the immediate gratification of the present while convincing us that the future will take care of itself. America is built upon a credit system promising instant fulfillment ... *no money down and forever to pay.* Then, we spend our entire lives trying to catch-up. Jesus told of a *rich fool* who had the Midas touch and who built his life upon his ability to succeed financially. He expands constantly and congratulates himself that he can finally relax and enjoy all he has produced. But God sadly shakes His head and says, "Your number's up ... it's time to go." He taps out and stands before God with nothing to show for His seventy or eighty years except *stuff* that he never even had time to enjoy. He traded in the purpose for which he was created for immediate bragging rights on what he had built but never got to enjoy.[1]

Don't fall for the silly idea of gabbing the gold ring now, and then later, when you've been there and done that, you'll settle down and focus on spiritual things. Why not believe God as the Psalm states, "at His right hand are pleasures forevermore?" Live your *whole* life ... don't trade in tomorrow for today!

---

[1] Luke 12:13–21

Lord, Did You Say Something?

"Call to Me and I will answer you, and I will tell you great and mighty things, which you do not know." Jeremiah 33:3 (ESV)

How do you know when God is speaking to you? I have struggled with this question for more years than I would like to admit. At times I've thought He has spoken, and it just turned out to be indigestion. Then there have been times I thought it was indigestion and it turned out to really be Him.

He tells us to "ask anything in His name" and it will be heard and answered.[1] It doesn't mean that we make certain to add *In Jesus Name* at the end of our prayer. His Name has to do with His character. When I pray in His Name, I am asking Him to respond in accordance with who He is … His character and nature. In college, I knew a guy who would ask God to lead Him to beautiful girls who were, "hot to trot." Obviously, God does not contradict His own character by granting such a request.

I have learned that the primary way God speaks to me is through the Scripture, but when a verse or word really grabs my attention I've learned to stop and listen rather than read on. If I ask you a question, I listen for an answer. But for years, I asked God something and just kept on talking, never stopping to listen. Maybe God

wants to answer right now if I would just shut up?

"Faith comes by hearing and hearing by the Word of God."[2] "Word" in this context means *freshly spoken revelation*. When we read the Scripture, it is God's Word, but until it is revealed to our heart, it is true information. The Bible is not a magical book that changes us simply by reading black print on white pages. Every Bible study you attend, book you read, or sermon you hear may be powerful and inspiring, but those words are not like *pixie dust* that suddenly changes your life. God must reveal it to your heart.

When you are really seeking and walking with Jesus and a thought comes to you, consider it a thought from God. Obey the thought as long as it lines up with His character. If someone comes to your mind, maybe there is a reason. Call them and just say, "I was thinking about you and wondered how you're doing." Their response may amaze you. Just as invisible radio waves constantly move through a room, God's voice is always speaking to your heart, so turn your *radio on* and listen.

---

[1] John 14:13   [2] Rom. 10:17

A Transparent Heart

"Behold, an Israelite indeed, in whom there is no deceit!" John 1:47

A serious-minded teenager named Nathaniel sat under the shade of a fig tree to pray and meditate on the Scriptures. It was a regular practice of most serious Jews. On this day, Nathaniel's thoughts were interrupted by his good friend Phillip, who had run to tell him some astounding news. He, along with Peter and Andrew, had just encountered, "the One whom Moses and the Prophets had written about."[1] Rather than share his friend's enthusiasm, Nathaniel makes a sarcastic response, "Can anything good come out of Nazareth?"

The hill country of Judea lies to the south of Galilee. Judeans were strict, staunch, serious people and Galileans were free spirits who danced and sang before the Lord. There was great animosity between them, but even the Galileans considered themselves superior to those who lived in the little village of Nazareth. Nathaniel's nasty response probably seemed incongruent to Phillip considering that he was meditating on the Scriptures, but Phillip does not debate; he simply says, "Come and see." The only reason people reject Jesus or make negative comments about Him is that they haven't met Him and don't know Him. To know Him is to love Him.

Jesus greets Nathaniel with a broad smile and says, "Behold, an Israelite indeed, in whom is no guile." One who is guileless is not deceitful. He's transparent; what you see is what you get. Jesus is contrasting this man with an Old Testament Israelite, Jacob, who was full of guile. He deceived his father and stole his brother's birthright.

"How do you know me?" asked Nathaniel. Jesus says he saw him meditating under the fig tree. He also knew what Scripture he was thinking about. This comes to light in verse 51, when Jesus tells him that the passage he was considering where Jacob saw a ladder with "angels ascending and descending" is peanuts compared to what he would see as the "heavens open and the angels of God descend on the Son of Man." No wonder Nathaniel cries out, "Rabbi, you *are* the Son of God."

Nathaniel was prejudiced toward Nazarenes. He didn't hide it, he dealt with it and became a devoted disciple of Jesus, the Nazarene. Transparency is the avenue through which our sins can emerge from the shadows and be redeemed. God will not change that which we will not acknowledge.

---

[1] John 1:43–51

Turtle on a Fencepost

"In their hearts humans plan their course, but the Lord establishes their steps."
Proverbs 16:9 (NIV)

You may have heard something like this before: "When my grandfather stepped off the boat as a young boy in New York harbor in 1909 he didn't have a dime in his pocket. Having come from the *Old Country*, he wondered the streets doing odd jobs to help him get by. He worked from dawn to dusk each day, slept little, but learned the value of self-reliance. Step by step he used every natural instinct he had, watched others and learned. Over the years, out of nothing, he built a multimillion-dollar business. He was truly a man who with bull-dog determination, beat the odds. He achieved the American dream and with help from no one. He pulled himself up by his own bootstraps!"

That is one of the biggest exaggerations you will ever hear, but it is one of the myths that has been handed down from generation to generation and often parades as a "Christian ideal." The truth is, no one pulls themselves up by the bootstraps. No one accomplishes great things without help ... and lots of it. They may have had determination, ingenuity, and discipline, but introductions were made, doors were opened, ideas were shared that paved the way. No one diapers, feeds, educates, and raises themselves without help from others. No one gives themselves the gifts and talents, physical and mental attributes to persist and succeed. To believe that first paragraph about yourself is an unknowing attempt to steal God's glory.

Jesus said, "Without me, you can do nothing."[1] It's either true or it's not. Proverbs says, "Many are the plans of a man's heart, but it is God's purpose that prevails."[2] There is nothing wrong with believing in yourself as long as you acknowledge the real Source. Paul writes to the Corinthians, "Who makes you different from anybody else, and what have you got that wasn't given to you? And if anything is given to you, why boast of it as if you had achieved it yourself?"[3]

A great athlete hones his skills, a politician may be prolific in his insight, and a business executive may seem to have the "Midas touch," but one thing you can always know about anyone's success ... It's like seeing a turtle sitting on a fencepost ... You know he didn't get there by himself.

[1] John 15:5 [2] Prov. 19:21 [3] 1 Cor. 4:7 (Phillips)

The Roots of All Problems

"Anxiety weighs down the heart, but a kind word cheers it up." Proverbs 12:25 (NIV)

What is the root of all problems? (It's not your mother-in-law!) Most believers understand that all problems are basically spiritual in nature. You and I struggle with relationships, decisions, patterns of thought, and continuous temptations every day. Every problem I have ever had, or have known anyone to have, is spiritual at its base. Someone hurts you in some way and you find yourself avoiding them ... that's a spiritual issue. You allow a child to continue in disruptive behavior, warning them over and over but never working with them ... that is a spiritual problem. From cheating on your expenses or gossiping about someone to overeating and lying ... all are spiritual offenses.

I began to notice years ago that every problem I encountered could be traced to one of three fundamental areas: *bitterness, sensuality,* or a *temporal value system.* In counseling with people, I have noticed the same thing. Relationships that have been damaged are almost always due to *bitterness* and *resentment.* The word means to *re-feel* a betrayal or some painful incident. It may have happened years ago but feels as if it happened two minutes ago. It is an emotional reflex that triggers anger in all directions.

Many problems can be traced back to *sensuality* in terms of guilt and memories that can tie us in knots. Other times the breach is due to a value system that is based on *temporal* rather than things that are eternal. We often see this in those whose whole identity is wrapped up in how they look, how their home is perceived by others, their portfolio, etc. The struggle is that too much value is given to things that are temporary and have no lasting value. There is great remorse when you wake up one day and realize that all those temporal things you reached out for rewarded you with nothing but a handful of air.

Take a minute and think of the three biggest problems or struggles in your life right now. Where do they fit in these three categories? If you do this, I think you will find that you will then understand how they must be dealt with. So many times I blamed someone for something only to realized that it was my resentment, not their action, that was causing the problem.

Every problem that exists in the world at this moment, God has the answer to. But, you can't deal with that which you will not acknowledge. If we don't identify the root cause, it will continue to grow. Identify it, confess it, and release it to God.

The Gospel: Beyond the Words

"In the beginning was the Word . . ." John 1:1–5

"We left our church because they didn't preach the gospel."

Rhetoric like this is very common, but I always wonder what the minister would have had to preach to meet the standards of this dissatisfied member. How many theological points make up *"the gospel?"* Who gets to decide? If you asked a hundred ministers, astute laymen, and believers across every denomination you will have a wide range of answers and very little agreement.

John's gospel begins, *"In the beginning was the Word ..."* The *Word* reflects a concept taught by Jewish theologians known as "Memra." It had six different meanings such as: being *the same but distinct from God, the agent of salvation, of creation, and the means by which God became visible.* John confirms that everything taught by the ancient rabbis was fulfilled in Jesus. The Word is a Person, not a tightly bundled package of doctrinal facts.

How do we export to the world that which the godliest among us cannot agree on? Which points are essential to a biblical definition of the Gospel? Agreement in the Church is essential; otherwise, it is like surgeons disagreeing on a procedure that holds a human life in the balance. God's intent is to *unite all things in Christ,* not in Christianity, and not around a set of precepts.[1] Because we have never been able to unite around a set of points, we have thousands of separate Protestant denominations and their splinter subsets in the world today. Why? They can't agree. What *can* we agree on? Jesus not only gives life, He *is* life! He died for the sins of the world. It is Jesus alone who draws the world to Himself. He, not a set of doctrinal facts; He *is* the Gospel.

The world will never gather around Islam, Hinduism, Judaism or even Christianity. Muslims are not interested in becoming Christians but have great respect for Jesus. They see Him as a prophet now, just as the disciples did until after His resurrection, but If the focus is on Him and not issues, they will eventually see Him as Lord. Jews see Jesus as a great Rabbi, but that will change one day. They will not become Christians but *completed Jews* as they accept Jesus as the true Messiah. Most atheists will discuss Jesus if we check our arrogance at the door. When we hold up our four, five or six points of the gospel, we reduce Jesus to a set of doctrinal precepts, and we diminish who He is.

---

[1]Eph. 1:10

Counterintuitive Thinking

"'For My thoughts are not your thoughts, nor are My ways your ways,' declares the Lord. 'For as the heavens are higher than the earth, so are My ways higher than your ways and My thoughts than your thoughts.'" Isaiah 55:8–9

In most areas of life, we are only limited by the way we think. God has built into the fabric of humanity the potential for almost unlimited creativity. Artists, poets, writers, and prodigies of technological marvels have created things we could only dream of years ago. Yet, we have never scratched the surface of the mind of God. He speaks to Isaiah, and to us, concerning the fact that our natural way of thinking—our perception of life, of death, of relationships, affliction, and even the normal issues we encounter daily—are antithetical to His way of thinking.

It's not hard to believe that if one doesn't have a relationship with God, sharing His thoughts would be irrelevant. But when a man or woman receives Jesus in his life, the potential to think God's thoughts after Him is available but does not magically engage with our brain. We each grow up in a culture that shapes the way we perceive the issues of life. This is why Paul warns believers to never allow the world (culture) to shape us into its own mold.[1] He goes on to say that we must allow Jesus to reshape our thinking from within. Put simply, we will become like that to which you are exposed. The world has shaped us, but the mind of God can, and will, reshape our thinking if we expose ourselves to that which reflects His perspective.

When we trust God with our lives, he creates in us a new heart. He also creates in us the potential to develop a pattern of thinking that mirrors His own thoughts. His dream for us is that we experience peace, not evil so that we will have a life of hope and confidence for the future.[2] As we allow Him to reshape our thinking we see reality through His eyes rather than through the eyes of our culture.[3] That way we will become representatives from His kingdom to our culture rather than representing our culture to His Kingdom.

It is comfortable and easy to simply attach God to our lives and our lifestyle. It may temporarily create a facsimile of authenticity, but when the north wind begins to blow, the façade will disappear and what is underneath will be exposed.

In the next few days, we will explore this further, because the way we think creates the pattern for everything we do.

---

[1] Rom. 12:2　[2] Jer. 29:11　[3] Rom. 12:2

Created from a Thought

"In their hearts humans plan their course, but the Lord establishes their steps."
Proverbs 16:9 (NIV)

You will never do anything contrary to the way you think. Our emotions, background, and culture in which we live generally sculpt our mindset. But a renewed mind recreates how we think.

I worked in the Empire State Building in New York for several years. It is an iconic structure that can house over thirteen thousand people. There are so many businesses it even has its own ZIP Code. In the late 1920s, someone had an idea. They took that idea to a draftsman and he came up with an *architectural rendering* of what the original guy envisioned. That massive structure originated from a thought! If it was destroyed, it could be built back exactly as it was as long as the original thought was kept alive. You and I are the results of a thought straight out of the mind of God.[1]

The power of the mind is astounding, but it must be recalibrated to reflect God's thoughts rather than those most natural to us. We can do all the right things, study the Scriptures, and be moral examples, but still not possess the mind of God.

Most of our philosophical perspective as a culture came to America from European immigrants whose ways of perceiving life goes back to Plato and Aristotle in ancient Greece. Education, religion, and social norms were deeply influenced by Greek philosophy. The problem is that the Scriptures reflects a Middle Eastern, Jewish mindset. They were written by Jews, to Jews, in a Jewish culture, about a Jewish Messiah. When we read the Bible, our default view is through the lens of Western thinking. In doing so, we impose our Western values and understanding not only on the Middle Eastern culture but on the perspective from which it is written. That's why all paintings of Jesus make him look like a WASP. We distance Him from His culture and impose our values on His words.

Rather than becoming like Jesus, we make Him like us. For instance, we look at a verse where Jesus says, "The poor will always be with you,"[2] and decide that He means that there are so many poor that we can't make much of a dent, so we shouldn't worry about it. But as you read, you discover that Jesus' heart throbs for the poor. Jesus is really telling His followers is that He will only be with them for a while, and they will have the opportunity and privilege to care for the poor the rest of their lives.

Let's look a little deeper at this tomorrow and the next day.

---

[1] Ps. 33:9   [2] John 12:8

Thinking God's Thoughts After Him

"For who has known the mind of the Lord that he may instruct him? But we have the mind of Christ." 1 Corinthians 2:16 (ESV)

The secular/spiritual dichotomy comes from Greek thought. Think of a dresser in your bedroom. One drawer is the religious drawer, one is social, another is family, and another is vocational. You pull out the drawer you need at the time. The modern version of that is, "In my Christian life I do such and such" That's why people see no conflict in acting differently in church than at the office or the golf course. One is *spiritual*, the other is *secular*. The Scripture teaches that God encompasses all of life. For believers, everything we do is spiritual and is done for God's glory.[1]

Western thinking is organized and conceptual. We like bullet points and outlines. The Middle Easterner thinks in story form … word pictures. The Bible is a story and the writers want you to step into the story, to feel the atmosphere and the emotions of the people, taste the food, smell the air. That's why Jesus insists that we become like.[2] Children think in pictures, not concepts. The genius of Jesus' teaching was that He walked people into the truth so that they experienced it, not by pounding it into them.

We tend to want to intellectually connect with the text. We want to get it into our head and hope it trickles down to our heart. We might ask our kids, "What did you *learn* in Sunday School? A Jewish mother would say, "What *moved* you? What *touched your heart* when the Rabbi taught?" Middle Easterners believe that if your heart is touched, you will run toward more knowledge.

Our culture is extremely individualistic. Our focus is on individual needs and wants. Our prayers are mostly all about us. The Jew is more concerned about the whole community. The prodigal son knew he could not return to his father's house in the same capacity in which he left because he had broken community.[3] To a Jew, what is good for God's family always surpasses that which is good for the individual. Joy comes from the health of the community. That is not a natural way for us to think. But this thinking must be built into the heart as God inclines it toward His concerns. The first step is to recognize the difference and then to ask God *to transform you by the renewing of your mind.*[4]

---

[1] 1 Cor. 10:31   [2] Matt. 18:3–4   [3] Luke 15:19   [4] Rom. 12:2

Two Different Worlds

In the Scripture, down is up and up is down. When we acquiesce to the mindset of the culture our lifestyle will follow. We have been taught to guard and protect our lives at any cost, but God says if you want to live, you have to die.[1] We aspire to greatness and are told to build our brand and advertise our accomplishments; God says we must become least.[2] We long to be well known and applauded, but the Scripture teaches that humility and anonymity are treasured values. Jesus' own brothers pressed Him to publicize Himself and He flatly refused.[3] We dream of being a great leader; we try to be more assertive and to let nothing deter us from what we want. God says if you aspire to leadership, the road downward as a servant is the road upward.[4] We've been taught that authority is gained by seizing control, but Jesus demonstrated in His life and in His death that submission is the key to having authority.[5]

Our government and political leaders believe that the answer to peace is a détente, a balance of powers with other nations. We seek to match nuclear capabilities with our adversaries, and we call it peace, but it is really coexistence. Paul says, "make it your aim to be at peace with God and you will inevitably have peace with one another."[6] Listen to people talk. Listen to the answers they offer for the problems we face as a nation, in our cities and our families. Rarely will you hear anything that remotely reflects the mind of Christ, even from believers.

Mother Teresa was invited by the Government of Yemen to come and help the poor of the southern portion, which is primarily Muslim. Almost any Christian Leader, if asked to do the same, would raise a ton of money and orchestrate an evangelistic effort and build churches across the Yemen landscape. It would immediately alienate the government and the people. But the first thing Mother Teresa did was to build a Mosque for the poor to have a place of worship. "Shame on her," you might think, but what she did was pure genius. She loved them in a manner that they could understand. No one ever walked in that Mosque without the haunting question, "why would this woman do this for us?" She is a follower of Jesus. And every day they saw the answer, "because she loves you and Jesus loves you too." A different way of thinking? You bet … but don't be too quick to write it off. You can't read the Scriptures and not see how differently God approaches everything in life.

---

[1] John 12:24   [2] Luke 9:46–48   [3] John 7:2–9   [4] Matt. 20:26
[5] Phil. 2:5–9; Heb. 5:8   [6] Eph. 4:3

Reshaping How We Think

"For as he thinks in his heart, so is he." Proverbs 23:7 (NKJV)

The Scriptures are replete with admonitions that may seem unreasonable and unworkable to us because we are so conditioned to think within the parameters of that to which we have been exposed. Historically, the church has always rejected the idea of mythical gods, but has mindlessly adopted secular concepts, merging them with Scripture and calling it "biblical."

Linear thinking is a Greek concept. For example, *we must get the right grades and get into the right college, so we can graduate at the top of our class and get the right job with the right income, buy the right house, take the right kind of vacations, retire comfortably, and leave an estate.* Nothing about that kind of perspective even slightly reflects the mind of God. Yet we have christened it "The American Dream" and made it synonymous with biblical values.

Believers give of their resources to support various ministries, their church, and the poor and disadvantaged. Why? We want to help people. But the purpose of giving is to help *you*! The blessing is aimed toward the giver.[1] The gift will no doubt help the recipient, but God wants you and me to grow a heart like His. Every time you give with the right motive, you grow that heart.

Most of us are obsessively concerned about looking good and coming off as smart, competent, and in control. Paul was happy to be considered a fool if by doing so it would deepen Jesus' impact in the world.[2]

I was taught many things in my early years by well-meaning people, but I've spent a long time unlearning many "good old American ideas" that don't line up with the mind of Jesus. It's a process, but it can only begin by learning to dive into the Scriptures for yourself. Don't rely on Christian books. Let God's Word speak to you.

First, begin a running list of daily thoughts you see in the Bible that are counterintuitive to that which we hear every day. Next, discuss it with trusted friends and critique everything in light of Scripture. Third, ask questions about what you read. God is never rattled by questions. Bring it on! Finally, keep a list of your questions and begin to read the gospels autobiographically. What are the disciples feeling in this scene? What is the atmosphere? Become part of the story; it will help you walk with them.

As you read these daily missives, consider the way you were taught to think. Does it reflect the mind of God?

---

[1] Acts 20:25　[2] 1 Cor. 3:18; Isa. 55:8–9

Fighting Fair

"Let everything you do be done in love." 1 Corinthians 16:14

One thing the unredeemed world resents about believers is that we often abandon our own principles if that's what it takes to get what we want. They are guilty of the same, but that doesn't absolve us from the responsibility to honor God by understanding both sides of an issue before we speak. Most debates or arguments on spiritual, political, or social issues do very little except to offend people and widen the gap in the relationship.

God's people must learn how to engage in a volatile discussion while holding fast to the truth and honoring the right of others to express a different view. The apostles did not always agree. Paul and Timothy didn't see eye to eye on everything.[1] Paul and Barnabas disagreed so vehemently at one point that they parted ways concerning strategy, but not relationally.[2]

A believer must not only know the truth, but he must also be able to communicate it in a kind, gentle and respectful manner.[3] We cannot allow the emotion of the issue to destroy the relationship. Some have said that many issues are important enough to warrant a breach in a friendship. That is both unfortunate and unbiblical. Think of your own history … the sins you've committed and the prideful ways you have acted. Any sin, whether it's gossip, adultery, theft, or even murder, is shaking your fist in God's face and saying, "I know it's wrong but I'm doing it anyway." Is there a time when, after you sinned, that God ever wrote you off and turned His back and said, "Don't call me or knock on my door; I'm no longer available?" Instead, He says, "I will never leave you nor forsake you."[4]

Our offenses are direct assaults on God Himself. The issues that divide friendships are often not personal. It might be abortion, gay marriage, gun control, or any hot button issue. God hangs tough with you; are you too fragile to disagree with a friend and work through it? I contend that the watching world sees little in this "Christian" sub-culture we've created that they want to be invited into. They can have broken friendships without Christ.

If we can't hold together fundamental relationships like our marriage, our children, and our friendships, we have no right to invite nonbelievers into that kind of fractured culture. If you are married you know that conflicts and arguments come up regularly. It's not easy to learn how to fight fair, how to disagree with your spouse without being petty and nasty, and creating a deeper breach. We must learn how to take a different view without destroying one another. No matter how important we may feel the issue is, the relationship should always trump the issue.

---

[1] Gal. 2:11   [2] Acts 15:37–41   [3] 1 Pet. 3:15   [4] Heb. 13:5

Temptation from a Different Place

"Look! All these years I've been slaving for you and never disobeyed your orders. You never gave me even a young goat so I could celebrate with my friends." Luke 15:29 (NIV)

This is the response of the prodigal son's older brother when he was welcomed back by his father after years of riotous living and blowing his inheritance. He is angry and hurt because while his little brother was out raising hell, he stayed home and did everything right. The sins of the younger brother are well documented, as is the unconditional love of his father. The prodigal was tempted by a world that he had never known. It was that which he imagined but had never experienced that drew him away from his family and community.

Because we tend to focus on the younger son, we don't usually give much thought to the elder brother. It's easy to identify with his pain. He had been the dutiful, perfect son he thought his father wanted. Now, dad is giving an extravagant party for the disobedient, punk younger brother who has blown every penny of the inheritance that he had demanded prematurely, and the brother has now slinked back home seeking a reprieve. Why *wouldn't* the elder brother be angry? He felt taken for granted. Did you ever work your rear end off only to get passed over for a promotion or job, losing out to a less responsible, less qualified person? The elder brother had been the good, responsible son and, it seems, the problem was that *his goodness* was his sin!

The father wanted his son's love, but the elder brother focused his energy on being good and doing everything correctly around the farm. Would you rather have your children love you or mechanically do all their assigned chores? God wants love and affection from His children, and the work we do should flow naturally out of that love. Our greatest temptations are not toward evil but toward good! Why would Satan try to get a workaholic to cheat on his spouse? It would be more damaging in the long run to get him to simply step up the pace even more and convince him it's all for the *family*. If the enemy wants to get to you he doesn't keep you from church or Bible studies, he will encourage you to do more of the same. Then there will be no time to live it out!

The father, in the parable, wanted affection from his sons first. The younger son was self-centered. He tried things his way, but he failed and hit the wall. Then, all he wanted was to be back with his father. The elder brother stayed with his father, did everything he was supposed to do, wanting his goodness to win his father over. God sent His own Son, not so that you would be good, but so that you would be His.

Unexplainable Apart from God

"One thing I do know, that though I was blind, now I see." John 9:25b (NIV)

Why did people follow Jesus? There were many reasons, but those who stuck with Him did so because they saw a life that was unexplainable other than by the power of God. What is it about your life that you cannot explain apart from the supernatural? You can become a good teacher a good athlete, an astute businessman, or even a good preacher apart from God. It simply takes a gift, some determination, and a few opened doors. Then you can tell people for the rest of your life that you were a self-made man or woman. People do it all the time. But one day when you stand before God, which of your *self-made* accomplishments will be impressive to Him?

Men seek to validate themselves by putting their names on buildings, hospital wings, academic and sports scholarships, or brass plaques on park benches. There is nothing evil about that but when I walk by a complex like Rockefeller Center in New York City, I wonder about the man, not his money or accomplishments. I wonder what he thought about during the uninspired moments when he was alone lying in his bed. I wonder if there was anything about his life that he could only point toward heaven and say, "I had nothing to do with this."

God builds into the fabric of each of us certain abilities, drives, and gifts to develop. We can use those gifts for our own glory or for His. We can operate in such a way that opportunities and circumstances work in our favor. But it is the invisible things that are remembered about us. It's the touch of my mother's hand, my father's unique laugh, the embrace I didn't expect, or the forgiving smile when I wrecked my uncle's car.

So, I ask again, what is there about your life that you can explain only in the manner similar to that of the blind man in John 9? "All I know is that once I was blind and now I see." What could you never have created or produced? It is that and that alone, that when you stand before Almighty God, He will say, "well done, my good and faithful servant." "Well done" doesn't mean you did anything. "Well done" will be that you trusted Him, you got out of the way, and allowed Him to accomplish through you that which you could never do.[1]

---

[1]Matt. 25:21

39

No Limits Means Unlimited Possibilities

"God is not unjust; He will not forget your work and the love you have shown Him as you have helped His people and continue to help them." Hebrews 6:10 (NIV)

When I was in college, I met a very fine minister; he was humble, affable, always available, and had an unusual level of wisdom. We later became friends. One Sunday night years later he was teaching at his large church in a very wealthy part of the city. His sermon was interrupted by a man who handed him a note. He apologized to the stunned congregation and made a hasty exit.

One of his members had taken her own life. When he arrived at the house, her body was just being taken to the morgue. He spent time with the family until they left to stay with friends. The woman had put a shotgun in her mouth, so you can imagine what the cleanup crew would have to face the next day. But when they arrived the next morning, the house had been completely cleaned. This kind and compassionate man hung around after everyone left, went in and cleaned the floor, walls, furniture, and carpet, finishing in the early morning hours. He left and never told a soul. I only know because a neighbor saw the lights at midnight and saw him through the window.

I've never known of such an act of radical servanthood. Tears welled up in my eyes when I heard the story because servanthood was merely a cliché to me at that point. It was one of those pivotal moments that found its mark in my life.

Years later, I was on a plane and was upgraded to first-class because of overbooking. I was shown to a seat beside a man whom I immediately recognized as Rod Carew, one of the greatest hitters to ever play Major League Baseball. Loving the game as I do, I plied him with questions about his amazing hitting. He said that for eighteen years he went to the ballpark before each game. He took batting practice before the other players arrived, then went out with the team and took batting practice again. He said, "I counted on the fact that no other player in the Majors was willing to pay that kind of price."

That encounter, coupled with my friend's humble act of servanthood, gave me a life principle from which I have never recovered. *If you are willing to do what no one else is willing to do, there is no limit to what God will entrust into your care.*

The Myth of Control

"'For I know the plans I have for you,' declares the Lord, 'plans for welfare and not for evil, to give you a future and a hope.'" Jeremiah 29:11 (ESV)

I remember taking my children to Disney World and watching how delighted they were with themselves as they "drove the old-timey cars around a winding track. Afterward, David, my youngest, said to me, "I think I'm a pretty good driver, Daddy." I, of course, affirmed that statement with relish, but as you all know, the track controlled and powered the car, not my children.

We rush through life with this dire need to feel that our efforts are that which turns the steering wheel of our lives and slams on the breaks to avoid the potholes. The longer I live, the more I realize that I can control nothing; I only nurture the fantasy that I am in control ... just like my kids at Disney World.

I remember an English Lit. Professor in college reading the Poem, *Invictus,* by William Henley, an English poet and humanist in Victorian England in 1875. It ends with this line: *"It matters not how strait the gate, how charged with punishments the scroll, I am the master of my fate, I am the captain of my soul."* The professor went on and on extolling the virtues of this poem, which has been quoted by many famous people over the years. It was the last words of Oklahoma City bomber, Timothy McVey, before he was executed. It is, in my opinion, the adult version of a child in a car on tracks thinking he controls where he goes. *Invictus* is the essence and definition of what *sin* really is. "I am the master of my fate; I am the captain of my soul." This perspective is the great folly of mankind. We are not the captain or master of anything ... *especially* ourselves. Paul laments in Romans that those things he wants to do, he doesn't, and that which he wants to avoid, he does.[1] It is the dilemma of man. Jesus said, "Without Me, you can do nothing."[2]

God does give us tracks to run on; He can move them in any direction He wishes but gives us the right to make creative choices along the way. The only sense in which we are masters of our fate is that God gives us the right to receive or reject Him.

Personal autonomy is not a bad thing, God gives us the freedom to decide our direction in life. The wise person seeks to understand the gifts he has been given and moves in that direction energized by God's thorough approval and power. To be captain of my soul would be like allowing a five-year-old to drive my car by themselves on a cross country trip. The thought may be exciting, but the reality would be devastating.

---

[1]Rom. 7:15–20 [2]John 15:4–6

When Truth Comes into Focus

"The path of the righteous is like the light of dawn, that shines brighter and brighter until the full day." Proverbs 4:18

I can't think of anyone I have known who dives into the Bible and begins to instantly understand everything they are reading. There's a rhythm and a harmony in God's story that connects us with His compassionate heart for a lost and erratic people, and the comfort and guidance of His instruction. It does not come quickly, but if we will be patient and persistent, in time, the path we walk "will become brighter and brighter until the full day."

Like most anything else that we want to do, if we fail to plan, we are planning to fail. Reading and studying the Scriptures often begins as a duty. We know we must if we want to grow spiritually, and we know that God desires to meet us in those quiet moments that we spend alone. To be honest, it began that way for me. I began reading a chapter a day in the gospels. As I continued and started reading in the Book of Acts, and then the Epistles, I noticed that during idle moments, particularly jogging, driving, or lying in bed at night, I would think about what I was reading.

I have never understood why people say, "I forgot *to do* my "quiet time" this morning or something to that effect. Imagine coming home from work and saying to your spouse, "After we get the kids to bed, I will *do* my time with you." What an insult! Those who "do time" are prisoners. Time with God should be an oasis, a shelter from the storm, a place to unload our burdens.[1]

I've experienced my share of failures in allowing God's words to impact my life, but little by little, I have begun to see some changes in my perspective and behavior. I began to meet people I wanted to listen to and spend time with. There were several men who revolutionized my thinking and started me on an exciting path where the light has become brighter and brighter as I have walked. There's no magic to it; you just carve out the time, be realistic, consistent and honest, and God will create a hunger in you. When you obey what He teaches you, He will give you something else, and eventually what God produces in you will begin to affect others. What began for me as a duty has now, for many years, become a joy ... a fascinating gift that keeps on giving and continues to remind me who I am and that God is always for me and stands with me.

---

[1] Ps. 91:1

Knowledge vs. Wisdom

"Christ Himself, in whom are all the treasure of wisdom and knowledge."
Colossians 2:3

What's the difference in knowledge and wisdom? The Scriptures indicate that both should be considered a treasure. In Jesus, we *find* both. Many people have vast knowledge. They've done the research and know the data and the variables involved. Their brain is a storehouse of information. Wisdom, however, knows the implications of that knowledge. If you are facing a walk through the desert, knowledge is knowing that the distance to the next town is 10.3 miles. Wisdom is discerning how much water you'll need to take on the ten-mile walk.

We live in a culture that obsesses over information. We want as much knowledge as is humanly possible. Today, with increased technology, we are a click away from answers to almost any question. Interestingly, with that access to information, we are more divided than ever. It is not the uninformed who start the wars or cause the Wall Street meltdown that almost toppled the American economy. Even the church of Jesus Christ is not immune to this thinking. We are often told that learning all the right theology and being equipped to answer any question is the key to effectiveness in the marketplace. If you buy that, you are saying that good information will change hearts. Understanding of Scripture must be tempered by the wisdom of the Holy Spirit.

Spiritual wisdom is different from knowledge and spiritual intellect. You can't cram for it or fake it, and a high IQ can't produce it. Yet, it is essential to living a life in harmony with God. "The fear of the Lord is the beginning of wisdom."[1] Jim Rayburn, the founder of Young Life, put it this way: "When you put God in His rightful place in your life, it's the first smart thing you'll ever do."

If you don't know the truth, you won't have wisdom; if you don't have wisdom, you won't have discernment, and if you don't have discernment you'll continually make reckless decisions and eventually self-destruct. Every critical decision you make and every winding path you travel will stand a good chance of being the wrong ones without the wisdom that comes from truth.

---

[1]Prov. 9:10

Clear Your Enemy List

"Do not repay evil with evil or insult with insult. On the contrary, repay evil with blessing, because to this you were called so that you may inherit a blessing."
1 Peter 3:9 (NIV)

Yes, you have one! You may not be conscious of it, but it is there lying in wait like a crouching tiger ready to attack when you least expect it. This subterranean monster can alter and damage relationships that are totally unrelated to the hurt and bitterness that wars within you. Why? Because resentment is the common denominator. It travels with you ... first-class!

The tendency for each of us is to minimize the pain from the past. It is an unspoken mantra that says, *leave it alone and it will go home*. But it won't go home. Hurtful words that were said to you dismissively, or in anger, a betrayal that destroyed trust, or even a suspicion that could never be proved ... all are like *chickenpox*. It is a virus that lingers in your system until you go to the pharmacy and get the shot that neutralizes it and keeps it from becoming *shingles*. The difference is that Chicken Pox that you contracted as a child may or may not become shingles as an adult. But an enemies list is guaranteed infection.

It's a spiritual problem even though most don't recognize it as such. It doesn't upset your stomach, though it may; it doesn't give you a headache, though it could. It is a subliminal thief that can, and will, rob you of the peace that God longs for you to experience "peace that surpasses all understanding."[1]

I've been there! I have had issues with someone that I thought was forgiven and solved, but something kept nagging at me that I couldn't explain. Finally, after racking my brain to figure it out myself, I gave up and asked God to reveal it to me. I told Him I would do whatever it took, no matter how humbling, to bring closure to this breach. Little by little a name kept coming to my mind. It was subtle but very uncomfortable. Finally, I called him and flew to see him. It was a small thing, but a misunderstanding that initiated other issues. Since then, we have a warm friendship again and are both at peace.

The Scripture is full of these kinds of breaches. King Saul had once admired young David. He had trusted him and Saul's son, Jonathan, had become his closest friend. But something grew inside of Saul. Jealousy and anger became his obsession to the point where he hunted David down with the intention to kill him. This seed of anger compelled him toward unrest and instability.

You and I respond to everything in life by either *love* or *anger*. Anything that you remotely believe is anger, must come off you're the enemy list. Peace and joy are what is at stake.

---

[1] Phil. 4:7

Sermon on the Mount

Chapters 5—7 of Matthew are among the most beloved sections of the Bible. Even people who are only nominally interested in spiritual matters find the teaching of Jesus challenging and deeply meaningful. The problem is that no human being can actually live out the words of Jesus. To see them as commands that we strive to conquer is a recipe for failure. Jesus is the only one who ever lived out these words He preached on that Galilean hillside. The Sermon on the Mount is impossible if it is read or studied as laws that must be obeyed. It can only be lived out through the eyes of grace.

In the next two days, before we begin the Sermon on the Mount, we will look at the purpose of the Law that God gave to Moses and which He wrote down and is contained in the Torah (the first five books of the Old Testament). On the following day, we will briefly look at the "Oral Laws" or "Hedge Laws" that were thought by the ancient Jews and were, by Jesus time considered by the Pharisees to have equal weight to the Law of Moses. They were said to have been orally given by God to Joshua and others after Moses died. These were the laws that Jesus railed against because they were man-made, impossible to obey, and held the Jewish people hostage. This will help us understand that the purpose of the Sermon is to show us that we are incapable of living it out. Only by the Spirit of God in us can we engage with the reality of these words. To read them under law will lead to utter frustration.

The Written Law

"'The days are coming,' declares the Lord, 'when I will make a new covenant with the people of Israel and with the people of Judah. It will not be like the covenant I made with their ancestors when I took them by the hand to lead them out of Egypt, because they broke my covenant, which they broke though I was a husband to them,' declares the Lord. 'This is the covenant I will make with the people of Israel after that time,' declares the Lord. 'I will put my law in their minds and write it on their hearts. I will be their God, and they will be my people.'"
Jeremiah 31:31–34 (NIV)

There is something about the word "law" that evokes thoughts of a policeman hiding in the shadows waiting to give you a speeding ticket, or the "meter maid" who nails you for being parked two minutes overtime. The idea of God being a type of policeman who nabs you for stepping out of line is a common image to many children growing up.

When Moses brought the Israelites out of slavery and across the Red Sea, they found themselves in unfamiliar territory. No longer in Egypt, and therefore no longer under Egyptian law, they were now seemingly free to create their own value system. But their values obviously conflicted, and soon Moses would meet God on Mt. Sinai and receive the Ten Commandments to protect the people from chaos, and to provide for their welfare. There were laws guiding relationships like the 10 Commandments, and dietary and hygiene laws were given to sustain their health. They were not given as a burden but, in a sense, for the same reason you would tell your child not to play in the street or touch a hot stove.

Some of the Israelites were faithful, but most violated God's laws and fell deeper into a quagmire of confusion and treachery of their own making. God never intended to guide His people by law. His intent was that He would lead them into the land which He had promised Abraham and his descendants. They would be a leadership governed by love to bring his children home. In sending His Son, God demonstrates His desire that their response to trusting and walking with Him be that of love, rather than rules. It's not that the Ten Commandments are now invalid, but that when Jesus introduced the New Covenant, it was better than the Old Covenant. Jesus repeats what Moses had said as he reduced the ten and replaced them with two: Love God and love your neighbor.[1] Jesus changes the concept of obeying God from an obligation to obeying God because of a desire.

---

[1] Deut. 4—5; Matt. 22:37

The Oral or Hedge Laws: Man's Laws

"For the law was given through Moses; grace and truth came through Jesus Christ."
John 1:17

The Law was instituted by God, through Moses, to protect and to provide for His people. Although equal justice under the law is the cornerstone of a just society, mercy is at the heart of God's character. Over time, the Law was perverted by those whom God had ordained to protect and fairly administer it. By the time Jesus came, thousands of additional manmade laws were added by the Jewish leaders, and the burden on the people was intolerable.

After the Jews were taken into captivity in Babylon for seventy years, a question arose … *If we are God's chosen people and He loves us, why are we here, being forced to eat food that's forbidden, forced to bow down to a pagan god and treated like slaves?* They concluded that the written Law of Moses (The Torah) was not strong enough to keep the people holy. After the Persians defeated the Babylonians, King Cyrus allowed the Jews to return to Israel, and eventually, *Oral Laws, or Hedge Laws,* were developed by the Jewish leaders to supposedly put a protective fence or hedge around the Mosaic Law. Jews claim that these thousands of Laws were given by God orally to Joshua and others after Moses died. There is no valid evidence for that. In fact, it is the Oral Laws that Jesus resisted and sought to break at every turn because they were from man, not from God. They were a burden that probably prompted Jesus to say things like, "Come unto me all you who labor and are heavy laden and I will give you rest."[1] Rest from what? The burden of these impossible laws! There were over fifteen hundred Oral Laws concerning the Sabbath.

We see God's grace throughout the Old Testament, but Jesus gave full expression to how it would look in human form. Because of His teaching, the Jews began to see obedience to God's laws from *desire* rather than *obligation*. Now, their praying, learning, and serving others wouldn't be because they had to, but because they wanted to. No longer would they draw on their own resources; no longer would the spotlight be on behavior but on the heart. Everything Jesus does is unmerited favor toward His beloved. He wants to build this in each of us. We live by grace (desire), not by law (duty).

[1]Matt. 11:28

The Sermon on the Mount: Its Purpose

"When Jesus saw the crowds, He went up on the mountain, and after He sat down, the disciples came to Him." Matthew 5:1

Keeping in mind the last two days, we now look at this great Sermon. Understanding law and grace have everything to do with properly understanding these teachings of Jesus in Matthew 5—7. He prayed all night and "chose the twelve to be *with Him*."[1] Overlooking the Sea of Galilee, He teaches principles meant for His disciples, but Jewish leaders and others are also present.

If this teaching is to impact our lives, it must be understood and taught from a standpoint of *grace* rather than *law*. Many have said, *I'm not interested in organized religion, but I try to base my life on the Sermon on the Mount.* My response is "Good luck, you'll need it!" The Sermon is not intended to be a moral barometer that governs our lifestyle. It is not our "standard for Christian living." The Sermon is the kind of righteousness required to enter the Kingdom. It's a picture of what life would look like if God's laws were lived perfectly, as Jesus did. So why would God expect us to do what only Jesus can do?

What if Jesus, who kept the law's demands perfectly, could somehow live His life in and through my life? I love golf, but no matter how much

I practice, I will never play like Tiger Woods. But what if Tiger could miraculously step inside my body with his swing and ability? I could then be a Tiger Woods, but it would not be me, but him through me. Grace means that through the energy of the Holy Spirit, within the life of the believer, we can trust God to be *in us* what we're not and to do *in us* what we cannot.

If you view the Bible as a set of directives on how to live, you don't need a resurrected Christ, you just need a rule book![2]

Why? Consider these images: The law is like a brick wall:[3] trying to crash through it produces only a headache. After many tries you say, "God, I can't do this," and he says, "I wondered when you would figure that out ... if you could do it my Son would be irrelevant." The law is like a plumb line:[4] It shows us how crooked we really are. It's like a high definition video ... it shows us every blemish that would otherwise be hidden.[5]

If you study the Sermon with a perspective of grace, you will see these principles, not as a hill to conquer, but a place of rest while God works within you.

---

[1]Mark 3:14   [2]Gal. 3:24   [3]1 Tim. 1:8—11   [4]Rom. 3:20   [5]Rom. 5:20

The Beatitudes: Matthew 5:1–3

Before He chose the twelve Disciples, Jesus had several confrontations with the Pharisees over their Oral Laws. Despite this, He begins his great teaching on a positive, upbeat note with eight blessed attitudes that will bring joy and completeness to human life. Because they are on the side of a mountain, it might be helpful to think of the first four blessed attitudes as markers ascending the mountain. These describe our initial "steps" in a relationship with God, and the character He wants to develop in us. The second four are steps descending the mountain and into the world, where character and perspective invade and, hopefully, impact the culture in which we live.

Notice that each of these perspectives cuts right across the ways we are taught to think and act. None of these blessed attitudes will qualify you for a job or promotion. They are considered liabilities in the world, not attributes.

First Step Up: "Blessed are the poor in spirit, for theirs is the Kingdom of Heaven."

Read these verses below.[1] The common thread is humility and brokenness. One who is poor in spirit recognizes his own spiritual poverty. The secular person sees this as weakness, a character flaw. The Nazis saw it as the great defect of the church. The Greek and Roman philosophers saw it as a non-virtue. Even some pastors have traded it for the gospel of self-esteem.

Why was King David "a man after God's own heart?"[2] He committed adultery, then to cover it up sent Bathsheba's husband to the front lines knowing he would be killed. But David was confronted by Nathan, the prophet, and hated what he had done; he was stunned by the sickness in his own heart. He said he was "poor and needy."[3] He said his "heart was wounded."[4] Humility was the only thing he brought to the table that could impress God. That he had been a prodigy as a kid, an undeniable leader as a young man, and was now King of Israel meant nothing to him. David was so shattered and remorseful over his sin that his sincerity touched the heart of God.

Being poor in spirit doesn't mean cowering in the corner; it is not pathetic and weak. It is just the opposite ... bold and courageous ... recognizing that you have nothing to offer God but your brokenness. Your spiritual bankruptcy is what qualifies you for friendship with God and eternity in the kingdom of God.

---

[1] Isa. 57:17; 62:2; Ps. 51:17   [2] 1 Sam. 13:14   [3] Ps. 40:17   [4] Ps. 109:21–22

The Beatitudes: Second Step Up

"Blessed are they who mourn, for they will be comforted."
Matthew 5:2

Mourn what? It certainly doesn't encourage us to be morose and pitiful. As I said two days ago, these teachings are a dramatic paradox. To grieve with gladness, to see joy amid sorrow, or to experience a strange sense of well-being while nursing a broken heart is an astonishing thought. As a young believer, I could never understand why Jesus was called a "man of sorrows."[1] I learned that it had to do with the devastation that sin and discord caused in people whom He loved. I then began to understand why Scripture says, "for the joy set before Him He endured the cross."[2] Going to the cross was a painful reality in His humanity, but He knew that in His Deity, His death would set men free, and it was a joyous reality to Him.

As you look at the current state of people's lives, do you identify with God's grief? Unlike the mourning with which we are acquainted, this is a deep spiritual yearning that won't subside until we experience the comfort and joy that only He can give.

When Hurricane Katrina devastated the Gulf Coast, many fled to wait out the storm in a safer place. Others stayed with their homes. When the storm cleared, many who returned were obsessed with the extent of their loss. Those who stayed, during great mourning and pain, seemed to experience a supernatural sense of well-being and thankfulness that they could not explain. Avoidance of pain and sorrow causes us to miss the comfort and joy of seeing God come through in impossible circumstances.

Envisioning Jesus on the cross, we know He feels our pain. But when you look at the cross, do you feel His pain? Do you also feel His joy in knowing what that pain would accomplish? When we see the Father watch His only Son brutally beaten and spat upon, we know He understands what a broken heart is all about.

---

[1]Isa. 53:3   [2]Heb. 12:2

The Beatitudes: Third Step Up

"Blessed are the meek, for they shall inherit the earth." Matthew 5:5

When I was a kid, I often heard the phrase, "Jesus meek and mild." Looking at some of the old renderings of Him in paintings I determined that He must have been a bit of a weenie until I learned what meekness meant.

As soon as Jesus makes this statement, Psalm 37 would have exploded in the minds of his hearers. Jews knew the Scriptures, so this Psalm would be familiar. It's about the "meek" who are uncommonly righteous and who wait with great expectation on the Lord. The meek are those who give liberally without any expectation of getting back, people so trusting of God, and so secure in His love, that they feel no need to manipulate circumstances that would benefit themselves.

To really understand meekness, we must look at Jesus as He moves among people. All that He taught, He was. In Jesus, you see God in human flesh. Imagine the power and energy of the God of the Universe compressed in a human frame. Imagine the human impulse in Jesus to just let it rip! But he kept that power and the full expression of God under control. It is a power like of a wild stallion that is broken and can be ridden. None of the power is lost, but it is now diffused and under control. Jesus could have called ten thousand angels to His aid on the cross,[1] but he tempered His will and submitted to the purpose for which He came. The Rabbis could understand that the Messiah would be a *Conquering King but* could never grasp that He would also be a *Suffering Servant*.

He had made blind eyes see and could have made seeing eyes blind, easily escaping the grasp of the soldiers who arrested Him. But He yielded His power to the will of the Father.[2] To view meekness as wimpish and weak is a gross misunderstanding. Meekness is having the ability to annihilate someone in an argument and make them look pathetic but instead, taking the high road. It is one who sees the weakness or vulnerability in another but walks away from exploiting it. It is choosing not to always be the hero.

It is those, says Jesus, *who will inherit the earth* ... not the brash, the arrogant, or the proud. Once again, we see the humility that defines Jesus and must define those who are His disciples.

---

[1]Matt. 26:53   [2]Luke 22:49–53

51

The Beatitudes: Fourth Step Up

"Blessed are those who hunger and thirst after righteousness, for they will be satisfied." Matthew 5:6

Have you ever been desperately hungry or thirsty? I haven't, but I have seen it up close and personal in Africa and India. Most of us gag when we see a survival show on TV and they eat bugs and yucca roots, but that's not real. They have cameramen, a director, a couple of assistants and a doctor on hand. The best most of us can identify is if we miss lunch, come home and say, "I'm starving." So, it's difficult to accurately relate with this teaching where Jesus speaks to desert people who probably have been there.

Well, how about this: Have you ever wanted something so badly you could "taste it?" That car in the show-room window, that promotion, the winning lottery ticket or maybe an accomplishment you crave? Our hunger and thirst is mostly for things ... Stuff! Jesus speaks here of a desperate longing for righteousness. Most of us can't relate to this longing because we think righteousness is a work assignment. We have been taught that it is praying and giving more, Bible memorization and more activity is what

will get us there. The truth is, righteousness is a perspective, a gift, not a spiritual achievement. Nothing that you do, or avoid doing, will make you righteous. Jesus' death is the only thing that qualifies you. Don't think of this as a religious word. It essentially means that we are *right* with God. When I was out there playing God, I was His enemy. But Jesus died so that I could become His friend. When I quit running and trusted him, I became right with Him.

Well, why does Jesus say we should hunger and thirst after something we already possess? If you really had been starving and someone gave you a meal, would it satisfy you for life? You would be hungry again in a few hours. Read the passages below.[1] God says He will open the gates of blessing for those who seek him. Righteousness is like the meal you can never forget. You tasted it, and now you can't live without it. When you pursue God, you will find a level of satisfaction and contentment that creates an insatiable desire.

---

[1]Ps. 22:26; 37:17; Isa. 55:1; 65:13

The Beatitudes: First Step Down

"Blessed are the merciful, for they shall receive mercy." Matthew 5:7

Jesus has taught four attitudes or perspectives He wants to build into His disciples: Those who are poor in spirit, those who mourn, those who are meek, and those who hunger and thirst after righteousness. Now we take four steps down the mountain to see how a disciple who possesses these character traits will impact the culture down in the valley.

We all tend to prefer justice or mercy, depending on whether the circumstances are favorable to our personal situation. If I get a speeding ticket and feel I wasn't speeding, I think I am being treated unjustly. However, when I exceed the speed limit and don't get caught, I don't remember ever driving over to the police station and demanding justice for the tickets I didn't get.

Imagine the first thoughts of the people on that mountainside who had experienced neither mercy nor justice from their Roman captors. Add to that the law-driven, judgmental attitude of the Pharisees, and we can understand how radical this teaching would have sounded falling on Jewish ears. Jews were basically under house arrest. They were hated by the Romans; they were cursed, spat upon, humiliated and forced to do everything they were told. Jesus is telling his new disciples that they will influence the world, even these horrible people ... if they have merciful hearts.

The Jewish leaders try to trick Jesus with a question concerning punishment for a woman caught in adultery.[1] Either answer He gives gets Him in major hot water. In the end, He asks the woman's accusers to throw the first stone if they have never sinned. They slink away, and Jesus does not condemn her. He doesn't acquit her or minimize her sin. He alone had the right to condemn her, but he pardons her. It is a sheer act of mercy.

The humility to forgive changes the forgiven. It also changes the forgiver. Letting an undeserving person *off the hook* lets me off the hook as well. Those who are merciful will see mercy return to them.

---

[1] John 7:53—8:11

The Beatitudes: Second Step Down

"Blessed are the pure in heart, for they shall see God."
Matthew 5:8

The first thing we notice about this blessed attitude is that it is about the heart. As Jesus spoke these words some of those who listened on the fringe of the crowd were Pharisees. These were people who Jesus confronted constantly concerning the heart. They took great pains to look good on the outside. Image was supremely important. They cared little for the motives and the inner parts that could not be easily showcased.[1]

Do you know, or have you ever known, anyone who you could honestly say is "pure in heart?" You might mention an aunt or grandmother who is kind and loving, but if you asked them if they had a pure heart they would probably laugh in your face. Why? Because they know thoughts, motives, and secrets that you could never know. Jesus' mission on earth was not to stop adultery, materialism, murder, or homosexuality. Why? They are symptoms of much deeper issues that are invisible in the human heart.

A pure heart is who you are when no one is around. The church is obsessed with behavior, but God's interest is in the heart.[2] No one can introduce you as a person with a pure heart because only God has ever seen your heart. The Psalmist wrote that someone with a pure heart does not deceive or lie.[3] That knocks me out, along with everyone I have ever met. To a Hebrew, a lie was not just the absence of truth; it was something false with the intent of being detrimental to another. Everybody lies … every day! It is usually to avoid embarrassment or to boost our ego. But Jesus did not come to cure our bad habits or make us more presentable.

How can we have a pure heart? Who never gets seduced by the exciting false gods of the world … money, cars, houses, power? Who is never false in any of his dealings with God or with man? Only Jesus. But if He is in you, and you yield to His life, He who is pure in heart will produce the purity of His heart in you. It will take time, but so does everything that matters.

---

[1]Matt. 23:25–26   [2]1 Sam. 16:7   [3]Ps. 24:3–4

The Beatitudes: Third Step Down

"Blessed are the peacemakers for they shall be called sons of God."
Matthew 5:9

Jesus is called the Prince of Peace.[1] At the announcement of His birth to the shepherds, the angel's greeting was "peace to those with whom He finds favor."[2] In His farewell to His disciples before His arrest, He told them that the peace He leaves with them is not like the peace the world gives.[3] The dream of God and His Son is that world He created would become a place of peace and that peacemakers would set that pace.

A true peacemaker is one who desires to introduce others to a level of contentment that only comes from God Himself. It is a kind of peace that is not temporary and does not depend on favorable circumstances. Like righteousness, peace cannot be created; it is an endowment that comes from within. You can't be a peacemaker if you don't possess peace. Peace has much to do with understanding and believing who we are from God's point of view. It requires that we reject the definitions given to us by a world that knows nothing of peace and contentment.

The Book of Judges was the lowest point in Israel's history. They had disobeyed God and had angered the Midianites who came in and destroyed their crops and killed their livestock. Hungry and beaten, the Israelites turned back to God and He sent an angel, not to the greatest of the twelve tribes of Israel, but to Manasseh, a tribe that had been split in two and was the weakest of the twelve. The angel went to Gideon, who was young and argued with God that he was the very least in his clan. He finally agreed to fight the Midianites and wanted to take thirty-two thousand soldiers, but God only let him take three hundred, which was suicidal. Gideon obeyed God and miraculously won the battle, restoring peace to Israel.[4]

The Israelites learned that God is the source of peace, not large armies or skilled warriors. But God also empowers ordinary people to become peacemakers. He had made a promise to Gideon, and through this "unimportant" young man from an insignificant family, peace was restored to all of Israel.

The life of a peacemaker can create a level of peace that permeates every atmosphere he or she enters. An ordinary person without pedigree or influence can create a calming culture that others will desire.

---

[1]Isa. 9:6   [2]Luke 2:14   [3]John 14:27   [4]Judges 6—7

The Beatitudes: Fourth Step Down

"Blessed are you when people insult you and persecute you, and say all kinds of false things against you because of Me." Matthew 5:11

Jesus is speaking to people who are well acquainted with persecution but don't see it as having anything to do with righteousness. The Jews resent their treatment by the Romans and see no positive outcome at the end of the tunnel. Today, as we follow Jesus, the journey won't be a cakewalk; we will be scorned and persecuted not only by the unredeemed but sometimes by those we thought were with us.

Jesus is saying to His followers, "My Father knows your pain. He understands rejection and misunderstood motives. Continue to honor Him in all you do, and He will open the gates of blessing to you because of your faithfulness."

Maybe you have never suffered persecution, but the world is running after a different set of values, and the contrast between their goals and ours will cause many to think we are a bunch of religious nuts. You don't have to be a prude to wince over the evolving attitudes and actions that adorn our culture. It doesn't take a scholar to look around you and see that we, and our children, will pay a great price because we are simply "going with the flow." If you speak out you will be considered intolerant and out of step. If you don't, they'll love you, but you'll lose respect for yourself and one day your kids will ask you why you kept silent.[1]

The key phrase is in verse 12: "because of Me." Being persecuted because you brashly offended someone with some spiritual rant is not what Jesus is saying. It is not our job to be as irritating as possible. Jesus is the truth and the truth will always be offensive to those who have created their own version.

I don't consider myself right-wing, left-wing, or chicken wing. I couldn't care less about those ridiculous labels. Their meaning is altered every decade, and on top of that, they are all extra-biblical. I simply want my life to honor God.

We are to be a light on a hill,[2] salt that flavors every atmosphere we enter,[3] and a healing presence,[4] but sometimes you must stand up and say, ENOUGH! Just make sure it is because of God's honor, and not the voice of the angry multitudes pulling you there. Blessed are you when you find the courage to stand tall when that time comes.

---

[1]John 6:26   [2]Matt. 5:14   [3]Matt. 5:13–16   [4]Jer. 8:22

Jesus Tells His Disciples Who They Are

"You are the salt of the earth, but if the salt has become tasteless, how can it become salt again? It is no good except to be thrown out and trampled underfoot by men." Matthew 5:13

Jesus is a Jewish Rabbi speaking to Jewish people. All rabbis communicated primarily in pictures rather than concepts as we do in the Western world. Jesus wants to show the twelve who they *already are* by virtue of their faith in Him, not simply what they *can become* if they try hard. He uses two images, *salt* and *light* to paint an unmistakable picture for His first-century hearers. These two images are not simply concepts; they are everyday realities with which His hearers were well acquainted. He wants them to see themselves as salt and light as they walk down into the valley.

We all know that salt is extremely versatile. It can clean brass, soothe bites and stings, keep wicker looking new, remove wine or grease stains. (It has more than sixty uses!) But salt is also a *catalyst*. It is never the main attraction, but without it, food can be tasteless and bland. Jesus tells His disciples that they *are* catalysts that will create thirst and add flavor to the world.

One of the chambers of the Temple compound was called "the salt chamber." This is where the salt from the Dead Sea was stored. If the salt lost its saltiness, its only value then was to sprinkle it on the floor of the altar of sacrifice to be walked on by the priests to keep them from slipping on the blood.

Salt is also a preservative. In the days without refrigeration, meat and fish were packed with salt to keep them in their original state. Despite the belief of many, Jesus never came to establish a new religion called Christianity. Nowhere will you find that in the Scriptures. Jesus came to seek and to save the lost[1] and to offer His life as a ransom for many.[2] We have created a religion that Jesus would not even recognize. God wants it to return to its original state where people would walk with Him daily, enjoy the creation rather than abuse it, and live in harmony with one another.

A catalyst is one whose foundation is reconciliation. We enter the atmosphere of relationships, and rather than antagonizing we bring together that which is alienated and aid the healing of that which is broken.

---

[1] Luke 19:10   [2] Mark 10:45

Jesus Paints a Word Picture of His Disciples

"You are the light of the world; A city set on a hill cannot be hidden, nor does anyone light a lamp and put it under a basket, but on a lampstand and it gives light to all who are in the house. Let your light shine before men in such a way that they may see your good works and glorify your Father which is in heaven."
Matthew 5:14–16

Again, Jesus uses the image of light to paint a graphic word picture of who His disciples are. Notice He doesn't say, *you can be salt and light if you really work on it.* Their identity in God's eyes is that of light. The degree to which that light will shine only depends on their willingness to allow it to shine through them.

The metaphors of light and darkness fill the Scriptures: Light points to truth, wisdom, direction, understanding. Darkness expresses death, confusion, evil, and falsehood. The expression, "a city set on a hill" is directly related to light. Fires were lit on the tops of mountains for the purpose of announcing the full moon. Unless the fires were set on the hills they could not be seen. To put a light under a basket defeats the whole purpose of the light.

Jesus' simple but profound message is that people whose lives have been illuminated with the life of God must allow the brilliance of that light to scatter the darkness. When you *strive* to become a light, it is like a thick dark cloud blocking out the sun. It is a light created by you and which illuminates you rather than Him. "Let your light shine" is the admonition, not *make* your light shine. There is no energy involved on your part, simply the willingness to be a vessel through which God's light radiates.

John, the youngest of the twelve, wrote that there is no darkness at all in God and that if we say we claim to be His friend and still walk in darkness we are lying.[1] The mistake enthusiastic believers often make is the same thing that happens if you shine a flashlight in someone's face. No one responds well to that. It forces people to look away. If however, you shine the light in front of them, they will see the pathway out of the darkness. If we allow our light to shine, people will be drawn like moths to a lamp … not because of us, but because of the Light in us.

---

[1] John 1:5–7

The Trap of Legalism

"Do not think that I came to abolish the Law or the Prophets; I did not come to abolish but to fulfill." Matthew 5:17

Although Jesus is teaching His disciples, there are Jewish leaders present. He makes this statement about the law to instruct *the twelve,* but also to speak to the Pharisees. To abolish the law meant to misinterpret it, and to fulfill the law meant to interpret it correctly. The Pharisees had corrupted the purpose of the law with their added manmade "Hedge Laws." The Law's purpose was to frustrate our attempts to be righteous on our own and recognize our need for a Savior. If we could keep God's standards on our own, we wouldn't need a Savior.

By the time of Jesus, righteousness had been reduced to three things: prayer, fasting, and giving alms. Jesus tells the Pharisees that if they are betting their righteousness on these three spiritual disciplines, they can kiss the Kingdom goodbye. Jesus posed a great threat to the Pharisees because things they held dear were being personified in Him. The Temple was the focal point of Jewish life, but Jesus *became the Temple*.[1] The sacrifice of a lamb was the atonement for sins, but Jesus was *the Lamb of God* who by His death atoned for the sins of the world.[2] When Jesus came, the Jewish leaders literally had come to see the Sabbath as an object of worship. Now Jesus declares Himself *Lord of the Sabbath.*[3]

Legalism is a deadly trap. It happens when people are so fearful of stepping over the line, they erect barriers to supposedly protect themselves from sin. But they become a hostage to their own legalism and in the process make themselves unattractive to be around. They cause a watching world to miss the love and compassion of God while only seeing a restrictive style of life.

It isn't that the Ten Commandments are invalid, but the new covenant that Jesus introduced was better. Jesus said that to Love God, and your neighbor fulfilled everything in the Law.[4] You can devise ways *not* to covet your neighbor's new car and wallow in guilt over adulterous thoughts about his wife … or you can obey Jesus and allow God's Spirit to create in you a new way to see your neighbors, and the ability to love them as He does. That's the difference. The Law was a "grit your teeth and bear it" style of life that was only meant to be temporary. Jesus offers a life that flows from the Father through Him that energizes and motivates the will of a man or woman to want to obey Him.

---

[1] John 2:19–21   [2] John 1:29   [3] Mark 2:27–28   [4] Matt. 22:40

Personal Relationships: Anger

"You have heard it said that the ancients were told, 'You shall not commit murder, and whoever does so will be liable in the court.' But I say to you, that everyone who is angry will be guilty before the court; and whoever says, 'Racah' shall be guilty before the supreme court and whoever says, 'You fool' shall be guilty enough to go into fiery hell." Matthew 5:21–22

The Bible is not a book of rules, a road map, or even a book of theological correctness. Every major word in the Scriptures is about relationships. Sin is a broken relationship with God. Love, peace, hate, resentment, even joy and hope, at their base, are relational words. The Bible is the story of two marriages: The Old Testament is about God's marriage to Israel and the New Testament is about the people of God being His bride. It's a relationship!

Jesus' concern for these young men was that they understand the relational connection between murder and anger. It is not just symbolic. Anger is the first step toward murder, but even if the act is never committed, the collateral damage of uncontrolled anger, slander, and gossip can be just as devastating. In those days, the word "racah" meant empty-headed and incompetent. The Hebrew word for "fool" meant a corrupt person, empty of knowledge who has turned away from God. In Rabbinic literature, it is an expression of scorn and contempt.

The issue to which Jesus speaks here is that there are certain matters of the heart that no human being has the right to challenge; it is God's prerogative, and His alone, because only He can know the content of human heart. Gossip or a slanderous word, either blatant or inferred, can overwhelm a human life. Hatred toward a brother is essentially the same as murder.[1] There are insults made in a moment of intense anger that can humiliate and devastate another human being.

We have largely lost the ability for civil discourse in our country. I believe that because we do not understand the destruction it causes on an individual basis, we are clueless on a national level. God cannot bless that which is divided and alienated. It violates His character and His purpose.

If there is any contribution one person can make to broken humanity, it is that we become ambassadors of reconciliation who pull people together rather than apart. Reconciliation is the mission of every believer; it is your ministry![2] There is no such thing as a ministry of alienation and retribution. We are called to be ambassadors of healing that pull people together.[3]

---

[1] 1 John 3:15 [2] 2 Cor. 5:18 [3] 2 Cor. 5:20

Personal Relationships: Conflict

"Therefore, if you are presenting your offering at the altar and there remember that your brother has something against you, leave your offering and go; first be reconciled to your brother then come and present your offering."
Matthew 5:23–24

We've all been in arguments or fights that seemingly cannot be resolved. One or both parties are unwilling to bring it to closure. Few things are as unsettling to me as when I walk into a worship service, speak at a gathering, or pull aside for time alone with God and know that somewhere a friend is seething in anger because I offended him. The Scripture is crystal clear. Even though he should have come to me[1] the ball is still in my court. I should say, "If I have offended you, I am very sorry and ask your forgiveness." Simple, but contrite and heartfelt words like that can not only heal the breach but take the friendship to a deeper level.

Why are we so afraid to go to someone with whom we have butted heads? It's because humility is required, but it is pride that holds us hostage. We lack the kind of vulnerability that is willing to take the blame, even if it is not all deserved. The question beckons; is the conviction that I am right of greater value than maintaining and even deepening my friendship with a brother or sister? I have never had wealth, but the wealth I have is in the friendships that have come my way over the years. I have

had a couple go by the wayside and it was probably my fault, but I grieve over those friendships even to this day. Don't let it happen to you.

Today people change friends almost as often as they change their underwear. They walk on as if it's no big deal, but it is the biggest of deals. If your children will not speak to each other and remain alienated throughout their adult life, it hurts you beyond words. Imagine the wounds God must feel. His Son, with whom He had never even had an argument, was battered, bruised, and died with the words of forgiveness on His lips for those who killed Him. But we won't forgive some petty issue that hurt our feelings.

Jesus teaches His disciples that their relationship with each other is paramount. Believers who walk together in harmony are very difficult to dismiss. If your *quiet time* has value to you yet you are unwilling to go to a friend whom you have offended, you may as well get up off your knees, close your Bible, and go play golf or watch a video. Your relationship with Him suffers when you are conflicted with another, but it flourishes when you are one.

---

[1] Matt. 18:15–17

Personal Relationships: Lust

"You have heard it said, 'You shall not commit adultery,' but I say to you that everyone who looks at a woman with lust for her has already committed adultery with her in his heart." Matthew 5:28–29

For me, the essence of walking down the path with God is this: *Father, transform my mind and heart to see people as you see them*. I believe that is the central issue in human relationships. There were certainly beautiful women with whom Jesus crossed paths. The Scripture tells us that He was tempted in all things, but didn't bend, so that includes lust.[1]

Jesus sat on a hill above Jerusalem and wept.[2] He looked at the people and had compassion for them because they were in turmoil, like sheep without a shepherd.[3] Jesus saw people far beyond the exterior trappings. He knew that in that culture, every woman he met was struggling with issues of her worth as a woman and understanding that her value was far more than simply being a vessel for procreation or recreation. He knew their understanding of God as a loving and kind Father had probably become lost in the quagmire of just trying to survive. His focus was on a woman's heart, not her body. He wanted her to see her unfathomable value to God.

An admiring glance at a beautiful woman as you walk down the beach is not necessarily lusting. It is the habitual, unbridled, out-of-control thoughts that debase the object of that desire. As we walk along with Jesus our desires will slowly begin to change. Temptations with our thoughts will always be relentless, but we should aim to consider every person we encounter as one for whom Jesus died, and for whom His single desire is wholeness and a life without regret and guilt.

Lust and even *sex at will* is not even part of the debate today. Sex is simply considered a recreational activity by many. Even among many followers of Jesus, it has become an accepted norm. For those who really desire to honor God with their lives, His principles never have an adjustable price tag no matter what year it is. There is not a person on earth who escapes the struggle with lust. It is a built-in attraction of how we were made, and if not under the control of the Spirit of God it can devastate people's present and future.

Following through with an emotional desire for another person is not about how far or how close to the line you venture and still be okay; it is more about the person you want to be.

---

[1]Heb. 4:14   [2]Luke 19:41–44   [3]John 9:36

DAY 51
Personal Relationships: Stumbling Blocks

"If your eye makes you stumble, tear it out and throw it from you, for it is better to lose one of the parts of your body than your whole body to be thrown into hell. If your right hand causes you to sin, cut it off and throw it from you."
Matthew 5:29–30

There is a common practice among those who are cynical or skeptical about the Scriptures to point out passages such as these and say that God is demanding self-mutilation. They point to Jesus' statement about eating His flesh and drinking His blood as a kind of cultic heresy. A simple investigation of the passage would reveal that He was speaking of Holy Communion or the Lord's Supper.[1]

When my grandmother was annoyed with me as a kid, she would jokingly say, "Neb, I could just spit in your eye and drown you." I have never heard that colloquialism before or since, but even as a little boy it never occurred to me that she was being literal. Sometimes there are idioms in Scripture that must be seen in the cultural context in which they were given.

These passages in the Sermon on the Mount are an ancient teaching technique used by Rabbis called *Kal va homer*. It literally means "light and heavy." It is hyperbole that was simply saying that the way to best deal with sin is to address it in its light or infant stages rather than waiting until it becomes a treacherous monster and devours you. If your eye strays into areas that are detrimental to your spiritual growth and health, don't wait until it becomes an addiction; deal with it now in its light stages. The same is true with the hand or anything that is harmful … don't play with it and soon find that it has become an obsession.

Imagine how different millions of lives might have been had they dealt with detrimental personal issues in the early stages. Alcohol, prescription drugs, sex, internet porn, and cell phone addictions may have been prevented and families saved by understanding and obeying this simple command. Imagine the beginning stages of something as simple as jealousy. Think of where that emotional sensation can take you. Consider how a mindless piece of gossip can literally destroy a life. Once that cat is out of the bag, it is almost impossible to stop. As that great theologian, Barney Fife used to say, "You've got to *nip it* in the bud!"

---

[1] John 6:54–56

63

Personal Relationships: Oaths and Vows

"Again, you have heard that it was said to the people long ago, 'Do not break your oath, but keep the oaths you have made to the Lord.' But I tell you, do not swear at all: either by heaven, for it is God's throne; or by the earth, for it is his footstool; or by Jerusalem, for it is the city of the Great King. And do not swear by your head, for you cannot make even one hair white or black. Simply let your 'Yes' be 'Yes,' and your 'No be 'No'; anything beyond this comes from the evil one"
Matthew 5:33–37

Why do we even *need* to make oaths and vows? It's because we are all prone to twist the truth and to look for a back door when it comes time to fulfill our promises. So, we swear oaths to assure others that we are trustworthy. An oath is a tangible way we guarantee our promises to be authentic. But, the truth about oaths and vows usually is a tell-tale sign that there is a hole in our story and the extra emphasis is an attempt to fill it. A minister, known for his fiery sermons, died and found in his Bible among many jotted notes was a passage underlined, and in the margin beside it, the words, "Weak point ... yell louder!"

Because of Jesus' words in the above verses, many believe that an oath or vow should never be made. However, we see many throughout the Old Testament Scriptures. Abraham swore an oath when he made a covenant with Abimelech.[1] Even God Himself swore to Abraham that He would keep His covenant promises.[2]

Obviously, since God Himself made a vow, oaths cannot be wrong in and of themselves. What Jesus was against were spontaneous vows like "I swear on a stack of Bibles" or "I swear on my mother's life." When a person goes to that level to persuade me of his sincerity, he is tipping his hand. When someone tries *that* diligently to make his case, there is usually a reason for concern.

When you make a vow, even one that is legitimate, you are assuming that you have the capacity to fulfill it ... and you don't! "I swear I will never do a dishonest thing ever again." Really? Jesus decries dramatic or superfluous answers. He wants His disciples to be straightforward without a bunch of tap dancing and ridiculous explanations. Our answer is to be a righteous "yes" or "no." You don't need to swear by anything; simply do what you say you are going to do, shut up, and walk on!

---

[1] Gen. 21:22–34   [2] Heb. 6:13–20

Personal Relationships: Hostility

"You have heard that it was said, 'Eye for an eye, and a tooth for a tooth.' But I tell you, do not resist an evil person. If anyone slaps you on the right cheek, turn to them the other cheek also. And if anyone wants to sue you and take your shirt, hand over your coat as well." Matthew 5:38–40

These teachings of Jesus are a hundred-and eighty-degrees counter to conventional wisdom. They defy the normal response of a person to insult, aggression, and malice. Turning the other cheek, offering your coat when someone takes your shirt, voluntarily carrying a Roman soldier's burden the extra mile, and acting with love rather than hatred toward your enemy is a revolutionary concept. This teaching was so radical and counterintuitive that to the unrenewed mind it must have seemed almost suicidal.

When someone speaks sharply or rudely to you, the immediate reaction is to respond in kind. Jesus wants his disciples to be under the control of His Spirit, not their emotions. A "slap" with the open hand in Jesus' day was more of an insult than an intent to injure. In Jewish law, an open-handed slap carried a penalty of two hundred denarii, which was about seven months' wages. It is our retaliation that offers control to the aggressor. Roman soldiers often taunted Jews and forced them to carry their load. The control returns from the soldier to you as you voluntarily go the second mile. This action creates a puzzling conundrum for the perpetrator: "Who is this person?"

Offering your coat after someone takes your shirt may appear to be passive indifference, but it is meekness in its truest form. You have every right to retaliate against this arrogant jerk, but you choose to give up that right. This may be the only kind response he will ever see. Vulnerability and humility have the capacity to touch the heart of another. A friend of mine in New York was accosted on an elevator by a guy with a knife. He demanded my friend's wallet. He handed it over and as the man was about to make his escape, my friend said, "I carry money in a clip, not in my wallet," as he handed the man a wad of bills. He looked at the money, looked at my friend, dropped the wallet, and ran. That's a true story. It won't make it into any of the self-defense booklets, but that is the power vulnerability can have.

Jesus' intent is always *reconciliation* rather than *retribution,* regardless of the situation. When we are treated with hostility, a calm, understanding response can have a dramatic outcome.[1] We are peacemakers;[2] we know what painful issues may be lurking in the dark corners of that person's life. We will never give a healing touch by retaliation,[3] only by love.

---

[1] 1 Thess. 5:15   [2] Matt. 5:9   [3] Rom. 12:17, 19

Perfection?

"Therefore, you are to be perfect, just as your Heavenly Father is perfect."
Matthew 5:48

How does that grab you? When I gave my life to Jesus, my Young Life Leader, Mal McSwain, gave me a Phillips New Testament and told me to read a chapter each night and mark passages I didn't understand, and we would discuss them later. I started in Matthew and at the end of the fifth day, I read verse 48 and threw my Bible across the room and broke a lamp. I just knew I had made a horrible mistake. No one can be perfect. I knew I was in over my head, and I didn't read again for several weeks.

Over the years I've heard many explanations for that difficult verse. Someone says," Well, you just have to try to get as close to perfection as possible. Another says that "perfect" means progressing ... getting better and better. The Greek rendering does hint at that, but that seems to weaken what Jesus obviously aimed at the Pharisees who were present. I've met people during my life who seemed like they were trying desperately to emulate perfection, but they weren't very likable people. They were boorish, way too serious, and I could never relax around them.

Years later I discovered that Jesus meant exactly what He said. He told those disciples to do something He knew they couldn't do. No level of spiritual disciplines will get you there. So, everything we have looked at so far in the Sermon on the Mount, we are incapable of doing. Only Jesus can live out these principles. It took me years to see that if He is in me and I will simply cooperate and yield my life to Him daily, He can produce in me that which is impossible through my own efforts. If I could live out this stuff, I would be the savior rather than Jesus.

When people say they are trying to live by the Sermon on the Mount, I read them the last verse in chapter five and ask them how it's working out for them. It's not about our efforts. Everything is about His life in and through us, without any assistance from us. Nothing we do on His behalf in our own strength will be pleasing to Him, because whether we realize it or not, what we are doing is basically what Adam and Eve reasoned in the garden. The serpent convinced them that God was holding them back. *"Don't you realize what puppets you two are? You try to do everything God says. Don't you realize you can be like God without God?"* That's what happens when we try to please God by doing things *for* Him rather than yielding our lives *to* Him and letting Him live in us.

The Value of Anonymity

"For promotion cometh neither from the east, nor from the west, nor from the south. But God is the judge: he putteth down one, and setteth up another."
Psalm 75:6–7 (KJV)

Have you noticed that everything Jesus does is without any attempt to seek attention to Himself? He never tries to draw crowds; they find Him. He never markets Himself; He rejects the multitude's attempts to make Him King. He has no organization, no letterhead, no national headquarters, no official title, and owns only the clothes on His back. How different He is from the religious leaders of today. He instructs His followers to practice individual spiritual disciplines secretly, without show or pretense, and to care for people quietly and without shining the spotlight on themselves. This makes no sense in today's world of self-promotion and "branding."

Consider the effectiveness of Satan in the world. He never advertises or draws attention to himself. He is the initiator of all evil, yet he disguises his efforts to imitate good. He is a master counterfeiter who influences us in ways so subtle and seemingly innocuous that we rarely notice. His influence in the world is undeniable but quite different than we think. We blame him when we overspend or overeat, have a flat tire, or fail to keep our New Year's resolutions. Satan becomes a convenient excuse for our own negligence or lack of discipline and has little to do with his plan to unhinge us. His works always thrive in the unexpected.

I have come to believe that anonymity is a critical posture for true effectiveness. If you want to have an impact on people's lives, do the opposite of what all the books and marketing people tell you. Don't seek attention or accent what you are doing. Let the deed and the knowledge that Jesus was honored be your reward. A profound quote I read some thirty-five years ago was by a fourteenth-century monk. Several young men asked him how they might become martyrs for Christ. He told them that it is much harder to live for Jesus than to die for him. Then he said, *"I will give you a true martyrdom to aspire to: To be a man of God but appear to be a man of the world; to be a man with a mission but not be called a missionary, and the hardest of all … to pass through the world unnoticed."* Meditate on that!

We enter the atmosphere of people's lives to encourage, be available, and help behind the scenes without hope of notoriety. If this is done faithfully, and as a natural extension of who we are, it will be impossible for the skeptic to write us off.

Anonymity in Giving

"Beware of practicing your righteousness before other people in order to be seen by them, for then you will have no reward from your Father who is in heaven."
Matthew 6:1–3

Why does Jesus address this in His great sermon? His young disciples had watched how their Jewish leaders had operated their entire life. By contrasting real giving with the egotistical motives of the Pharisees, Jesus shows heartfelt generosity as opposed to the token variety.

When you give, don't hire a trumpeter to alert people to your generosity, says Jesus. In the court of the woman at the temple were vessels that were wide at the bottom with a narrow opening at the top, giving the appearance of a trumpet. The larger the number of coins put in, the greater the noise. People would immediately look at the source of such a "generous" display. It was called "sounding the trumpet." This was a favorite activity of the Pharisees and gave them the notoriety they craved.

"The poor still got the money," you might say. True, but it misses God's primary intent for giving. The gift is to be a blessing first to the giver and secondarily to the one who receives it.[1] God is a giver by His very nature. He wants to build His perspective about money into the lives of His people. He doesn't *need* our money, but he wants to help us overcome our tendency toward selfishness and self-adulation. He goes on to say that our giving should be such a natural part of our thinking and so unconscious that your right hand should be unaware that your left hand did something kind and generous.

For those whose motives mirror that of the Pharisees, he is saying that any adulation they gain by these intentional public displays of pseudo-generosity is all they will get, while God will personally reward those who give secretly. Giving is not a program, and if it is a spiritual discipline, we have missed the essence of grace. To give out of *obligation* is law; to give out of *desire* is grace. Giving is the foundation of God's character. "For God so loved the world that *He gave* ..."[2] We can never become more like Jesus without a generous heart.

---

[1]Acts 20:35   [2]John 3:16

Prayer: The Ultimate Act of Privacy

"And when you pray, don't be as the hypocrites, for they love to stand and pray in the synagogues and on the street corners in order to be seen by men. Truly I say to you, they have had their reward in full. But when you pray, go into your inner room and when you have shut your door, pray to your Father who is in secret." Matthew 6:5–6

A conversation from your heart to the heart of God is the most private and intimate thing you will ever do. It is deeply personal, laced with raw honesty and with groanings too deep for words.[1]

I felt more in harmony with God in the first months after I learned to pray then in the next few years that followed. I knelt by my bed and had no idea what to say or how to say it. I just blurted out my deepest hurts and yearnings and unburdened my soul. In college, I was *taught* to pray by listening to those further along than me. The spontaneity and honesty began to disappear. I was given the "ingredients" of prayer *like praise, thanksgiving, confession, and petition,* and in my quest to do it properly, it became mechanical. When it was just God and me, I felt like I connected, but in a group it became SHOWTIME! The spiritually mature would moan, "Yes, Lord," or say "Amen," affirming the prayer that was prayed. I realized that I had begun praying for a verbal acknowledgment from the group. If no one responded I thought I had messed up. Don't misunderstand, praying with friends is wonderful, but deepening our friendship enables us to speak candidly with God while allowing our friends to listen in, rather than the reverse.

The Pharisees prayed long, ornate prayers; the more elaborate and poetic the better. It was a show, and Jesus called it out! When I was a kid in school, prayer and Bible reading over the intercom was a joke. If that's what people are assuming will get God back in the schools, count me out. No one listened … no one cared. It was not only irrelevant but irreverent. It cemented in us the idea that prayer and Scripture were activities rather than part of a relationship. We figured out that it was something that the adult world hoped would intimidate us into raising a little less hell. And besides, how does man take God out of anything?

Sometimes our attempts to help kids grow spiritually ends up being counterproductive. If you want your child to pray, do what Jesus did. He never coaxed or commanded the twelve to talk to God, He simply did it Himself. They began to connect what He did in private with how He lived in public. Prayer is a private and sacred relationship, and we must allow others to come to that place of need without coercion or intimidation.

---

[1] Rom. 8:26

When You Pray . . .

"And when you are praying, do not use meaningless repetition as the Gentiles do, for they suppose they will be heard for their many words. Therefore, do not be like them, for your Father knows what you need before you ask him." Matthew 6:7–8

On numerous occasions, I have gone to the ER to be with the family of someone who was in an accident or very sick. Often, several friends will circle up and pray the Lord's Prayer. It is the one moment when people, regardless of their personal belief, will stand in solidarity on behalf of the hurting family.

A football team enters the locker room after a game and the coach says, "Let's all take a knee," and the players and coaches echo the Lord's Prayer in unison. Just as the prayer at the hospital was not about the afflicted family, the Lord's Prayer in the locker room expresses nothing related to the game or the players. "Thy will be done" is the only phrase that could remotely connect with the previous two hours. Wasn't anyone there able to just talk to God?

After Jesus told the twelve not to use meaningless repetition and flowery words to impress God, He teaches them to pray "in this way."[1] He then prays what we have labeled, "The Lord's Prayer." The phrase, "in this way" (or manner) is key. He does not say, *"In times of difficulty or every Sunday, pray this prayer."* But that's exactly what we do. This prayer expresses the heart of what God wants us to bring to him. He never intended it as a *one size fits all* prayer for any occasion. Jesus wants us to understand, "You're talking to your Daddy!" If your daughter was crying and you put your arm around her and said, "What's the matter honey, how can I help?" What if she blurted out, "Our Father who feeds me, clothes me, and gives me shelter, etc."? Would you not say, "I'm your Daddy, for goodness sake, just talk to me?"

This is a wonderful prayer, but it was never meant to be an emotionless parade of words devoid of passion and meaning. When we pray by *rote*, it is like saying "I love you" to someone in a flippant manner. "Love ya" has been said to me by people I hardly know. Do I believe they really love me? Of course not, but when we throw a word around it will soon become irrelevant. I appreciate their gesture, but it's just a cliché.

Jesus is teaching us to offer up our hearts along with our words. Repeating prayers isn't wrong, but we should never forget you're addressing your Heavenly Father. If I really know Him, I feel free to express any emotion, even anger or doubt. The point of Jesus' teaching was intimacy over mindless repetition.

---

[1]Matt. 6:8

Forgiveness: The Secret Sauce

"For if you forgive men for their transgressions, your Heavenly Father will also forgive you. But if you do not forgive men, your Father will not forgive your transgressions." Matthew 6:14–15

In the Lord's Prayer, Jesus clearly says, "Forgive us our trespasses as we forgive those who trespass against us." He immediately reiterates this after the prayer. It is imperative that the twelve understand that being forgiven by God is directly connected to forgiving others.[1] This is not saying that your salvation is in jeopardy, but it is saying that unwillingness to forgive another is a sure sign that you haven't really experienced God's forgiveness or you have a very convoluted understanding of it. Some may feel they are too bad to be forgiven. They have never felt the freedom and joy of that liberating release. Others may be riddled with pride and feel they don't *need* forgiveness.

Forgiveness of others does not let them off the hook, but failure to forgive keeps you *on* the hook and imprisons you for the rest of your life. How could God believe the sincerity of a person who asks for forgiveness but harbors great bitterness against someone? Bitterness causes us to relive and replay every remembrance of the offense. God hates the sin, but He never holds bitterness toward the sinner. When sin is confessed and forgiven, it is separated from the forgiven one as far as the east from the west.[2] God even says that He will not only forgive us but will no longer even remember what we've done.[3] That's a blank check if there ever was one!

The following is one of the most moving expressions of forgiveness I know of. It was a note found in the pocket of a child incinerated at Ravensbruck Concentration Camp in 1944.

"Oh Lord, remember not only the men and women of goodwill but also those of ill will. But do not remember all the sufferings they have inflicted upon us. Instead, remember the fruits we have borne because of this suffering, our fellowship, our loyalty to one another, our courage, our generosity, the greatness of heart that has grown from this trouble. When our persecutors come to be judged by you, let all these fruits that we have borne be their forgiveness."

---

[1] Eccles. 28:2   [2] Ps. 103:12   [3] Heb. 8:12

Anonymity: Fasting

"And when you fast, do not put on a gloomy face as the hypocrites do, for they neglect their appearance to be seen fasting by men. Truly I say to you, they have their reward in full. But you, when you fast, anoint your head and wash your face so that you may not be seen fasting by men, but by your Father who is in secret; and your Father who sees in secret will repay you." Matthew 6:16–18

Fasting is not some ancient ritual that is out of date and overrated, but it is misunderstood and has received a bad rap because of its abuse. During the time of Moses, a national day to honor the Day of Atonement was initiated. Five more national days were added, and by the time Jesus came, it had gone to at least twice a week and was a burdensome tradition.[1] Jesus was not against fasting in its original intent, but the Pharisees had turned it into a legal requirement rather than a voluntary act of devotion to God. It also became another platform for them to display their counterfeit spirituality. They would smear ashes on their face and look as disheveled as possible, seeking to put their "devotion" to God on display. Jesus hated this kind of pseudo-piety and hypocrisy or *play-acting*. He called them out during His Sermon as He teaches His disciples.[2]

Fasting became a burden for a Jew trying to provide for his family because it required all work to cease on the second and fifth days of each week. Additionally, no washing or bathing was permitted, as well as abstinence from sex during this period. I imagine the *no washing* made the *no sex* part more tolerable.

Few believers practice fasting today, but if done with the right intent it can be a tremendous blessing. Most people who fast do so because of a major decision or a life and death issue where they want God to know of their sincerity and devotion. Real vulnerability and genuineness of heart always pleases God. The true intent of the heart is the issue. It is a secret matter, not a chance to show off. To deny oneself a legitimate appetite for a time to cleanse the spirit and focus on connecting uniquely with God is a gift to Him and to you.

---

[1] Lev. 23:27–29   [2] Luke 18:12

Investing Wisely

"Do not lay up for yourselves treasures on earth where moth and dust destroy and where thieves break in and steal; but lay up for yourselves treasures in heaven, where neither moth nor rust destroy and where thieves do not break in or steal. For where your treasure is, there will your heart be also." Matthew 6:19–21

People who have money spend a good portion of their time trying to make it grow into more money and keeping others from taking it away. Money is the medium of exchange between people. You see something you like and you say, "How much?" Jesus knew that owning, possessing, and protecting one's holdings is the preoccupation of human beings. He also knew that it had a greater potential to destroy friendships, marriages, and the souls of men than anything on earth.

More than two-thousand-three-hundred verses in the Bible concern money. Eleven of the thirty-nine parables Jesus taught are about money. If the Bible is God's story, you could say money is one of the main characters ... a hired gun used by the anti-hero to create chaos and destruction.

God is not against money and holdings, but He knows what the *love* of it can do to people.[1] To invest and to plan for the future is a responsible thing to do, but it has enormous limits. When you go, it stays; when your kids go, it stays. A friend of mine once watched Mother Teresa refuse a check for a million dollars from a businessman who was visiting in Calcutta. She realized that the man was riddled with guilt and was hoping that giving the money would somehow appease God for the sins of his past. She said to him, "God doesn't want your money, He wants your heart."

Jesus says, "Lay up for yourselves treasure in heaven." Every scammer out there spends his waking moments trying to figure out how to take your money away from you. How do we lay up treasure in heaven that cannot be destroyed or stolen? The only way I know is to invest in that which is going there. When you invest in the lives of *people* who spend their energy, time, and gifts caring for others, you are laying up treasure in heaven. Why? Because it will lead to others hearing about the love of God. Money is so central to our lives that no matter what we may say about our love for God, how we handle money is the real priority of our heart.

---

[1] 1 Tim. 6:10

Singleness of Purpose

"The eye is the lamp of the body. If the eye is clear (healthy), the whole body will be full of light." Matthew 6:22

As we have been seeing through Jesus' teaching on a side of a mountain in Galilee, he constantly warns His disciples about the tendency to try to live within two life perspectives. If you want to be a leader don't exalt or promote yourself, because true leaders move downward serving people. You cannot do both. We tend to hide our flaws and never show weakness, but it is those flaws that qualify us for a relationship with God.

"The eye is the lamp of the body." If it is healthy, clear, and rightly focused, the rest of the body will reflect that health. It is seen in several ways. Many teach about guarding your intake ... what you allow your eyes to see. They cite movies, salacious books, pornography, etc. This is certainly legitimate, but we just saw in the preceding three verses how an unhealthy view of money can affect the heart.[1] Immediately following this passage about the eye, Jesus says you cannot live in two worlds, serving God and obsessing over money.[2]

After spending many years studying the Jewish mind and Jewish culture, I don't believe Jesus sandwiches a verse about *the lust of the eyes* between six verses about money. The Jewish Mishnah is not Scripture, but it can help us understand Jewish thinking. In *Terumoth 4:3* it says, *"The person with a good eye gave the 40th part of the first fruit of the heavenly offering for the maintaining of the priests, while the person with the evil eye gave only a 60th.* Avot 5:15 says, *"He that gives but wants a monopoly on giving and does not want others to be able to give too is considered to have an evil eye."* It seems that Jesus continues his teaching on money, saying that one with a good (single, healthy) eye is a *generous giver* and one with a bad *or evil eye* is stingy.

Giving is the essence of God's character, and He wants to produce that character in us. Jesus is saying when a person has a generous attitude about giving, *his* entire body, as well as the family of Christ, prospers. Those with a dualistic (bad eye) and stingy view of God and money hurt their own body and the entire Body of Christ as well. Nothing we do as believers is a solitary act. We may think it is, but actions and attitudes affect other people. Generosity can permeate an atmosphere and touch others in a way that few things can.

---

[1]Matt. 6:19–21   [2]Matt. 6:24

Anxiety: The Enemy of Faith

"For this reason, I say to you, do not be worried about your life, as to what you shall eat and what you shall drink, nor for your body as to what you will put on. Is not life more than food and the body more than clothing?" Matthew 6:25–34

It makes perfect sense for Jesus to address stress and worry after speaking about the healthy way to deal with money. Nothing causes more marital discord than issues over finances. Nothing causes more sleepless nights, more breaches in relationships with friends than the almighty dollar.

Jesus says, "For this reason, I say to you ..." What reason? The reason for not trying to serve God and money. If you focus on making it, keeping it, growing it, and protecting it, the obsession will make you sick. You will entertain every "what if" scenario imaginable. You will be frozen with fear, and it will impact every relationship you have.

For many years I had the privilege of meeting every week on Capitol Hill with Dr. Richard Halverson, Chaplain of the U.S. Senate. A very wise and wonderful mentor, he made this statement many times: "Anxiety and stress is God's gracious invitation to come and spend time with Him." We worry about our kids and how to pay for their education, we compete with friends and neighbors to be *the king and queen of stuff*, whether we admit it or not. Because most of us live beyond our means, debt creeps in and causes even greater angst. While teaching, Jesus points to a familiar sight. He tells his listeners to consider the flowers whose beauty adorns the landscape; He points to the bird who never sweats his bank account balance because he relies completely upon a loving Creator to supply his needs.

He then says the same basic principle that Dr. Halverson said: "Seek first ..." Not when you find the time but seek right now, the Father who made you and loves you ... Sit on His lap as a child would with a loving Daddy and spill every anxious thought out to Him. He knows the mountain you are facing, but He wants you to tell Him the unabridged story, holding back nothing. He will say, "make this your first thought every day and you will see the anxiety begin to melt away and worry will be replaced with confidence and trust." He whispers to us constantly, "Cast your burdens on Me because I care for you."[1]

---

[1] 1 Pet. 5:7

Judging or Caring: The Divide

"Do not judge so that you will not be judged. For in the way you judge, you will be judged, and by your standard of measure, it will be measured to you."
Matthew 7:1–5

Jesus is teaching His disciples, but Jewish leaders are in the crowd. They had set themselves up as the ultimate authority and the standard by which they pronounced the verdict on the marginalized of the day, such as tax collectors and prostitutes. Jesus speaks to them indirectly.

This passage about judging has become both the most popular and most misunderstood verse in the entire Bible. It is the first line of defense when a person's erratic behavior or dubious lifestyle is questioned. A young couple lives together unmarried; a guy cheats on his wife, or a woman abuses her children ... do we have a right to make a judgment? The truth is, we judge constantly. We pass a house with a car on blocks in the front yard and shake our head, we see an obese woman walking by in the mall and we wince, we hear a politician say something absurd on TV and we throw our "remote" in the air and call him a moron. We judge people all the time.

So, what is Jesus saying? Obviously, He is not saying that we have no right to call out sin. Knowing truth from error is critical.[1] Knowing the truth initiates wisdom, and wisdom enables discernment, which helps us determine what must cease to continue and what is none of our business. So, what is Jesus talking about?

If I see a man strike a woman, he can yell "judge not" to me all day, but it won't work in his favor. The Bible tells us to "speak the truth in love."[2] When you make judgmental statements toward others, you are setting yourself up to be judged by that same standard. How many times have we heard politicians wax eloquently about family values only to be later found cheating on their wife? They have not only set themselves to be judged in kind but have also silenced their own voice on that subject.

I have no right to pontificate on the sins of others but building a friendship with them and earning the right to come in love and confront the erratic behavior of their actions is not judging ... it's caring. If I feel compelled to confront a friend, am I willing to ride it out with him, or is this going to be a drive-by kind of love? The judgment Jesus speaks of here is more about questioning the motives or intent of someone. I have never seen a motive and I have no right to say, "I know what you're thinking." No, I really don't know! I can only call into question that which I am certain of, and only then with love and discernment.

---

[1] 1 Kings 3:9   [2] Eph. 4:15

Ask, Seek, and Knock

"Ask and it will be given to you; seek and you will find; knock and it will be open to you. For everyone who asks receives, and he who seeks finds, and to him who knocks it will be opened." Matthew 7:7

Now there is the winning ticket if there ever was one! "Ask and you will receive; knock and the door will open." Jesus draws a parallel of God answering His children's requests to a father giving a gift to his beloved child. Is there anything more satisfying than watching a child, wide-eyed and expectant, tearing into Christmas wrappings and finding the toy he has longed for? What kind of father would give his son a poisonous snake instead? But what if the child asks for something he thinks is fun, but that you know will be harmful to him? I believe God's predisposition is to always say "yes," but He knows that "yes" is sometimes a very harmful answer.

A child would not expect a lavish gift from a neighbor down the street who he barely knows. There is no relationship there. It is the level of the relationship that ensures the response. God's intent is to love His children deeply and give to them generously, but His primary aim is the relationship. To give a gift and never have a mutual love relationship is hollow.

God wants to give us every gift, but until we develop an intimacy with Him, our desires will move in a direction that may seem exciting but will prove deadly. Did you ever secretly ask God to let you win the lottery? Most have. But winning the lottery and paying off debts, buying things you always wanted, could derail your life. Watch the documentaries about former lottery winners. They experience horrors you wouldn't believe. Most will say it's the worst thing that ever happened to them.

We are often much like a child who wants that special toy. It looks so attractive and we think it will give us pleasure for the rest of our life. But it may be the very thing that keeps us from ever trusting God moment by moment. If God gave you a boatload of money, why would you think of trusting Him for your needs? The broker who always pushes *financial independence* is unknowingly encouraging you to circumvent trust. The unspoken idea is that you can have enough money that you never have to depend on or trust anyone ever again ... even God.

God does want you to ask and He wants to deliver, but He desires intimacy with you first. The more intimate you become with Him the more your heart and mind will be in sync with His desires for you. Then when you ask, the door will swing open, because His desire has become your desire.

The Narrow Path and the Wide Path

"Enter through the narrow gate; for the gate is wide and the way is broad that leads to destruction, and there are many who enter through it. For the gate is small and the way is narrow that leads to life and there are few who find it." Matthew 7:13–14

Religion is often defined as a system of ethics, a code of conduct, an ideology, or a creed. To a Hebrew, it is none of these. A Hebrew understood his daily life of faith in terms of a journey or a pilgrimage. A Jew's faith was tantamount to the way he chose to walk. If a person knows God, he is daily at God's disposal and walks in an intimate relationship with Him along the road of life. Manmade laws and ritualism crept in, and in Jesus' day took over, but to a true Jew, it was walking with God in His path of wisdom and righteousness. In this Sermon, Jesus used this familiar Hebraic imagery to teach about the two potential ways to walk. One is Law, the other is Grace.

This verse seems very straightforward, but remember, Jesus is speaking to Jews who had not only been oppressed by the Romans but harassed daily by the Jewish leaders. Their shepherds, the Pharisees, pummeled them with laws and oral traditions taking them down an impossible path toward ultimate destruction. Normally, when you think of the "wide way" of which Jesus speaks, it is the easy way because it's the path of least resistance. However, these Jews would never have considered the path they walked easy. Through the eyes of grace, the wide way is the *hard way*. In fact, it's *an impossible way!* You can't manufacture salvation by keeping the Laws. The narrow way is the easy way because it is not about us, nor is it up to us. Grace means that we come through the narrow gate on the shoulders of Jesus who, by His sacrifice on the cross, allows us to enter by faith.[1] It's not what we do, but what He did.

If salvation is a free gift, why would it be hard? What *would* be hard is if we had to work and jump through all the hoops to get it or try to make ourselves worthy to receive it.

When you consider your own life, are you making something difficult that was intended to be easy? Has your notion of following Jesus always been predicated on your efforts on God's behalf, rather than *His efforts* on your behalf? The narrow way leads to life, but the only effort you need to exert is the willingness to trust God moment by moment, limp by limp.

---

[1]Matt. 11:28–30

Those Who Would Deceive

"Beware of false prophets who come to you in sheep's clothing, but inwardly are ravenous wolves. You will know them by their fruits." Matthew 7:15–20

You don't have to look far to find multitudes of "experts" claiming to hold the answer to life and all its complexities. Thousands of *How-To* books sit resplendent on bookstore shelves to give you the perfect solution to whatever ails you. But Jesus is speaking of something much more sinister; it is discerning truth or deception in someone's word and actions.

The function of the Prophet was to hear from God and accurately communicate that truth to the people. He would, in a sense, sit at the King's gate and discern if the King's decrees were or were not of God. If they were, the Prophet gladly encouraged the people to support the King's decrees. If he determined that the decrees did not reflect God's perspective, he urged the people to stand against it.

Today false prophets abound, just as in biblical times. They are those who create an audience of needy, searching people, many of whom have been deeply hurt and disappointed. They are susceptible to words appearing to offer hope and are hard to resist. It is not always the cultic movements or the prosperity preachers on TV; it is often the one who is warm and soft-spoken, but who adds something to Jesus. He is one who isolates his followers and subtly creates a we/they atmosphere. He will exclude and marginalize people. The message is never completely wrong; it always has a measure of truth, and yet, not the whole truth.

Jesus says, "You will know them by their fruits." Fruit is the byproduct of a life occupied by the Spirit of God. But when we begin to list fruit that we deem is absent in other people, we walk the line between legalism and accusation. It is easy to pick out flaws in others and say they are wolves in sheep's clothing, but I have read some horrendous attacks on good and faithful people who simply have a different perspective. They are not wolves, just people whose theology may be tilted a bit.

The Secret Service not only guards the President, but a primary focus is the detection of counterfeit money. They learn how to spot the bogus twenty-dollar bill by studying the real thing, not by studying the fake bills. Evangelicals are often quick to spot a "conspiracy." The way to know the truth is by studying the real document, not by listening to the "experts" on the radio and TV.[1] This will keep you from being at the mercy of every character who steps to the microphone.

---

[1] John 8:32

Whistling in the Wind

Not everyone who says to me 'Lord, Lord' will enter the kingdom of Heaven, but he who does the will of my Father in heaven will enter." Matthew 7:21–23

The standard line from parents at Christmas time is, "Be good or Santa Claus won't come." Every child knows that Santa is coming whether you're good or not! In a world that is super-sensitive to anything that might offend the suggestion that anyone with the exception of Hitler, Osama Bin Laden, and Charles Manson would wind up in Hell is soundly rejected. The notion that a loving God would cast one of those He created aside for eternity would be considered by many as narrow, judgmental, and mean-spirited. So, we posture the same notion about heaven that we tell the kids about Santa. The world says, *live and believe as you will because in the end God will pat you on the head like a doting white-bearded Santa and give everyone a free pass.*

I don't like the concept of hell. Any believer who applauds it is like the Pharisees who believed that God rejoices in heaven when a sinner bites the dust and goes to hell. The truth is, it breaks God's heart! Consider this ... if a man or woman live secular lives with little concern to know God and follow Him, why would they suddenly want to be with Him for eternity when they die?

Does God send people to hell? This Scripture in Matthew says many will come and outline the good things they did, and God will say "Who are you? We've never been introduced."[1] Those accomplishments and traits which they thought sufficient will be empty tokens from empty hearts without a relationship with God's Son. He gives us the opportunity to live with Him or without Him. If we choose the latter, we also choose the consequences, and He will sorrowfully allow us that choice. If we choose not to eat for a month we die. Who sentenced us to death? We did! Death is the natural result of no nourishment in the human system. When darkness fills the room, what insidious being caused it? Darkness is the consequential result of not having light. Think about it! No one dumped it on you.

It's a hard reality, but God will not be mocked.[2] He loves fiercely and will pursue His created with passionate diligence, but in the end, He will allow those who choose to do so to walk away.

And when they walk away from Him, they will continue that path, both in this life and in the life to come. The choice was theirs.

---

[1]Matt. 7:21–23   [2]Gal. 6:7

Something to Brag About

"Let not the wise boast of their wisdom or the strong boast of their strength or the rich boast of their riches, but let the one who boasts boast about this: that they have the understanding to know me, that I am the Lord, who exercises kindness, justice and righteousness on earth, for in these I delight." Jeremiah 9:23–24 (NIV)

What is it that makes us want to brag on ourselves and our accomplishments? The answer is simple: insecurity. Anyone who must continually extol his own virtues is filled with self-doubt. He is a person who believes that *what he does is who he is.* It means that the value of his existence on the earth is predicated on what he achieves. It is a terminal sickness in our world. When we think that way, every potential good day teeters precariously on how we performed. Our perception of ourselves is governed by whether we win or lose.

People who boast about themselves fail to realize that they set themselves up for ridicule when they fall short. They create unrealistic expectations they can never fulfill. Solomon wrote, "Let another praise you, and not your own mouth; a stranger, and not your own lips."[1] If you excel in something others will soon notice and if you display true humility people around you will participate in your success. If you are arrogant fellow believers will likely be resentful of you because one who boasts constantly is seeking to *steal God's glory*. God gave us our gifts and talents so we could enhance the lives of those in our sphere of influence and celebrate His glory. Why boast as if you pulled it off yourself?[2] Paul even says that if he is to boast, he will boast of his weakness. Why would anyone do that? Because Paul's goal was the glory of God not the glory of Paul. God had told him, "My strength is perfected in weakness."[3] In other words, when we are weak, recognize it, admit it and refuse to cover it up. God's strength will be magnified, and the world will know it came from Him and not us. Friendship with God is a non-earnable gift.

So, if you must boast, says the Lord, *boast that you are learning to understand and know God as a friend*. The difference is that if you are His friend you did nothing whatsoever to earn or deserve it. There is no greater prize in the universe than that.

---

[1]Prov. 27:2   [2]1 Corinthian 4:7   [3]2 Cor. 11:30

A Foundation That Won't Crumble

"Therefore, everyone who hears these words of mine and acts on them may be compared to a wise man who built his house upon the rock."
Matthew 7:24–27

Jesus goes on to describe the contrast between a house faced with wind and floods standing firm as opposed to one built on sand and falling apart. Notice that He is not saying the strong foundation is being a student of the Bible. He says failing to *act* on His words will result in a life that will eventually crumble.

It is possible to build your life on what you think are scriptural principles but run more parallel to cultural axioms. Many will follow these cultural adages faithfully only to find that they cannot hold up against the north wind. Sayings like, *"God helps those who help themselves"* and values like, *rugged individualism, you can have it all,* and if you win, *you're a winner;* if you lose, *you're a loser* may be American ideals, but they are certainly not biblical. *Competition* has its legitimate place within the right context, but *cooperation* is the biblical value. Giving ten percent of your income back to God and considering that the remaining ninety percent is yours is as ludicrous as the donkey that Jesus rode on Palm Sunday thinking all that adulation was for him. A solid foundation can't be built on cultural notions. The more we act on bogus principles the more rapidly our house will crumble.

A friend of mine tells a comical story about trying not to laugh when his young son came downstairs dressed for church. He had started the first button of his shirt in the second buttonhole. It won't work any more than hanging wallpaper without a plumb line does. A small quarter inch off on the first piece will cause cumulative error that creates a major slant by the time you go around the room.

Our foundation must be built on the strong and life-giving fundamentals of Scripture. As we act on the knowledge we are given God will entrust us with more. Each time we trust and obey Him the foundation becomes stronger and we will be able to stand firm when the storms come and the waters rise. Those storms will not be able to decimate our lives and distract us from moving on in a positive direction. The pursuit of happiness is guaranteed in our Constitution. We have the right to pursue it, but if we chase after happiness … disappointment will be the guarantee! True happiness and completeness come only by stepping into the purpose for which you were created. This is the "Rock" of certainty on which believers must build.

Authority and Power

"When Jesus had finished these words, the crowds were amazed at His teaching; for He was teaching them as one having authority, not as the scribes."
Matthew 7:28–29

Jesus ends the Sermon on the Mount and the people were stunned. They had never heard anyone speak with such authority. When the Scribes and Pharisees spoke, they generally quoted Rabbis. When Jesus spoke, the words that cascaded from His lips were of such an intimate quality that it reminded them of no one else. He only quoted His Father.

Have you ever heard a great message and been awed by the knowledge and delivery of the speaker only to forget what he said a day later? I know a man who was not a great speaker. When he would talk it was so natural and powerful that when he finished it was a talk you could never forget. His own intimacy with God and the principles he shared rang with a level of authority that was undeniable. There were two main types of Rabbis in Jesus' day; Torah Teachers who emphasized the value and significance of the Law, and a handful of exceptionally wise and highly respected men who were known as Rabbis with *S'mikhah*. They were deemed to possess unearthly wisdom and deep understanding of the mind of God. These Rabbis could interpret the Scriptures in new ways as opposed to Torah teachers who could only teach accepted doctrinal precepts. *S'mikhah* represented ultimate authority on earth. They saw the difference between their leaders and Jesus because Jesus was seen as a Rabbi with *S'mikhah*.

Hitler *seized* power … Mother Theresa had authority, but no power. Presidents have power, but limited authority. Jesus had all the power of God but chose to "empty" Himself of it.[1] A Roman soldier who met Jesus understood that to have authority, you must be *under* authority. He knew instantly that Jesus was under the authority of His Father,[2] and Jesus said this Roman officer's faith was greater than anyone in Israel.

Few people in positions of leadership understand the concept of being under authority. You cannot have true authority in the life of another by taking it; it must be freely given. This is where many "accountability groups" go astray, and marriages as well. The members boldly confront one another and usually offend because they fail to give each other the right to ask the hard questions. Grasping authority always ends badly, but if given freely it can offer guidance, protection, and a deep sense of security that someone is watching your back.

---

[1]Phil. 2:5–8   [2]Luke 7:1–10

The Secret of the Early Believers

"What we have seen and heard we proclaim to you also, so that you too can have fellowship with us; and indeed, our fellowship is with the Father and with His Son Jesus Christ." 1 John 1:3

When Jesus ascended back to heaven He left a small cluster of disciples who He had commissioned to make other disciples as they ventured into the world. Even after three years with Him they never truly understood the import of who He was. They were basically teenagers, ordinary and mostly uneducated, except for their training in the Torah as children. How would they convince a still antagonistic world that Jesus was exactly who He said He was? Why was His death not an accident or a failed mission?

John wrote the above verse. The reality of what the disciples had personally experienced, what they knew for certain, what could not be explained away was the intimacy of the personal message they spoke. It was not secondhand; it was not from a sermon or talk they had heard or a book they read. It was a message they witnessed in action. It was a reality from which they would never recover; a reality so powerful and real it became non-negotiable for them even in the face of death. So, they lived among people from every walk of life, and the power from their lives was then explained by their words as an indelible expression of what had happened to them. Who can argue with the reality that is seen in another's life? This was their secret!

Had you met the Samaritan woman years later, she would not have peppered you to death with theological jargon; she would have told you about that day when she encountered Jesus at the well. The same would be true of the man born blind from birth, or the leper, or the woman with the hemorrhage. Each would tell you their story, and no matter how skeptical you might be, you could not refute the reality of their personal history—what they absolutely knew for certain.

Yes, we need to study the Scripture and know what we believe, but someone with an experience is never at the mercy of someone with an argument. A great exercise would be to take a sheet of paper and write down those things you absolutely know for sure—things that you would not recant even if a gun was pointed at your head. Then begin to build your message around those few things in accordance with God's Word. God will bless it and give you a new truth, and then another along the way. If authenticity matters to you, your life will be framed not only by the truth of God's Word but by that same truth that has found its home within you.

Does Truth Still Set the Pace?

"Then you will know the truth and the truth will set you free." John 8:32

Our children are grown now and have children of their own, so we stand outside the circle of confusion that many of you must confront every day. The demands of trying to balance work, civic and church obligations with the needs of your children and their busy activities are enough to make you try to pinpoint the actual moment when you began to lose control of everything.

Balancing all these issues has been a huge problem for generations, but the difference today is the dominance of social media. Our children and grandchildren are pummeled with blogs, Facebook postings, and tweets. No matter what is posted, it is assumed to be true. The battle for truth has always existed but never has error come from so many directions with such force.

Like it or not, we are living in a "post-truth era." If your circle of involvement is limited to church, work, a few friends and your family, you may have a hard time believing this. But all it takes is walking on almost any college campus, and it will literally scare the hell out of you. For many years, the debate was about whether truth was absolute and never changing, or fluctuating relative to the circumstance, generation, or culture. Among young people, the thought that sex is intended for marriage is almost totally rejected. In fact, living together has become a basic assumption.

I believe the problem for many people is not so much that they never consider what is true and what is not, but they don't know *where* to find the answer. In the last twenty-five years, young people have lost the ability to reason ... to think through an issue with clarity. They have become lost in this world of cyberspace and have created their own reality. Objects like phones have become so personalized that if taken away it would be like the death of a friend. When truth becomes a personal choice like a buffet line and is only a matter of what's good for you and what's good for me, abject confusion will result.

The answer is not to sequester ourselves or our children away from dissenting opinions. On the contrary, when we know the truth it sets us free from the fear of facing what is *not* true. I'm not afraid to watch any particular news channel. I want to hear both sides of the issues. We seem to forget that God loves the people who stand on the other side as much as He loves you. To understand them does not mean to agree or comply. To see their point of view helps me understand and approach them with the truth. The truth sets us free to differ while still respecting their right to their opinion in an atmosphere void of hostility.

Approaching the World as a Learner

"Although He was a Son, He learned obedience from the things which He suffered."
Hebrews 5:8

The term *disciple* means learner or apprentice. However, the Jewish perspective of being taught by a Rabbi was far more than simply accumulating knowledge from Him. When Jesus said the words "Follow me" it was a supreme compliment. It literally meant, "I see in you the potential to become *like* Me." It was far more about character than knowledge. Learning is a lifelong process that never ends, and it comes not primarily by knowledge but by watching a live model. Former Senate Chaplain Dr. Richard Halverson often said, "Spiritual truth is learned by atmosphere, not by intellect."

The Apostle Paul was imprisoned by Nero during the last days of His life. He wrote to Timothy instructing Him to bring the coat and book he had left, but *especially the parchments*.[1] Down to his last breath he wanted to learn and grow. It was not intellect, but about more deeply knowing His Savior. He was a learner to the end. Even Jesus learned through His suffering.[2]

When people go on mission trips they usually say they are going to help the poor. But if you go to another country, mission trip or not, take the posture of a learner and it will change the whole atmosphere. Mother Teresa said that the poor taught her how to love Jesus. When we go anywhere thinking of ourselves as teachers rather than learners, we may miss the most unique opportunity of a lifetime. Everyone you meet, even the homeless guy on the street has something to teach you if you will be humble enough to listen. If you allow him the opportunity it will be a gift to both of you. With everyone you meet, think, *what can I learn from this person?*

It is said that Francis of Assisi would submit himself to the youngest monk in the order. It sounds foolish until you think of someone like Billy Graham coming to you and asking for guidance and wanting to put himself under your authority. Imagine the humility it would take for him to do it. Imagine what it would do for your prayer life and your dependence on God if you accepted that challenge. Always crave learning, not simply for intellectual stimulation, but for the deepening of your character.

---

[1] 2 Tim. 4:13   [2] Heb. 5:8

The Value of the Individual

"Then Satan stood up against Israel and moved David to number Israel . . . "
1 Chronicles 21:1–8

We measure almost everything today. *How much and how many* are the universal questions asked in any transaction or event. In King David's life, Satan encouraged him to count his troops. God punished David because he trusted in the size of his army rather than trusting in God. You're in a Sunday School class, and a man is at the door ... counting. You are later in church and another man wanders up and down the aisle ... counting. Then you listen to a sermon that challenges you concerning God's love for *the individual.* The sermon ends: "If you had been the only person on earth, Jesus would still have come and died just for you." Can you see the contradiction in what is being said and what is being done?

Without being able to measure we become very insecure. We are not sure how we did. We can't tell where there's a hole we dug, and therefore we struggle to convince ourselves and others that anything significant has been accomplished. This flies in the face of biblical thinking. Jesus never called together a crowd; he only went to individuals. "Follow Me," he said to this one and that one. He never counted or considered the size of anything.

In the Hebrew language words have a numeric value. We use numbers to denote quantity, Hebrew numbers are primarily used as symbols. Real faith means that we do not have to always see the results. God says that His Word will never return empty and it will accomplish its mission whether we see it or not.[1] If we're insecure, we need to see the final tally; but if we trust God, we know that the results are God's business, not ours.

The early believers grew up within small groups and matured quickly and deeply because they could not hide among large numbers. They knew each other's strengths and weaknesses; they always had each other's back. It is very difficult to do that with large crowds. Never forget the value of the individual. Discipling one to one is the slow way, but people's hearts don't respond on cue. It takes time and much individual attention, but it is the way Jesus did it. We can't improve on that.

Who are you taking under your wing? In whose life are you helping to build the truth? Friends on Facebook and followers on Twitter don't count. Who are you walking with and nurturing? Never forget the value of one person. You never know who that one person will turn out to be.

---

[1] Isa. 55:11

Assessing Value

"Because you are precious in my eyes, and honored, and I love you, I give men in return for you, peoples in exchange for your life." Isaiah 43:4 (ESV)

You stand with your child on the sidelines with last-minute instructions as she waits to run out on the soccer field. "Okay Ginny, go out there and make Mom and Daddy proud." In my opinion, that is the worst possible thing that could be said to a child. Our society is built on affirming performance. "Be a winner," comes a husky voice of another father behind you. We have created an axiom that if you win you are a winner, and if you lose you're a loser. I was taught that in college football. It is pure baloney. Abraham Lincoln was faced with defeat throughout his life. He lost eight elections, twice failed in business and suffered a nervous breakdown, and yet he persisted and became one of the greatest Presidents in American history.

Who can say how many children have grown up in the rancid quagmire of that kind of "performance thinking"? Not only does performance play no role in your salvation, but also has nothing to do with your value or worth as a person. In business, athletics, politics, and almost anything you can name, your ability and accomplishments are what propel you upward. But in God's economy, what qualifies you for the Kingdom of God is your deficiencies. God sees through the failures, the missteps, and the sins in your life, and he sees an irreplaceable creation that he loves unconditionally.

Why is it that we affirm a child for a home run but not for the character he displays when he strikes out? Maybe he will become a man or woman who understands how to comfort someone in the face of loss. Why is the character of a person celebrated far less than his ability? Why do we seldom hear, "I love your compassion for people?" How about, "I learn so much by watching you interact with your wife?"

Maybe you have noticed that character has been all but eliminated from the discussion concerning what really matters in the leadership of our nation. It is all about accomplishing and getting what we want. How we do it has become irrelevant.

God loves you not because you always do well; He loves you in spite of the fact that you don't.[1] Focus on affirming the essence and character of people and less on their accomplishments. Heroic performances come and go, but a look, a touch, a kind affirmation can literally alter a person's life.

---

[1]Rom. 5:8

A Critical Life Choice

"Humble yourselves before the Lord and He will lift you up." James 4:10 (NIV)

Throughout the average believer's life, many questions will surface as he encounters challenges along the way. One critical life choice is this: *Will I seek to distinguish myself among people, or will I humble myself before God?* Both cannot happen simultaneously. The difficulty is that humility is the most disruptive checkpoint on the road to fame and recognition. This road of humility, many believe, is the highway leading to mediocrity. How do you become successful and competitive in a *take no prisoners* world that beats on its chest after every touchdown, demanding adulation? Where does a man or woman put God's glory on display in this world without appearing to concede every battle?

I have known business and political leaders through the years who have brought excellence to the marketplace. They have done it with the utmost integrity and humility and have also enjoyed enormous success. Each of them believed that they were not in charge of the ultimate results. Their job was to value their employees or staff, build a sense of pride and confidence in the company, and never compromise the quality of their products. They used their gifts, trusted their managers, and recognized that if God did not build the enterprise they labored in vain.[1]

People in business, politics, and medicine often forget that despite what they have been taught, it's *not* up to them. Obviously, we must learn, prepare, take risks, be creative, and make hard decisions, but we cannot control the results. Yet many still give it a shot. In politics today, we believe we must vote the perfect candidate into office and if we don't, the country is doomed. That perspective is shared by many believers, and it is basically an atheistic point of view. It unknowingly assumes that God has *left the building*, and it's now up to us.

Jesus highly prized humility and reflected it in all He said and did. True humility is a lifestyle. It is one of the most attractive features you will ever witness in a person. It was framed in the life of John the Baptist: He took the hits in paving the road for the Messiah and then turned his loyal disciples over to Jesus. His great confession rings throughout history: "I must decrease, and He must increase." He knew who he was; he knew his role. His life screams, *It's not about me, it's about Him.*[2]

---

[1] Ps. 127:1–2   [2] Luke 7:28

A Great Man with a Slender Resume

"Enoch walked with God; and he was not, for God took him." Genesis 5:24

We know very little about Enoch, but what we know is fascinating. His life should be both an encouragement and a challenge to any believer. He lived for three hundred and sixty-five years during the time preceding the great flood. One of his sons was Methuselah, who lived longer than anyone.

Anyone who is considered great has a long resume listing one stellar accomplishment after another. We do much the same within the realm of faith. How many books have they written, how many people were saved, or what great leaders were influenced by this person? In sports, those with super-human statistics make the Hall of Fame. In acting, they win an Oscar or a Golden Globe, and in business, a building may be named after them.

Enoch, as far as we know, never did much of anything that we would brag about! He founded no universities, he invented nothing, no one quotes anything he ever said, and he never shook hands with a king or a president. But in Hebrews 11, where members of God's Hall of Fame are found, Enoch is listed. He's famous for never dying;[1] that fact is connected to the only thing we know of this man. He *walked with God.* And apparently, God was so *pleased with his friendship* that He wanted more time with His good friend, so one day ... He just took him!

Can you imagine anything more satisfying and thrilling than for God to feel that way about you? He just can't get enough of personal time with you. If you think you can please God by great works for Him, think again! It *pleases* God if you walk with Him as Enoch did. During one of your strolls, He may say, *I want you to do this or that.* He may ask you to be an elder in your church, start a prayer breakfast group, or volunteer helping with urban work in your city. If He does ... do it! But wait for *His* answer. Anything you do will obviously be helpful, but the real impact comes when you hear that "still small voice" telling you to go. And if by chance He never gives you a great task wouldn't it be enough to just keep walking along and enjoying His companionship for the rest of your life? When you can answer "yes" to that question you will be in a position for God to use your life at a level you never imagined.

---

[1] Heb. 11:5

Are You a This or a That?

"But you must not be called 'Teacher.' You are all brothers and sisters together. You have only one Teacher. And don't call any person on earth 'Father.' You have one Father. He is in heaven. And you should not be called 'Master.' You have only one Master, the Christ." Matthew 23:9–10 (ESV)

Little in our culture seems to be more perplexing to people than trying to figure out who everybody is. We do it by labels such as position, rank, affiliation, occupation, race, nationality, and status. "What do you do?" is the first question at a cocktail party. "What church do you attend?" is a favorite once we've determined their level of spiritual interest. "Are you a Democrat or Republican?" is high on the charts, but a bit more volatile these days. Each of these groupings has various subsets that are designed to zoom in on a more accurate profile of our identity. It drives us crazy if we don't know where to mentally *file* each other.

These attempts to label people are irrelevant to who they are. Once we are filed in a category, we become a *Lifer,* incarcerated in an identity prison from which few ever escape. Somehow, we don't feel comfortable unless we know a person's occupation, denominational affiliation, and expertise. Early on, we develop assumptions that place a certain value on each label.

Interestingly, in the Scriptures, there is no superficial division or distinction of any sort between people except whether a person is *in Christ* or *outside of Christ*.[1] Terms like Presbyterian, Republican, Evangelical, and Liberal are extra-biblical words that falsely define us and distract from who we really are. We learn the true heart of a person by intimate companionship in an atmosphere of freedom and trust. Was Jesus a conservative or a liberal? Yes! Was he a disciple maker or an evangelist? Yes! The minute you define Him, you marginalize who He is. Defining people with labels limits them and cuts off their ability to step across these manmade lines of demarcation. If you're a *this,* you can't be a *that*! But if you are content to simply be a person who loves God and cares about people, you can be with anyone at any time, and in any circumstance.

We are called to go into the world. You'll never reach the world as a conservative, a Baptist, a Presbyterian, a Catholic or even as a Christian. Why not be known as a person like Enoch, a man or woman who is a *friend of God* and who *walks with Him* daily?[2] Once you wrap a label around yourself and seek to identify with an institutional group you lock in limitations. When others in that "group" go off course they take you with them, whether you want to go or not. Enoch's calling card was "Friend of God." How can you improve on that?

---

[1]Gal. 3:28   [2]Gen. 5:21–24

Ask . . . in Faith, Believing

"Therefore, I say to you, all things for which you pray and ask, believe that you have received them, and they will be granted you." Mark 11:24

When I was a young believer, I could never understand the idea that God knew everything about me, even my thoughts, but I was still supposed to ask Him for what he already knew I needed. It wasn't until I got married and had children that I began to understand. I would see one of my sons working on something and when he asked me to help or show him a better way, I noticed that it began to cement our relationship bit by bit. I knew what he needed, but it thrilled me as a dad to have him ask me. As they became adults, Susan and I still want them to ask.

God wants us to ask, in faith, believing that He will answer and takes great joy in meeting our needs. Sometimes prayer can be little more than whining. When we whine in asking something of God, it is usually because we don't believe he will say yes. Somehow, we think the whining will touch Him and make Him more sympathetic. Faith is not throwing darts blindfolded toward a target and hoping you hit something. It is not simply believing that God *can* answer, but that He *will* answer. If a father or mother anticipates all the needs of his children, they will never learn to ask for and boldly communicate their needs. Yes, God does know all our hopes and dreams, but He loves to hear us tell Him. He never gets annoyed, flustered, or tired of our petitions; He delights in them.[1]

As you walk with Him through the years, you may well notice that the questions you are now asking are the very questions He wants you to ask. It is because you are embracing His character and perspective. His will and your will are gradually becoming one. This is the essence of "praying in His name." It is not simply saying it at the end of your prayer, it is praying in His character. It may be praying for someone you don't particularly like and asking that God bless his or her life mightily. You are then praying in His name because your character and perspectives toward that person are lining up with His. This is when prayer becomes a real adventure!

---

[1] Isa. 58:11

The Issue is Never the Issue

"Who do men say I am?" Matthew 16:13 (NIV)
"But who do you say that I am?" Matthew 16:15

We live in an issue-oriented world. We become embattled in contemporary issues, many of which may spawn grave consequences: same-sex marriage, immigration, terrorism, minimum wage, gun control, and whether the accomplishments of our political leaders carry greater weight than their character. When I counsel with a couple, I ask them their version of the problem they are having. After they each say their piece, I know the problem is not what they say it is. The issue is never the issue!

Jesus was born into a melting pot of problems and struggles the likes of which most of us have never even imagined. Almost half of the babies born in Jesus' day died by the age of five. The Romans' imposing foot was on the neck of the Jews to a degree not dissimilar to the Gestapo of Nazi Germany.

Jesus had as many issues that demanded answers as we do today, and yet he seldom, if ever, addressed them. Though strictly forbidden by the Jews, homosexuality was rampant among Greeks and Romans. Racism, unfair taxation, and deception were common. It wasn't that Jesus had no position on these matters, but he knew the issue is never the issue. He never lectured the woman caught in adultery or demonized the immoral tax collectors. He took the twelve right into the heart of man's most despicable sins, but as far as we know, never lectured them about what they saw. He knew that the *issue is never the issue!*

What's wrong with the world is people, and what's wrong with people is their heart! If we solved all of the issues, there would still be *the issue*: the heart of man. Every division in life … families, marriages, political ideology, racism, labor, and management are of our own making. Jesus took twelve teenagers to Caesarea Philippi. It was a horrible place that had been founded as an international center for pagan worship. Sex was part of the pagan ritual. Thousands of people would copulate in front of one another as they celebrated and beckoned Pan, the God of fertility, to return and replenish their crops and livestock. What an ideal time for Jesus to give these young men His sex talk, but he didn't. He asked them a question, "Who do people say I am?" Peter answered, "You are the Christ, the Son of the living God."[1] Why? Sex was not the issue. The issue with these people was their heart. If the heart is the issue, and if Jesus can change a heart, then everyone who becomes one with Him can begin to become one with each other.[1]

---

[1]Matt. 16:13–16

Training and Encouraging Our Children

"Train up a child in the way he should go; Even when he is old, he will not depart from it." Proverbs 22:6

The Proverbs clearly teach that the true measure of a mature believer is the ability to relate and apply God's Word to everyday life experiences. Raising children to honor and trust God in a world that considers faith old fashioned and backward is an awesome task. Few things are more heartbreaking than a child who has not been taught the right path by loving parents.

I've watched many faithful parents claim this verse as an absolute promise and scour the bookshelves seeking "the way" their children should "go." Many are devastated as Junior rejects that direction when he leaves the nest. What happened?

Proverbs is not a book of absolute promises. It is a book of practical wisdom that gives every possibility and opportunity for that wisdom to be realized in a human life. It is not an absolute pledge any more than the wisest financial guru in the world could absolutely guarantee a great financial return every year.

Our approach is part of the problem. The Hebrew rendering says "Train up a child in his own way ..." We read the books, listen to the experts and they all tell us what "that way" is. They all have a formula that sounds perfect. We settle on one of the lists and off we go ... making the kid go to Bible studies, special Christian Camps, giving gold rings for purity, avoiding R-rated movies, etc. ... and it doesn't work. God is saying that we should *study the child; learn his tendencies, his gifts, his personality, and work with it.* In other words, don't try to create a Christian clone. Allow God to be as original with him as he has been with you. Don't try so hard! Nothing will be more resented later than a frantic parent trying to make little Sally into the perfect Godly princess.

The second part of the verse says, "and when he is old, he will not depart from it." The Hebrew can be translated, "it will not depart from *him*." It helps me to know that if the truth is initially understood by the child, it will always be there and any circumstance later in life can jar it back into reality. You and I can't change ourselves or anyone else. That is God's prerogative.

Our job is to give them space, keep them close, honor their privacy, listen to them, love them, and give them the freedom to fail. If you do, there is an excellent chance that if they stray from the path at some point, they will return. They will never be able to refute the realities of a loving home, no matter what some college professor says to try to undermine their faith. They will never be able to explain away the love and faith of a mom and dad who cherished, accepted, and were always there for them.

Success

"For where your treasure is, there your heart will be also." Matthew 6:21 (ESV)

What constitutes success? Our culture has concocted a confusing and warped definition. Success is the one who makes the highest grade, crosses the finish line first, ranks at the top of his class, has a large home, and dies with the most toys. What makes this damaging to people is that we create the notion that anything less than an absolute win is a complete loss. Defining a human being as having less value than another because he lost the match, flunked a test, or got passed over for a promotion is absurd. Parents routinely tell their children that they can be anything they want to be. It sounds progressive and positive, but it sets the child up for real disappointment and suggests that they can be master of their own destiny. That is God's prerogative. Coach John Wooden said, "Success is peace of mind which is a direct result of self-satisfaction in knowing you did your best to become the best that you are capable of becoming." Winning is not wrong, nor is striving to be the best you can be. But, when you define someone as a winner or a loser based on the outcome of a competition, the size of a portfolio, or a position or title, you have *left the building* biblically.

I am very competitive by nature; I try to win when I play golf, Ping-Pong, and if you want to race down the street I'll try to beat you. But, if I lose, it has nothing to do with who I am. Sadly, that is not what is being taught to young people. When you hear national leaders call people losers simply because they have a differing opinion it is reminiscent of fourth-grade bullies harassing kids on the playground.

Just before King David's death, he gave this advice to his son, Solomon: "Do what the Lord your God commands and follow His teachings. Obey everything written in the Law of Moses. Then you will be a success, no matter what you do or where you go."[1] David does not define success as building his kingdom and armies and trying to acquire more wealth. It was simple ... success is walking with God and obeying Him. Let God oversee the outcome. Who knows, if you fumble on the two-yard line and lose the game, maybe God will use that so that all those who have "fumbled" their marriage will have someone to talk to.

When we stand before God one day, nothing we bring that defines success in this world will ever see the light of day. God's Kingdom is about faithfulness and nothing but the friendship you have established with Him through Jesus will carry any weight. So, as they said to us freshmen when we arrived for our first practice at Alabama, "Leave your press clippings at home!"

---

[1] 1 Kings 2:2–3

Our Three Great Adversaries

"Do not love the world or anything in the world. If anyone loves the world, love for the Father is not in them. For everything in the world—the lust of the flesh, the lust of the eyes, and the pride of life—comes not from the Father but from the world." 1 John 2:15–16 (NIV)

In writing fiction, the first rule is that it must have conflict. Writers love their main characters like a son or daughter, but he must throw every difficult circumstance in their path in order to give the story depth and realism and create drama. That is what real life is! You are the protagonist. The person you marry becomes an equal lead, the children you have and the friends along the way are vital supporting cast, but only you can perform your part. There will be adversaries and roadblocks along the way, and you can recognize and use them as teaching opportunities.

There are three enemies, or roadblocks, with which we must contend: the world, the flesh, and the devil. This passage in John's first epistle speaks of a love that God hates. It is not hatred for the created world;[1] God said it was good. It is not the people; He gave His life for them.[2] But this *world* that we are instructed not to love is about a pattern of thought. It is a style of life that excludes God; a perspective that ignores or abuses every good thing He created. It is the world that envisions total autonomy with concern for only self. Loving both God and the world is incompatible.

The flesh is what causes us to sin. That's why when you die you will have no more problems with sin. The flesh wants everything now. This temporarily makes us feel good and gives us a false sense of dominion. It seeks a high that never ends.

The devil is our ultimate adversary, but unlike the hideous monster we see in the movies, Satan is the most enticing and beautiful personality in the universe. He is a counterfeiter ... an "angel of light" who knows he has been defeated by the cross but wants to destroy as much as he can while there is still time.

If you were the devil and wanted to destroy *you*, why would you not study the ways that you were enticed by the world and the flesh, making them readily available, and simply sit back and let those two enemies do the job? Most of us never engage in hand to hand combat with Satan because we are so entwined in the world and flesh that we have rendered ourselves ineffective. When trusting Jesus becomes our default position the devil gets personally involved. But remember, He that lives in you is greater.[3] The final chapter has been written, and the bad guy loses!

---

[1] Gen. 1:1–25   [2] John 3:16   [3] 1 John 4:4

Gumby

"But when he asks (for wisdom) he must believe and not doubt, because he who doubts is like a wave of the sea, blown and tossed by the wind. That man should not think he will receive anything from the Lord. He is a double-minded man, unstable in all he does." James 1:6–8 (NIV)

My kids grew up during the rising popularity of a little green animated humanoid named "Gumby." He had a happy little face, and you could bend him in all directions. Gumby is who I think of when I read this passage in the Book of James. He is speaking of the fact that God wants each of us to be mature and complete, lacking nothing. He goes on to say that if we lack anything, we need only ask, but to do it in full belief and not with secret doubt.

Have you ever heard someone say, "I am praying, but I really don't think it will make any difference?" For the life of me, I can't understand why they bother to pray in the first place. Thinking God *can*, but not believing that He *will* is not faith. This is a "double-minded person." It means "of two minds." When we have divided loyalties, we are placing one foot in the Kingdom of God and the other in the world. The result is instability because with each issue you face you will bend back and forth like Gumby.

Divided loyalties pull us in two directions in the critical matters of life. Let's say I am a journalist and a believer. My goal is to make it on the national scene. To do that will require hard-edge stories that will get the attention of my editor. If I fail to turn up the cutting-edge news, I will not get my shot. I want to be honest, but I am on a story that, if I tweak a little by using some *hearsay* over facts, it could put me over the top. What to do? Do I bend?

Let's say I'm an executive for a huge pharmaceutical company that produces cancer medicines. A revolutionary cutting-edge natural cure is discovered and will be available in a year. Thousands of lives will be saved, but I will lose my job and my company will suffer drastically. Am I conflicted?

We see doublemindedness played out every day. Do I stand firmly in the Kingdom or bend toward the world when it is more profitable or convenient? As Elijah asked God's people, "How long will you hesitate between two opinions?"[1]

James writes that God wants to give us everything we need, and we have only to ask Him in faith. This means releasing the outcome into His hands without trying to manipulate and bend it to our benefit. Despair occurs when we finally get what we were determined to have only to see it fail to deliver what we expected.

---

[1] 1 Kings 18:21

A Love with No Expiration Date

"Anyone who does not provide for their relatives, and especially for their own household, has denied the faith and is worse than an unbeliever."
1 Timothy 5:8 (NIV)

I often ask people to tell me their story: how they grew up, about their family, and the journey that brought them to where they are now. Numerous times I have heard unfortunate words recounted when I asked about their relationship with their brothers and sisters: *"I really haven't seen my brother and sister in many years. We don't talk on the phone and stopped sending Christmas cards years ago. It's complicated."* There are few things sadder and more unsettling than to hear words like that. My wife was told by a woman years ago that she had four siblings and did not know where two of them were or whether they were alive or dead.

I don't understand that! I can't imagine a breach that could cause that kind of alienation. How do you grow up together in the same house for some eighteen years or so and then create a new life that does not include the ones who know you best?

Our three grown sons live in different states but communicate and keep up with each other's families. They are not only brothers but friends. They were very close growing up and have always been very protective of each other. Family loyalty is very important to me. If I was forced to choose,

I would almost rather they love each other than love me! We taught them to ask forgiveness when they hurt each other, and it wasn't always easy. But you can't have any real unity without forgiveness. If the matter is swept under the rug, you can coexist and live in denial, but reconciliation will be impossible.

I have always loved the fact that my Dad, his brother Tom, and sister Carolyn were so close. I remember the confidence and feeling of security it gave me and my sister, Melissa, and the desire that our children might experience the same.

Relationships are hard, sometimes inconvenient. Our life may be busy and complicated, but nothing should get in the way of being there for our family. We set the tone for them by our attitude and loyalty. I love Italian and Jewish families. There is a level of love and sacredness that they have for one another. In the best of those homes, the family is celebrated as a God-given gift that you never take for granted. I love that, and it saddens me when I see families that are alienated. All we have is God and each other ... everything else is temporal and will one day disappear.

Together without an Agenda

"As iron sharpens iron, so one person sharpens another." Proverbs 27:17 (NIV)

If you *walk with a limp*, as I do, you have probably realized that you need friends in your life from whom you can request and give help in times of need. No one has all the answers, but a collective cadre of people who are trustworthy and who want the best for each other can have a dramatic impact.

Many men and women are in Bible study groups, breakfast groups, prayer groups, and the like, but all of us need more than that. I've been to many of those groups, and though they can be very encouraging, they can also be a place to hide. A Bible study can be a place to learn the Greek words for this and that; it can be a source of knowledge and encouragement, but often we go in hurting and come out still hurting. Prayer groups are wonderful, but you may have noticed that most are about physical issues and seldom delve into the deep matters of the heart because we have not developed a level of trust and intimacy.

I believe that the best way for a small group of trusted friends to deepen their own faith, and even become a beacon of encouragement to others, is by first learning to be together without an agenda. Women naturally do this much better than men. A woman calls up a friend, "Let's have lunch together on Tuesday," and

the answer will be, "What time?" The same call is made from a man and he will say "What's up?" Every encounter does not have to be driven by an agenda. Have you ever tried to plan quality time with your family? It never works. But sometimes you just hang out together and realize quality time happened.

I used to travel constantly. Most of the time I would ask a couple of people to accompany me. There was no real reason for their going along except for our chance to spend time together. I also wanted them to meet friends of mine in the places we would travel to. I knew from experience that there would be mutual encouragement to one another. I also knew that those we met along the way would be stunned that these friends would travel all this way with me, at their own expense, but had nothing to sell and wanted nothing from them. Being with people without an agenda is one of the most powerful tools of impact I know.

When believers care about each other and pray for each other, they don't have to have a reason to get together. Almost always, in that atmosphere quality things will happen … healing and freeing things that are impossible to plan or orchestrate.

A Brother Offended

"A brother offended is harder to be won than a strong city, and contentions are like the bars of a citadel." Proverbs 18:19

Why do little boys love superheroes? It's probably because as children they feel powerless and they are able to vicariously become Superman or Spider-Man and garner respect, as well as vanquish the bad guys. Little girls play with dolls and play dress up, which empowers them in a different way. As we get older and mature in our faith, we become more concerned with matters of the heart. But regardless of what age you are, you can be offended, and you can offend. Once we are offended, it becomes a matter of pride as to whether we are willing to reconcile with the other. If the offense remains on a slow boil and unresolved, it is as difficult to repair as conquering a strong city.

Most offenses are personal. If you don't like my shoes, I really don't care. If you say I am a disingenuous person, that really hurts. A child would care that you think his shoes are ugly but could care less about being called disingenuous. The Scripture tells me that *if I offend someone* I am to go to the offender and reconcile.[1] It also tells me that *if I am offended by someone* I am to go to the one who offended me and reconcile.[2] The ball is in my court either way; it is also in the other person's court as well, so it is easy to see why Jesus says it must be solved immediately ... not when you have time to get around to it!

Alienation runs like spider veins throughout relationships between family, friends, colleagues, and teammates. It is the number one problem in all of humanity. We have all kinds of soft-shoe approaches to solve it, and they all amount to nothing. The answers are an attempt to circumvent the only thing that will solve the alienation that exists between us. It requires vulnerability, and we have been taught that vulnerability is a weakness. Of course, that is pure baloney, but we buy into it anyway. The answer to alienation is *forgiveness*! It is the *only* way reconciliation can occur. Anything less than that is simply a band-aid on cancer, and all we can do is co-exist with the disease.

People who are unified in Christ and who refuse to allow the sun to go down on the offense[3] become a strong city that can stand firm against any intruder. Alienation is a weakness in the city wall. When we lock arms and face the world, it's no contest!

---

[1]Matt. 5:21–24   [2]Matt. 18:15–17   [3]Eph. 4:26

Self-Expression

"In the beginning God expressed Himself. That personal expression was with God and was God, and he existed with God from the beginning." John 1:1 (Phillips)

Green or purple hair, tattoos, hats worn sideways, hoodies, and multiple varieties of clichés and offensive words are simply a sign of our need for self-expression. It is easy to be critical and judgmental of new styles and avenues of individualism that blow through our lives like locusts, but if you think back a few years we've all been there. I remember penny loafers, leisure suits, platform shoes and Villager blouses for the girls as *must-have* items. When I was a freshman football player at Alabama, Joe Namath lived in Tuscaloosa in the offseason and would come out to our spring football practice. One day he showed up in a buckskin coat with fringe hanging off. The next day, we all had one. My good friend Jerry Leachman and I were in San Francisco in the summer of 1968 and each bought two pairs of bell-bottom pants and wore them the next fall at Alabama; we thought we were hotter than a twenty-dollar pistol. Everyone wanted a pair and we were the only guys that had them.

We live in a crowded, salad bowl world. We feel as lost as last year's Easter egg, with few distinguishing characteristics, and we long for some kind of uniqueness. As we get older, we try to express ourselves with money, cars, houses, position, and power, but it all simply says, "I don't want to be a cog in a machine; I want to be *me*, but I'm not sure who *me* is."

"In the beginning God expressed himself." He didn't do it with platform shoes, a silk suit, or a funky haircut. He expressed Himself by wrapping skin around Him and becoming a man ... the honest original, so unique and different that those who encountered Him wanted not only to follow Him but to be like Him. He expressed Himself by loving as no one had ever loved, thinking as no one ever thought, living as no one has ever lived, and dying as no man ever died.

Fads change, and those icons of self-expression become tired and old, but the ultimate expression of humanity is when the invisible God becomes visible in a man or woman. The trick is to allow Him to be Himself in the real you ... not the you that is a version of someone else or the one that seems more appealing. Christ in you is the hope of Glory.[1] The authentic Christ in the authentic you is the hottest commodity this side of heaven.

---

[1]Col. 1:27

Teach Children Along the Way . . .

"These words, which I am commanding you today, shall be on your heart. You shall teach them diligently to your sons and shall talk of them when you sit in your house and when you walk by the way and when you lie down and when you rise up."
Deuteronomy 6:6–7

Few things frustrate learning more than a row of chairs and four walls. Learning is a natural process; you learn as you take a walk, have a conversation, or play golf with friends. Why separate life lessons we want to convey from the ordinary functions of life?

Jesus took twelve teenagers on a field trip. There were no classroom sessions, and instruction was integrated into life. Questions arose, and challenges were made along the journey. It was *on-the-job training,* and twelve kids later changed the world.

When our three boys were very young, my wife suggested that we begin family devotions rather than just reading at bedtime. A disastrous time resulted before dinner and after much whining, we tried the den. We sat in a tight circle on the floor that our kids called *knee-knockers*. We all hated it! Susan and I agreed that if we continued, we could well be the first couple to divorce over family devotions. I later stumbled across the above passage in Deuteronomy. I began to see that the world is filled with natural opportunities to guide rather than push, but you must engage.

When I traveled I began taking one of my boys with me. That they understood little of the meetings I was irrelevant; they were with their dad, and situations constantly came up that offered me natural opportunities to help them see life and relationships from God's perspective. To Susan's dismay, I put off giving the dreaded *birds and bees* talk but when I took them with me on these trips that and other issues came up naturally as we traveled.

Spiritual growth is not a session amid four walls; it's a natural relationship that can develop and grow while walking in the woods, sitting by a lake, or even driving to the mall. To the degree we segment growth as a *sit-down* session, we reinforce the absurd notion that we have both a spiritual and secular life. I believe the same is true of making disciples in your community. You can have about five quality hours playing golf with someone. If you focus on encouraging your partner rather than worrying about your score, an exciting friendship can develop that is based on things that matter. As you go along your daily pace, make disciples.[1] It doesn't preclude specific preplanned times to look in the Scriptures together, but it will feel more relaxed and in tune with real life the more natural it is.

---

[1]Matt. 28:19

Walking with God
Over the Long Haul

For the next couple of weeks, I would like to focus in on a metaphor that is used in the Scriptures to describe the ultimate companionship God wants to have with us. It's not a sprint, a jog, or marathon; it is a lifelong cross-country journey that requires a consistent "walk." The Scriptures are replete with the notion of walking in a certain manner. We will look briefly at a number of ways that will hopefully be helpful and encouraging to you.

A Man Who Walked with God

"This is the account of Noah and his family. Noah was a righteous man, blameless among the people of his time, and he walked faithfully with God." Gen. 6:9 (NIV)

The classic illustration in the Scriptures of someone who walked with God is Enoch, who I mentioned previously. But there is another man who walked with God in those early days of recorded time. Noah is generally known for building a boat out in the middle of a desert. From a human perspective, it was a stupid idea, and the locals called him out on it. But Noah was a righteous man, blameless among all the people who were now mocking him. Even though he couldn't explain the logic of it he pressed on because He walked with the One who gave him the command.

What also impresses me about this man was his family. Imagine coming home after your daily stroll with God and telling your wife, "The kids and I are going to build a boat." She may have said, "Where?" He answers, "Right here." She stares out at the dry landscape and says, "But there is no water close by," and he says softly, "Not now there isn't." And what touches me is that Noah's wife was so certain of her husband's walk and friendship with God that she gladly moved forward with him. The kids did the same, probably not because of any level of maturity with God that they had at this point, but they trusted

their parent's relationship with God. What a tribute to this man.

I have known people engaged in various ministries whose families hate what they do. The kids are embarrassed at school and their spouse constantly says, "Why don't you get a *real* job?" Few things can be more painful than a divided family.

We all know the story of God's instructions after the ark was built and the animals that were taken on board. But we marginalize the story with children by not helping them understand that the story is not about the animals, but the obedient heart of a faithful man and a family who *trusted* his relationship with God.

As the rains came and the waters began to rise, those friends who had questioned Noah's sanity began to see the wisdom of Noah's boat building project. Friends and neighbors cried out from the raging water below the ark, and Noah could only watch with a broken heart. God's heart was broken too because He desires that no one should perish.[1] But He had to purify His creation because it had become out of control. He chose this old patriarch to walk with Him and be His instrument for a new world.

---

[1] 2 Pet. 3:9

Walking in Love

"And walk in love just as Christ also loved you and gave Himself up for you, an offering and a sacrifice to God as a fragrant aroma." Ephesians 5:2

Love has become a cliché these days. "I just love your shoes, and "love your new car," and of course, "Love ya!" Love was intended to be the most cherished reality in the world. Love is a Person, a description of who God is as well as the actions He has taken to prove it. Catastrophic events often produce the standard, "our thoughts and prayers are with the families." A nice sentiment, a kind thought, but it is hard to imagine Jesus using ready-made clichés rather than real love coming from the heart.

The central thrust of this great word, "love" that we often use and sometimes abuse, literally means, *to will the best for another.* If I *say I love you,* I am saying that I desire the absolute best for you unconditionally. It's not simply an emotion or warm feeling, and its value is in the demonstration of its true essence … the life and death of Jesus. Had God simply said, "Love ya," mankind would have been left without any hope of redemption.

Ephesians is about *unity.* These new Gentile believers had a shallow sense of God's love. Paul urges them to *walk in love* toward others just as Jesus paid the ultimate price because of His love for them. Drop the shallow rhetoric and demonstrate to the world what real love looks like in a human being. The great "Love Chapter" Paul wrote to the Corinthian Church is not simply a description of real love; it is a picture of Jesus.[1] You can't be or do what is written in those verses in and of yourself. They were meant to show who Jesus is and how His life in you can be a life that exemplifies love.

You know someone who is hurting, and you say, "We're praying for you during this difficult time." That's great, but why not walk the path with them? Don't text or e-mail; go see the person. Ask how you can help. Ask how the family is coping. If you genuinely persist, a door will open for you to specifically demonstrate love to that family.

There is an unlimited number of ways to walk in love when you walk with Jesus. When you pray, ask God to open a pathway for you to really engage with someone who desperately needs you to walk with them in love. There will never be a gift so great as the deposit of time that you give them. To put aside your own agenda in order to give yourself to another will pay dividends you never imagined, both for you and for the person in need.

[1] 1 Cor. 13

Walking Worthy of Your Calling

"Walk in a manner worthy of the calling to which you have been called."
Ephesians 4:1

Paul has just said at the end of the previous chapter that God is able to do more than we could possibly imagine by the power of His Spirit in us.[1] The word *worthy* has to do with a balancing of the scales. It is one thing to be equal or balanced with another, but to be balanced with God is something else entirely. Our word "worth" comes from *worthy*. If you are paid to do a job, the pay should be commensurate with the task. To walk worthy of all that God has done for us is impossible! The only way we could walk in a manner worthy of our calling is if God created in us the desire to trust Him to do in us what we can't do and be on our own.

What is our calling? You may sense a specific calling to the medical, legal, business or educational profession. You will utilize your God-given gifts and talents in that calling. But *all of us* have a calling to be a beacon of hope within the circle of influence where we live and work.

The verses that follow in Ephesians 4 tell us that we should *make allowances for each other—being patient, gentle, and tolerant, staying unified in love.* We can do this by allowing the fruit of the spirit to come through us toward others. When we walk in humility, gentleness, and patience ... as it comes through us from the Spirit of God, we are walking worthily. It is impossible to walk in this manner if these fruit of the Holy Spirit—gentleness, humility, and patience are not present in us.

Later in this chapter, Paul warns the Ephesian believers to no longer *walk in the vanity of their minds.*[2] Given free reign, most of us, because of our ego, would walk according to whatever would benefit us the most and show us in the best light. Paul is saying that as the humility of Jesus takes hold in us, we begin to realize that everything we have is a gift, not an entitlement. Everything good comes from God's grace and generosity toward His beloved children.

---

[1]Eph. 3:20–21   [2]Eph. 4:17

Walking in Wisdom

"Therefore, be careful how you walk, not as unwise men, but as wise, making the most of your time, because the days are evil." Ephesians 5:15

As believers, we learn and grow as we begin to connect with the Scriptures and engage in the community of faith. The danger seldom addressed is *tunnel vision*. The King James translation uses the word *circumspect,* from which we get the word spectacle. It means to see all around you. In other words, wisdom doesn't simply mean the ability to discern the truth in a vacuum. It sees the truth amid an understanding of opposing views and seeks to understand where they miss the mark without denigrating those who take that position.

We live in a world that creates its own reality. In doing so, it plays right into the hands of the enemy.[1] Satan is not a cartoon character in a red jumpsuit holding a pitchfork. He is a personality in the universe that wants to counterfeit every notion of truth. That which you read in the news, hear from the "experts" and even non-circumspect believers, must be critiqued in light of God's Word. Wisdom means not simply buying into what the articulate commentator on TV or the radio says. They have an agenda and are not looking for truth as much

as they are looking to win. Liberal or conservative ... they first have to stay on the air, and that often will drive their point of view. Critique even the highly regarded pastor by God's Word. They have just as much capacity to misunderstand and compromise truth as anyone. We must do our own homework and learn to discern truth from error.

Jesus associated with people most believers would run from, but these people were not the main source of His fellowship. He knew the truth and could not be coerced. For us, being circumspect is being aware of the company we keep.[2] We are warned by the Psalmist not to walk in the counsel of the ungodly.[3] That doesn't mean to watch only one news channel or never listen to the reasoning of those who have a different point of view. It means don't *walk* in their counsel! We must understand why we believe the positions we take and why we disagree with those of a different opinion. Know the whole story ... not just the side that you already agree with. Walk circumspectly but love your enemies as you walk.

---

[1] 1 Pet. 5:8 [2] Prov. 13:20 [3] Ps. 1:1

Walking in the Light

"But if we walk in the light, as he is in the light, we have fellowship with one another, and the blood of Jesus, his Son, purifies us from all sin." 1 John 1:7

Throughout the Scriptures, the metaphor of *light* is a recurring theme, particularly in the Gospels. It can symbolize good just as darkness can evoke evil; it was the first of God's creations. Light can also represent truth, wisdom, and understanding. Nothing is hidden, darkness is scattered, and everything is illuminated. Walking in the light will give us the clarity to recognize that which was hidden to us when we walked in darkness.[1] Light is truth at an angle that allows us to see what was previously hidden.

When we walk in the light, our path is "like the light of dawn; it gets brighter and brighter until the full day."[2] As we walk along the path, the light is dim at first, but as we go, the light will create greater wisdom, and in turn, greater discernment as we walk.

After college, I was on Young life Staff working with high school kids for eight years. After three years I met and married Susan. High school kids came over constantly and continued to do so after we married. We would all sit together and talk, but to my shame, I never noticed that the questions were almost always directed only to me. Susan suffered silently until one morning in my core group one of my closest friends, Robby Rowan, asked if we all were sure we made our wives feel fully included and appreciated. I asked Susan that night if she had felt left out and the flood gates opened. I was insensitive and didn't even know it until God used my friends to shine a light on my insensitivity.

Walking in the light moves us into fellowship with one another. Criticism, resentment, and judgment cannot exist in the light. Strife cannot tolerate the light, because the Spirit of God in one another is always in harmony. The light purifies our motives and chases the darkness that may originate from things we have been taught. Take a risk and ask your spouse or a close friend if there is any shadow of darkness they can see in you that needs to be brought into the light. It may be hard to hear, but if you will receive it, you may well see great changes take place in your relationships.

If you live to impress people, you will block the light for fear of being known. My parent's generation wasn't conscious of hiding anything; they had just been taught to keep their cards close to the vest. Speaking about matters of the heart or asking for help was unheard of. Most lived with issues that could have been healed. I'd rather accept the help now and walk in the light.

---

[1] Ps. 56:13   [2] Prov. 4:18   [3] 1 John 1:7

Walking in the Truth

"Teach me Your way, O Lord; I will walk in Your truth; unite my heart to fear Your name." Psalm 86:11

This prayer by David reveals his heart. This kind of desire caused God to say that David was a man after His own heart.[1] The second part of this verse tells us more: "He will do everything I want Him to do." David told God that if He would show him His way, he would walk in that truth and his heart would revere God's name. There is nothing complicated about this; it's just a matter of the will, the desire. It is one thing to tell a friend, or your spouse, that you want to live out the truth in everything you do. It's quite another to say that to God. In Ecclesiastes, Solomon said, "When you make a vow to God, do not delay to fulfill it. He has no pleasure in fools; fulfill your vow. It is better not to make a vow than to make one and not fulfill it."[2] Strong words! Did David walk in the truth? Not all the time; he sinned just as we do, but his heart was committed to truth.

Pontius Pilate asked the ultimate question, "What is truth?"[3] Ask that question on any university campus and you will hear more baloney per square inch than you can imagine. The secular world and even some people of faith believe truth is relative. They say it ebbs and flows and changes from generation to generation. The fundamental conflict is *desire versus truth*. A person's obsession, that which he truly desires, will ultimately be the reason he walks away from the truth. David wanted the truth to drive his value system, but those who argue for relativism want their value system to drive what is true.

Truth is that which is consistent with the mind, the character, the glory, and the Personhood of God. It is impossible to make sense of truth without God as a starting point. You have no moral authority, no prism of truth through which the idea and thoughts of man can pass. One idea is as good or bad as another because there is no standard. The writer of Hebrews says Jesus is the Incarnation of Truth.[4] Truth is a Person, and David prays that if God will reveal truth through His Word to him, and guide him, he will walk in the light of the truth.

Meditate on this and consider saying to God what David said.

---

[1]Acts 13:22   [2]Eccles. 5:4   [3]John 18:28   [4]Heb. 1:3

Walking in the Spirit

"If we live by the Spirit, let us also walk by the Spirit." Galatians 5:25

According to the Scriptures, every person is born without the life of God in them. At some point, a man or woman, boy or girl, must personally and individually trust Jesus Christ with their life. In a real sense, we *transfer title* of our life over to Him.

What now? In the days immediately following my surrender to Christ, I thought it was up to me from then on. God was patting me on the rear and saying, "Go get 'em, tiger." But I slowly began to learn that my former life, desires, perspectives, and habits were *a bridge too far* for me to contain. I was overwhelmed! The disciples must have been scared out of their sandals just before Jesus resurrected. But He told them that He would not leave them alone, but would send the Comforter, the Holy Spirit, to teach them and to live in them.[1]

After my initial epiphany and adjusting to college, I was concerned about how I was going to reboot my life when I had so many issues that certainly were not pleasing to God. I learned that if I would follow the lead of the Spirit to change me from within, He would take care of those old desires.[2] I never dreamed that I could really enjoy reading the Bible or listening to people talk about their faith. Someone showed me a passage that opened my eyes. It said that God would take the old heart of stone, that I guarded like Fort Knox, and replace it with a heart of flesh that would cause me to want to honor and obey His commands.[3] The old desires still pop up, but to the degree that I yield to the Spirit within me, I am walking in the Spirit and will honor him.

Many have crashed and burned by thinking that by exercising more discipline they would be able to drive themselves to overcome the desires of the flesh. Discipline is essential in life, but it can take you just so far.

Paul says we are not under the law.[4] Grace means that we are no longer burdened by the "have to" of the law. Walking in the Spirit is not about gritting your teeth and dutifully doing what you don't want to do. Grace means that I don't *have* to study the Scriptures, pray, and share my faith anymore. I *get* to do those things because that which I once considered a task or duty, has now become a privilege. As an old friend of mine used to say, "When you learn to walk by the Spirit, God changes all of your *want to's*."

---

[1]John 14:16, 26   [2]Gal. 5:16   [3]Ezek. 36:26–27   [4]Gal. 5:18

Walking by Faith

"For we walk by faith and not by sight." 2 Corinthians 5:7

In our culture, faith has become an anemic sentiment that simply means, "Hang in there!" It's more akin to positive thinking than to the framework of what it means to trust God. People have *faith* in all sorts of things. "I believe in love, I believe in you, I believe for every drop of rain that falls a flower grows," and on go the clichés. But faith is only as valid as its object. Great faith in thin ice will ruin your day. Tiny faith in thick ice can keep you dry.

Paul says believers walk not by what they see, but by what is invisible. Holding out for no-risk guarantees and foolproof fixes is like refusing to play an athletic event unless you are assured of victory. Trusting God for the visible is no trust at all. We put *In God We Trust* on our money, but our faith is in the federal government that the green paper bills in your wallet are worth what they say they are worth. We trust the visible, but to trust God for that which we do not see is a far safer bet than trusting in what you can see. God has a far better track record!

Walking in faith will eviscerate fear. The more we see God come through against all human odds, the more confident we will become. Blind faith is not blind at all if it is placed in the right object. Jesus trusted His Father in His life, His death, and His resurrection. Without faith, it is impossible to please God.[1]

"My faith isn't strong enough," you say. The truth is, we all have tremendous faith! We demonstrate it every time we open a can of soup. We have no idea what is in there. Every time you get in your car and press your foot on the brake, you demonstrate incredible faith. Can you guarantee the car will stop? To walk by faith simply means that we are transferring that which we lean on daily to the One who is worthy to be leaned on every day. It's not a gamble! It has the backing of the whole created order behind it. Walking in faith by trusting God is the most reasonable thing you will ever do.

---

[1]Heb. 11:6

111

Walking in God's Ways

"Oh that My people would listen to Me, that Israel would walk in My ways!"
Psalm 81:13

David sat out under the stars one night and prayed, *"Make me know your ways, Lord; teach me your paths."*[1] Have you ever prayed that prayer? Is becoming a man or woman who walks in God's ways a high priority? Men like David didn't have the distractions we have. There was no buzzing, beeping, vibrating, texting, or tweeting in his life. He was a shepherd. But aside from the simplicity, his life in many ways was more difficult. How would God teach Him? Verbally, I suppose, in those days, but there was much stumbling and falling in his quest to walk in God's path. What an advantage we have! How do we walk in God's ways? Look at Jesus, the perfect model.

The closest most of us get to David's plea is to ask Him what His will for us is concerning what job to take, what house to buy, what school to attend, etc. The truth is, God's will has little to do with those questions. His will is primarily internal, not all the stuff we can't figure out. If we genuinely ask God that question and begin to walk in His path, those "God's will" questions would be a piece of cake. I believe that God has a passion that we walk with Him as did Enoch and Noah. God would probably say, "Keep walking with me and choose the job you like, the house you can afford, and the college that best fits what you want to study."

Can you imagine following Jesus in an intimate fellowship and not eventually learning His perspective on everything? David really wanted to know, and he wasn't blowing smoke. He wanted to be intentional. My guess is that those words would please God more than anything you could ever come up with.

To walk in His ways we must *know* His ways, and we often get sidetracked by well-meaning people who simply repeat to us what they were told. Others drag us into the latest hot-button issues that everyone is buzzing about. Don't get distracted; go back to the source. I remember asking Billy Graham once how he approached His times alone with God. He said that no matter which book in the Scriptures he was studying, he always read the gospels every day. He wanted to saturate himself with the perspective of Jesus. So, read the gospels no matter what else you may presently be reading. Fill your mind and heart with the thoughts and principles Jesus lived and taught. He will show you His ways. Don't sell out for anyone else's idea of what He desires ... including mine. Ask Him!

---

[1] Ps. 25:4

Walking in Newness of Life

"Therefore, we have been buried with Him in baptism into death in order that, just as Christ was raised from the dead through the glory of the Father, we too might walk in newness of life." Romans 6:4

There is nothing like a new car or a new house, or even a new coat. Old things, as well, can hold great memories of days gone by. I look back and relish much of my early life and the friends and family that helped shape who I am, but the newness of life I've experienced since high school is beyond anything I could have imagined. My first memorized verse was, "If any man is in Christ, he is a new creation; the past is finished and gone; everything becomes fresh and new."[1]

I have noticed something in many lives over the years that is more of *sameness in life* than newness. It is possible to make the *decision* to follow Jesus but never experience an authentic *conversion*. I've known people who learn the spiritual language, attend the right functions, and do some caring things, but something seemed strangely amiss. They seemed mechanical and robotic. I don't have the ability to see their heart so only God knows, but I do know that when the Holy Spirit is in a person, the fruit of the Spirit will begin to emerge as well.[2] Obligation and duty are replaced by privilege and opportunity.

Something else that is all too common is seeing someone meet Jesus and come out of the gate like a young colt, only to sputter and run out of energy and enthusiasm somewhere around the second turn. There is a reason life with Jesus is defined as a *walk* rather than a *run*. A man or woman who is untutored in the Scriptures, never learning to trust God, never having close companions for encouragement and accountability, will drift until the north wind blows them away.

Walking in newness of life means that selfishness turns into a giving heart, a unilateral person will learn to walk with brothers and sisters, a slothful person will become more energized, and an undisciplined mind will be renewed. Newness of life is not simply attaching Jesus to whatever you already have going; it is a revolutionary way of life where "everything becomes fresh and new." If you were obsessed with money and things and continue that pattern, you have missed the essence of real life in Christ.

God's compassion is new every morning,[3] problems won't cease, but God will open a new path when you wander in the wilderness.[4] It is a promise from a Father to His children.

---

[1] 2 Cor. 5:17 (Phillips)   [2] Gal. 5:22–23   [3] Lam. 3:23   [4] Isa. 43:19

113

The Parables of Jesus

Parables were a primary way of Rabbinic teaching long before Jesus was born. There are over four thousand parables found in Jewish literature and about forty that Jesus taught in the gospels. In fact, of those forty recorded in the first three gospels, only three are original with Jesus. The others are those the Rabbis had taught for centuries, and Jesus tweaked them and took them in a new direction to illustrate a spiritual truth.

Jewish Rabbis spoke and taught in story form. They painted word images so that their audience could get a mental picture of the teaching. The Scriptures contain great theological truths, but they were perceived in story form by their hearers. In the western world, we think in a more abstract manner. We like outlines, bullet points, and very orderly progression of thought.

When we come to the Scriptures, it is important to realize that we are reading a Jewish document. It was written by Jews, to Jews, in a Jewish culture about the coming of a Jewish Messiah. We are stepping into alien territory, and therefore we gain the intended impact of the Scripture by seeing it through Jewish eyes rather than westernizing it as we tend to do.

Failing to see through a middle eastern lens causes us to miss much of the flavor of the text, and we also separate Jesus from His own culture.

Initially, Jesus used parables to paint a striking picture to the multitudes so they would more deeply understand His meaning. After the Jewish leaders claimed that Jesus performed His miracles by the power of Satan in Matthew,[1] His ministry changed in several ways. He knew that the multitudes were too far down the road with the distorted form of Judaism that the Pharisees had sculpted and would never accept him as Messiah. This is when he turns His attention to the Gentiles. He will no longer use His miracles to reveal His identity and will now perform healings privately and will now focus more on training the twelve. Additionally, He would now speak in parables, not for clarity, but to hide these truths for those Jews and their leaders who were dedicated to unbelief.

Scholars have studied the parables for centuries and debates still rage. I have no corner on the truth, but in the next ten days, I will try to give you the flavor of what Jesus is trying to convey in some of these word pictures through a Jewish context.

---

[1]Matt. 12:22–37

The Parable of the Garments and Wineskins

"No one sews a piece of unshrunk cloth on an old garment. If he does, the patch tears away from it, the new from the old, and a worse tear is made. 22 And no one puts new wine into old wineskins. If he does, the wine will burst the skins—and the wine is destroyed, and so are the skins. But new wine is for fresh wineskins."
Mark 2:21–22 (NIV)

Jesus is approached by some people who notice that the Pharisees, as well as John's former disciples, were fasting. They ask Jesus why *His* disciples are not doing the same. Fasting was done on the Day of Atonement, the one day of the year when Jews could know their sins were forgiven. The Jewish leaders, however, had made fasting a mandatory act twice a week. Jesus agreed with fasting, but it was to be voluntary and not a law. He answers by saying that it is pointless to expect people to fast at a wedding. The whole idea of a wedding is to enjoy the food and wine and celebrate the marriage. *"What wedding?"* they ask. Jesus becoming one with the believing body, the bride called the church, is the wedding He is referring to. Why would anyone fast at such a celebration? They will have ample time to fast when the Bridegroom is gone.

Jesus then gives two parables that are basically the same. You never put a patch of new cloth on an old garment or put new wine in old wineskins. The cloth will shrink, tear, and the new wine's gases will expand and burst the old wineskins. Jesus' new teaching of grace and liberty will never fit into the Pharisee's law-driven works-oriented perspective. The truth that He brings will never be compatible with the old Pharisaic legal system.

Why are there so many people who don't understand grace? If you were raised in a more legalistic, works-oriented atmosphere and later learned about the unmerited favor of God, you would find it impossible to merge the two. Law comforts us because we feel secure with very specific fences or boundaries. We don't want to trust ourselves to the direction and power of the Spirit of God within us. Learning and functioning by grace require *unlearning*[1] that which you were taught by good and loving people who were probably victims themselves. Grace and law are not compatible, because under law you obey because of obligation—*you should, you have to.* But under grace, it is obedience by desire and privilege. There is a vast difference!

God not only accomplished it all for us on the cross, but He also keeps us and holds us up by His power as well. We can add nothing to what He has done! It is a gift that keeps on giving.

[1]Eph. 2:8; Rom. 6:23

115

The Parable of the Sower

Matthew 13:4–9

When the truth is spoken, it must have a place to land. When God speaks, the reality of His words is not primarily meant for the mind, but for the heart. It must be openly received in order to penetrate and change a human life. This well-known parable told by Jesus is more focused on the soil than on the farmer who sows it. Jesus is speaking to a group of people about four kinds of soil. They are standing in a volcanic area that was well known for the richness of its soil. It also had very rocky soil, and during the summer months, it produced many thorns. In addition, the shoreline was also the major highway for all north-south travel, making it easy to imagine seed falling on the beaten path.

No matter how important and life-changing a message may be, it has no chance to penetrate the soil of the human heart unless it is received. The farmer sows his seed and some fall on the hard path which has been beaten down by many travelers. The birds (the enemy, Satan) swoop down and devour it before it can work its way into the soil. So it is with a heart that is unreceptive. It may be hardened from a bad experience early in life, a disappointment with God, or a misunderstanding. Whatever the circumstance, the truth is not received.

As the farmer continues to sow, some of the seed falls in rocky areas where there was minimal soil. Some of it takes root quickly in the thin soil, but the sun scorches it and it withers away because of a shallow root system. It is common for people to hear the truth and become enamored with Jesus but are so busy and distracted with personal agendas that the truth never really penetrates. You will often hear words similar to what a well-known celebrity in New York once said to me: "I tried God once, but it didn't work for me. It's just not my thing."

Some of the seed settled among thorns and as it grew, they choked the life out of it. We live in an information age, and everybody has a theory of what makes life tick. A person who is not grounded in the Scriptures, prayer, and fellowship is up for grabs. A man or woman untutored and constantly exposed to the thinking of the culture will soon lose his moorings and become like that to which he is exposed.

Some seed falls on the rich earth, a receptive heart that is hungry to grow and become like Jesus. This person is one who can grow into the full measure of the stature of Christ.[1]

---

[1]Eph. 4:13

The Parable of The Hidden Treasure

"Again, the Kingdom of Heaven is like treasure hidden in a field, which a man found and hid, and for joy over it, he goes and sells all that he has and buys the field."
Matthew 13:44

During the time of Jesus, valuables were very difficult to keep safe from robbers. There were no banks as we know today and money, jewels, coins, or precious metals had to be easy to transport or sufficiently hidden in a secret place.

In this parable, a man finds a treasure of extreme value in the ground, possibly buried in a field by someone who died before being able to retrieve it. The man knows that the value of the treasure is beyond measure. He does not steal it but re-buries it and sells everything he has to purchase the field.

There are several ways to look at this parable as well as the parable about "The Pearl of Great Price."[1] They convey the same message in a different way. The most obvious is that someone like you or me stumbles onto something that we have longed for our entire life ... the assurance and peace of knowing that we are loved and desired by God to be part of His kingdom. We realize its value and want it more than anything. To possess it, the cost will be handing over the title of our own life to God.

But consider the way a first-century Jew might have heard this parable from Jesus. The man (Jesus) finds a treasure in a world that is not his own. Satan currently holds title to this world. He is the *god* of this world[2] and is called the prince and power of the air.[3] God created the world and will one day take it back, but it has been in the hands of Satan since the fall of Adam and Eve. The man (Jesus) finds the treasure which is Israel.[4] What did He do to purchase the field (the world) and gain the treasure? He paid a terrible price, His own life in order to rightly gain the treasure. This means that in the fullness of time many Jews will one day receive Jesus as Messiah.

Whichever way you see it, don't overlook the fact that the one who finds the treasure does not simply come back under cover of darkness, snatch it away and claim "finders' keepers." He does the legitimate and honorable thing. He pays the full price of His own life to purchase the treasure.

---

[1]Matt. 13:45–46   [2]2 Cor. 4:4   [3]Eph. 2:2   [4]Exod. 19:5; Ps. 135:4

The Parable of the Mustard Seed

"It is like a mustard seed, which is the smallest of all seeds on earth. Yet when planted, it grows and becomes the largest of all garden plants, with such big branches that the birds can perch in its shade." Mark 4:31–32 (also Matthew 13:31–32)

This parable is paired with the Parable of the Leaven, which follows these verses. Jesus is painting a verbal picture for His listeners about the miracle of the Kingdom of God.

The mustard seed is about the size of a grain of salt. This tiny seed can grow up to ten feet tall, which can provide shade from the scorching sun and in which birds can build their nests. Jesus came as a baby from the womb of a peasant girl in what was considered a backwater, insignificant province of the Roman Empire. He grew up in utter obscurity and began His ministry at age thirty with a handful of ordinary teenagers. The Jewish hierarchy was threatened by Him and the Roman Empire ignored Him until Pilate was convinced by the Jewish leaders that He could become a threat to Caesar. Today, there is no place on this planet that has not heard about Him.

The natural progression of growth is for the tiny seed to thrive in rocky soil in between rocks and literally push away large stones in its process of growth. This is meant to be a vivid description by Jesus to encourage and point out to His hearers that what they now see around them will grow mightily in time. It may appear small, insignificant, humble and almost invisible in its present state, but it will progressively grow and spread throughout the world in ways that they cannot even comprehend.

For us, the astounding growth of the family of Jesus Christ is undeniable. Even having been infiltrated by cults, and its message perverted by many, the miracle of its power to radically change a human heart is attested by millions across the earth.

Consider how you came to faith. Maybe you heard about Jesus from your earliest memories, but maybe you were more like me without any spiritual moorings as a child. The miracle that I have witnessed in my own life, that took me down a path of virtually non-existent spiritual beginnings, is much like the growth of a mustard seed.

Tell your story to people no matter where you are along the path of faith; you are a miracle in the making! Never think your journey is uneventful to share. It is unique. Don't be intimidated by the dramatic conversions of others. Your story is just as real and important because just like any other person who has come to know Jesus, you miraculously have gone from *death to life*.

The Parable of the Rich Fool

"And he told them this parable: 'The ground of a certain rich man yielded an abundant harvest. He thought to himself, "What shall I do? I have no place to store my crops." Then he said, "This is what I'll do. I will tear down my barns and build bigger ones, and there I will store my surplus grain. And I'll say to myself, 'You have plenty of grain laid up for many years. Take life easy; eat, drink and be merry.' 'But God said to him, "You fool! This very night your life will be demanded from you. Then who will get what you have prepared for yourself?'" Luke 12:16–20 (NIV)

This is a powerful parable that strikes at the heart of any generation, gender, or nationality throughout history. It is not as much about money as it is about false security and arrogance.

A man experiences great success in life; he has the Midas touch and every venture he attempts turns to gold. He has distinguished himself as a man with enormous talents and is highly respected for his accomplishments. He reaches the point in life where he is almost overwhelmed with his own success. He must build and expand again in order to contain it all.

In the days of Jesus, wealth was not measured by stacks of cash and boxes of gold coins. It mostly had to do with land, crop production, and livestock. In taking inventory of his estate, this man realizes that he is set for life. No need to work anymore; in fact, he already has a storage problem. He feels secure and untouchable by any looming catastrophe that might occur. The rest of his life will be a virtual Disneyland! He even brags to his own soul that he has made his own dream come true.

But he misses two things ... the fragile nature of life and the vulnerability of a soul ignored. Later that evening and without his consent or approval, he will die of a heart attack or some unexpected event he cannot control. Within a split second, after his last heartbeat, he will stand before God and give an account of his life. None of those accomplishments will matter, and God will be forced to say, "Depart from Me, I never knew you."[1]

The man was a fool, but there are many who follow his lead. Any sense of security in life can be gone in an instant. Nothing is guaranteed except God's indelible promise that on the last day of the life of someone who has entrusted all that he is and has to the Savior, he will hear the same words spoken to the thief on the cross: "Today, you will be with me in paradise."

---

[1] Matt. 7:21–23

119

The Parable of the Barren Fig Tree

"A man had a fig tree planted in his vineyard, and he came seeking fruit on it and found none. And he said to the vinedresser, 'Look, for three years now I have come seeking fruit on this fig tree, and I find none. Cut it down. Why should it use up the ground?' And he answered him, 'Sir, let it alone this year also until I dig around it and put on manure. Then if it should bear fruit next year, well and good; but if not, you can cut it down." Luke 13:6–8

The context of this parable is that it is initiated by a confrontation between Jesus and some Jewish leaders in verses Luke 13:1-5 prior to the parable. Two tragedies had taken place; one was caused by an evil, paranoid man and his soldiers, and the other was caused by an accident.

We read that Pilate had "mingled the blood of the Galileans with the sacrifices." Pilate was paranoid and mistakenly believed that Jews from Galilee were planning an uprising. He dispatched soldiers to sack the city. It was late in the day when the sacrifices were being made. During the carnage, some of the Galileans hid in the temple but were found and also slaughtered. "Their blood mingled with that of the sacrifices."[1]

The second tragedy was the collapse of a tower in Siloam that killed eighteen people. Jesus uses these two tragedies that would have been well-known in order to say, "Unless you repent, you will all likewise perish." He is referring to what would happen in 70 AD when the Romans will destroy Jerusalem and over a million Jews are slaughtered by the Romans.

With that backstory, Jesus gives this parable. A man planted a fig tree and later came looking for fruit but found none. God planted a tree ... the Nation of Israel. He deeply loved them and wanted them to be fruitful. He came to them personally, in the form of a man, and saw that His beloved people were producing no fruit. Year after year the owner saw nothing but the barrenness of his fig tree. The *tree* was simply taking up space in the vineyard. Rather than cut it down, the *gardener* asked for time to fertilize the tree to see if his nurturing and care might still produce fruit.

We see the patience of God on one hand, and the judgment of God on the other. He desires that no one should perish,[2] but also warns that His patience is not unlimited.[3] God's kindness is meant to lead us to rethink our direction![4] Jesus warns the Jews that unless they repent (change their minds in terms of the path they have chosen) they will suffer the natural consequences of a life without meaning, one that is simply taking up space and producing no fruit for the Kingdom.

---

[1] Luke 13:1   [2] 2 Pet. 3:9   [3] Matt. 7:19   [4] Rom. 2:4

The Parable of the Lost Sheep

"What man among you, if he has a hundred sheep and has lost one of them, does not leave the ninety-nine in the open pasture and go after the one which is lost until he finds it? When he has found it, he lays it on his shoulders, rejoicing. And when he comes home, he calls together his friends and his neighbors, saying to them, 'Rejoice with me, for I have found my sheep which was lost!'"
Luke 15:4–6

What triggered this parable from Jesus? In the first two verses, we see that the Pharisees were critical of Jesus because He ate with sinners, something a *righteous* Pharisee would never do. The Pharisees were "the separate ones," experts in the law and even more expert in singling out those who broke it. They believed that God hated those who strayed away from Him. In the Mishna, it says that God rejoices when a sinner bites the dust. This is what the disciples and all Jews had been taught.

Jesus will give three parables in a row to drive the point home that, on the contrary, God will go to the ends of the earth to rescue one who has strayed. In this first parable, as the Shepherd, He will leave the ninety-nine sheep to go after the one who strayed. In the second, a woman will search for the one lost coin until she finds it, and in the third, he will receive back a self-absorbed son who had left home and broken with his family.

The Jewish culture is driven by a *shame* and *honor* way of thinking that developed over the years as a sort of pecking order. The primary motivation for what, and how, things are done is based on seeking honor for yourself and avoiding shame. Jesus knew that the Pharisees would have considered going after one lost sheep or a rebellious person as a colossal waste of time. Jesus re-frames the disciples' understanding of God with a message insisting that God has a tender, personal concern for one sheep that is lost and "when he finds it, he puts it on his shoulders and carries it home." God has an extravagant love for individuals who are lost and are found.

Jesus makes it clear that the Pharisees who thought themselves righteous and close to God were far away, and the *shameful* prostitutes and tax collectors they hated were the ones God was pursuing for His Kingdom.

It is exciting to know that God never gives up; He is the "Hound of Heaven" who will pursue the one who has strayed until His last breath. He searches and seeks even the most arrogant and hopeless person and longs for him to return.

The Parable of the Prodigal Son

Luke 15:11–32

This is probably the most well-known and popular of all Jesus' parables. It strikes at the heart of what it means to be a forgiving father and highlights the even stronger reality of how our Heavenly Father feels about his children.

The younger of two sons was getting tired of waiting for his elderly father to die. He had dreams of his own and wanted to try out his wings and fly solo in a new zip code. The first-born male in a Jewish home would receive a double portion of his father's estate, so this young man asked his dad for his third now, rather than after his father died.[1] The arrogance and selfishness of this young lad are astounding. His father's wealth would have been in land and livestock, so he would have been forced to sell a third of his estate in order to honor the son's wishes.

The son goes to "the far country," which is the Decapolis area on the other side of the Sea of Galilee. He blows all his money and raises all the hell he can until he is finally reduced to eating pig slop, a low point for any Jew. His shame is overwhelming as he realizes what he has done and that he can't fix it! By Jewish law, he cannot return to his father's house in the same capacity which he left. He has broken community, which is one of the strongest and most enviable bonds in Jewish culture.

He is lost, hungry and has shamed himself and his family. With no other options, he begins the long walk home to hopefully be allowed to return as a hired hand. The brokenhearted father sits on his porch looking out in the distance longing for his son. One day he sees a figure walking slowly, tentatively, closer and closer. He recognizes his son's walk and does what elderly Jewish men never do ... he runs down the road toward his boy.

This was an ancient Jewish parable, but in the Jewish version, the father sits the son down and tells him he cannot take him back because he has broken community. But Jesus startles his hearers by having the father greet the boy with open arms. Before the lad can give his prepared speech, his father calls his servants to celebrate and have a gigantic party because, "my son was lost, but now he is found!" It was as if he had never left.

The elder son was angry. He had done everything right. He stayed home and worked the farm, and now the old man was throwing a party for his rebellious little brother. The truth is, the elder brother had counted on his righteousness to gain favor with his father, just as the Pharisees thought they could please God by good works but would never receive His own Son. This parable would have dismantled the theology of the Jewish leaders.

---

[1]Deut. 21:17

The Parable of the Good Samaritan

Luke 10:25–38

A young Pharisee asks Jesus a most critical question: "What must I *do* to have eternal life?" Jesus says *you are a lawyer ... what does it say in the law?* The young man quotes the great commandment, "Love God and love your neighbor as yourself." Jesus says, "Do this and you will live." The key to this encounter is the word "do." It is used in two different ways. The Pharisee uses the *aorist tense,* which conveys a onetime action, like slamming a door. In other words, he asks, *what one-time big splash can I make that will give me eternal life?* In Jesus' affirmation of the man's answer, He uses the same word "do" in the *present tense,* which means continual action. The Pharisee wants to do one big dramatic thing, and Jesus is saying, "Love God with all your heart, soul, mind, and strength and your neighbor every minute of every hour of every day of your life and you will have eternal life." He gives the man a task he cannot possibly do so that he will realize he needs a Savior.

This leads to the final question, "Who is my neighbor?" and Jesus gives this famous parable. A man is robbed and left for dead, and two different Sadducees pass by without helping. Why? One of the great debates of Jesus' day was concerning the *weight* of various commandments. To love God was agreed by all to be the greatest command. The issue was the second. Pharisees believed that loving your neighbor was next, but the Sadducees did not. It ranked down the list, and purity ranked higher. The injured man was "nearly dead," and Jewish law required a priest not to touch any dead or nearly dead person. These two were simply obeying their understanding of the Law.

The young Pharisee would have certainly known what was to come next in the story because this was a common parable where a Pharisee is always the hero who helps the injured man. But Jesus throws him a curveball and changes the parable. A "half-breed" Samaritan is the hero who saves the victim's life. Jesus asks the young man, "Who among the three was a neighbor to the victim?" The man answered, "The one who showed mercy to him." What is this parable really saying from the perspective of its context and the people involved?

The most hated enemy of the Jews were Samaritans. The young Pharisee's answer confirms that this is a parable about *loving your enemy,* loving the one with whom you have the greatest animosity. Your neighbor includes those whom you intensely dislike, not simply a neighbor with whom you are socially congenial, spiritually similar, or politically aligned.

The Parable of the Rich Man and Lazarus

Luke 16:19–31

Each day a homeless man named Lazarus sits in front of the gates leading to a lavish home owned by a fabulously wealthy man. Lazarus survives on the trash that the rich man throws away. This wealthy man is indifferent to the plight of Lazarus, showing no compassion or concern for him. Passing through his heavy iron gates, he shrugs and rolls his eyes at the inconvenient "clutter" lying at the edge of his property. Eventually, they both die, and both go to Sheol. It means the *place of the dead.* There were two sides or compartments there. One is the *redeemed* side, which is called *Abraham's Bosom,* where Lazarus went, and the unredeemed side, which is *hell,* where the rich man went. (All Old Testament believers went to Abraham's bosom initially until Christ was resurrected and was the first to enter heaven, the firstborn of the resurrection. Then, other believers from Abraham's Bosom would follow).[1]

From the horror and intense "agony of this fire," the rich man sees Lazarus from across the abyss in Abraham's Bosom and appeals to Abraham with two requests. First, that he would send Lazarus, whom he had ignored in life, to dip his finger in water to cool his tongue. Abraham reminds him that he focused all his attention and priority on the good things he had in life and cared nothing about eternity. Secondly, he asked that Abraham would send Lazarus back to warn the rich man's brothers not to make the same mistake he had. Abraham replies that if they would not listen to Moses (The Torah) and the Prophets, they would never listen to a man like Lazarus, even raised from the dead.

Though it is not popular or politically correct to believe in a literal hell, Jesus unequivocally teaches that heaven and hell are literal realities. I don't like the concept of hell, but I cannot escape the reality that it is spoken of throughout Scripture. I know many people who are as indifferent to hell and to the plight of the poor as was the rich man in the story. They too will be as surprised and as remorseful as this man when they are confronted with that reality and realize it is too late to change their mind.

We also see in this story that God is deeply offended at our neglect toward the poor.[2] Our time on earth is like a vapor that appears briefly and vanishes.[3] Jesus teaches a stark truth that if a person books passage on the USS UNBELIEF, he will have to sail all the way to its destination.

---

[1] 1 Cor. 15:20–23   [2] Prov. 17:5; 29:7   [3] James 4:14

A Decision of Faith Over Expertise

Luke 5:1–11

Every day we face choices. Many of them are unconscious and so repetitive that we simply react. But there are others that push the boundaries of our comfort zone. They are not easy. Maybe they should be, but nonetheless, they force us to choose not simply right versus wrong, but good versus best. To trust God in all things is the most supreme of all the choices we make.

As Jesus walks one day by the Sea of Galilee, boats line the shore and fishermen are busy washing their nets after fishing all night. Jesus sits down in a boat belonging to Peter. He is pushed out from shore and begins to teach the ever-present crowds. His voice carries easily and evenly over the still waters. When He finishes, He tells Peter, who was eagerly listening, to row out to deeper water and let down his nets. This, for Peter, is one of those uncomfortable choices.

Simon Peter wants Jesus to respect him as proficient in his chosen field, just as any of us would. He is already embarrassed in that he and his companions had been skunked and caught nothing all night. He knows Jesus is a great and learned Rabbi and he knows Jesus means well, but after all, what does *He* know about fishing? Herein is the crux of Peter's dilemma, and ours

as well. To obey Jesus is to admit in front of all his fellow fishermen that he is listening to a non-fisherman concerning the art of fishing. His reputation and image are on the line. What will he do? The big decision is whether to trust his own training, vast experience, and professionalism or trust Jesus.

Imagine that you, as a professional in business, medicine, education, athletics, or politics face a decision that you deal with constantly. You know the upside and downside, and you are very much aware of the consequences of a wrong choice. But you hear a *"still small voice"* in your head. You dismiss it but it doesn't go away. It leans against every normal instinct of professional expertise you know. It is the Holy Spirit directing you. But it doesn't make practical sense. This is where Peter finds himself. *Do I trust my professional knowledge, or do I trust God?*

Peter leaned against his natural instincts and trusted God. The result was a boatload of fish. But this wasn't about food or economics; it was about the man Peter was to become. Trusting God is not really about the outcome of the decision; it is about the man or woman you gradually become as a result of decisions like this.[1]

---

[1]Prov. 3:5–6

Lip Service

"Because this people draw near with their words and honor Me with their lip service, but they remove their hearts far from Me, and their reverence for Me consists of tradition learned by rote." Isaiah 29:13

To most of us, there are few things more annoying than to listen to someone constantly chattering "Christian smack", with little or no evidence in their life to give validity to their words. We are all guilty of that to some degree. I have heard myself extol the virtues of prayer only to be asked by someone to pray for them. With a big smile and a furrowed brow of concern, I nod my head, go on my merry way and forget to do it.

Jesus makes statements very similar to these words that God spoke to Isaiah seven-hundred years prior to His coming.[1] Many of the Pharisees were good people who began with good intentions. But over the course of time, the lure of self-importance, the reverential treatment by the Jewish multitudes, and their resolve that *image is everything* put them at odds with Jesus. They were very serious about keeping the rules because they had come to believe that the one who dies with the least broken commands wins. Jesus came and taught that the issue was the condition of the heart. This they could not comprehend, so they continued to double down on doing everything right rather than allowing God to give them a new heart.

Today the unfortunate result is that the emphasis in much of the church is on knowing and doing the right thing rather than allowing God to make us the right people. God says to Isaiah, "their reverence for Me consists of tradition learned by rote" (repetition, memorization). None of this impresses God. Verse memory is valuable; repetition of the truth is helpful in learning, but God reads our intent. Is it to impress or does it spring from a heart eager to know God more intimately? God knows when the motive of His people was obviously the latter.

Creating a spiritual image is always detrimental to you, to those who really know you, and to God's reputation in the world. Endless clichés are not helpful in lifting up Christ. They marginalize Him. I remember a high school girl giving a testimony in a church service saying Jesus was "a really good guy." I get where she was trying to go, but Jesus being *a good guy* is like saying Mozart and Beethoven wrote some *snappy tunes*. The tip of your hat to God with little or no real substance behind it is like showing up at church at Christmas and Easter and feeling you have done God a favor. It accents a cliché relationship that is hollow and empty. Allow your words to spring from a full heart.

---

[1]Matt. 15:8

Faith and Works

"Even so faith, if it has no works is dead, being by itself. But someone may well say, 'You have faith and I have works; show me your faith without the works, and I will show you by my works." James 2:18 (ESV)

There is no contradiction here to Jesus' statement that "the work of God is to believe (trust) in the One whom he has sent" (see Day 8). James argues that the position of simply believing and being otherwise passive in the face of human need is a sham. He challenges that notion by saying that faith that is not naturally driven toward a desire to serve is not faith at all. James asserts that his desire to serve is a natural by-product of his faith and intimacy with God. Faith without works is dead because if our beliefs do not drive our passion to care for and serve others, there is reason to question whether we are spiritually alive.[1]

We often hear people speak of the *balance* of faith and works. I believe this is unfortunate and leads many to think that trusting God and doing things on God's behalf is a dual responsibility. James clearly tells us that faith is what motivates, and drives works.

Trusting God every minute of your life is the essence of what it means to "follow Jesus." Doing great things for Him is in no way equal to that kind of trust; it should flow naturally *from* that trust. Faith that comes from intimacy with the Father initiated everything Jesus did. He said, "The words that I say to you I do not speak on My own initiative, but the Father abiding in Me does His work."[2] Jesus said nothing and did nothing on His own. Every miracle He performed was done *not* by Him, but by the Father working through Him.

Every good and lasting thing in life comes through faith. Faith without works is dead but works without faith will one day burn up unless it possesses the *quality* that can only be initiated by faith.[3] Work done in our own strength will not pass the test.

Let's say a sixteen-year-old girl wants to go on a weekend camping trip in the mountains with her boyfriend and two other couples. Her parents say, "absolutely not." Upset and still determined, she goes upstairs, cleans her room, launders her dirty clothes, washes her parents' cars, and volunteers to pick up her little brother at soccer practice. Friday afternoon she sneaks out to join her friends and they head for the mountains. Everything she did was pleasing to her parents, but she circumvented their decision and tried to substitute good works over trusting her parent's decision. Good works must spring from faith in God's wishes, not as a substitute for trusting Him.

---

[1] James 2:14   [2] John 14:10, 24; 7:16; 5:19   [3] 1 Cor. 3:13

127

The Power of Compassion

"The Lord is gracious and compassionate, slow to anger and rich in love. The Lord is good to all; he has compassion on all he has made." Psalm 145:8–9 (NIV)

We have seen time and again how God thinks and operates far outside the boundaries of conventional wisdom. He solves problems in ways we would never even consider. Joshua saw that firsthand when God gave him the battle plan to invade and overtake Jericho. He was to have his army march around the city walls six times every day and on the seventh day they were to march seven times around and, on his command … shout! You certainly won't find that strategy in the West Point Military Manual.

The Syrian army was moving briskly toward Israel. They outnumber Israel's army and are stronger and better equipped. But Israel has something they don't have … Elisha, the Prophet. The Syrian army came by night and surrounded the city. Elisha's servant panics when he sees the chariots and soldiers, but Elisha is calm and confident. He prays that his servants' eyes would be opened to see what he sees. Suddenly, the servant sees the hills around the enemy filled with horses and chariots and fire all around Elisha. The prophet prays again and asks God to strike the Syrian army with blindness and He does. He leads them to Samaria, the capital of the Northern Kingdom. Inside the city, Elisha's prayer this time was that

their eyes would be opened again. The King's son wants to execute all of the Syrian soldiers, but the King will not allow it and reprimands his son. Instead, he orders that the captured soldiers be fed and then send back to their home.[1] Again, not a strategy we would tend to employ against an invader. But here is the kicker: as a result of this King's actions, the Assyrian army never again invaded their land.[2]

The *compassion* of the king did what men and weapons could not. There are times that compassion will gain a victory when nothing else can. When compassion is demonstrated, it not only deals with the immediate problem, which is giving the soldiers food, but it transforms the perspective of the aggressor. The King's kindness was so strong, it made the enemies of God lose their aggressive desire. When you show sincere generosity and compassion toward an adversary it awakens in them the awareness of what God has already written in their hearts.[3]

Has anyone ever done for you something so unexpected and so caring that you were left speechless? Compassion, especially to the undeserving, is one of the greatest assets we possess.

---

[1] 2 Kings 6:8–23   [2] 2 Kings 6:23   [3] Rom. 1:20–21

Nothing Added

"But even if we, or an angel from heaven, should preach a gospel contrary to what we have preached to you, he is to be accursed." Galatians 1:8–9

Every now and then you see an add on TV that makes claims that their juice is real juice, "with nothing added." "Real chicken," they say touting their *nuggets* as if it's a bonus for us. We do the same with Jesus. There's the Methodist and Baptist version, the Presbyterian and Catholic and literally thousands of highly touted reproductions of the original. All are sincere and mean well, but by adding our denomination or theological twist we have introduced a conundrum to the world that is difficult to untangle. The apostle Paul has strong words to the Galatian Church for those who either add to or take away from the message or the Man. Everything about Jesus and the principles He taught is the final unvarnished truth just as it is written.

Oswald Chambers said, "Jesus plus anything else is heresy." This is more than simply adding your own *take* to the Scriptures. Denominations began because of the dissatisfaction with certain doctrinal issues and perspectives on worship, communion, social issues, and modes of Baptism. Now we have Jesus plus or minus this or that doctrinal precept.

Jesus plus nothing means exactly that. How can you add anything to Jesus or His finished work on the cross, or His authentic, inspired, personally breathed words? You cannot improve perfection; you can only *diminish* it. When you add your own *twist* to Jesus, we can't make Him more attractive; we can only distort and marginalize His majesty. When we try to add to the truth, we dilute and therefore weaken it.

The truth is a Person, not some beautifully articulated dos and don'ts. The Gospel is not a list of essentials that must always be preached in order to offer redemption to a lost world. If the gospel was four, five, or six points God would have expressed it that way. As it is, few can agree on what the essential points are.

If Jesus walked into your living room, how much information would you need from Him before falling on your face before Him? His presence alone would take your breath away. The atmosphere would be mesmerizing, and you would intuitively know that you were in the company of God Himself.

Don't add to that! No perfectly articulated words can change a heart; only the presence of God can do that. The knowledge and understanding will come as we walk with Him along the way.

Unity and Harmony

"Behold, how good and pleasant it is for brothers to dwell together in unity."
Psalm 133:1

The idea of Unity—of "coming together as one"—is echoed in churches everywhere and has provided themes for campaign slogans since the First Continental Congress sought to shape a new nation. But like so many commonly used words, it is rarely defined and as a result, its true essence all but disappears. Unity in our culture has come to mean . . . *everybody who agrees with me.* As the matter is discussed and debated, we draw a line in the sand and stand shoulder to shoulder apparently "united" against the treachery of the other side. Unity? In the church, we draw the same kinds of lines but add our denominational and theological spin into the mix. We stare across the abyss . . . steely-eyed at our foes and shake our heads at their obstinate refusal to see the truth and *agree* with us.

Unity is a concept on which our nation and our faith are based, and yet, I fail to be moved anymore when I hear our political and religious leaders wax eloquent about it. If real unity is understood and practiced, it will embrace diversity; it will applaud the right for others to disagree, and it will seek common ground. You and I don't have to concur on an issue for you to remain my friend. William Penn said we must have "Unity in essentials, liberty in non-essentials, and love overall."

Unity is not uniformity on all political or theological issues. It's not picketing outside an abortion clinic or marching on the Nation's Capital while demonizing the other side. Once you play that card, communication and any possibility of harmony are severed forever. Don't confuse locking arms and singing *kumbaya* for authentic oneness. Often, that which appears as unity disappears after the issue loses steam, the crowd disperses, and everyone goes home. The unity we felt at the gathering will never hold people together over the long haul.

Jesus' last prayer before his arrest by Roman soldiers was that those who follow him will be one "as He and the Father are one."[1] Did his disciples agree with each other on every point as they faced the Roman Empire? No way! Different people with different gifts in different circumstances equals different strategies. But what was their common identity? They knew Jesus; He was their life, not the issue; it was not their manner of worship or their level of faith; it was their common love for Him.

---

[1] John 17:21

Unity and Harmony (2)

Did you know that the Trinity, the Father, the Son, and the Holy Spirit have never had an argument; they have never disagreed and turned away from each other in disgust for even a millisecond. The Trinity exudes harmony at every level. Unity is the fulcrum on which healthy relationships pivot. To say we desire to follow Jesus but are unhinged from this person or that group of believers is a mockery. It compromises the very heart of what we say we believe.

One reason the secular world is unimpressed and even alienated from us is that we speak of the Trinity as one, yet we remain divided and fractured. It used to be subtle, but no longer. Politics is no longer a lively debate; it has now wrapped its divisive tentacles around biblical truth and sought to redefine it and bring it in line with Party and personal agendas.

Consider our brothers from another mother: Have you ever seen the Methodist Church concerned about the budget deficit in the Episcopal Church down the street? Have you ever seen the Presbyterians speaking charitably and lovingly about the Catholic church around the corner? Is there any love lost between the Charismatics and the Bible Churches?

God cannot bless disunity. He cannot sanction that which is so central to the mission of His body of believers any more than He could help a thief steal a car. Paul says that unity among believers makes His joy complete.[1] Few things in life are more attractive than love and affection among people who ignore socio-economic, ethnic, and political differences because their unity in Christ exceeds those differences. If you continue in disunity with your spouse, you nullify everything you say you believe. It's like saying, "It doesn't work for us, but why don't you give it a try?" We spend millions on evangelistic efforts and then neutralize our message by negative remarks about a brother or sister who thinks or worships a little differently than us.

Words are not what draw people to Jesus. It is the Spirit of God that draws them.[2] But our negative swipes at others can easily make a serious seeker spin around and do a one-eighty.

A dear friend, Bob Warren once said to a group we were meeting with, "If you have something critical or negative to say about someone, please don't say it to me. If you do, I will never trust you again, because if you will say it to me about them, you will say it to them about me." Who are you at odds with? Who do you resent? You can't afford the luxury of grudges or judgmental attitudes against our family of faith. The price is far too great.

---

[1]Phil. 2:2   [2]Acts 4:23–31

131

Sabbath Rest

"There is, therefore, a Sabbath Rest for the people of God." Hebrews 4:9

I grew up in the era of the Blue Laws, or Sunday Laws. They are laws that restrict or ban, certain activities on Sunday. This was done to promote worship and a day of rest. Thirty-eight states have rescinded the law, but it is still a law in the remaining twelve.

Even as a kid, I could not understand the sanity of such a law and later as a believer, I understood it even less. It was started in Philadelphia in 1933 primarily to force people to abstain from alcohol on Sunday in the hope that they would attend worship services, repent, and maybe give it up altogether.

The inference is, *you can't get liquor on Sunday so you'd better stock up on Saturday so you won't run out!"* The attempt to legislate morality and create symbolic images of godliness not only failed miserably but also flies in the face of biblical teaching. You can create speeding laws and enforce them, but you cannot make people stop speeding. Even if you could, there is no reason to believe it would change their heart.

Yes, God created for six days, then rested on the seventh.[1] But Jesus is "Lord of the Sabbath."[2] When he arrived, Pharisaic Judaism had become obsessed with the Sabbath. They literally worshipped it. Jesus confronts this thinking by saying, the Sabbath was made for man, not the other way around.[3] One reason for their hatred of Jesus was that He personified everything that was dear to them. He *was* the Temple, He *was* the Sacrificial Lamb, and now he claimed to be the fulfillment of what the Sabbath was intended to be.

If we love Him, we have fellowship twenty-four seven. So, every day is the Sabbath! Sunday is a great day to gather with friends and family to worship, but it is no longer some special religious time to dress up and be ultra-spiritual. Every day is a day of rest while the spirit of God is at work within you. There are fast food and other retail stores that do not open on Sunday. That's fine; it gives the workers a day off. But to think that it somehow magically makes them go to church or become better people is to misunderstand God's intent. As with the Blue Laws, you can only create the illusion of morality and spirituality, but you can't make it happen by not buying alcohol on Sunday or not opening your business establishment. Sabbath rest is a *state of being*, where effort and striving are no longer part of the equation. It is a place of spiritual relaxation where God *in you* works while you are at rest.

---

[1]Gen. 2:2–3   [2]Matt. 12:8   [3]Mark 2:23–27

The Reason for It All

"Seek first the Kingdom of God and His righteousness and all these things will be added to you." Matthew 6:33 (ESV)

It's the age-old question that never quite seems to get answered and is often used as a punch line. Why are we here? What's the purpose of it all? Often you will hear that "everyone must find their own purpose." The Scriptures teach that we do all have a purpose and it is the same one for all of us. Individually, we may have different gifts and talents that translate into different careers, but God's intent is that those gifts and abilities be wrapped around one central theme. The purpose for which we are made is to enjoy an intimate friendship with God. That's it!

It is expressed in many ways in the Scripture, but with the same meaning. Moses said, "Love the Lord your God with all your heart, soul mind, and strength."[1] Jesus repeated this in the gospels when asked about the greatest commandment of all.[2] Paul said the purpose is to know "Christ."[3] Peter said, we are to sanctify or set Christ apart in our life[4]; Jeremiah said that "glory of God is the reason we are here.[5] John said we are here "that we might have fellowship with Him"[6] All say, *Intimacy* with God.

You often hear people say that serving God is our purpose but consider this: When Susan and I first married I hated yard work. One hot muggy summer day I was pulling weeds, sweating and muttering to myself, and I looked at her, took her hand, and said, "This is too much for two people, let's have children!" Obviously, I didn't say that, or I would be an old bachelor now. You don't have children because you need a labor force around the house. Children come as the natural result of the love relationship you have with your spouse. God didn't give us life because He needed help. It was for the same reason you had or will have children. You want to enjoy them, love them and help them grow. When there is a healthy relationship with your kids, what may have initially been a labor for them should, as they mature, become an act of love. Helping around the house should be the natural by-product of the relationship they have with us.

The purpose is not to fix each other, and not even to evangelize people. You can't export or give away what you don't own. Everything flows from personal intimacy with Jesus. Don't make the mistake I made for many years and allow your desire to serve and care for people to outpace the primary desire of God's heart … intimacy! Otherwise, you will give out of an empty vessel.

---

[1]Deut. 6:5   [2]Matt. 22:37; 6:33   [3]Phil. 3:10   [4]1 Pet. 3:15
[5]Jer. 29:13   [6]1 John 1:3

This One Thing I Know!

"Then my enemies will turn back in the day when I call. This I know, that God is for me." Psalm 56:9 (ESV)

I have always told my three sons that as long as there is a breath in my body, I will have their back and be there for them. There are no conditions on that promise. Regardless of their behavior, that promise will never be revoked. They are my sons, my flesh and blood and that will never change. God feels even more so about His children. When our hearts belong to Him there are no lengths to which He will not go *to be for us*.

I have heard many people invoke the same certainty about our nation. Their assumption is that because America was founded by men and women who loved God and wanted it to be a "Christian nation," God stands on our side against all who oppose us. America is the greatest country in the world, but we have only to look at the news and at our own secret lives to know that we have not reflected the intent of the Founding Fathers, let alone the intent of God. Do you lock your doors at night? Do you have a password on your computer? Why are cameras needed on your front door, in stores, and at stoplights? Everywhere you look, we are protecting ourselves. From who … a nation of godly people? God stands with righteousness. He cannot validate our lifestyles just because we put "In God We Trust" on our money and call ourselves a

God-fearing nation? That may have been the intent, but sadly, it is not the present reality.

Joshua was preparing for a siege of Jericho.[1] He leaves his army and goes to the city to see what he is up against. Across from him stands an impressive warrior, sword in hand and dressed in full battle gear. Joshua ascertains that the side on which this *man* fights will win the battle. "Do you fight with us or with our adversary?" Joshua asks. The man answers, "No, but as the Captain of the Lord's host have I come." In other words, the *man* (a Christophany of the coming Christ) is saying, *Joshua, I'm not on your side or theirs, because in my Kingdom, I don't take sides, I take over!* Remember, Joshua was the leader of the chosen people and the Warrior would not simply bend his way.

As His beloved child, God is always for you, but just as an individual must bow the knee before Him, we must do the same as a nation. We must stop trying to convince ourselves that He *rubber-stamps* everything we do simply because of great men and women who came before us. It will take a level of humility that we are sorely lacking. *"Humble yourselves under the mighty hand of God, that He may exalt you at the proper time."*[2]

---

[1] Josh. 5:13–15   [2] 1 Pet. 5:6

The Miracles of Jesus

What was the purpose of the miracles Jesus performed? The obvious answer is that they gave people another shot at a quality of life they had either lost or never had. Miracles showed Jesus' power over nature, disease, and circumstances beyond their control. But in the mind of Jesus, miracles were performed primarily to reveal His identity. He had no intent to publicize Himself or to gain attention. In fact, after He is accused of performing His miracles by the power of Satan in Matthew 12, He performs no more public miracles with the Jews. Those He does perform on an individual are done in private. Why? It is because He knows that the Jewish multitudes have journeyed so far down the road with their misguided leaders that they will never recognize Him as Messiah.

Miracles are not new and are certainly not confined to the New Testament. Throughout the early beginnings of biblical history, we can see vivid accounts of the way God uses miracles as a source of guidance, protection, revelation, and for the general welfare of His beloved people. From the plagues that God visited on the Pharaoh to convince him to release the Israelites to the provision of *manna* to feed them in the desert, we see God come through in miraculous ways.

Do you believe God still does miracles? We usually think of the miraculous today as some physical healing, but the human body itself is a miracle; the created order is a miracle; salvation is a miracle, birth is a miracle. We take so much for granted that is all around us but cannot be logically explained apart from God.

In the next ten days, we will look at some of Jesus' miracles and the context in which they are performed as well as several that God used to aid and guide His people in their journey. This will help us step into the story and become those people to whom the miracles were directed. Jesus' miracles were not simply giving a person a few more year of quality life; they were much more.

What might the beneficiaries of Jesus' miracles have been thinking? How did what they saw Him do impact their life? If we read these miracles and imagine being there, we will gain a much more intimate understanding of what was happening on a human as well as a spiritual level.

The Replenishing of the Hooch

John 2:1–11

Ninety percent of what you read in the Gospel of John is not found in the other three accounts. It is the only book in the Bible that is expressly written to nonbelievers.[1] John writes to the people of Asia Minor. He presents Jesus as the Son of God. But the people in this area had their own gods. John knew of their beliefs, but rather than confront them head-on and draw offense, he uses this knowledge to compare and contrast the miracles of Jesus, of which he was an eyewitness. John records only seven miracles in his gospel. The first four are directly related to Asia Minor's top four mythical gods.

Dionysus was the god of wine. Each year on his birthday, he was said to turn water into wine. Jesus' first miracle was the result of being invited, along with His disciples to a wedding in the little village of Cana in Galilee. It could well have been a relative of Jesus since his mother, Mary seems to be specifically involved in the arrangements. The wine runs out, and besides being a social blunder, court records show such incidents as often causing litigation in courts by the bride's parents. Mary is deeply concerned and tells Jesus that there is no more wine. His first miracle is to be performed in Jerusalem, but He understands her concern and she tells the servants, *"Do whatever He tells you."* Jesus instructs them to fill six stone water pots of twenty to thirty gallons each with what would have been brackish water, good for foot washing, ritual cleansing and not much else.

Jesus tells the servants to take a dipper of the *undrinkable water* to the wine steward. I'm sure the servants expected to lose their jobs when their wine steward gives it the taste test. But to their surprise, he praises the quality of the wine. Quality and depth can only develop over time by the process of fermentation. Jesus shows His power by compressing years into a brief moment.

It's a simple story with a simple but profound message for all of us. For many, the wine has run out in their marriage, their faith, or their dreams. An old Jewish saying is *"Where there is no wine, there is no joy."* Where does that fit for you?

John is showing the people of Asia Minor that their belief in Dionysus to bring joy in their lives is a myth. His story is saying, "your god supposedly creates joy, but you have never seen this miracle performed. I was at this wedding when Jesus turned water into wine." Joy comes from the real thing, not a facsimile.

---

[1] John 20:30–31

The Healing of the Paralytic by the Pool

John 5: 1–15

Bethesda is a place in Jerusalem that archaeologists denied ever existed until 2005. Then it was unearthed exactly as described in John 5. *Bethesda* means "house of mercy," but in Jesus' day, it was anything but. It was a place of suffering and misery, with hundreds of people sick and dying sitting and lying beside a pool of water two to three feet deep, waiting for a long-believed legend to occur. An angel would supposedly stir the water, and whoever stepped in first would be healed.

It's festival time, probably the Feast of Tabernacles in the early fall, and rather than two to three hundred sick people, the festival would have produced possibly a thousand more, many coming from far away and all hoping against hope to be healed. As Jesus' disciples walk with Him into the city, they ponder His recent teaching that the new wine will never fit in the old law-driven wineskins of the Pharisees. The miracle will cause a critical turning point in His relationship with the Jewish leaders regarding their misplaced *worship* of the Sabbath.

Jesus walks up to a man who had been hopelessly disabled for thirty-eight years, powerless to help himself. Amid the stench and sight of disease-ridden humanity, Jesus asks what would appear to be an insensitive question, "Do you want to get well?" But, if you consider the ability human beings have to adjust and adapt even to horrible circumstances, the question is very insightful. This man has had to depend on the charity of others for food, his daily needs, and basically everything. Jesus knows that if he is healed, he will no longer be able to rely on the help of others. As strange as it seems, it will be a new world bidding farewell to a thirty-eight-year habit.

Some reluctantly make peace with an unhappy marriage and fake happiness while living separate lives rather than reaching out for help. A healed marriage may be a bridge too far for hearts that have become hard.

Jesus tells the man to pick up his bed and walk. This incites the Pharisees to attack Jesus as breaking the Sabbath, not because of the healing, but because the man picked up his bed. John includes this miracle as he writes to the people in Asia Minor who have a strong affection for *Asklepios*, a Greek god who was known to heal over moving water. This directly corresponds to the miracle John witnessed that day at the Pool of Bethesda. John is saying, *I was there; I saw it, and Jesus didn't even need the moving water.*

The Feeding of the Five Thousand

John 6:1–13

In John's quest to show the people of Asia Minor that Jesus is Lord of all of Creation, he writes about a miracle that is in direct proportion to the third most important of the mythical gods, Demeter, the goddess of the harvest.

It had been a long day. The crowds of people coming to Jesus teaching in Galilee had swollen to 5,000, not counting women and children. The disciples had returned from a mission, going out two by two around the countryside as part of their training. Upon their return, they learn that John the Baptist had been executed by Herod Antipas, and Jesus takes them across the lake to rest and to grieve.

Earlier that morning in a small village nearby, a mother packs a little boy's lunch. A man named Jesus, who had gained great acclaim was in the area and the young boy could hardly wait to see him in person. The lunch was simple; bread and dried fish, but adequate for the day

Phillip, who was from the nearby town of Bethsaida, asked Jesus how they could feed the huge crowd with two hundred denarii (equivalent to about six to seven months' wage for an average man) It was an impossible situation. Andrew, Peter's brother, brings this young boy who had five fish (a little larger than a sardine) and two barley loaves. The boy freely gives up his lunch, and Jesus instructs the disciples to have the crowd sit in groups. He may have prayed this common Jewish blessing, *"Blessed are you, Lord God, King of the Universe who brings forth bread from the earth."*

When that mother made her little boy's lunch, she could never have imagined that Jesus would multiply it to feed possibly 15,000 people until everyone was satisfied. Twelve baskets were picked up. Yes, there were twelve disciples as some suggest, but the story takes place in an area called the "the land of the twelve" where devout Jews, descendants of the Twelve Tribes of Israel, lived and worshipped God.

All four gospel writers tell the story, but only John mentions the little boy. John may have been close to the boy's age at the time. Again, John challenges his readers to look at Jesus' power and authority over and against their goddess Demeter. The food was more than enough. God will always bless His children beyond their wildest dreams. Paul may have had this story in mind when he said to the Ephesians, "God is able to do, exceedingly abundantly above all that we ask or think according to His riches."[1]

---

[1]Eph. 3:20

The Healing of a Royal Official's Son

John 4:46–54

This is a story of faith at a level that most of us never experience. It is a story that we need to step into emotionally in order to understand the human elements that are in play.

An official, high in the royal court of Herod Antipas, has a personal problem; his son is ill and nothing he and his wife have tried is working. Be this man for a moment ... feel his anguish ... sense his frustration of having to report to the palace each morning with no means of monitoring your son's condition. Your position gives you access to the best medical care, but no doctor has had any success. When you're home your wife sleeps, and when you sleep, she keeps vigil over the boy. There is no ice to trick the fever down. You try to pray, but your prayers seem hollow and impotent.

Your wife is a strong woman, accustomed to hard work and the difficulties of life, but as options run thin, as any mother would, she cries out in frustration, "DO SOMETHING!" Do you remember a man that everyone is talking about? Herod's palace has kept a close eye on His whereabouts. You learn that He is presently in Cana, seventeen miles away, where He had previously turned water into wine. Can He help your son? *Will* He help your son? You face a horrifying decision:

If you go to Jesus, and the boy dies as you travel, you will not be with him in his final moments. But if you stay, he will surely die.

Ordinarily, people would not travel alone, and traveling seventeen miles is a day's journey. But when your child's life is at stake, you run, you walk, you crawl ... whatever it takes! You reach Jesus at 1 p.m. and beg Him to come and save your son's life. He doesn't go; He simply says, "Go home, your son lives." How can this happen simply by saying it? There's no way to verify it. Do you insist on visible evidence or trust Him?

The man believes Jesus and begins the journey back home, but the story accelerates here. His servants meet him on the road and tell him the news that his son is well. He asks them what time he recovered. They said 1 p.m. yesterday. One word tells us of a level of faith with which most of us are unfamiliar. The word *yesterday* tells us that this royal official was so certain of Jesus' words, he went somewhere and got a good night's sleep and started out the next morning. Could you do that? I doubt I could. I would run back to my son faster than I got there.

The faith this man showed is the kind of *full-on* trust Jesus wants from us!

The Touch that Changed a Human Life

Luke 5:12–16

Of all the diseases and deadly infections a person in the ancient near east could contract, leprosy was the most feared. Not only was it incurable, but its victims were ostracized from society. They could not offer sacrifices in the temple, their fingers and toes generally dropped off in time, their skin lost its color, and swelling and deep grooves on the face produced a distorted look and an intolerable odor. Because the Jews considered it a disease, leprosy could not be healed, only cleansed. However, from the time Moses wrote the Torah, no Jew had ever been cleansed or healed from the dreaded disease. Its cause was thought to be the result of some secret sin.

The coming of the Messiah was the hope of every Jew, but with that expectation came the question, *how will we know it is really the Messiah and not a fraud?* There were two categories of miracles: one which God performed through a Rabbi or godly person and one which could only be performed by the Messiah. In ancient rabbinic teaching, three specific miracles performed by Messiah would verify His authenticity. The first was to be the healing of a Jewish leper.

The Scripture says Jesus encounters this leper in the latter stages of the disease, near death. The man flings himself on the ground in front of Jesus, pleading, "If you are willing you can make me clean." Jesus responds, "Of course I want to," and He touches the man and he was healed. Jesus had performed many miracles without any need for physical contact. But this man had not experienced human touch for most of his life, and Jesus knew this would be part of his healing.

Moses spends a good portion of Leviticus 13 and 14 detailing what must be done if a Jew is healed of leprosy. Jesus asks the man not to tell anyone and to go to the priest for an eight-day examination where he would be declared cleansed. Since a Jewish leper had never been cleansed, the priest would never have performed the ritual. But upon completion, would have had to declare him clean and thereby affirming Jesus' Messiahship.

A touch of Jesus' hand changed everything for a lonely, isolated man. Imagine those you see every day who experience some hidden loneliness or guilt that has driven them into the shadows. They long for a compassionate touch. If you take a risk, listen intently, and return for a second and third time, it will be the first step that may move them toward a real encounter with the same Jesus who healed the leper that day.

The Miracle that Changed Everything

Matthew 12:22–37

Have you ever known people who were predisposed to unbelief even in the face of undeniable evidence? Faith is a matter of the will, and the Jewish leaders willed themselves not to believe that Jesus was the "Coming One." In this second Messianic miracle, He heals a demon-possessed man who also could not speak. This had never been done before and was a sign of Messiahship taught by the ancient Rabbis. The people are stunned by what they witness. They expect the cynical Pharisees to finally agree that Jesus is the Messiah.

Not knowing how to refute this unprecedented miracle, they accuse Jesus of doing it by the power of Satan. Jesus responds by asking them how it is possible for Satan to cast out a Satanic demon? It is illogical, but we are seeing classic *cognitive dissonance* here. If they agree, they are admitting that Jesus is the Messiah and they will lose their power base with the Jews.

This hurtful and offensive response to Jesus initiates a critical moment in His ministry. He realizes the Jews will never accept Him because of the depth of the Pharisees' influence. From this point on, His ministry will radically change: He will immediately begin to speak in parables; He will step up His training of His disciples; He will turn His attention toward the Gentiles; and will no longer perform public miracles. He will respond to individual Jews coming to Him privately in personal faith, but not publicly.

Two passages in this account have frightened many people over the years. Jesus speaks of *blasphemy of the Holy Spirit as being unforgivable,*[1] and says that *every careless word will be held accountable at the judgment.*[2] Many have been taught that an angry tirade directed at God or a careless word spoken in haste could condemn them to hell. These verses are related to *that specific generation of Jews* who believed their badly mistaken leaders. They blasphemed the Holy Spirit by saying that Jesus' miracles were "done by the power of the devil." Their careless words charged that He was an agent of Satan. These leaders had unknowingly turned the gun on themselves and took an entire generation of Jews down with them.

Being in a leadership position is an awesome responsibility. Whether you are officially considered a leader is irrelevant; if you have children and grandchildren they watch everything you do. When I consider that my words and actions could potentially mislead another human being, I am reminded of this story. Although these stark comments were made to that generation only, it illustrates the power of careless words.[3]

---

[1]Matt. 12:31–32   [2]Matt. 12:36–37   [3]Matt. 12:39 ,41, 42, 45

A Man Who was Born into Darkness

John 9:1–41

Jesus and His disciples enter a town and encounter a man who had been blind from birth. He is reduced to begging because he was unemployable in that time and culture. Blindness was far more prevalent than you might think and far more debilitating than today. There were no guide dogs, no braille, and no special school to teach a person how to cope with his blindness. This is the third of three miracles the Rabbis taught that the Messiah would perform when He comes. We see in this story the images of light and darkness. Jesus has proclaimed that He is the "Light of the World." Now He will bring this man physically out of total darkness into the light.

The disciples reveal the type of warped perspective of God one would have in order to assume that any malady, such as blindness, was caused by a sin of his parents. Jesus assures them that, on the contrary, this man will be the vessel through whom God's glory will be displayed.

Do you believe that God can receive glory from failure or adversity? There is much to this story, but let's focus on this question. As an athlete, I was often told that "God loves a winner." When a celebrity wins an Oscar, they will often thank God. When Miss America is crowned, she thanks God for her tiara. Why not thank God when you lose, if you really believe that *"all things work together for good?"*[1] Do you believe Paul's admonition to be thankful *in all things, for this is the will of God"*[2]? Let's play baseball. You are at bat in the bottom of the ninth with men on second and third; your team is behind by one run. A hit will win the game. But what if God had you strike out so that everyone who ever failed to come through in the clutch will have someone who has been there and can empathize and feel their pain? Our "top-down culture" celebrates only winners, but you and I operate by a different standard and live from a different Kingdom.

Jesus heals the man, and when he is grilled unmercifully by the Pharisees the man simply answers, *I don't know what you guys want me to say, all I know is that I have never seen the light of day until this man, Jesus, touched my eyes.* They question the neighbors, the man's parents, and twice come back to him, unsatisfied with his simple answer.

After the inquisition, Jesus meets the man again. Now, he realizes that the removal of physical darkness is not his real problem. Now his heart sees the light of day for the first time. As a result, he would have been barred from the synagogue and ostracized in the city forever. Was he a winner or a loser?

---

[1]Rom. 8:28   [2]1 Thess. 5:18

Do You Believe What You Believe?

"Anyone who listens to my teaching and follows it is wise, like a person who builds a house on solid rock. Though the rain comes in torrents and the floodwaters rise and the winds beat against that house, it won't collapse because it is built on bedrock." Matthew 7:24–25 (NLT)

Most of us grow up with beliefs that have been handed down from our parents and grandparents. They may be solid beliefs we have built upon or unpleasant memories that we now reject. When I was a kid I threw up while eating a pimento cheese sandwich and have never been able to eat one since. Our belief system is generally fashioned by either positive or negative experiences from our youth, but rarely are our beliefs shaped and developed by personal study. We generally build on whatever foundation we have been exposed to, and without realizing it we add in cultural assumptions that are not true.

Theoretically, every believer, either serious or nominal, would place prayer at the top of any list of the most important personal practice of a believer. When tragedy strikes, prayer is the first thing we do, even if it is not a normal part of our daily routine. We may know little about the Scripture except for some isolated verses and stories, but everyone who believes there is a God also believes in prayer. But what if, in your church, the Pastor wanted congregational approval to hire a bright young man or woman who was a real "prayer warrior" for a $40,000 annual salary. Their job would be to pray eight hours a day for the needs of the church and the city. Would you vote "yes?" The truth is we would hire a youth worker, an assistant minister, man's or women's ministry person, or a janitor, but never someone to simply pray all day. Prayer has been theoretically built into the foundation of our lives, but the reality of prayer as our essential lifeblood is missing.

We believe in unity within the body of Christ until a volatile social, political, or theological issue creates a divide. Then, we become more adamant about our side of the issue than we do about keep the unity of the faith.

We are taught unconditional love which means love with no designs, stipulations, or hoops to jump through. However, if a gay couple wanted to attend our church, many would have a very hard time accepting their presence there. I realize it's a process, but every Sunday in the pews around us sit people who are abusive to their spouse, adulterers, and unethical people and we never bat an eye. The point is, we don't really believe what we say we believe. It's one thing to give mental assent to an idea passed down, but quite another to build a belief system that you step into with wholehearted commitment.

Jesus: Steady and Unhurried

Mark 5:21–43

A friend of mine used to say, *"Slow down, Neb; remember, Jesus wore sandals, not Nikes."* It's true! You never see Jesus scurrying to make up lost time or frantically rushing past people to get somewhere. We see this vividly illustrated in the story of a synagogue official. A Sadducee named Jairus, in great distress, falls at Jesus' feet. His daughter is at death's door, and he implores Jesus to come and lay His hands on her. We don't know if Jairus was a believer, but we can understand that when your child is in danger it trumps everything, even your theology.

Step into Jairus' sandals and walk with Jesus toward your home. A huge crowd presses in as Jesus and his men move along the crowded street. You are stressed beyond words and want to yell at the crowd to disperse so Jesus can step up the pace, but you know it would be arrogant and out of place. Suddenly, Jesus stops and turns around. He speaks to an old woman. "Come on!" you mutter under your breath. You hear Jesus say he felt power surge from Him at the touch of this woman's hand on the tassels of His robe. Someone who knows the woman tells you she has been hemorrhaging for years with no improvement. You are not an uncaring person but your little girl, with her whole life in front of her, is dying. You hear Jesus say, "Your faith has made you well," and you remember that Malachi writes of the Messiah having "healing in His wings."[1] All rabbis had five tassels at the hem of their garments representing the five books of the Torah, but the Messiah's would have healing in His.

Weaving through the crowd is a messenger from the house telling you that your daughter is gone. Your stomach tightens, your mouth is dry, and tears fill your eyes, but before you can speak, Jesus puts His hand on your shoulder and tells you to hold to the faith that brought you to Him in the first place. The entourage proceeds slowly to the house where professional mourners are wailing, and they all laugh when Jesus says the child is simply sleeping. Jesus forces them all out of the house, and you and your grieving wife lead Him into your daughter's room. The sight of her lying motionless and pale makes you gasp. Jesus takes her hand and says softly, "Wake up, little girl." Your heart is about to burst as your little girl sits up, then walks around the room. "Get her something to eat," Jesus says.

Don't you love the human touch here? Kids are always hungry, and Jesus even cares about that. The little girl has a new life, and all at God's pace.

---

[1] Mal. 4:2

"I Was Dead, But I'm Much Better Now!"

Read John 11:1–46

Mary and Martha sent an urgent message to Jesus who was with his disciples in an area called Perea, just outside the jurisdiction of the Sanhedrin Council. Their brother, a close friend of Jesus, was seriously ill and the two sisters fear that if Jesus does not intervene, their brother will surely die. Jesus does a curious thing; he waits two days longer to make the thirty-five-mile, two-day journey to Bethany. Jesus loved Lazarus and his sisters, but he is purposely allowing time to run out on His friend. At times God may do something that seems like He does not love us in order to show us the extravagant degree of His love for us.

Mary and Martha knew Jesus was from God. They believed He can *prevent* death, but not that He can *overcome* it. Jesus had said and demonstrated that He was the *Bread of life*,[1] *the Light of the World*,[2] *the Door*,[3] the Good Shepherd,[4] the Vine,[5] the Way, the Truth, and the Life,[6] but everything He said and did was a lead-in to His ability to conquer death. If Jesus heals Lazarus, He will be to them a great healer; if Lazarus is raised Jesus will be the *Resurrection and the Life*.

Jesus arrives in Bethany after Lazarus has been dead four days. He is angrily confronted by Martha for His delay in coming. The Jews believed that the spirit of the deceased hovers over the body of the dead for three days and during that time a miracle was still possible. In their minds, Jesus was a day past even God's ability to restore life. In Matthew 12, when the Pharisees claimed Jesus' power was from Satan, He has said He would give no more signs (miracles) except one. This was the "sign of Jonah."[7]

Jesus goes to the tomb of Lazarus and tells the officials to roll the stone away from the entrance. You can almost hear the gasp of those gathered. Martha knows how "ripe" her brother will be by now, but Jesus assures her that her brother's death is only temporary. She thinks He is speaking of the last days, but Jesus quickly responds, "Did I not tell you that if you believe, you will see the glory of God?" A common cliché today is *seeing is believing*. Jesus is saying that true faith is the opposite. "Believe and then you will see." Commitment comes before knowledge.

Lazarus is raised, and what happened that day is the foundation of our faith. Without this, and Jesus' resurrection six weeks later, our faith is a colossal waste of time.[8]

---

[1] John 6:35   [2] John 8:12   [3] John 10:9   [4] John 10:11   [5] John 15:6
[6] John 14:6   [7] 1 Cor. 15:14   [8] 1 Cor. 15:13–14

A Different Way of Thinking

When we read the Scriptures it is impossible not to notice how contrary God thinks compared to the way we think. His perspective is completely different in every area of our life, death, and suffering. In fact, our natural perception of daily existence is one hundred and eighty degrees opposite that of God's view.

In these next ten days, we will briefly touch on some of these differences in Gods thinking and ours, and how He wants to renew our mind so that we have His very thoughts.

The Counter-Intuitive Mind of God

"'For My thoughts are not your thoughts, nor are My ways your ways,' declares the Lord. 'For as the heavens are higher than the earth, so are My ways higher than your ways and My thoughts than your thoughts.'" Isaiah 55:8–9

Left to my own designs, very few perspectives I have would find any resemblance to God's point of view. The man who mentored me for many years used to say that *if you'll notice the thoughts that guide the decisions of the average believer and determine to do the complete opposite, you will be much closer to the mind of Jesus.* As over the top as that may sound, over many years I have found that to be true. The way Christians approach everything usually has little to do with biblical thought because it usually reflects that which is more expedient, cost-effective, and "sensible." It may look similar on occasion, but upon closer examination will fall far short.

The big deal about this is that not only do we betray our stated beliefs on everyday matters, but we betray those who stand on the perimeters of faith and see little difference in the way we think and act. That means that we have very little to call them into. Of the tens of millions of *born-again* people, most of us would crumble under close scrutiny. There are few of whom you could confidently say, "Watch those two in any situation and you will see how Jesus thinks." We know that if you followed them around for a day the disappointment would grow even wider.

We will never live our life differently than the way we think! If the Spirit of God truly changes a heart it will gradually be accompanied by a renewed mind.[1] You and I cannot afford to have a thought or perspective in our heads that does not come from God. There is too much at stake. Much of what we hear in the commentaries and opinions on the radio and TV often sound reasonable and convincing, but they are professionals and that's their job. They have to keep us watching long enough to get us to support their sponsors so that the Parent Company will make money. The only voice you and I can trust emphatically is the voice of God. Without His wisdom, we lack the discernment to know the difference from who sounds right to what is right.

For the next nine days, I would like to discuss some basic examples of the counter-intuitive thinking of God.

[1] Prov. 23:7

Moving Downward Toward Success

"Truly I tell you, unless you change and become like little children, you will never enter the kingdom of heaven. Whoever takes the lowly position of this child is the greatest in the kingdom of heaven." Matthew 18:3–4 (NIV)

Two chapters after this verse, Matthew records another shocking statement. Jesus tells His disciples that the great Roman generals and those in authority make sure everyone knows who is in charge. They hold their authority and position out as a badge of honor over the heads of the multitudes. But, the one who is great is the one who is the servant of others and will voluntarily move downward and go to the back of the line and allow God to move them forward.[1]

You will never see that perspective in a corporate leadership manual. It is counter-intuitive to everything we are taught, and it is an absolute guarantee. In principle, we all concur, but when it comes to taking this admonition into the marketplace, we really don't trust it to hold up. A businessman I know once said to me what most people think: *"I get that Jesus washed His disciple's feet when they should have done it to Him. I get that humility is a valued character trait, but I live out there in the real world! I understand this as it relates to serving in church-related things, but I would get creamed if I didn't fight and claw like everyone else in the business world."* When I hear people echo those sentiments I'm always dismayed

that anyone could think that Jesus' world was a fantasyland and not the real world.

My friend forgot a critical element. He assumed, as do many, that he had to make things happen and if he was laid back and passive, his competition would crush him like a bug. He assumed that God is simply patting him on the rear and sending him out there with a wink and a kiss for good luck. God doesn't do that! All through the Scriptures, God tells leaders going into battle, to take no thought of the enemy … *the battle belongs to Me, not you!*[2] God does not send you out in the world with a bag of clichés and Bible bullets. If you have done your homework and are prepared for the task ahead, go out *with* Him, and in His strength be a servant. Then, watch God deal with the competition.

God's principles work! If you apply them and trust Him, why will He not act on your behalf, especially if you aim the glory away from yourself and toward Him? His reputation is at stake! You don't have to cut and slash; become like a child and move humbly downward and you will be amazed by what will happen.

---

[2]Matt. 20:25–28   [2]2 Chron. 20:17

Save it and Lose It . . . Lose It and Save It

"For whosoever shall save his life shall lose it: and whosoever will lose his life for my sake shall find it." Matthew 16:25 (ESV)

This makes absolutely no sense from a natural perspective. If you want to save your life, you must self-protect. You create an atmosphere surrounded by everything you need and want. You eliminate anything disagreeable, painful, and inconvenient. But, the consequences of building that kind of self-indulgent cocoon is that you will lose it all! Every blessing, every level of joy, peace, and the certainty of eternal life will have evaporated like mist on the highway after a summer rain. A wasted life!

The second part of Jesus' statement is the contrasting, counter-intuitive words that seem equally ludicrous to the natural mind. It is that you will *find* life at its most abundant and most satisfying pinnacle when you loosen your grip and *let it go*.

Jesus illustrates this mystery in nature as He explains to His disciples that a grain of wheat must die in order to be transformed into a plant.[1] It will never experience its intended purpose and will never flourish unless it dies. A dream must die in order to live. If you try to force dreams to happen, they disappear like a puff of smoke.

If a man or woman gives up and "dies" to all that they have been taught by the world that is supposed to create and maintain a successful life, that willingness will be taken by God and transformed into its intended shape. Many of us have known people who were unable to have children. When they finally made peace with that dream and decided to adopt, suddenly junior comes along. It's not a perfect illustration but it underlines the necessity of letting your dream die and allowing God to act.

All the euphoria, contentment, and those things we thought would produce life will be crushed and reconstituted into the true and authentic version of what God always wanted for us. The world promises life but delivers incompleteness both on this earth and throughout eternity.

This is the greatest paradox ever revealed in the universe ... that life is gained not by frantically holding on with white knuckles to what you want, but by loosening your grip and allowing God to give what you can never produce yourself. It is in this release that life is given, and eternal life is secured.

---

[1] John 12:24–25

Image: Wise or Foolish?

"Let no man deceive himself. If any man among you thinks that he is wise in this age, he must become foolish, so that he may become wise." 1 Corinthians 3:18

Another great paradox of the Scriptures is the nature of true *wisdom* and how it is achieved. It is often confused with intelligence but has little to do with knowledge or intellect. Wisdom comes from being firmly rooted in truth. As truth is recognized and obeyed, discernment will emerge. If you weigh a decision solely based on its visible merits, it becomes a "best guess" scenario. Paul makes a strong statement by saying that it is possible to deceive *yourself.* It is one thing to deceive others ... we do that all the time, but to deceive yourself means that you have defrauded others for so long that in the process, you have ended up defrauding yourself.

Paul then explains that in deceiving ourselves we have created an imaginary world where our perspective becomes the standard. Therefore, when we hear God's perspective it appears to us as foolish. It does not fit in the world we have created. We have *snookered* ourselves!

Once a person's heart is changed, he or she will begin to see ordinary matters through a different lens. That which we saw as foolish will begin to make sense as God renews our mind.

If standing with Him and allowing His life to permeate through mine is foolish ... bring it on! The wisdom of God and the "wisdom" of the world cannot co-exist. You can't put "new wine in old wineskins."[1] My view of life without Jesus can never be merged with the perspective I have gained *in* Jesus.

The paradox of life is that you and I must become "foolish" to become wise. If the world sees us as wise, we are a fool. If the world sees the new path you and I walk with Jesus as foolish and ridiculous, we are on the path to true wisdom. What halts us in our tracks is that we long to be taken seriously and seen as wise and capable. To take a chance of being seen as foolish dismantles the dream!

"We are fools for Christ's sake," says Paul.[2] A popular song of my youth was titled, *Everybody's Somebody's Fool.* It's true! People are fools for money and possessions; people are fools for sex, ambition, power. The greatest self-deception is that you will find fulfillment and joy in the illusion of these things. Everybody's somebody's fool. Whose fool are you?

---

[1]Mark 2:18–22   [2]1 Cor. 4:10

Self-Centered or Other-Centered?

"Do nothing from selfishness or empty conceit, but with humility of mind regard one another as more important than yourselves; do not merely look out for your own personal interests, but also for the interests of others." Philippians 2:3–4

It is neither natural nor normal to wake up each morning with thoughts of how you can help lighten the load of other people. We are programmed to think first of taking care of our own needs and then if we have the time, shift our attention to the hurting masses. Churches don't normally put the needs of the place of worship down the block ahead of their own, especially if it is a different denomination. But consider how Jesus thought: He never thought of His own comfort; He never sought the most prominent seat in the Synagogue and in fact, preached against it.[1] He never turned people away because He was tired and hungry. He awakened each morning and closed his eyes each night focused on others.

One of the saddest verses in the Scripture is what the Apostle Paul wrote to the believers in Philippi when they heard he had been thrown in a Roman prison. He writes to thank them for their kindness and adds this: *"But I hope, in the Lord Jesus, to send Timothy to you shortly, so that I also may be encouraged when I learn of your condition. For I have no one else of kindred spirit who will genuinely be concerned for your welfare."*[2]

Paul had faithfully proclaimed Jesus from the time of His Damascus conversion until his death. Many had responded, and churches were formed across Europe and the near East. Still, something was missing. They gladly received the guarantee of salvation that God offered, believing that Jesus was the Messiah. However, they apparently attached Jesus to their normal self- focused way of operating and continued as usual. They learned the hymns and the right words to say, but their interest and focus remained on their own needs. Despite the multitudes who had received Jesus, Paul knew of no one but Timothy who had the same love and concern for the Philippians and therefore, had no one to send. What a sad commentary. To think like Jesus is to be other-centered … even when it is not convenient.

I knew a man who was discipling a young couple. They had to transfer to another city. My friend took a leave of absence from his job and moved into the same apartment complex for six months to help them adjust and find like-minded friends. This is a man Paul needed. This is the kind of man I want to be!

---

[1]Luke 14:8–9   [2]Phil. 2:19–20

Grab It Now . . . Forfeit it Later

"Beware of practicing your righteousness before men to be noticed by them; otherwise you have no reward with your Father who is in Heaven." Matthew 6:1

Recently, I saw an article on the Internet entitled, *Seventeen People Reveal the Heartwarming Good Deeds They Have Done in Secret*. How ironic. They were nice stories, and everyone said they had never told anyone until now. The stories were an encouraging reminder concerning the power of compassion, but there was no mention of any spiritual motivation, the acclamation clearly rested on those "anonymous" people who were listed.

What tugs at all of our hearts is the natural desire to be recognized and appreciated. We want people to believe that we are loving, selfless, and spiritually living on the cutting edge. It is hard to be excited about the aid you gave someone and not share it with others. But Jesus said when we advertise our good deeds, we forfeit the reward we would have received in heaven for keeping it secret. He follows by saying that when you give, don't *toot your own horn* so that people will notice how generous you are. In fact, it should be so secret that your left hand doesn't know that your right hand wrote the check.

Then, Jesus says when you pray, don't make an event of it so that people will think you are spiritual. Go in private; it's not showtime! It's a sacred conversation between you and God. We have all seen people make a show of praying in public or seeing kids gathering around the flagpole to pray for their school. Nothing wrong with that, but nowhere in the Scripture will you see God endorsing a spiritual spectacle. Some view this as a form of evangelism, but the *motive* should be private devotion from you to God rather than a backdoor way of saying to others what you're unwilling to say to them face to face. The same goes for fasting. Don't showcase it with a pitiful, look. It's a waste of time![1]

Finally, Jesus says, when you give a party, it is common to invite those whom you know will reciprocate. Jesus says to invite the poor who could never be able to invite you back.[2]

The point about the reward is that if you make sure that you are in some way honored by men, you will have made a choice that the honor of men is more important to you than the honor of God. If you settle for acclaim now, it will not be available as your reward in heaven, according to Jesus. So, keep a lid on it and in the privacy of your own heart, you will know that you have truly honored God with no secret agenda that would steal His glory.

---

[1]Matt. 6:2–18   [2]Luke 14:12–24

153

Cover It Up or Confess It

"Whoever conceals his transgressions will not prosper, but he who confesses and forsakes them will obtain mercy." Proverbs 28:13 (ESV)

It is a basic human characteristic that when we sin or make a mistake that carries consequences, our first inclination is to deny or cast blame. Had President Nixon confessed about the Watergate cover-up, he would probably never have had to resign in shame. America would have forgiven him.

Even in the simplest of matters … in our homes, on the golf course, or who broke the coffee cup at work, our first thought is to deny rather than to confess. There is something about this false persona of presenting ourselves as sinless and blameless in every circumstance that stalls our growth and impeaches our integrity … even if we are never found out.

Confession of sin honors God because it agrees with His diagnosis of the error we have made.[1] When we deny or place blame elsewhere, we are seeking to deceive Him and explain away or hide what He already knows anyway. Confession is really *for* us. Every time we confess or agree with God we are developing a pattern of coming clean, and we are then able to start over. Conversely, when we deny we create a pattern in the opposite direction, and it becomes the norm of our behavior rather than the exception. It damages our relationships.

What can help greatly is to open up to a trusted friend or two and share your negative tendencies. To hide them will diminish our credibility with others. "Don't even ask her if she did it, she's just going to lie." This type of sentiment can tear your credibility to shreds. God promises that honesty is the road to healing.[2] To share our failures and weaknesses … to confess your sins to someone is one of the most liberating things you will ever do. To come clean and find that you are still loved and still respected is a great emancipation of the soul.

Have you ever prayed by yourself or with others and a little voice in your head says, "You big fraud!" I have done it many times and I find that it is because there are issues that have been swept under the rug that needs healing. Nobody expects perfection, but they appreciate honesty. Give up the sham of trying to appear as something you are not, and let God re-make you by agreeing with Him and moving forward without the mask.

---

[1] 1 John 1:9   [2] James 5:16

The Pathway to Authority

[The Centurion said] "For I also am a man placed under authority, with soldiers under me; and I say to this one, 'Go!' and he goes, and to another, 'Come!' and he comes, and to my slave, 'Do this!' and he does it." Luke 7:8–9

Jesus had set up His headquarters in Capernaum after being rejected in His hometown of Nazareth. A Roman Centurion sends some Jewish elders to ask Jesus to come and heal the Centurion's servant. This official had a great love for the Jews and had even paid for the building of their Synagogue. He loved his servant boy who was apparently close to death. As Jesus arrives at his house, this Gentile Centurion sent friends to tell Jesus that he felt unworthy for Him to enter his home. "Just say the word, and my servant will be healed." This man understood that as a Gentile, he had no right to even ask. Jesus is deeply impressed as the man says he understands that Jesus has authority over illness because He is also under the authority of His Father. He tells the man that He has been teaching about faith all over Israel and that he understood it better than any Jew. He gladly heals the servant.

Power and authority are different. Power seeks to control the outcome and authority seeks to influence it by a relationship that is built and a trust that has been established. Politicians can create a bad law and we are forced to obey it; that's power. But if the value of a law is explained to us and we trust the people who enact it, that's authority! Hitler and Marx had power; Mother Theresa and Gandhi had authority. They lived and modeled what they professed, and people followed volitionally. Authority cannot be taken; it must be given. The mandate for wives to submit to their husbands is grossly misunderstood. To the degree that my wife trusts me to make the final decision when we are at an impasse does something in me. I want to be very certain I am worthy of her trust. She influences every corner of my life. Why? She doesn't constantly challenge me. If you want to move up in your company or get more playing time in a sport, gripping and complaining will ensure that it never happens. Deferring does not mean compromising or giving in. I have deferred to my sons on many occasions because I know they have more wisdom and expertise in some areas than I. Only a fool thinks that because he is a man or has seniority that all decisions necessarily fall to him.

The key to authority is not rebellion or insurrection, but submission! Jesus yielded to the will of His Father[1] and no greater authority has ever stepped foot on this planet!

---

[1] Luke 22:42

The Secret Sauce of Effectiveness

"Let this mind be in you, which was also in Christ Jesus, who, being in the form of God, did not consider it robbery to be equal with God, but made himself of no reputation, taking the form of a bondservant and coming in the likeness of men." Philippians 2:5–8 (NKJV)

If you want to be influential, successful, and effective, the experts will tell you that you need maximum exposure, consistent branding, and thick skin. God's perspective is quite the opposite. The world that He created was for man to enjoy.[1] But It took a hard-right turn with its first two inhabitants. Many who have come in their wake have also thought they knew better than God and could accomplish more on their own. So, they create their own reality and wave to God on Sunday but manage their own lives.

Everything Jesus did was without fanfare. From the announcement of His birth to lowly shepherds to the discovery of an empty tomb by a few nondescript women, His entire thirty-three years on earth violated every common notion of success. To Jesus, people were and are far more valuable than agendas; faithfulness always trumps success, and compassion is more desirable than sacrifice. We run, Jesus walked; we stress out, Jesus lifts His concerns to the Father. We focus on the visible things around us, Jesus focused on the invisible. The key that unlocks the door to things that matter in life is *subtlety*, not *pomp and ceremony*. It is that "still small voice" that awakens the heart to the truth that trust will always produce blessing.[2]

In their desire to have a great impact by drawing many people, churches and ministries commonly try to get Miss America, a wealthy businessman, or an All-Star athlete to speak at their gatherings. The implication is that Jesus will bring you similar success if you accept Him. But, the point of identity of ninety-nine percent of people is not with people like this. Why not have the church janitor to tell about how he cleans toilets and mops floors to the glory of God because he loves his family so much? Why not have someone who lost his business or a football player who fumbled on the one-yard line, so they can tell us what God is teaching them and how He has sustained them in this defeat?

Why are men and women rarely discipled one on one? Because we think it is a better use of time and resources to disciple a room full. But it's impossible to disciple a room full of people. You can only give them information. To build into the life of another involves giving them access to your own life as you walk with them. Jesus never tried to draw crowds; He moved quietly in the shadows, made Himself of no reputation, gave Himself to twelve men and everything He touched was never the same.

---

[1] 1 Tim. 6:17   [2] 1 Kings 19:11–13

Forgive or Retaliate?

"Bear with each other and forgive one another if any of you have a grievance against someone. Forgive as the Lord forgave you." Colossians 3:13 (NIV)

Miss America contestants always want "world peace" when asked what their greatest wish is. Who wouldn't want the world to be at peace? But would that change marriages, or help our political leaders work out their issues? Would racism and sexism come to a halt? The problem is more fundamental than world peace. Our State Department sends representatives to other countries to negotiate peace accords, but they don't even get along with the guy in the next office or with their own wife and kids. The problem that plagues mankind is alienation at every level of society: black vs. white, rich vs. poor, Arab versus Jew, liberal versus conservative, labor versus management, let alone husband verses wife, and children verses parents, etc.

Reconciliation is the answer and it is to be the mission of every believer,[1] but how do we achieve it? Unity is far more than a sleepover and painting each other's toenails or lighting candles and singing *Kumbaya*. It cannot happen unless and until someone takes the step and says, "Will you forgive me?" You can sing "We Are the World" all day and it will be a nice gesture, but that's all. Genuine forgiveness is the *only* pathway to reconciliation. Anything short of that may look like oneness for a time but will not last because it is only *co-existence* or *mutual tolerance.* That's not reconciliation!

Every movie you see where someone has suffered loss at the hands of some sinister person or group will always devote the remainder of the movie to payback or revenge. It is the normal response when we have been wronged, but it is completely counter to everything Jesus taught. I'm sure He would agree that we were terribly mistreated, but He wants the pain in us to stop there. To retaliate and refuse to forgive gathers only momentary relief. It will plague us forever.

Imagine Jesus forgiving the hatred and betrayal He suffered. How could God endure the unfaithfulness of the Nation of Israel for thousands of years and eagerly wait for the right time in history to send His Son to redeem the very people who had abandoned Him? Forgiveness is not just a good idea; it is as essential as your next breath and there is no peace without it.

---

[1] 2 Cor. 5:18–21

The Will of God

"Trust in the Lord with all your heart and lean not on your own understanding; in all your ways submit to him, and he will make your paths straight."
Proverbs 3:5–6 (NIV)

"How can I find God's will for my life?" I suppose this question is one that every believer has asked at one time or another. We have taken something God wants us to know and made it a conundrum of great mystery and complexity. It was never intended to be something hidden or lost that we must search diligently to uncover. God's will is not a treasure hunt where after centuries, one lucky person finally stumbles upon the scroll containing the secret message. Why would God hide something that can sculpt our life into its intended shape?

What do we already know? God's general will is that we become more and more like His Son so that when people look at us they will see what the invisible God looks like in a person.[1] Jesus' teachings in the Gospels explains it. They are God's will. The mystery exists for most of us because we assume that God has a specific school for us to attend, a certain career to pursue, a city to live in, and a specific person to marry.

When we speak of God's will we're generally thinking of these kinds of external things. Do you really believe that God is in heaven stressed out that you'll attend a State University over a Christian College? Do you suppose that He is having acid reflux over the

fear that you might choose law over medicine (Well, maybe!). And who does God want you to marry? Some leader of a singles group long ago probably said *God has one special person picked out for you, so wait on that person,* and everyone thought it was in the Bible. I know of no passage that says anything like that. Love is a decision, not something you fall into. You meet someone and find that you enjoy their company; you learn that he or she loves God as you do; you see in them characteristics that you are drawn to; you find that you have similar interests and are a better person when you are with them. Yes, physical attraction matters. God never said, "go find the ugliest woman or man in the village with no teeth and a hump on their back." Don't over-spiritualize it! Get counsel from trusted friends, listen to the Holy Spirit, make your choice, and trust God.

I really don't think God cares where you go to school or what you choose as a career. The question is, *what do you want? What are your gifts? Where can you maximize your relationship with Christ?* God's will is that you love Him and walk with His Son. Where you do it is irrelevant. So, love God and do what you really want to do!

---

[1] 1 John 4:12

The Will of God: A Thankful Heart

"In everything give thanks, for this is the will of God for you in Christ Jesus."
1 Thessalonians 5:18

In a world where anger and resentment are the norms, maintaining a spirit of gratitude can push the limits of almost anyone. But we want to know God's will for our lives, so here it is: become a person who gives thanks *in everything*. When my dog dies, I'm supposed to be thankful? No, the passage says, "*In* everything give thanks," not *for* everything. I have lost good friends and family members that I loved deeply. I could never be thankful for their death unless they were suffering and in severe pain with no chance for recovery. I can, however, embrace the great memories we had together. I can be grateful for the love we shared and the impact of their life on mine.

Our daughter-in-law, Kristin, is one of the most gracious people we have ever seen. She takes nothing for granted. Even the smallest and most insignificant of things garner a "Thank You" note from her ... not a text or an e-mail, but a hand-written note. In fact, we have received notes from her thanking us for our thank you note. It is a trait I deeply admire and respect.

Why would Paul say that thankfulness is the will of God? I believe it is because of God's understanding of mankind. He knows that we tend to complain incessantly when things do not fall into place. We tend to feel sorry for ourselves and often a spirit of discontent can engulf us. It can almost reshape our personality. Discontentment is the opposite of gratefulness. When you focus and dwell on what did not happen as you hoped or expected, or what you did not receive, you open the gate to legitimize doubt and unbelief.

John the Baptist was in prison. He was a front-line guy who was hearing news about Jesus. He began to question if he had tapped the right man. He knew better, but his focus was on what had *not* happened (his release) rather than on the great miracles that *were* happening.[1]

A thankful heart will power through disappointment. It is what God will use to help you stand against the north wind when disappointment comes at you like a category-five hurricane. A thankful heart changes the atmosphere in the room and shames the nay-sayers who obsess on what has not yet occurred rather than rejoicing in what has. A thankful heart is the will of God!

---

[1]Matt. 11:2–5

The Will of God: Silencing the Skeptics

"For it is God's will that by doing good you should silence the ignorant talk of foolish people." 1 Peter 2:13–15 (NIV)

This is a tough one, especially in the current political atmosphere where very often outlandish statements and proposals are made by those in authority. Still, this is God's will that by obeying the elected and appointed leaders in our city, state, and nation, we will silence those who are examining us to find holes in what we say we believe. You may disagree with the Governor, Senator, or the President. His policies may be putrid. I hear you; I have trouble with this one, but I know it's true.

What we tend to forget is that when our elected officials make decisions that are self-serving and unethical, God is still in control. It is not ultimately up to them or us; it's up to Him. "The King's heart is like channels of water in the hands of the Lord; He turns it wherever He wishes."[1] Every leader believes that he or she has the power to change the destiny of a city, state or nation. Every leader believes that their way is the best way.

Pontius Pilate stood face to face with Jesus and arrogantly told Him that he had to power to free Him or crucify Him. Jesus said, "You would have no authority over Me except that which was given to you from above."[2] God is not nervously counting on these people! He has not bet the house on the fact that they will do what is right. If He finds it necessary, He can intervene at any time He desires. He wants those who lead others to look to Him for instruction. If they are arrogant and refuse He is perfectly capable of removing them from authority. God's will is *submission*. Hard words to hear, but absolutely true. All of life in Christ is about yielding my self-interest and agenda to a God who never fails. We speak of submission as if it is the exclusive job of women, but it is the essence of following Jesus for everyone. We silence the critics by continually exceeding their preconceived notions. Every action and reaction we have should be the opposite of their expectations. That is why Jesus said that *when someone smacks you on the cheek, give him a shot at the other*.[3] The world expects you to react the same as everyone. When you don't, it catches them off guard and takes them off the defensive.

Make it your aim and a habit to consistently, but respectfully, confound the world by your reaction to their absurdities. You are *free to disagree* and to respond in love, but not to react as they have come to expect. This is the will of God.

---

[1]Prov. 21:1   [2]John 19:10–11   [3]Matt. 5:38–39

The Will of God: A Certain Kind of Suffering

"For what credit is there if, when you sin and are harshly treated, you endure it with patience? But if when you do what is right and suffer for it, you patiently endure it; this finds favor with God." 1 Peter 2:20

Why in the world would it be God's will that his followers suffer? At first blush, it sounds mean spirited and even sinister. You and I live in a culture where people do everything possible to make themselves comfortable to the greatest possible degree. We go to massive lengths to ensure that we will never suffer. So, how do we make peace with "suffering according to God's will?"

Peter is speaking of the fact that everyone suffers at times; no one gets a free pass. But it is one thing to suffer for a sin we committed because actions do have consequences. But what about suffering for what you *didn't do*? There's no justice in that. But, the mind of God again collides with the way we have been taught to think.

God is not happy when we suffer, but He is happy to use that suffering to help us grow. God knows that we learn from losing, not from winning. When we win, we party! When things go as we wish, we celebrate just as anyone would, and as a result, we look the same. When people of the world lose, they pout, become angry, and often resentful. Our natural tendency is to do the same, but as God matures us, we learn to suffer with dignity and grace. It is even more powerful to the skeptic when it is undeserved.[1]

How does the world handle undeserved suffering? They throw a fit; they run and hide and get drunk. How do believers deal with it? Much the same way. "What did I do?" we explode indignantly. We have been taught that if we do the right thing there is always a pot of goal at the end of the rainbow. Yet, Jesus suffered greatly, and it was not for doing evil, but for doing good. That is what bothered one of the thieves on a cross beside Jesus. "We deserve this," he said; "He has done nothing wrong."[2]

When Mary was made aware that she was pregnant with a son, she knew immediately of the gossip and innuendos that would follow. Yet, she never once defended herself or became a victim. It is in this undeserved pain that we see her true character.

God's wants to display His glory in us in such a way that the world will take notice. If when we are falsely accused, we endure it patiently, that is God's will because it boldly proclaims, "It is not about me, it is about the power of Christ that lives *in me*."

---

[1] 1 Pet. 2:20   [2] Luke 23:39–41

The Will of God: Control Your Body

"It is God's will that you should be sanctified: that you should avoid sexual immorality; that each of you should learn to control your own body."
1 Thessalonians 4:3–7 (NIV)

Yes, this is God's will that many would rather skip over or explain away. After all, we are well into the twenty-first century and sleeping with multiple partners and living together doesn't even rate a denial, or even a slight blush anymore. And yet ... truth is truth, and it never changes with the times, or ebbs and flows with the current morality adjustments. To say to God, "Show me your will for my life," and continue in sexual immorality is a mockery. Why would God show us the deep recesses of His desire for us if we ignore that which He has already told us? Sanctification, or *being set apart,* so that God's glory can be displayed in you is His heart of hearts.

I know of no harder command to obey in a world that has decided to ignore every principle that God had set concerning sexuality. Regardless of the years that one has walked with Christ, or the length of time one has lived, the issue never dissipates and never goes away. It is in our face every time we turn the television, read a book, go to a cocktail party, or stroll down the beach.

The solution is as old as the issue. Your actions will eventually mimic that which you continually expose yourself to. To the degree that we allow our mind to be filled with uplifting thoughts that honor God and contribute to the care and nurture of people, our thinking will begin the change.[1] Secondly, understanding who you are in Christ helps you begin to see that what God is building in you will never be compatible with using others for your pleasure. The temptations will always be there and will always appeal to our flesh, but as a son of God, a brother or sister of Christ, and a new creation, we do not have to give in to them.

Dick Halverson, former Senate Chaplin, often said that love literally means, *to will the best for another.* I think of many instances in my life when I willed the best for me. I thought only of myself and my gratification. This is not the will of God! I have learned through the years that He wants to set us apart from the world's point of view because it is self-absorbed and interested in gratifying its own desires first. God's will involves creating givers, not takers ... those who *will the best* for others.

[1]Phil. 4:8

162

Parenting Really Does Take a Village

"All your children shall be taught by the Lord, And great shall be the peace of your children." Isaiah 54:13 (NKJV)

Discipling a son or daughter is the ultimate responsibility of a parent.[1] But that doesn't mean we can't enlist others to aid us in the process. I have had many great friends through the years, and each of them has something valuable to give my children that my wife and I don't possess. I know them well enough to know that they would not undercut the principles we have taught our sons but would add a flavor and a perspective from a different voice and life experience.

When someone compliments Susan and me on our children's character and lifestyle, we are quick to say that others have probably made greater contributions. As they grew up in the Washington, D.C., area we had many wonderful people through the years live with us, and others who visited from all over the world. Each of them took an interest in our boys and helped them see faith through a lens that Susan and I were not able to give.

Through the years and even as I write this, good friends have taken an interest in helping my sons form a deeper faith. I've always coveted the opportunity for them to get to know and draw from people who have had an influence on *my* life. I'm not jealous in the least if I hear them say how much a certain friend of mine has encouraged them. It thrills me more than I can say.

As a family in Jesus Christ, we are in this thing together. That's why the congregation pledges to help the child grow when he or she is baptized. When I was growing up if I misbehaved my mother would get a phone call from a friend or even a neighbor whom we barely knew. Today, it is seen as an intrusion because we don't understand community. A community helps each other raise the children. It was intended by God to be a shared responsibility. Certainly, the buck ultimately stops with us as parents, but to refuse valuable input from friends we love, and respect is the height of arrogance in my opinion.

I encourage you not to be afraid to expose your children to different opportunities and don't feel that you must be the *Grand Pooh-Bah* of all wisdom and knowledge to them. Allow trusted friends to help. If you have built a solid foundation with them, they will grow stronger rather than weaker. Jesus shielded his twelve from nothing. He wanted them to be able to stand firm in every type of circumstance.

---

[1]Deut. 6:6–9

A Heart That is Completely His

"For the eyes of the Lord move to and fro throughout the earth that He may strongly support those whose heart is completely His." 2 Chronicles 16:9

What an incredible picture! The eyes of God scanning the earth like searchlights seeking men and women who have hearts that are receptive to His truth. As His eyes come to rest on that person, He seeks ways to encourage and strengthen them.

What would it mean to have a heart like that? Is it something we can produce by discipline? Is it a random gift that God gives, and then waits in the shadows to see who responds?

There was a king named Asa of Judah to which this passage refers. His fatal mistake is that he trusted in the monetary help of another King in order to fight a battle rather than completely relying on God. His commitment was half-hearted. That is the problem with being "committed" to God. When I first began to seriously investigate faith in Jesus, the words I heard were about *yielding* myself or my heart to Him. Over the years the admonition became "commit your life to Him." The difference is that when you make a commitment, *you* decide what that means. You decide how much and to what degree. Yielding yourself is a complete transfer of ownership of your heart to Him. *A heart that is completely His* cannot be a heart committed or dedicated at certain levels; it is a heart submitted or yielded completely.

David was said to be "a man after God's own heart."[1] God made a covenant with David promising him an eternal dynasty, an eternal throne, an eternal son, and an eternal kingdom. God had blessed him. "Then David, the King, went in and sat before the Lord and said, 'Who am I, O Lord God, and what is my house that you have brought me this far?'"[2] David did not take for granted what God has done for him. He didn't feel entitled; he never ran over people with the wealth God gave him. There is nothing wrong with wealth or power; the question is whether it was given or sought. David's humility is what touched God's heart. His heart was supple. He knew where his assets came from and he held them with an open hand.

Can you imagine a greater thrill than God's eyes scanning the horizons looking for a yielded heart, and His eyes coming to rest on you?

---

[1] 1 Sam. 13:14; Acts 13:22   [2] 2 Chron. 17:16

It Seems Right to Me

"In those days there was no king in Israel; everyone did what was right in his own eyes." Judges 21:25

This is the last verse in the Book of Judges. It is a commentary on the chaotic state of God's people during the worst time in Israel's history. When Moses led the Israelites across the Red Sea they were in a land where everything was new. The laws and customs of Egypt no longer applied to them. God gave His Laws through Moses as a basic standard for living. It is a standard for protection and provision for His people. Moses dies and Joshua takes them into the Promised Land. There were no courts or police force to arrest and bring to trial those who ignore the law. Judges were established to create order and administer justice. By this time many Jews had even succumbed to idol worship. The people did what seemed right to them. That is about as subjective as you can get. Some guy decides that your wife was meant for him rather than you. It seems reasonable to him. Another man feels that he works harder than you and it makes sense to him to take some of your earnings and leave you with less. Thinking like this began the lowest point in Israel's history, simply because "everyone did what was right in his own eyes."

We live in a world today that is moving like a downhill racer in the same direction. "We each have our own truth," they say. "You have your truth and I have mine." We are encouraged to follow our heart and each of us should do what we feel is right with no standard for truth except our feelings. This was essentially the lie that the serpent told Adam and Eve. "Don't you realize that you can be like God without God. Don't you two get it? You can be your own god and whatever you want to do will always be the right thing because you say it's right, and you *are* god."[1]

The Scripture says we can't trust our heart because it is desperately wicked.[2] It will trick you because it operates on a feeling level and can change like the weather. There must be a standard of truth by which all "ideas" and "beliefs" are measured. I believe that standard is the Word of God. It is "living and active and sharper than any two-edged sword."[3] If it's not, we live helplessly alone in a world of constant contradictions with no standard or authority to guide us and where everyone does what is right in his own eyes.

---

[1]Gen. 3:4–6 [2]Jer. 17:9 [3]Heb. 4:12

Welcome Conflict as a Friend

"When all kind of trials and temptations enter into your lives, my brothers, don't resent them as intruders, but welcome them as friends. Realize they come to test your faith and to produce in you the quality of endurance." James 1:2–4 (Phillips)

We all secretly believe that if God would just remove a couple of the nagging obstacles in our lives, we could live the life of our dreams. Tired of conflicts, frustrated with having to *walk on eggs* around a spouse or family member, we nurture the illusion that a boulevard of green lights would open to us the doors of heaven. We compare our circumstances to that of others and become resentful as we fantasize about this idyllic life that could be ours.

Imagine your life without conflicts or roadblocks. Imagine living in a "Stepford Wives" atmosphere where problems and struggles are disallowed, and everyone and everything is spit-polished and shiny. It would be the most boring, mechanical existence where every day would be the same with no problems to work through and no reason to trust God. Answers would become irrelevant because there would be no questions. There would be no surprises because around any corner and with every action would be an infallible guarantee. Life would be more miserable and insipid than any of us could possibly imagine.

Conflict and struggle are what gives life mystery and intrigue.

There *must* always be two trees in the garden. Why do we wrap gifts at Christmas? The mystery is what creates excitement. Will it be door number one, number two, or door number three? When you read a novel, what you don't know is more important than what you know, because *not knowing* is what makes you turn the page. In writing a story an author must throw every roadblock at his beloved main character that he *doesn't* want to happen. Conflict is the engine of the train. *Welcome struggle as a friend, don't resent it as an intruder,* says James. Peter tells us not to be surprised or think it strange when the bullets whiz past our head.[1] Struggle creates the fascination of life. It is unpredictable in its timing, but it keeps us turning the pages and walking with courage and anticipation around the next corner. As we trust God, we have the privilege of seeing Him come through in impossible situations. Once we begin to see His track record in these potential calamities, we will trust Him more and grow deeper in our appreciation and love of Him. Life is a great adventure. Why resent the very thing that makes it that way?

---

[1] 1 Pet. 4:12

Helping the Body of Christ Flourish

Who just wants to exist? You and I were meant to flourish ... to live abundant lives with our head high, our back straight, and with confidence in who we are, and whose we are. As we grow in Christ why would we not want to help others flourish as well? Discipleship was never intended to be a solitary endeavor. We all need models that have wrestled with God and walk with a limp. We need to learn from their mistakes; we need their counsel and encouragement.

The next four days speak to the idea of authentic discipleship and how we can help one another.

For ten days following that, are principles that Jesus taught His disciples when they had private times together. To teach these principles to the nominal believer is a waste of time. These principles are for those who desire to become more like Jesus and are willing to help others do the same. They were taught to me many years ago and I pass them along to you. They are not from a book on discipleship, they are the actual principles Jesus taught His twelve privately.

Authentic Discipleship

"And He appointed twelve so that they would be with Him . . ." Mark 3:14

Have you ever wondered why God didn't just send Jesus as a solitary redeemer, teaching, healing and speaking across the country as many ministries operate today? His teaching would have been just as effective and His healing power just a potent. But after he resurrected and ascended, who would He have left in His wake? One of the saddest things to me is the great leaders and men and women of God, some of whom I have known who, when they died, had no one to take their place. Often the son or daughter takes over the ministry, but there is seldom anyone else who has been trained and nurtured as Jesus did with His twelve.

What was a disciple in Jesus' day? A Rabbi would usually be asked by a young man somewhere around fifteen if he could "sit at His feet." It did not mean the young boy simply wanted to gain the knowledge and wisdom of the Rabbi; the question, "May I follow you ... may I sit at your feet" meant, "do you think I have it in me to become a man like you?" The Rabbi would usually test the boy with questions and then say yes or no. When Jesus said, "Follow Me" to His young men, He was giving the greatest compliment a person can ever hear: "I see in you the potential to be like Me." The young boy would then be with the Rabbi constantly, watching his every move and listening intently. This could go on for years.

How far we have come from that kind of authentic discipleship. First of all, no one wants to give that much time to one person. Secondly, few be willing to be vulnerable enough to allow another to become that close and intimate. Thirdly, we would feel very uncomfortable saying, "I think you can be like me." That, of course, is Jesus' prerogative; we want others to be like Him, not us, but they can feel our love, our passion and the reality of God's heart throbbing within us. John's disciples loved him and were deeply loyal, but He pushed them toward Jesus. People follow people to Jesus. Paul said, "Follow me as I follow Christ."[1] Will Paul make mistakes and violate his own teaching at times? You bet! That's what made him approachable. Jesus didn't sin, but He fully allowed the twelve to see His pain, His suffering, even His anger, and with those emotions, His passion to do His Father's will. Real discipleship is allowing them to see you, warts and all. "Jesus chose twelve to be with Him."[2] Yes, He would eventually send them out, but that was secondary to their simply being *with Him*! He knew that by this exposure alone they would never recover. In this context, we learn true discipleship.

---

[1] 1 Cor. 11:1 [2] Mark 3:14

The Cry of God's Heart

"Sanctify them in the truth; Your word is truth." John 17:17

When you intentionally delve into the gospels you discover that the manner of Jesus' training of the twelve is quite different than in the books we read on discipleship. Their physical presence with Him was a seminal factor in their training. The books and the eight-week discipleship classes can subtly inoculate us from authentic discipleship. These guys had to *be with* Jesus, so they could observe what made him tick. This is why He chose them.[1] During His last moments with His Father before His arrest, He asked Him to sanctify, or set apart, these men by His truth. This is far more involved than learning verses. Real discipleship is up-close and personal. They must see how you treat your spouse; how you resolve conflict; how you handle criticism and praise. They must see how you treat the clerk in the store or the homeless man on the street? We are far more comfortable thinking in pictures, and this is on the job training that can't happen in a classroom.

Jesus wanted the twelve to learn to *trust* and *depend* on Him just as He had with His Father.[2] Just as Jesus did nothing other than what the Father did through Him, He wants the twelve to trust Him in the same manner. That trust will be built as they observe Him in multiple circumstances. They will begin to see that becoming like their Rabbi is not by trying to imitate his actions, but by allowing His perspective to be built in them. It is not about trying to decide how Jesus would vote if he was here today. It's not about the church He would join, the college He would attend, or about the kind of car, He would drive. If we learn what it means to yield to Him in complete trust and allow that to permeate our mind and heart, it doesn't matter what you drive or what career you choose.

Jesus wanted his men to understand that words and knowledge do not change people. They will not become like Him by memorizing everything He teaches. Scripture memory is great, but it is not a magic wand. "Faith comes by hearing and hearing by the Word of God."[3] Faith rests upon revealed truth, *never* upon information. The Greek word here for "word" is not *logos* as in John 1:1, but *rama*, meaning "freshly spoken revelation." Information will stimulate your mind, but revelation will penetrate your heart.

In the beginning, the twelve wanted to know what Jesus knew, and do the things they saw Him do. In the end, they wanted to be *like* Him. Don't allow discipleship to degenerate into taking notes, reading books, and memorizing verses. It's a one on one journey.

---

[1]Mark 3:14   [2]John 14:10   [3]Rom. 10:17

Helping Another Grow

"The things that you have heard from me in the presence of many witnesses, entrust these to faithful men who will be able to teach others also." 2 Timothy 2:2

It's astonishing when you really think about it. We pay exorbitant prices to buy organic foods for our family; we pay for gym memberships, personal trainers, Yoga, Pilates classes, and recommend medicines and doctors to each other, but seldom do we take another under our wing for spiritual nurture. The greatest weakness in the church is that we don't know how to help another deepen their walk with Jesus. We recommend a book or say, "I'll pray for you," but that is far cry from what Paul is saying to Timothy.

After His resurrection, Jesus spent forty days with His disciples teaching them. He tells them that *as they go* on this great mission into the world, they are to make disciples.[1] Years later, Paul tells Timothy that the things he has taught him must be passed on to faithful people who will repeat that process with others.

There are hundreds of books on discipleship and everyone has a curriculum they believe is the best way to build disciples. But I will pass along to you what has become the greatest gift I have received when Doug Coe began to work with me individually over forty-five years ago. "If you want to help people grow," he said, "don't go a bookstore, study how Jesus did it with His twelve." In observing Jesus, you have a man who spent more than three years, twenty-four/seven with twelve young men, and His input and example empowered them to impact the whole world.

Discipling another has little to do with methodology and everything to do with presence. When you find someone who sincerely wants to know Jesus better, he or she will first need access *to your time*. Meeting an hour or so a week in some restaurant for breakfast is great, but it's not discipleship. You can only give them information there. I believe you must spend time in different life situations and circumstances in order for the principles you teach to connect with reality. When you disciple someone, you are saying to them what Paul said, "Follow me as I follow Christ."[2] This is not an arrogant or boastful statement. People follow people to Christ. They need to see vulnerability. They must see you fail as well as succeed. They need to see you ask forgiveness of someone you have offended. You can't do this in a meeting.

Tomorrow we'll look at this a little deeper ...

---

[1] Matt. 28:19   [2] 1 Cor. 11:1

Helping Another Grow (2)

Few things frighten believers more than the thought of sitting eyeball to eyeball with someone and talking about matters of the heart. We feel unqualified … fearful we will not be able to answer their questions, and numbed by the notion they will discover that we too have "feet of clay." Yes, you will have to continue to grow and learn yourself. You begin by passing on what God has and is teaching you, but eventually, you will become companions and will learn from them as well. I taught my three sons about Jesus mostly by spending time with them and taking them with me whenever possible. When I used to travel a lot, I would always take someone with me, and we learned from each other, as well as from the people we spent time with. I believe we do a great disservice to Jesus' admonition to make disciples by always assuming it should be weekly meetings. Nowhere in the Scripture do we see Jesus or Paul rush out for an early discipleship meeting. Sure, it was a different culture, but the truth is, we influence people regularly and don't even know it. Your kids, your friends, and those you work with are either drawn or repelled by your values, your reaction to failure, or simply by the way you treat the waiter in the restaurant.

The argument I often hear is that we could be far more productive by discipling a group of people rather than just one at a time. Well, if you were training a team of salesmen to go out and sell insurance or vacuum cleaners that might be true. But you can't disciple a group of people in a class. You can give them information, but that won't translate into disciples. As I mentioned yesterday, you must give a person access to your life; they must walk with you. You can't do that in a classroom, and rarely in a small group. One on one is the slow way, but it the sure way.

I can't encourage you enough to ask God for someone to disciple you, no matter how far down the path you may have traveled. When I was twenty-five, a man named Larry Nicastro, who was twice my age, asked me to disciple him. In the process, he taught me many things I needed to know about marriage. Ask God to lead you to someone who has a deep desire to grow and who is willing to see your times together as a priority. No matter how busy you both are, if you both want it, you *will* find the time.

Jesus often pulled His disciples aside and taught them privately, away from the crowds. I believe what He taught them in these private times is where we begin in "making disciples." He reinforced these principles as they walked together. In the ten days that follow, I want to share with you the principles that Jesus taught to His disciples privately.

Principles Jesus Taught: The Word

"If you continue in My word, then you are truly disciples of Mine; and you will know the truth, and the truth will make you free." John 8:31–32

After Jesus chose His twelve, He immediately began to expose them to the life they will face after He is gone. Critical to their ability to stand face to face with the opposition of the secular world will be their understanding of truth. They must have a standard for their beliefs, and that standard is the Word of God. They will have to unlearn much of what they have been taught by Pharisaic Judaism. They will also need a firm grip in their understanding of grace. It is a radical concept that would shake the foundations of the Middle East, Asia Minor, and Europe.

If we "continue" in God's Word, we are truly disciples of Jesus; we are slowly becoming like our teacher. To continue is a call to *step into* the mind of God. Allow the truth to become a natural extension of all you think and do. It means that these twelve, and all disciples, will walk along and encounter every philosophy known to man. Much of it will sound reasonable, enticing, and will often counterfeit the Scripture. It will make your walk feel out of step, old fashioned, and irrelevant to the current trends ... but "continue." Eighty-three percent of adults believe that man is basically good,

but "continue" in His Word. Seventy-seven percent of born-again people believe *God helps those who help themselves,* but "continue in His Word." Many professors in Universities will penalize students if their papers differ from a secular, humanistic point of view ... but "continue in the Word."

Every world view you encounter in these arenas will say that ultimate fulfillment and freedom is to be found in the absence of moral boundaries. Jesus categorically refutes that in promising that knowing and acting on *the truth will set you free.* If we don't have a standard of truth by which all ideas, philosophies, and perspectives are measured, we are hostage to our own feelings. "Follow your heart" is horrible advice! When continuing in God's Word you find that the heart is the one thing you *never* want to follow.[1] Ask anyone who has experienced the pain of divorce if their heart made the right choice. The heart must be informed by the truth, not simply the emotion of the moment. God's Word is true. Jesus' last prayer for His disciples is that "they be set apart by His truth."[2] The Scripture is the very foundation of truth and is a principle central to following Jesus.

---

[1] Jer. 17:9–10   [2] John 17:17

Principles Jesus Taught: Prayer

"Until now, you have asked for nothing in My name; ask and you will receive that your joy may be made full." John 16:24

Ask any random person on the street, "What gives you joy?" Let's say you are walking your dog, sitting by the fire on a cold night, or cutting the grass. Suddenly, you feel an overwhelming sense of joy. Where does it come from? What is its source? Most of us mistake joy for happiness or sudden elation. This happy feeling is always temporary as well as circumstantial. It comes with good news and departs with bad news. Joy is an overriding sense of contentment that never depends on what does or doesn't happen.

In this verse, we learn that the disciples had asked for nothing in Jesus' name and that they did not know that asking was related to their being full of joy. We also learn something about the heart of Jesus; He *wants* them to be joyful, not simply happy, and it is His pleasure to give it. Now it makes sense when Paul says, "Pray without ceasing."[1] I used to think this meant I would have to become a monk and do little else. I finally realized that it means to continually open the lines of communication with God and as long as I do continual joy will follow. Prayer is the source of joy!

Prayer is not easy. It has either been learned as a flippant cliché ("I say a little prayer for you") or relegated to a level of piety that seems far beyond the reach of most of us. Prayer is not

difficult, but our lifestyles … the frantic pace we keep, the addiction of our cell phones, and the inability to ever be alone, as Pascal says, "amid the silence of four walls," is tearing away the joy that could be ours. Prayer is a stranger to many of us because it requires us to be vulnerable. God knows our thoughts; we can't lie to him … and so we must be open and willing to address secrets that are hard to even think about much less bring to Him.

My senior year in high school, I began going to a weekly Bible study with Mal McSwain, the patient and persistent Young Life Director in Charlotte who introduced me to Christ. In the end, he had everyone pray for the person on their right. I had only recently uttered the first payers I had ever prayed and wanted to run out of the room. But my friend Billy Farthing, to my left, prayed the kindest, most generous prayer for me and a sense of value came over me like I never imagined. It relaxed me, and I prayed for the guy to my right. The rest of the day nothing threw me off course, and my thoughts we radically different than usual. Prayer draws us together and initiates a sense of caring that nothing else can even approach. It's a principle central to following Jesus.

---

[1] 2 Thess. 5:17

173

Principles Jesus Taught: Unity

"That they may all be one; even as You, Father are in Me and I am in You, that they may also be in us so that the world may believe that You sent Me. The glory which you have given to Me I have given to them, that they may be one just as We are one." John 17:21–22 (NIV)

When someone looks death in the face, that which matters most to them bubbles to the surface. Jesus is in the Garden of Gethsemane, in an area where olives were pressed to make oil. In a very real sense, He is being pressed as He prays before the soldiers come to arrest Him. He prays for His disciples and what surfaces in His deepest concern to His Father is that His disciples *will be one* just as He and His Father are one. There is no request that they become great speakers and teachers, no concern about who should be the key leaders and no regrets. His concern is that they would love each other as He had loved them and that they would operate with the same undivided harmony and compatibility as they had seen in Him with the Father.

Unity demands *compromise*. No two people will ever agree on everything all the time. Even the best of marriages must compromise. The principles of Jesus that we are discussing are inviable they are not up for a vote. How we go about it and how we deal with non-essentials along the way is a matter of discussion. Unity requires that egos be checked at the door. Arrogance is a game-changer in the wrong direction. Real unity requires that I may have to defer my position on a non-essential matter for the cohesion of the group.

We have thousands of church denominations today. Within these are hundreds of subgroups that have split due to theological or ecclesiastical issues they could not agree on. If the split came as a result of a disagreement on a matter like the centrality of Christ or authority of Scripture that's one thing. However, it usually is a matter of preference about modes of worship or baptism, the role of women, and even the preaching style of the minister. The world laughs all the way to the golf course every Sunday.

They will know we are His, not by our political position or the issues we are for or against, but the love we have for one another.[1] That is our calling card. Nothing makes a more profound case for the genuineness and power of God. Anyone who thinks that the correctness of their theology and the flawlessness of their lifestyle will be what draw a lonely, alienated world will be disappointed. That we stand together as brothers and sisters is central in our ability to make an impact in the world. Unity can't be created; it happens mysteriously as we stand together in God's presence.

---

[1] John 13:35

Principles Jesus Taught: Jesus Before Things

"In the same way, those of you who do not give up everything you have cannot be my disciples." Luke 14:33 (NIV)

Happily reading along in Luke 14 you come to this verse and suddenly, your mouth gets dry, your throat tightens, and you feel nauseated. If Jesus was a marketing executive He would have just violated a cardinal sin of persuasion. You never accentuate anything but the positive. Forsaking all your stuff doesn't fit the profile. But Jesus is not selling a product, looking for votes, or trolling for new members. He is making disciples. Discipleship is not a hobby, a part-time pursuit, or something you do on a rainy day; it is a radical lifestyle that by its very nature, calls into question the thinking of the modern world.

When you give this mandate some serious thought, leaving it out would have been a travesty. He has already said that no one can have two masters.[1] Dual affection never works. You must decide if your master will be Jesus or possessions. It takes only the turn of your head to see what Jesus is saying. Look around you. We are flooded with things we don't need, but which capture our imagination, distract us from reality, and dominate our time. Jesus is not commanding that you sell everything and live on the street in order to be an authentic disciple. But this is a serious principle that we should meditate on and discuss. Ultimately, you must hear from the Holy Spirit what is being said to you. I must do the same.

Consider this … when you look at the full counsel of the Scripture, passage after passage relates to how possessions can, and will, derail our desire to follow Jesus. Why? Two masters! The appeal of all that is shiny and bright can be more potent than any drug. It appeals to our insecurity that we are not enough without the expensive car, the jewelry, the huge house, etc. It appeals to our need to keep up with the Joneses and the fear of not being accepted. I encourage you to take this as seriously as Jesus did when He said it, but don't become legalistic. Do what God tells you to do but don't go and lay this on someone else. Give them the freedom to wrestle with this and make their own application.

What Jesus does not say is important. There are no specifics. There are no examples. It is an issue you must decide in your own heart regardless of what your friends decide. It is a requisite decision of discipleship so please don't write it off.

---

[1]Matt. 6:24

Principles Jesus Taught: Jesus Before Others

"If anyone comes to me and does not hate father and mother, wife and children, brothers and sisters—yes, even their own life—such a person cannot be my disciple." Luke 14:26 (NIV)

At first blush, this doesn't seem to line up with anything Jesus has said about loving one another and the commandment to honor your father and mother.[1] It is similar to God's statement that He loved Jacob and hated Esau.[2] It means Jacob have I loved, and Esau have I loved less. God's love for His people, Israel, is unparalleled. Jacob and Esau were twins and Jacob cheated Esau out of the birthright that should have been his. Jacob wrestles with an angel of God and when confronted he confesses that he is a deceitful man. God forgives Him and gives Him the name *Israel* which means, "Prince of God." The descendants of Jacob happen to be Jews. Esau's descendants are Edomites. Paul says in Romans 9 that God loved Israel more than Edom.[3] That seems unfair. But consider this: If God will have a Son, he had to have a wife. God married Jacob's descendants, the Israelites, at Mt. Sinai. Would it be offensive to you if I said I love my wife more than any other woman alive? So Paul is speaking of nations, not people. Did God love the Jews more? Yes. They were married.

How could I love God that much more than my wife and children? God wants us to love Him to such a degree that by comparison, it would seem as if we hated the next closest people in our life. The truth is that loving God with *all* my heart, soul, mind, and strength is the only way to love my family with a pure love. All my love would seem to leave nothing with which to love others. But when I love Him that much, He gives me back a level of love I am not capable of giving on my own. To love God gives us the capacity to receive back, and give enough love for, not only my family but with every person I meet ... even my enemies!

This is another paradigm that is opposite of the way we think. It is anything *but* a call to hate your family as some critics often assert. The more I love God, the greater the capacity I have to love my family and others. This is a principle that is critical in following Jesus.

---

[1]Exod. 20:12   [2]Mal. 1:2–3   [3]Rom. 9:13

Principles Jesus Taught: Jesus Before Self

"If anyone comes to me and does not hate father and mother, wife and children, brothers and sisters—yes, *even their own life*—such a person cannot be my disciple." Luke 14:26 (NIV, emphasis added)

The second part of the verse we read yesterday is our focus. It's the same idea. *Hating your own life* is to love God more than your own life. Think of it this way: From the moment we are born, the default position of every human being is the protection, maintenance, and preservation of ourselves. When a baby is hungry his only concern is satisfying that hunger. All philosophies wrestle with the question, "Even if we solve all the human dilemmas of knowledge, reality, and existence, what do we do with the problem of *self?*" E. Stanley Jones, a great missionary to India once said, "Everywhere I go I take me with me and have a bad time." In other words, you may develop the *Midas Touch* in making money, possessing power, and have enormous gifts and talents, but at the end of the day, when you are alone in your own thoughts, how do you solve the problem of *you*?

Socrates said, *know yourself*; Rousseau said *express yourself*; Buddha said, *suppress yourself*; Mohammad said, *submit yourself*; Confucius said, *control yourself*; Epicurus said, *enjoy yourself*. In the 20th century, Hitler came on the scene and *extolled himself*;

women's liberation said *free yourself*; the "hippie" movement of the sixties and seventies was about *finding yourself* and today everything is about *branding yourself*. Everything in life circles around "how do I handle me?" This is why Jesus used such strong language as *hate*. The pull of our flesh is so great that only if our love for Jesus is so singular and deep that by comparison, it would seem as if we hated our own life. If you ever saw Susan and me around our grandchildren you might think we hated all the other kids on the playground. Of course, we don't at all, but by contrast to how we feel about ours, you might think so. To love God to that degree will mean that the purpose and meaning of our lives will come crashing through, and our destiny will take its intended shape.

How do we do that? All I know is that when I carve out specific times to focus my heart and mind on the Person of Christ, I begin to see things differently. Truth has the winsome ability to allow us to see, bit by bit, the way God sees. Gradually the needs and interests of others become a dominating force, leaving our own desires secondary. This is a principle Jesus taught.

Principles Jesus Taught: Love the Brethren

"A new commandment I give to you, that you love one another: just as I have loved you, you also are to love one another. By this, all people will know that you are my disciples if you have love for one another." John 13:34–35 (NIV)

Does it surprise you that Jesus called this a *new commandment?* We all know that love is the essence of our faith, but to these twelve men who had grown up under the dominance of Pharisaic Judaism, keeping the law was the drumbeat that defined their lives. Loving your neighbor was the second part of the Great Commandment but Jesus now deepens its meaning in defining love by the standard of His own love.

The question we must ask is *how* did Jesus love His disciples? First, Jesus' priority was not his disciples but His own intimacy with the Father. God *is* love, so to the degree we love Him, we then have the capacity to love our spouse, our children, and others. Jesus' love for His disciples was predicated on His love for His Father. He never nagged these guys to love more; He simply kept loving them, and eventually, they caught on.

Secondly, Jesus loved them despite their deficiencies. They saw Him perform miracle after miracle and still waffled in their ability to fully trust Him. Despite this, He never wavered in His love for them. He opened His life to His disciples by the way He lived both privately and publicly. His teaching was a seamless explanation of His deeds.[1] We tend to rely too much on our words to teach. Words change no one; they only add information. Smoking causes cancer. Is there anyone who doesn't know that information? Yet millions continue to smoke. The disciples felt the heartbeat of what he said because it was reflected in everything He did and everything He was.

Finally, He loved His disciples sacrificially. He never *saw* it as a sacrifice; it was the natural expression of who He was and the affection He felt for them.[2] To love as He loved will often insist on extending ourselves inconveniently on behalf of others. This may mean exhibiting the kind of unconditional love that will not give up on someone because of a social, political or even a theological difference. Jesus' disciples knew next to nothing. They thought of Him as a great teacher, a prophet, and healer, but did not fully believe He was the Messiah until after the Resurrection. They scattered like a covey of quail after He was arrested and did not even believe the women who reported that He had risen, Yet, He still loved them as brothers.

Are you prepared to love ... not as *you* define love, but as His life defined love? This is a principle Jesus taught.

---

[1]Luke 24:19   [2]Matt. 9:13; Hosea 6:6

Principles Jesus Taught: Be Fruitful

"I am the vine and you are the branches; he who abides in me and I in him, he bears much fruit for apart from me you can do nothing." John 15:5

You and I were placed on this planet to put God's glory on display in our lives. So, Jesus uses a metaphor of something that middle eastern people see every day. Wine was the common beverage of rich and poor alike, and grape vineyards were therefore very common. Had Jesus been talking to insurance salesmen or bankers, He might have said something like, "It's up to you men; as the CEO, my father wants to double sales by the end of the year. To be fruitful and to prove your value to the company, you will have to try harder and be more aggressive."

But Jesus isn't selling anything. He is telling these young men that what has happened to them over three years is not simply a moral upgrade accompanied by a song in their heart that they will hopefully pass on to others; it is a living breathing Person in the form of the Holy Spirit that has begun to transform who they are from the inside out. That transformation is similar to the grape vineyard Jesus is describing. He says, "Consider Me as the vine and consider yourselves as the branches that connect from the vine. How much work do those branches do in order to produce grapes? None at all. But, at the same time, the natural expression of a branch properly nourished by the vine is to produce fruit. The *Fruit of the Spirit* is "love, joy, peace, patience, kindness, goodness, faithfulness, gentleness, and self-control."[1]

The problem is, we can't make any of this fruit happen, and that is very distressing for proactive people who are used to kicking things into gear. Jesus says we must abide in Him and He in us. How does that work? You never see a branch gritting its teeth and straining to produce fruit. Fruit comes not as the result of *effort* but of *connection* with the vine. Its only job is to soak up the sun, absorb the water and the vine *will* produce fruit.

Think of a woman in her last trimester of pregnancy. The main counsel from her doctor is good nourishment and adequate rest. She has no control over the natural process that is slowly taking place within her womb. She must relax in the knowledge that God is at work while she simply abides or rests in that reality.

When we *yield* our natural tendencies to try to make things happen fruit will develop and grow in us. At some point, birth will occur and transform us into the likeness of Jesus.[2] Our responsibility is to be at rest as we absorb the nurture of the vine. Fruit is produced through a *branch* that is yielded to Him.

---

[1]Gal. 5:22–23   [2]Rom. 8:29

Principles Jesus Taught: Filled by the Spirit

"But you will receive power when the Holy Spirit has come upon you; and you shall be my witnesses, both in Jerusalem, and in all Judea and Samaria, and even to the remotest part of the earth." Acts 1:8

Jesus makes this statement to His disciples before He ascends back to heaven. They are finally convinced that He is the promised Messiah and now want to know if this is the time when the Messianic Kingdom will be restored to Israel. Jesus responds that it's not for them to know the time; that is the Father's business, "but you will receive power when the Holy Spirit comes upon you."

They are now motivated and ready to go after spending forty days with the resurrected Christ, but He says, *not so fast; you have the will, but you lack what it will take to face an angry and cynical world.* Jesus has already told them that He will not leave them alone but will send the "Comforter" to live in their hearts forever.[1] The Holy Spirit will come upon them and they will be living models of what it looks like when the Spirit of the Living God inhabits a human body. Apart from the Holy Spirit, they have no chance … nor do we. Trying harder, being good, and living a moral life will simply say to the world that you are a dedicated, good and moral person and they will say, "Good for you."

The hardest truth for believers to understand is that it is never about your ability, your drive, or your dedication on God's behalf that will impact the world. It was a wonderful friend named Tom Skinner who taught me this many years ago. He said *it is the Spirit of Christ in you, living His own life through you, without any help or assistance from you.* The passage says, "All power is given to *Me*." We tend to think that if we are called to go make disciples, we need power. Jesus is saying, "No you don't!" You need Me and I have "all power." What God wants from you and me in order to influence the sphere of the world where we are called is for us to say, "Lord, you drive, I'll ride." He neither needs nor wants a co-pilot. He wants a man or woman who listens for the inner voice of the Holy Spirit and is willing to obey whatever He says. Wherever you go in the world, or if you just go around the block, you can know with confidence that because you have Jesus in you, you also have power. He is not a fuel pump where we come and fill up when we run out. He is the fuel and has all power. All we need is Him. This is a principle Jesus taught to His disciples.

---

[1] John 14:16

Principles Jesus Taught: Disciple All Nations

"Go therefore and make disciples of all nations, baptizing them in the name of the Father, the Son, and the Holy Spirit, teaching them to observe all that I command you; and lo, I am with you always, even to the end of the age." Matthew 28:19–20

When the Spirit of the Living God enters a person's life, his perspective begins to change. When the Spirit comes, the Fruit of the Spirit comes with Him. It's not something you receive from somewhere else.[1] Don't pray for more patience, love, or joy, etc.; These are the fruit that comes with the Holy Spirit. *"Then, why do I have such a short fuse?"* You're in the way! Step aside from your natural tendency toward irritability, and yield your responses concerning people and situations to the Holy Spirit. Do this intentionally until it becomes a natural extension of the character of Jesus within.

As a new heart forms in you, caring about others will follow. If God has done a great work of redemption in your life, you are indeed a new creation.[2] If you begin to love your neighbor as yourself, it naturally follows that you would want him or her to experience the joy and freedom you have found. I realize many have been put off by well-meaning, but overly aggressive believers. Aggressive evangelism is actually an oxymoron. The Scripture is clear that you and I can convert no one! It is solely an act of grace by the drawing power of the Holy Spirit.[3] Being more aggressive may induce a *decision,* but only the Holy Spirit can bring about a *conversion.* For God to give you a burden for people you know, or those whom God brings in your life, is a natural expression of love ... so be natural about it!

The phrase "Go, therefore, and make disciples" is a command, but it is not meant to make you nervous or give you an upset stomach. If you have an honest concern for people, they will sense it and God will open a door for you to express naturally and without judgment what happened to you. Do you ever pray for a country? I don't mean a *bless the missionary* prayer. Do you ask God to raise up a man or woman to stand in the gap for that country? Get a map and circle a country, read about it, and ask God to show you the needs there. You may really be amazed at the collision course he will put you on to meet someone from that country. It sounds crazy, but you can have an impact simply believing God for that country. I could tell you some stories that would curl your toes. This is a principle that Jesus taught His disciples.

---

[1]Gal. 5:25   [2]Phil. 4:13   [3]John 6:44–45

181

Road Trip: On the Job Training

Then he said to his disciples, "The harvest is plentiful, but the workers are few. Therefore, beseech the Lord of the harvest to send out workers into his harvest." Matthew 9:37–38

The previous ten days have been about principles of discipleship that Jesus gave privately to His disciples over a three-year period. This passage is critical in considering God's passion to bring the world to Himself. Jesus saw the multitudes as "sheep without a shepherd," and His great compassion shows us the depth of His human emotions. There were priests, Levites, and Pharisees across the land; but they were *idol* shepherds as we read in Zachariah.[1] The multitudes were drawn to Jesus, but He was limited because of their misguided loyalty.

Jesus wants His disciples to feel as He does about the lost and marginalized of the world. He knows they will not learn this in a classroom; they must learn it "on the job." Before He sends them out, He tells them that as they look at the bountiful harvest before them, the answer is not to rush out and try to meet every need. He tells them to pray to the Lord of this great harvest for laborers because He knows that if they pray for laborers, they will become a laborer as well. He intends to send them on a road trip and endow them with authority to heal the sick and cast out evil spirits,

but this will not be a magic wand; they will have to trust Him even though He will not be physically with them.

Today we have eight-week classes called *discipleship training*. Consider the ten principles we have recently discussed. Each of these takes a lifetime to digest; they must be much more than cerebral. They must be taken out on the road, in all sorts of situations, and with all kind of people. What Jesus wants is for these twelve to multiply themselves in people like you and me who will not simply pray a prayer of salvation and go back to business as usual. The prayers are that we become men and women with a mission who make a lasting difference.

If you want to become an authentic disciple, don't buy books or go to seminars on discipleship; study the life of Jesus and how he worked with His men. Very few believers meet with another person, one on one, with the intent to help them grow spiritually. It is the most critical need in the church.

In the next few days, we will look at how Jesus sent the twelve out to test their wings and, hopefully, we will learn along with them.

---

[1]Zech. 11:17

Road Trip: Sent Out . . . Two by Two

"Jesus summoned His twelve disciples and gave them authority over unclean spirits, to cast them out, and to heal every kind of disease and every kind of sickness." Matthew 10:1

The entire account we will look at over the next few days is found in Matthew 10:1-23, but also in Mark's account. Mark includes what I feel is a critical element which is very instructive for us. *They went out in pairs.*[1] Later, on the way to Jerusalem and the cross, Jesus will send them ahead two by two.

Why is this significant? Matthew tells us that he gave them the authority to cast out unclean spirits and to heal every kind of sickness. It is easy to misuse or abuse authority; it is easy to compromise or to give up when no one is around. But Solomon says, "Two are better than one, for if one falls the other will lift him up."[2] The chances of both who walk together being down at the same time is minimal. Also, together they bring a sense of accountability and encouragement to one another. They will encounter different kinds of people from a variety of circumstances. Having a partner with different gifts and different life experiences doubles the possibility that one may speak with greater authority than the other to those they encounter.

Throughout the Scriptures, even the testimony of a single person is not considered acceptable to God.[3] In the Old Testament, the testimony of one person was not considered sufficient to convict someone of murder. In fact, two or three witnesses were required in order to establish that a person committed a sin worthy of punishment. In verse 7, Jesus states that these disciples are to preach that "the Kingdom of Heaven is at hand." In other words, they are to say that everything about the coming of the Messiah that they heard from their parents and grandparents for generations is happening! This really is "good news" because it is the fulfillment of a promise from God to His beloved people.

I have had the unique opportunity to travel all over the world and I always take another man with me. It is the greatest form of exposure and teaching that you can have. Even on a simple road trip to visit other believers or to go on a mission trip you and your partner will never be the same and your friendship will grow by leaps and bounds. Apart from using the bathroom, two is *always* better than one.

---

[1] Mark 6:7   [2] Eccles. 4:9–10   [3] 1 Cor. 14:29; 2 Cor. 13:1; Deut. 19:15

183

Road Trip:
The People, the Place, the Message

"These twelve Jesus sent out after instructing them: 'Do not go in the way of the Gentiles and do not enter any city of the Samaritans; but rather go to the lost house of Israel." Matthew 10:5–6

Why is Jesus doing this? He wants these young men to grow; He wants them to take a risk; He wants them to recognize the way people think and to understand their hang-ups. Only then can these men understand how to approach people with a message of grace and hope they have never heard from their leaders.

They are told to fan out and go to various cities in pairs that are inhabited by fellow Jews. Jesus commands them not to go into Samaritan areas and not to Gentiles. Doesn't God love these people? Absolutely, and Jesus will deal with them later, but for now, they are to visit with fellow Jews.[1] There are a couple of very practical reasons for this. Jesus wants them to face some hard realities so that they might mature, but he does not want them to be overwhelmed and discouraged. Except for Peter, they are almost certainly teenagers. For young and inexperienced men to face an angry crowd of Samaritans with generations of hostility toward full-blooded Jews would be a disaster. For them to go to Gentiles who saw them as inferior and believed Jesus was only for the Jews would be way over their heads at this point.

These young men are to go to Jewish areas and say that the long-awaited Messiah has come. This was not an evangelistic mission as we might think of it today. They were to preach in public and private gatherings and tell what they had seen and heard while walking with Jesus. It was a way to get their feet wet. Often, many of us are timid about sharing our faith because we are fearful someone will ask a question we can't answer. We are also paranoid about being labeled as a religious nut case. But if you saw someone driving toward a bridge that was unsafe, would you be embarrassed to warn them?

I have seldom met anyone who, in a relaxed atmosphere, would be offended by someone showing genuine interest in them.

It is only when we make people a target or a project to be completed that resentment sets in. The disciples were not given a script to follow. They had watched how approachable and natural Jesus was as He interacted with people. Nothing was forced. Why not just relax and tell people your story? Listen actively, then respond appropriately. As a friendship forms and trust develops few things, if any, will be off the table. You will be amazed by the result because honesty and compassion are irresistible!

---

[1] Rom. 1:16

Road Trip:
Removing All Avenues of Escape

"Do not acquire gold, or copper, or silver for your money belts, or a bag for your journey, or even two coats, or sandals, or a staff; for the worker is worthy of His support." Matthew 10:10–11

It was common in the first century for travelers to carry such items as a purse, a staff, a girdle, and sometimes a second tunic. Jesus says don't take any of these things with you. Why? Because these things will get in the way of the purpose of the journey. This is an experiment in faith; these young men need to move beyond soaking up information and watching Jesus teach and perform miracles.

The natural tendency for all of us is to plan a fallback strategy when we are faced with a difficult task. These guys are no different. They were probably planning to take extra money just in case, a staff to make walking easier as well as the possibility of facing opposition that could become hostile. They would take the tunic they wore plus an extra one to use as a cover on cold nights. But Jesus knows that it is the lack of these things that will ensure the value they will gain from the trip. Money is something we all tend to lean on. Jesus wants them to lean on the Father as they must do after He is gone. Napoleon Hill wrote that *to be successful you must cut off every avenue of escape.* Jesus wants these men to trust God, not their ability to buy or manipulate their way to success. The same is true of taking a second tunic. Jesus wants them to stay in a home until they leave rather than retreat to a secluded place to spend each night. This way they will build a relationship and will be expressing truth to a friend rather than an acquaintance.

I still travel frequently and always try to stay with friends along the way. The most fruitful and moving conversations I have ever had have come around the breakfast table. You get to see people in their natural environment, meet their families and hear stories about what's really going on in their life. The façade breaks down and wonderful things can happen.

Jesus wants these men not to go solely as teachers with a message, but to allow others to teach them as well. He wants them to learn how to receive as well as how to give. Pride often disallows us from receiving from others. If you go as a *learner* there's no person on earth who can't teach you something you never knew. A reciprocal relationship is the kind that endures.

Road Trip:
Go with the Intent to Bless

"And whatever city or village you enter, inquire who is worthy in it and stay at his house until you leave that city. As you enter the house give your greeting. If the house is worthy, give it your blessing of peace, but if it is not worthy, take back your blessing of peace. Whoever does not receive you, or heed your words, as you go out of that house or that city shake the dust off your feet." Matthew 10:11–15

Middle Eastern homes were, and are today, given to extreme hospitality. Many homes were open to traveling Rabbis and others who came in town to teach. The disciples are told by Jesus to find a home that is *worthy* and stay there the *entire* time. There was a Pharisaic practice of staying in homes that were faithful in their financial giving of tithes and offerings and, therefore considered worthy. Why should we think of this as a home where people of good character reside? Where your treasure is there will your heart be also.[1] If a person is faithful with their money, they can usually be trusted with anything. Luke adds that they were to stay at this home the entire time and not change houses. Jesus did not want them to "weigh their options" and choose a house they liked best. This is not only rude but also reflects a respecter of persons which Jesus will not tolerate.

They were to give a blessing of peace to a home of gracious people but take back the blessing of peace and shake the dust from their feet as a sign of protest toward a home where they were not received. This sounds harsh until we realize the times and the culture in which they lived. Shaking off the dust from your feet was a Jewish act that says," I have done all I can, but everything that is true is being rejected so I have no choice but to wash my hands of the whole matter. From Jewish writings, we know that dust refers to "teaching." If the person will not listen to the truth and holds firmly to his beliefs, shaking off the dust is a symbolic act of protest because of the damage their erroneous position does to others. We see this in the Book of Acts when the Jewish leaders stirred up persecution against Paul and Barnabas on their first missionary journey.[2]

In the context of our own culture, this may also seem brash, but this was a life and death issue, not a minor disagreement. The truth was not optional and still isn't, and our willingness to compromise on the essentials is still regrettably alive and well.

---

[1]Matt. 6:21   [2]Acts 13:51

Road Trip:
Fearless in the Face of Opposition

"Behold I send you out as sheep in the midst of wolves, so be shrewd as serpents and innocent as doves." Matthew 10:16

"Well … thanks a lot," the twelve probably thought after Jesus made this statement. Sounds like a suicide mission. But Jesus is teaching them the posture of a citizen of the Kingdom. We are not, as some people assert, intended to seek out and vanquish Satan and all the enemies of our faith. I remember many years ago laughing at a "Peanuts" cartoon where Charlie Brown and Lucy stood looking at the vastness of space. Lucy says, "Well, it's you and me against the world, Charlie Brown, and personally, I think we're going to get creamed!" Apart from the power of God on our behalf, that would certainly be true.

I believe the key to understanding this statement has to do where responsibility begins and ends. Jesus these young men that they are to go out like sheep. Sheep are basically defenseless. They have no means to protect themselves. Where they are going in the world are hungry, savage wolves who eat "sheep" for lunch. There is no contest! But their responsibility is to be a sheep. Jesus is saying, *"You guys just go out like sheep and My Father will deal with the wolves. You don't have to do anything but focus on being sheep. I am the Good Shepherd and I will give my life for my sheep."*

He continues by saying that His disciples must be as wise as snakes and as harmless as doves. Snakes are crafty; they don't generally attack and only retaliate when they have no place to go. Otherwise, they are smart enough to get themselves out of the way. Vulnerability is our position. Without God, we will get creamed as Lucy said. But the battle is not ours. We are to stand firm against those who would seek to humiliate us, and then watch God stand strong on our behalf.[1]

When you and I look across the landscape of your life, never forget that we do not have to win! We don't have to bare our teeth and talk tough about taking down those who oppose us. On a human level, we are vulnerable. This is why Jesus said, "Without Me, you can do nothing."[2] But then we remember Paul's great affirmation of the power of Jesus. "I can do all thing through Christ who strengthens me.[3]

---

[1] 2 Chron. 20:15–17   [2] John 15:5   [3] Phil. 4:13

Freedom to Fail

"My flesh and my heart may fail, but God is the strength of my heart and my portion forever." Psalm 73:26

At first glance, it sounds like an oxymoron. Free to fail? The American Dream is about the freedom to achieve, succeed and *exceed* all the accomplishments of your parents. How can that happen if we make peace with falling short?

I grew up in a home where I always felt loved, but my insatiable desire to succeed was partly self-induced and partly a product of my generation. I am competitive by nature and was very driven to excel in everything I did. I put great pressure on myself and would not tolerate doing less than my best. My dear friend Bob Warren, who is in heaven now, told me I was so hard on myself because I thought it was up to me rather than it being up to Jesus. He held up his Bible and said, "Who is this book about anyway? Is your name in here?" That simple but loving rebuke helped me see that I had put my value as a person in what I was able to achieve rather than who God created me to be. It is a death trap in our culture where a person's whole identity is wrapped up in his performance.

Freedom to fail gives us the freedom to walk down a road we have never trod or dream a dream we never thought possible. It's not the checkered flag, it's the journey. If you live in fear of failing, you will never take a risk. If you define yourself by what you produce, who are you when you fall short?

One of the saddest things I have seen over the years is watching a father at an event say, "Go out there and make Daddy proud." That is far more damaging than most of us realize. It says to a child, *Daddy will only be proud of you if you perform well.* What a message! No wonder kids are afraid to fail. If you compliment kids on their character or some caring or insightful thought they have, it will encourage them in the right direction, and they will become confident in who they are.

Failure not only helps you learn and grow as a person, but it releases you to explore new avenues. Some of the great achievements have come after multiple failures.[1] You can do nothing to impress God or to cause Him to give up on you. You are always free to fail and therefore ... free to grow!

---

[1]Prov. 24:6

Satisfied with Life

"Abraham breathed his last and died in a ripe old age, an old man and satisfied with life . . ." Genesis 25:8

As I've grown older, this passage has become prominent in my thinking. Imagine coming to the end of a long life with no regrets, no hovering guilt and only the anticipation of an eternity with God. I have been with many people during their final moments on this earth and have yet to hear anyone say they were satisfied with their life. They have things that were left undone; relationships that weren't mended or opportunities that were missed. Abraham seems to even exceed that. He was satisfied with living.

If you look closely at Abraham's life you see an uncanny willingness to trust God where there were huge consequences. But you also see Him lie about his relationship with Sarah to save his own skin. Here was a man who the Scripture a say was "God's friend."[1] Here was a man who wrestled with God and *walked with a limp*. We don't meet him in Genesis until he was seventy-five years old. God tells Him to leave his home and family and go to a place He will soon reveal. He tells Abraham that he will make a great nation and will bless and stand by him every step along the way.[2] Abraham obeys without question. But he was

also impatient for the child he and Sarah never had. He accepts Sarah's suggestion that he should have a child with her servant, Hagar. As a result, Ishmael is born.[3]

Later, we see a level of faith in Abraham that few of us could ever understand. He and Sarah had finally been rewarded with their own son and now God commands him to sacrifice Isaac on Mount Moriah.[4] It is something that even the thought of renders us speechless, but as we know, God stopped Him. This old patriarch had been blessed in every way possible and he loved God more than the life of His Son. Hebrews tells us that Abraham believed God could bring Isaac back from the dead.[5]

Being content with life is not about perfection, nor is it about being successful or performing well. Abraham was a flawed man. He lied, he became impatient with God, but he was confident that God would never break His promises. He was unafraid to ask questions and never hesitated to obey Him. He was a man content to be who he was created to be. Abraham is a great example of a man who lived well and died satisfied with life.

---

[1] James 2:23   [2] Gen. 12:1–3   [3] Gen. 21   [4] Gen. 22   [5] Heb. 11:17–19

The Power in a Name?

"A good name is to be desired more than great wealth." Proverbs 22:1

We give names to hurricanes and boats; we often give family names to our children, but more and more these days, we give children a name we think will sound good with our last name. Ancient Jews were very serious about names. They understood that a name represents a person's identity and in a real way, defines their essence. Jews believe that when you name a child, it is the outworking of a partnership with God. The Hebrew word for "name" is *them*. It has the same numerical value as the word for "book." So, your name is really a book that tells a story about you. It speaks of your spiritual potential as well as your calling. A name is so important to observant Jews that they believe when you leave this earth and stand before God, one of the most profound questions you will be asked is, "What is your name … and did your life reflect the name you were given?"

The first name given after the creation was "light."[1] God spoke and *light* appeared. God creates with a word, a name. God spoke the world into existence[2] and he holds the world up, not like a giant Atlas, but by the "*word* of His power."[3] Things are what they are because of what they are named, not the other way around as we might assume. We see something and give it a name, but God has a name and purpose before it was created.

Abram lived in a culture of many gods. When He realized there was only one God, God changed his name to Abraham (Father of many nations) before he ever did a thing.[4] The name Jacob comes from the root word meaning "heel," which was appropriate in that he was always a flight risk when faced with a dilemma. He always ran away. Suddenly he is faced with a situation where he had to fight rather than flee. He demands a blessing in order to release the Angel of God and God renames him *Israel* (Prince of God). As is the title of these daily thoughts, he always *walked with a limp* to remind Him of His true identity.

Names are important. To say that your name defines who you are is not a cliché. "As his name is, so is he," writes Samuel.[5]

Your name does not force you to be or live other than how you choose, but it is the legacy you leave behind. May your name be remembered as a blessing that touched the lives of others and made the world a better place.

---

[1]Gen. 1:3 [2]Ps. 33:9 [3]Heb. 1:3 [4]Gen. 17:5 [5]1 Sam. 25:25

The Name Above All Names

"For this reason, also, God highly exalted Him and bestowed on Him the name which is above every name, so that at the name of Jesus every knee will bow and those who are in heaven and on the earth and under the earth and that every tongue will confess that Jesus Christ is Lord to the glory of God the Father." Philippians 2:9–11 (ESV)

As we saw yesterday, *names* are extremely important and none more important or powerful than the name *Jesus.* One of the most appalling slights that we have made in the Body of Jesus Christ is in substituting the Name of Jesus or making it interchangeable with the religious nickname of *Christian.* This name appears three times in the Scriptures, but never in the manner it is used today. It was coined in Antioch and was done so by the enemies of Jesus, not his disciples and followers.[1] It was generally used as a negative slur to describe "Christ ones." Throughout the New Testament, it is never used by Jesus, Paul, or the New Testament writers for specific reasons. There is power in the Name of Jesus, but no power in the name, *Christian* or *Christianity.* Those names have created more divisiveness and misunderstanding than any word you can imagine.

The name *Jesus* and *Christian* in the mind of most are interchangeable. We say Christian and mean everything that pertains to Christ. But most of the world is confused by that. Look at the news reports today. Christian is a word linked with all sorts of positions, alienations, and idiotic statements that have nothing to do with Jesus.

It's confusing if you're on the outside looking in.

There is a reason you don't end your prayers in the name of Christianity, Amen, or that Peter and John did not say to the paralytic, *in the name of Christianity, take up his bed and walk.*[2] If you ask fifty people what a Christian is, the answers will almost match the number of people. Why would we continue to use an extra-biblical word, coined by first-century enemies of Jesus to describe the Name above all Names? It won't be at the name of Christianity that every knee will bow.[3]

If you tell a stranger you follow Jesus, He or she may ask, "how is that possible?" If you say you are a Christian, you will never be asked because everyone already has their own definition depending on their personal experience and background. How do we ignore a Name that appears hundreds of times throughout the Scriptures? When we substitute something else, we diminish who Jesus is. There is power in "the Name" so use the Name and you'll be amazed by what happens. It is not Jesus that the secular world rejects … it's Christianity!

[1]Acts 1:26   [2]John 5:8   [3]Phil. 2:10–11

A Man with a Big Question

"For God so loved the world that he gave his one and only Son, that whoever believes in him shall not perish but have eternal life." John 3:16 (NIV)

It happened at the first Passover Feast that Jesus attended after His ministry began. Nicodemus, a respected Pharisee, and teacher had been part of many discussions about the new Rabbi, His miracles and His teaching. By the dark of night, He comes to Jesus because he is troubled. His own theology may have betrayed him and left him wondering if he had somehow missed something. Jesus knows what this man believes and what he has taught to others over many years. Jews believed that as a "son of Abraham, having been circumcised on the eighth day, and having meticulously following the 613 Laws of the Torah gave him automatic entrance into heaven. Nicodemus begins the conversation by assuring Jesus that the Sanhedrin members know He is from God because of the things he had done. Jesus knows that this learned older man has a hole in his heart. He cuts right to the chase saying that unless a person is "born again" he will never see the kingdom of heaven.

Nicodemus is very familiar with the term *born again*; it was a common Jewish saying that had at least six meanings. It was used when a gentile converted to Judaism; it was true of a newly appointed King; it was used when a boy had his bar mitzvah at thirteen; when a Jewish man married usually between eighteen and twenty-five. This term would be used when on becoming a Rabbi at age thirty, and finally when a man became a teacher at a Rabbinical school at age fifty. Nicodemus clicked each of these off in his mind and all were true of him. This is why he asks, "how a man can be born when he is old."

Nicodemus' given name was Nakdimon Ben Bonai. He was one of the wealthiest men in Jerusalem. All Pharisees believed that their wealth along with their Jewish credentials qualified them for heaven. The conversation continues, but Nicodemus cannot understand. However, he never forgot the encounter or the words of Jesus. He will later become a secret disciple. It is he who will help Joseph of Arimathea take Jesus body to the Tomb. Nicodemus paid a great price for his loyalty. History tells us that he lost his wealth, was dismissed from the Sanhedrin, and spent the rest of his life digging wells in Jerusalem.

It takes a certain amount of humility for a senior Rabbi to sit at the feet of a Man half his age, admitting that his whole life had been predicated on error. Nothing qualifies a person for eternal life except their sin, their weakness, and their inability to fashion their own life into its intended shape.

Return to Me

"I have swept away your offenses like a cloud, your sins like the morning mist. Return to me, for I have redeemed you." Isaiah 44:22 (NIV)

I became a follower of Jesus just prior to my senior year in high school as a result of becoming involved with Young Life. It is the best ministry focused on disinterested high schoolers I know of. The Young Life leader, Mal McSwain, built a casual friendship with me as he did with hundreds of other kids. It's what piqued my interest. I started going to Young Life Clubs every week. They were light, upbeat, and non-threatening with a thoughtful but kid-friendly message at the end. I don't remember the talks after so long, but I knew that the truth Mal spoke defined his life.

There was one illustration I never forgot. It was simple but profound, even now. A young boy built a little boat. He worked on it every day after school and on weekends. He painted it, attached a sail and took it to a nearby lake. It worked just as he imagined until a wind came up and pushed it far out on the lake. Frantically he yelled, "Come back, little boat," but it plunged over a waterfall and disappeared forever. A year later he was walking with his mother in town. He looked through the Pawn Shop window and there it was … the little boat that he had made. He told the shopkeeper this is his boat, but the man tells him that if he wanted it, he must buy it back. The little boy immediately runs home, breaks open his piggy bank and returns with the money. As tears of joy fill his eyes, he hugs the little boat tightly and the Pawnshop owner hears him say, "Little boat, now you are twice mine. I made you, I lost you, and now I've bought you back."

I understood nothing about redemption then, but I never forgot that simple story. It is the essence of God's amazing love. He created us for a relationship with Him. We wandered off and were lost, but He found us and bought us back and the price was the life of His only Son.

The dictionary defines redemption as "the action of regaining or gaining possession of something in exchange for payment or clearing a debt." Do you realize that no religion on earth offers or even mentions redemption except the message of Jesus? In Islam, Hinduism, Buddhism, etc., you must pay! The good must outweigh the bad at the end of your life. There is no forgiveness of sin, no second chances. You are hostage to the life you lived.

Only God the Father buys back that which was His in the first place. Isaiah says it beautifully: *"I have swept away your offenses like a cloud, your sins like the morning mist. Return to me, for I have redeemed you."* Return to me," says God, "I want you back!"

A Complex Man

"Thus King Solomon excelled all the kings of the earth in riches and in wisdom. And all the kings of the earth sought the presence of Solomon to hear his wisdom, which God had put into his mind." 1 Kings 10:23–24 (ESV)

I doubt there is a more complicated person in all of Scripture than Solomon. He had the uncanny ability to see the financial potential of the empire that his father David had built. However, he showed a blind stupidity in other areas that brought the Northern Kingdom to its knees. He was born and raised under the cloud of consequences that His Father had created by his sin with Bathsheba and the cover-up he orchestrated by having her husband sent to the front lines.[1] We don't know for sure, but many scholars feel that some shady dealings by his mother and the Prophet Nathan may have put him on the throne.

Despite the cloud of suspicion accompanying his coronation, he was a gifted man. God gave him unusual wisdom. Ravi Zacharias says that in Solomon, "we see the untamed passions of a gifted man." This was his Achilles heel. God has specifically outlined a mandate for a ruler of His people.[2] But Solomon accumulated massive amounts of Gold, took 700 wives and 300 concubines. He was a man who you never had to ask, "Whatcha been up to?" He was so wise that his writing flowed naturally from his fingertips. He built a Temple unparalleled in human history, but he was a bevy of contradictions.

In my hometown of Charlotte, North Carolina, in 1999, Hurricane Hugo came inland with devastating power. Charlotte has always been known as a city of huge beautiful trees that line the older parts of the city. Many were uprooted during the storm and when I flew there from a meeting in Chicago, I was stunned by how shallow the root system was on trees 4-6 feet in diameter.

Solomon was enticed by his passions. He had a shallow route system. During his reign, Solomon was the only King who had no Prophet to hold him accountable. Men especially must have a brother to confer with about their dreams and plans. We all will answer to God one day, but I would rather a caring brother ask me now. Nathan was there for David, but Solomon had no Elijah's or Jeremiah's to ask him the hard questions.

Our passions and temptations will always be there. We must have a prophetic voice in our lives or the wisdom and gifts we possess will be nullified by our inability to control those tendencies that can derail us.

---

[1] 2 Sam. 12:9–11   [2] Deut. 17:14:17

Sacrifice

"But go and learn what this means: I desire compassion and not sacrifice, for I did not come to call the righteous, but sinners." Matthew 9:13

Matthew was a Customs agent in Capernaum. It was a small but important city on the Sea of Galilee. A major trade route called the Via Mares passed just outside of the city and many people from various countries would have stayed in the city for at least a night or two as they traveled. The Romans levied many taxes on travelers as well as residents and used Jews to do their dirty work.

After Jesus was rejected in his hometown of Nazareth, He made Capernaum His home base. Peter lived there with his wife and Jesus stayed there often. Matthew would have certainly seen Jesus' miracles and heard His teaching, so when Jesus said to him "Follow Me" it would have been a compliment like no other. From a Rabbi, this meant "I think you can be like Me."

That night there was a party at Matthew's home celebrating his decision to be a disciple of Jesus. Only tax collectors, prostitutes, and Jesus with his disciples attended. Those professions were considered unredeemable by the Jewish leaders and were ostracized accordingly. Some Pharisees stood outside and asked the disciples why Jesus would dine with such sinners.

Jesus overhears them and says that it is the sick who need a doctor, not the healthy. The Pharisees considered themselves in the healthy group. Their focus was trying to please God with a sacrificial lifestyle. Jesus asks them a rhetorical question and then tells them it is compassion that God wants, not sacrifice.

In the church, we hear the word sacrifice often. We are to sacrifice our desires for His; we are asked to give sacrificially, and we know the sacrifice Jesus made on the cross. But when Jesus hung there, do you really think He considered what He was doing was a sacrifice? It certainly *was* from our perspective, but Jesus did it out of love and compassion. If someone came in my home, held a weapon on my family and just before he pulled the trigger, I dove in front of them and took the bullet, tomorrows news would say "Local man sacrifices life for family." Never would that thought have entered my mind. I would react to save my family out of my love for them. When you see a sacrificial act, observe it will see as such, but if the one who does the act sees it as a sacrifice, he has missed the whole point.

We do what we do out of love and compassion, not because we perceive it as a great act on our part. A woman risks her life to save a drowning child … was it sacrifice or compassion? Those focusing on their sacrificial efforts have missed the point entirely.

195

"Just Follow Your Heart" . . . Really?

"Many people saw the signs he was performing and believed in his name. But Jesus would not entrust himself to them, for he knew all people. He did not need any testimony about mankind, for he knew what was in each person."
John 2:23–25 (NIV)

For generations we have all been exposed to the collective "wisdom" of Hollywood celebrities on Late Night Talk Shows, Self-appointed Guru's giving seminars on TV, and Top-Forty songs musically advising the world on love and relationships. The abysmal ignorance is staggering, yet we still watch and sing along. We all do it! But when you stop and really listen to the words of the songs and the philosophies echoing the world views of the celebrities, you might wonder what planet they're from.

One of the all-time favorites is "just follow your heart." It sounds so right no one will ever question the wisdom of that advice. That line has been used in more movies than you can count and the weight it carries only depends on how much you like the actor who said it. If following your heart is legitimate, why was there a divorce in America every thirteen seconds in 2018, and why does the average marriage last only three years?

The truth is . . . the heart is the last thing you want to follow or trust. King David's heart was messed up and it cost him dearly That's why he asks God the create in him a pure heart.[1] David's son Solomon says that we must guard our heart because everything we do flows from it.[2]

You can't trust your heart because your heart is not trust-worthy. Artful words strung together in a popular song or greeting card sound sweet and soulful but there is no substance there. Jeremiah makes a stark statement saying that the heart is deceitful and desperately wicked and however much you may know; you can never be sure of a deceitful heart.[3]

The good news is that the heart is not simply a blood pump, but the place that the Holy Spirit chooses to live. A heart that is under the control of the Spirit of God will be reshaped and changed. The is the great hope we have, and our children and grandchildren need to understand that they will hear the "follow your heart" philosophy from cradle to grave. It will sound fluffy and sweet, but the writers of the Hallmark cards are simply stringing beautiful words together to sell cards.

God is in the business of changing hearts and growing them into their intended shape.

---

[1] Ps. 51:10   [2] Prov. 4:23   [3] Jer. 17:9

Becoming One: Maintaining Unity

"Being diligent to preserve the unity of the spirit in the bond of peace. There is one body and one Spirit, just as also you were called in one hope of your calling." Ephesians 4:3–4 (NIV)

Have you ever noticed the propensity of God's people to fall into the trap of affirming and passing on *biblical* thoughts and principles that aren't so biblical? I mentioned previously the often quoted nine fruit of the Spirit in Galatians 5 as a characteristic of our life that we want God to give us. We ask Him for more *peace,* and yet Isaiah says a person whose mind is focused on God will be "kept" in perfect peace.[1] The Hebrew root for peace means *to be complete* or *to be sound*. We possess peace from the moment that the Prince of Peace enters our lives. We make the same request of God about receiving more patience, more love, more gentleness, etc. All these nine fruits are contained within the Holy Spirit who is in you from the moment you receive Jesus. There is no place to get any more of what you already have.

Unity is something we all desire for the Body of Christ so that our love and oneness will cast a light among the unredeemed of the world. Notice in this verse above that we are to preserve or keep the unity that we already possess. You don't pray for more unity within the human body because it is already perfectly organized. If the brain is not communicating with the arm or leg it is because something is broken. Perfect harmony is the norm.

To "keep" or "preserve" the unity of the faith means to "guard" it. This is why we can never let the sun go down on our anger because it gives Satan a foothold on the relationship.[2] Don't criticize or speak evil of others[3] or engage in gossip.[4]

Unity with our brothers and sisters does not come from voting for the same candidates, agreeing on every issue, or even by lining up on every theological issue. It is not about being carbon copies.

Unity is what we possess from our new birth onward and preserving it despite differences should be a top priority. It is this unity that the world cannot achieve. When they see our desire and insistence on overlooking differences with one another and staying together even in diversity, they will know it comes from a Source beyond human capability.

[1] Isa. 26:3 [2] Eph. 4:26–27 [3] James 4:11–12 [4] Exod. 23:1; James 1:26

197

Guarding the Unity of Our Faith

Unity is not something you produce by diligence and hard work. It does not thrive by rallying around political or denominational issues. Paul tells us to "guard" the unity of our faith. How do we do that? First, by the natural and uncontrived characteristic of *humility*. It is the hallmark of all virtues. Imagine a group of believers together on a trip, at a party, or at a retreat. One or two in your midst become insufferably arrogant and dominates every conversation. They continually interrupt and make everything about *them*. How probable would it be for real unity to exist? They will have created an unsettling atmosphere of division that even the most patient among us could not tolerate.

Humility guards the unity of faith because it requires vulnerability. It is this that draws people inward in the same way that arrogance and pride repel them. Humility is not thinking negatively about yourself; it is aiming the attention away from yourself. Paul said that he put no confidence in the flesh.[1]

Another way that naturally follows in guarding unity is by being *other-centered*. Self-centeredness is a dominant thrust in a fallen world. Just as arrogance separates people, self-absorption will make people head toward the exits. There are few things more distasteful than someone who seeks credit for every accomplishment and even non-accomplishment, and whose ego takes all the air out of the room. If you believe the Scriptures, God cannot bless that type of person.[2] They break the unity of the Spirit and cause division. The reason divorce is so devastating is that friends, and even children, are usually forced into taking sides with the man or the woman, and that creates an even deeper breach with the community of faith.

I believe we guard our unity by never allowing criticism of someone who is not present. Little things are said, or innuendoes are subtly alluded to, and they always get back to the one who is the object of the criticism. We've all done it and even if you think you came through unscathed ... you didn't! If you will say something negative to me about someone, what would give me the assurance that you wouldn't say something negative to them about me? Trust would be nearly impossible from then on.

---

[1]Phil. 3:1–4   [2]James 4:6–7

World View:
How Do You See the World?

"As you, therefore, have received Christ Jesus the Lord, continue to live your lives in him, rooted and built up in him and established in the faith, just as you were taught, abounding in thanksgiving. See to it that no one takes you captive through philosophy and empty deceit, according to human tradition, according to the elemental spirits of the universe, and not according to Christ."
Colossians 2:6–8 (ESV)

Almost every important decision you and I make, and every conclusion we draw in life comes from a *worldview* we have consciously or unconsciously developed. It usually comes through the grid of our parents, teachers, clergy, friends, and media. A worldview is a framework or lens through which we view the world and the manner in which we live within that world. It is the philosophic grid through which we understand the big questions like *where we came from, what is our purpose,* and what, if anything, is on the other side of our last heartbeat?

Most people sort of *drift* into a philosophy of life that is based on the dominant voices they have heard since childhood, as well as those they have come to admire. Research by George Barna since 1984 indicated that only four percent of Americans has a "biblical world view," and out of those who defined themselves as *born again* believers, the result was an embarrassing nine percent. *"Although most people own a Bible and know some of its content, our research found that most Americans have little idea how to integrate core biblical principles to form a unified and meaningful response to the challenges and opportunities of life."*

Do you understand your faith enough to clearly and simply explain to your children or a friend what you believe and why you believe it? I'm not speaking of books you have read or sermons you may have heard. Do you *own* your beliefs? Could you explain God's character? Do you believe in absolute truth or does it ebb and flow with the times and with circumstances? A mom or dad tells a child that he or she can do and be anything they want to do and be. As positive as that sounds, do you realize those parents are teaching them that they can control their own destiny? Why can we trust the Bible? How can a loving God send someone to Hell? You don't have to be a theologian, you just have to do your homework and get a firm grip on what you believe and why. How can we confidently believe Jesus over the endless absurdities we will hear on Twitter, blogs, TV and from their friends.

World View:
Origin . . . How Did We Get Here?

"In the beginning God created the heavens and the earth." Genesis 1:1

Right out of the shoot in Genesis, which means "Beginning," we are told categorically that there is an intelligent Being behind everything we see when we look out the window or drive down the road. As you read in Genesis, you will find that God also made the person who is looking out the window or driving down the road. However, in the universities today you will almost certainly hear that there was a cataclysmic event millions of years ago that is responsible for your view out your window. You will hear that man evolved by emerging out of the primordial slime and all the complexities of the human body somehow organized themselves perfectly so that he became one who *could* look out the window. He could then look out at the happenstance world that accidentally emerged and smell the accidental flowers. In many colleges, if your term paper alludes to anything contrary to this scientific theory, your grade will suffer. You will be laughed at, mocked in many instances, and treated as a naïve simpleton.

Can you explain to your son, daughter, or a friend, in simple language, the reason for your hope? Can you help them to build a deep intimacy with Jesus so that their love for God will motivate them into the Scriptures and give them the confidence to one day say with the Psalmist, "I have more insight than my teachers."[1]

People whose worldview does not include God are summarily creating an amoral society. We would never so blatantly say that there is no right or wrong, but either side of that issue would depend solely on the mood we are in, the climate of the culture at the time, and what we are willing to live with. Where there are no moral absolutes there will be chaos. It would be like standing in a room with hundreds of people screaming out their personal opinions. No one is listening to anyone else and it is just a matter of time before a riot breaks out and chaos ensues. Who brings order to this disconnection? How do we all agree on any standard of civility? Was the Holocaust wrong? Was slavery? Not if we have no moral authority. You can't definitively say anything is wrong because the standard for these atrocities is you and me and millions of others rather than a moral God. Our origin, where we came from, is critical in establishing our worldview.

---

[1] Ps. 119:99

World View:
Meaning . . . Why Are We Here?

"Everyone who is called by My name, and whom I have created for My glory, whom I have formed, even whom I have made." Isaiah 43:7

In his classic book, *Man's Search for Meaning,* Victor Frankl says, "Those who have a 'why' to live, can bear with almost any 'how'." Imagine living your entire life on this earth without a clue as to why you are here. After college, I joined the Young Life Staff and was sent to Huntsville, Alabama to start the ministry there. Each summer for seven years, I took two busloads of high school kids on a 25-day Western Tour which ended with a week at Frontier Ranch in Buena Vista, Colorado. I was standing at the South Rim of the Grand Canyon with a teenager gazing across the vastness of this incredible wonder. Finally, he said, "Is this *it*? I thought there would be more to it." As ludicrous as his reaction may sound, it is a perfect metaphor for the way millions view their lives.

Day after day men and women slog through a meaningless existence repeating the perfunctory tasks and routines of life, interrupted by occasional moments of happiness, but never connecting with the reason why they were created. G. K. Chesterton said, "Meaninglessness does not come from pain; it comes from pleasure." We can endure and fight through the pain, but no one can explain why the pursuit of pleasure becomes such a disappointment. It never delivers what we are desperately looking for.

God created man and gave him authority as steward over all the earth.[1] His intent was to display His glory, His brilliance, and magnificence in and through that which he created.[2] In other words, He wants to put His glory on parade in your life so that when anyone looks at you, they see the greatness of God. To allow Him to live this magnificence through your life is to fulfill the exact purpose for which you were made.[3] The astounding truth is that this lifestyle is anything but boring and restrictive. The Bible says everything God created was for man to enjoy richly.[4]

Life was meant to flow like a river in an unsinkable boat. Storms will come, the river will rise, but the boat will arrive at the harbor and those watching will say, "What a God you have ... He always seems to deliver!" This is why we are here. Step into it!

[1] Gen. 1:26–28   [2] Isa. 43:7   [3] 1 Cor. 10:31; Matt. 5:16   [4] 1 Tim. 6:17

World View:
Morality . . . Is There Right & Wrong?

"Woe to those who call evil good and good evil, who put darkness for light and light for darkness, who put bitter for sweet and sweet for bitter!" Isaiah 5:20 (NIV)

Who are these people that call evil good and good evil? Well, click on your TV, surf the internet, or just engage a few people in conversation and you will find that the standard for right and wrong ebbs and flows depending on who you talk to.

When I was in college in the late sixties' demonstrations about Viet Nam dotted the landscape on almost every college campus. The horrors of war intersected a culture that was saturated with drugs and the sexual revolution. But there was a puzzling bifurcation of morality, not only among college students but also among their parents. If you asked students about the morality of the war, you would get a decisive *thumbs down*. If you asked about the morality of free sex, you would get a very relativistic answer . . . "well, you can't be dogmatic about these things; it all depends on the relationship." If you asked their parents about free sex they would say, thumbs down . . . "Absolutely not!" How about the morality of undeclared war? "Well, you can't be dogmatic about that; it depends on a lot of things." So, if you either dodge or eliminate a moral standard, good and evil would depend on which group you talk to. In other words, your morality will be driving your theology instead of the other way around.

People whose worldview does not include God are often unaware that if there is no God, there is no moral authority for anything. Murder becomes okay. Why? God established that moral boundary on Mt. Sinai. But murder is still against the law, isn't it? Who says so . . . you? Me? The Children of Israel weren't in Egypt anymore. They were free people in a new land and no longer under Egyptian mores. Until God gave the Law to Moses, as far as the Israelites were concerned, to murder or not murder your neighbor was a matter of personal choice. If you like your neighbor's wife better than yours, go for it . . . there's no law against it because there is no infinite moral voice of justice to create the boundaries to protect us. Where there are no moral absolutes there is chaos. If *man* can eliminate God, he thinks he can fill that position. Everything becomes a matter of personal choice. Theft and adultery are legitimate if you can get away with it. This is why God gave Moses the Law.

Trying to rightly determine good from evil and light from darkness without moral authority is like trying to assemble pieces of a jigsaw puzzle after you have thrown away the box.

World View: Stepping into Your Destiny?

"'For I know the plans I have for you,' declares the Lord, 'plans for welfare and not for evil, to give you a future and a hope.'" Jeremiah 29:11 (ESV)

This is a very popular verse and often misunderstood. People often quote it without understanding the context and it suddenly becomes a personal promise of protection and a destiny of nothing but good things. Without question, God does have a beautiful plan for our lives and the plan is a good one. But we must be careful not to inadvertently turn God into a superimposed Santa Claus who we expect to deliver all the goodies to us over a lifetime.

The Prophet Jeremiah writes this at a time when Israel had been taken into captivity by the Babylonians. To the Jews, it is a deathblow to their existence. They were God's beloved people; how could He allow them to be taken from their homeland and enslaved by a pagan nation? Back up a few verses and we will find God's real intent. Beginning in verse four, God tells His people through Jeremiah that they are to carry on their lives in captivity just as they would in Israel. Then in verse seven, He says that they are to "seek the peace and prosperity" of the city where they will live for seventy years. As the city prospers so will

they. *Listen to none of the naysayers*, He tells them *because they are liars.*

He does not bail them out. Israel had been unfaithful and had become vulnerable, and because of this, they were taken. God did not cause this, *they did*! He knows that as a nation they will learn and grow from this experience if they receive it with an open hand. After seventy years, God will bring them back to their land and fulfill His promise. Now we get to verse 11 and the beautiful promise He makes to His people about His plans for them.

Our struggle is that we don't want to go through the pain to get to the plans. It is easy to embrace the Scriptures that seem to indicate that life will be a boulevard of all green lights, but God is interested in character and it doesn't come from dancing through life unscathed. God has a destiny for you. Don't sell out for the American Dream. Don't settle for happiness that ebbs and flows with circumstances. Let God fill your life with a level of joy and hope that you have never known. That is what lies at the end of the rainbow.

World View:
What's at the End of the Road?

"And if Christ has not been raised, then our preaching is in vain and your faith is in vain." 1 Corinthians 15:14 (ESV)

The question that has plagued mankind for thousands of years concerns the afterlife. Is there anything on the other side of our last breath … our final heartbeat? Is death like an endless sleep? Is there a heaven and a hell? Any philosophy that a person lives by must be adequate for living, for dying, and for affliction. If it does not provide a reasonable and verifiable answer in these three areas, it is not worth the energy to pursue.

If our existence is simply *matter plus chance plus time*, then purpose and meaning go up in smoke.

God's intent was to create people in His image and death was never meant to be part of the equation. But man rebelled against God and chose his own way. Essentially every evil, senseless thing that has happened in human history resulted from that first man saying, "I choose to be my own god." But God refused to give up on His creation. He sent His only Son to be the payment for the debt man owed.[1] All who receive Him by faith are redeemed or bought back by His death on the cross.[2] As believers, we can know that we will be with the Father and the Son after we die because Jesus rose from the dead. The resurrection is the foundation of our faith and without it, we have no hope beyond the grave and have wasted our life on earth.

A Hindu never knows if he has *earned* enough karma for paradise; a Muslim must live precisely by the law of the Koran and never knows if it will be enough to rate heaven. Only Jesus assures those who believe in Him that they can know for certain that we will be in heaven because it is on the merits of His work, not ours, that qualifies us. But how could a loving God send those He created to Hell? He doesn't! God invites us to live with Him through Jesus. When you or I say, "No … not interested," He loves us enough to allow us to make that choice. Having said "no" to Him, why then would we suddenly want to live with Him throughout eternity after being disinterested during our whole life on earth? Hell is not the choice of God; it is the choice of man!

Jesus came to give life, and this is His focus in the gospels. However, He refers to hell directly or indirectly almost sixty times. Our worldview must recognize the reality of the consequences of a life that rejects a loving, compassionate Father. "For God so loved the world …" His desire is that *no one* should perish.[3]

---

[1] John 3:16   [2] Eph. 2:8–9   [3] 2 Pet. 3:9

The Privilege of Caring for One Another

Almost every word you read in the Scriptures is a relational word. God's story is about people and their relationship to God, one another, their adversaries, and the Kingdom that God is building. It is not by accident that God links our relationship with one another to our love and affection for Him. One cannot exist without the other.

For the next fifteen days, I would like to explore some of these relationships and the ways God wants us to connect and be a part of one another's lives.

"Be at Peace with One Another"

"Salt is good but if it loses its saltiness, how can you make it salty again? Have salt in yourselves and be at peace with one another." Matthew 5:13 (NIV)

"Salt" is what Jesus called twelve young kids at the beginning of His teaching in the Sermon on the Mount. It is a statement of their identity, not simply what He hoped they would become. It is the same with us who follow Him today. Salt is a purifying and seasoning agent that also has the ability to resist corruption. Jesus speaks of this first and finishes with His call to be at peace with other believers.

What is this peace to which Jesus is referring? Paul states it this way: "Live in harmony with one another."[1] He goes on to say that this means that pride must be replaced by humility, retribution or payback must be a thing of the past and doing what is right is not optional.

When the average believer defines peace, it generally sounds more like co-existence. "You don't bother me, and I won't bother you!" This shows a cynical world nothing at all. From 1945 until 1991 we lived through what was called the *Cold War*. It was basically a standoff or "balance of powers" where both Russia and the United States had an arsenal of nuclear capability to blow each other off the map. We considered it "peaceful co-existence."

That has nothing to do with the peace of which Jesus and Paul speak. Paul told the Ephesians that if they would make it their aim to be at peace with God, the inevitable result would be peace with one another.[2] Peace with God produces peace within oneself and that kind of peace produces an atmosphere where peace with your brothers and sisters becomes a true option.

Being at peace with others is not a passive matter. As Paul said, it requires humility. The relationship must have greater value to you than always having to be right. Paul also said that we must pursue the things which make for peace and the building up of one another.[3] Is your focus on being right and coming across as the smartest person in the room? If so, peace will remain simply a nice idea. Actively look for ways to find agreement rather than trying to accent your differences.

It is said that when a herd of horses is cornered by wolves, they face each other and kick outward at the predator. When donkeys are attacked, they face the enemy and kick each other.

We spend way too much time acting like donkeys.

---

[1] Rom. 12:16–18   [2] Eph. 4:3   [3] Rom. 14:9

Devotion and Honor Toward One Another

"Be devoted to one another in brotherly love. Honor one another above yourselves." Romans 12:10

I got up this morning and my first thought was, I'll cook breakfast for all my neighbors before work. Driving to my office I realized I was low on gas. At the gas station, I filled up several cars and paid the tab. Upon arriving at my office, I told my boss that the guy down the hall deserved the promotion more than me. By midafternoon I was hungry but gave a homeless man on the street all my cash. This has become a regular day to me as I seek to devote myself to others and honor them above myself.

That didn't happen and anyone who reads this verse and thinks he can pull something like that off by his own tenacity and discipline is nuts. Paul's intent is that this way of thinking will become a lifestyle. But it must be understood in light of the full counsel of the Scriptures.[1] Jesus' life on earth was a picture of dependence on His Father.[2] Every miracle He performed, His Father did through Him. He wants us to rely on Him as He relied on the Father. You will never *naturally* think of honoring others over yourself unless it is empowered by Jesus.

When we think of devotion, we generally think of our love for God and our family, but seldom would we use that word about other believers. Yet, if we believe the Scripture, they are precisely that ... our family. Honoring our extended family above ourselves is about developing a certain sensitivity toward their needs and sometimes needs of which they may not be aware. I have had friends in the FBI. When they are being trained, they will be in a restaurant and may be asked by their mentor, *how many people are sitting at the bar behind you? What color is the coat that the man at the far end wearing? Is the couple behind us eating or just having a drink?* These guys must be aware of everything around them. How much less should we sensitize ourselves to one another? You notice a sullen look by a normally gregarious person, an agitated glance by one who is usually laid back and affable, or a friend who avoids eye-contact.

Jesus was going to the cross in a few hours, yet He washed His disciple's feet. He was on the cross in agony, but He was concerned for His mother's welfare. Build this kind of awareness into your life. It's not about solving every problem with money. It might be the stewardship of a listening ear, a touch or a smile. Honoring another is about seeing with the eyes of your heart.

---

[1]Acts 20 27 (KJV)   [2]John 14:10

Stop Judging One Another

"So then each one of us will give an account of himself to God, therefore let us stop passing judgment on one another." Romans 14:12–13a (NIV)

Other than gossip, which is basically the same thing, judging people is the favorite indoor sport of the Body of Christ. There seems to be a built-in voice that whispers *if you take him out, it will give you a leg up!* I think it has something to do with the idea that we live in a dog-eat-dog world and I have to do it unto them before they do it unto me.[1] Whatever it is, as Steve Brown often says, "It's from the pit of hell and smells like smoke!"

To stop judging does not mean that you don't call sin what it is. Obviously, if you know that a friend is in flagrant violation of God's commands he or she must be confronted. But there is a way to do that, and it doesn't include public humiliation. Paul has, in the previous verses, said that one day "Every knee will bow before Jesus and every tongue will confess." Each of us will stand before God. None of us have the right to be the judge because we don't know the full story and are in no position to do so.

We seem to have this idea that we have been hired by God to help Him get the *bad guys* and we never include ourselves in that group. You and I are hard-wired to always insist that the blame should be placed elsewhere or, at least, that your offense is much bigger than mine. Judgment not only damages but often severs relationships; It also deletes credibility. Who will ever trust such a person or believe that the accusations they make are anything more than a personal vendetta?

The problem with gossip, in addition to the fact that it is a sin abhorrent to God, is that those who are told seldom ever stick around for the restoration of the person after they have confessed their sin. So, in their minds, the object of the gossip is always defined by an offense that God and those directly involved have forgiven and moved on. Paul lists such deeds of the flesh as drunkenness, immorality, idolatry, and sorcery, but alongside are such things as envy, strife, dissension, and jealousy.[2] The judgment spoken of is when we act as if we know the intent of another. "I know why you did it!" No, you don't. "I know what you're thinking." You couldn't possibly. No one has ever seen a motive.

Paul is simply saying, "Stop it!" Stop judging one another! Stop acting as if your sins are less offensive than that of another. We are a family, built for companionship ... built to encourage and love one another, not to destroy others and dishonor Jesus.

---

[1] 2 Conundrum 1:17   [2] Gal. 5:19–21

Building Up One Another

"So then let us pursue things which make for peace and the building up of one another." Romans 14:19

What could possibly be a reason for tearing down another believer rather than building him up? What would be the payoff for such a thing? Unhappiness? Misery *does* love company. Envy? Wanting what another has and the willingness to crush them to get it. How about competition? We have a built-in obsession to come out on top, to be vindicated and validated. When these desires are in play, strife is an absolute guarantee. Conversely, if we actively pursue avenues that welcome and enhance peace, it automatically encourages those around us.

How do you build up others? When you are with someone or a group of people, never participate in any level of gossip about those who are not present. In fact, look for genuine ways to counter the negativity. The statement of support, or affirmation of another person, will always get back to the person who is absent. It will build them up. People who tear down their brothers and sisters, on the other hand, are looking for someone to agree with their assessment. If you refuse to join in, they will often feel shame and stop.

Pete Moore is a college friend who remains a good friend today. I have never heard him say a negative word about anyone … ever! People like him

and like to be around him. No one would feel comfortable being negative or critical in his presence. It would be awkward because his character sets the tone.

Bob Warren, another close friend, and I were speaking to a group of people in Nashville. His words are seared in my brain. "If you have something negative to say about someone, please do not say it around me … because if you will say it to me about them, you will at some point say it to them about me, and I will never be able to trust you again." They were hard words but when you allow gossip and innuendo to continue, it is more destructive to the body of Christ than any sin you can name.

John the Baptist was a front-line warrior who was stuck in prison. He began to wonder if he had tapped the wrong man. He had one mission in life and feared he may have blown it. Jesus sends word back that convinces him that Jesus was indeed the Messiah. Afterward, Jesus is speaking to the crowds … a perfect time to shame John for his doubts. But Jesus gives him the greatest compliment. "No greater man has ever been born of woman."[1] This is how we build up one another.

---

[1] John 11:7–11

Accept One Another

"Accept one another, then just as Christ accepted you." Romans 15:7 (NIV)

Is there a difference in acceptance and acquiescence? Yes, a big difference. To acquiesce means to agree or to finally be won over. It is more of a reluctant agreement. Acceptance is to recognize the right of another to hold an opposing position but respectfully disagree with it. Paul is not saying that we must agree with one another up and down the line. Can you accept the choice and position of a friend even if you disagree?

As I write this, our three branches of government and both political parties are wallowing in a quagmire of disunity unparalleled in our history with the possible exception of Watergate. Friendships that have lasted decades are struggling under the downward pull of the political undercurrent. Unlike in the past, many relationships hinge on political agreement. Acceptance and respect for a colleague's position was once the norm. In fact, the phrase, "at the end of the day," which is simply a media cliché today, was coined in the 1980s. Members of Congress would fight it out on the floor of the house and senate, but would say, "*at the end of the day*, we're still friends."

Paul's admonition of acceptance rests on the phrase, "just as Christ accepted you." You and I often do not agree with Jesus. We violate our friendship with Him, we disobey His commands and even abandon Him, but He still accepts us without condition.

I have friends with whom I disagree on issues such as abortion, gay marriage, immigration, absolute truth, and even what it means to walk with Jesus, but I still love them and would fight for their right to take a different view. Yes, we must have unity on essentials but rejecting a fundamental premise should not mean the rejection of friendship. I have known people who have spent a lifetime violating almost every principle of truth only to meet Jesus late in life because of the persistent love of a friend who would not give up, even if they disagree.

If you are honest and will consider the darkness of certain areas of your own life and how graciously Jesus still accepts you, maybe it will be easier to be patient with others. It is unfair to equate a person's entire life with a single point of view. Don't let the angry voices on radio, TV or in the marketplace deter you from this principle that will, in the long run, produce lasting unity.

Serve One Another in Love

"For you were called to freedom, brethren; only do not turn your freedom into an opportunity for the flesh, but through love, serve one another." Galatians 5:13

When a man or woman yields their life to Jesus Christ and becomes a new creation, something revolutionary happens. Motivations, desires, concerns, and priorities slowly begin to change. Those things that were always responsibilities and obligations gradually, but steadily, transform into desire and opportunity. Duty becomes pleasure because life is now lived from the inside out … from a heart filled with gratitude for what God has done. Religion creates guilt which obligates us to do the right things and be the right people in our own strength, but a new life in Christ changes duty into desire.

Serving one another was never intended to be a burden. Most of us serve fairly naturally in certain circumstances. A neighbor is sick, and we bring a meal or two; an elderly friend cannot get to the grocery, so we go for her. These are wonderful acts of kindness but are usually occasional circumstances. I don't think this is what Paul is saying to the Galatians. Paul says, "serve one another in love."

Let serving become a natural and even unconscious extension of who they are in Christ.

You may find that if you listen carefully people will often say something inadvertently that gives a clue to something they need but are embarrassed to ask. If you develop a habit of seeing between the lines and listening for the unspoken word, you will often be an unexpected answer to a great need.

Jesus is called the "Suffering Servant" in the Old Testament.[1] During His time on earth and in His death, He came not to be served but to serve.[2] His service was not a burden; it was an act of unconditional love. Even going to the cross was a joy, not an obligation[3] To us it was a sacrifice, but in the mind and heart of Jesus, it was motivated by love.

If you feel that things you do to serve God and others feel like a sacrifice, you are missing the point. Love for God engenders a deep affection for everything and everyone He created.

---

[1] Isa. 52:13–53:12   [2] Matt. 20:28   [3] Heb. 12:1–2

DAY 195
Bear the Burdens of One Another

"Bear one another's burdens and thereby fulfill the law of Christ." Galatians 6:2

One of the saddest verses in the Bible is when Paul was writing to the Philippian Church about sending Timothy to aid and encourage them. He says, "I have no one else of kindred spirit who will genuinely be concerned for your welfare. For they all seek after their own interests' and not those of Christ Jesus.[1] When we shoulder the burden of another, we are fulfilling the law of Christ which is to love one another.[2] The law commands us, but the Spirit of God creates the desire in us to be involved with people and to seek ways to help them with their burdens.

I have been to India several times. One of the times that I traveled there I found myself in an isolated village in Hyderabad. The translator for our small group introduced me to a young woman because he wanted me to hear her incredible story. She lived in a Hindu culture, but she had met Christ through a missionary many years before. Others followed and they began to save money to build a church where they could meet and worship. Years went by and they were unable to save enough money to build. This woman loved her village and made a radical decision. She took an

eight-hour bus ride to Delhi and went straight to a hospital and sold one of her kidney's. Three days after the operation she took the long ride back to her village and gave the money to the elders to build the church. This was her way of bearing the burden of her village for a place to grow and thrive spiritually.

I once asked my friend and mentor what he considered the most important thing he had learned. He said, *"Growing in my ability to trust Jesus was what I want most. I found that trusting God with money was critical to that goal. When I began, it was tough, but through the years that which kept me on my knees became easier as I went along. I wanted to keep growing, so I decided to trust God for the financial needs of another person as if it was my own. Great things began to happen, and one person turned into two, then three and eventually it became a way of life."*

I was deeply moved and later found it to be true. Where your treasure is, your heart will be also.[3] Most will bear other's burdens in small ways, but when it comes to money, it is guarded like Ft. Knox! Yet, it is money that is probably the greatest vehicle we have in learning to trust God.

---

[1]Phil. 2:19–21   [2]Gal. 5:14   [3]Matt. 6:21

212

Be Humble and Gentle Toward One Another

"Be completely humble and gentle; be patient bearing with one another in love."
Ephesians 4:2 (NIV)

Humility, gentleness, and patience are not generally the hallmark of most men. Women have much to teach men in this area. If you study the Person of Jesus of Nazareth, you will see these characteristics flowing through Him like an electric current.

The thirteenth chapter if 1 Corinthians, often called the "Love Chapter," is one that is often read at wedding ceremonies. It is not uncommon in youth groups to have the kids insert their names in place of the word "love" in describing their character. "*Bobby* is patient and kind; *Bobby* does not envy or boast, etc." I suppose this is to make Bobby more aware of how he falls short. But this entire chapter is really a portrait of Jesus. This is who He is and what He is like. You and I are incapable of pulling that off.

I love golf and I would love to play like Tiger Woods. But, no matter how much I practice it will never happen. But what if Tiger Woods could live inside me and simply play golf as he normally does, only now it would be through me? I would then be able to hit shots like him.

The kind of humility, gentleness, and patience of which Paul speaks is not something achievable by us. If that was so, we wouldn't need Christ. Humility is recognizing your limitations in every area of life. Some may have a measure of these traits, but never to the level of which Paul is speaking. Jesus walked away from every attempt to be hailed as King. One reason Muslims cannot accept the cross is that they can't understand the humility of a God who would willingly subject Himself to scorn, humiliation, and death at the hands of mortal men. But this is not a human trait; it is a Godly trait and Jesus wants to live that level of humility, gentleness, and patience in us.

Paul tells us to consider others as better than ourselves and to consider their interests before our own.[1] Try as you will, you will never pull that off consistently. Jesus did it every waking moment and He wants to continue doing it in you and me.

Ask Him to be that person in you; to develop the willingness to take yourself out of the picture and let Him be Himself in your body. It's not magical; it's not easy; it is the willingness to yield my tendencies to the Spirit of God in me. This, I believe is the only road to true humility.

---

[1] Phil. 2:3–4

Speak Truth to One Another

"Therefore, laying aside falsehood, speak truth each one of you with his neighbor for we are members of one another." Ephesians 4:25

Speaking the truth to someone can be terrifying because people's reactions are so unpredictable. But it can also be the most liberating, conciliatory act you will ever experience. It may be in a conversation where someone makes a statement that is blatantly in contradiction to the truth. It may be gossip that embellishes the facts or in a small group where the Scriptures are distorted by personal opinion. It generally involves the need for a private *sit down* with a friend.

The context of this passage in Ephesians 4 is that Paul is calling for unity within the Body of Christ. He speaks of humility, gentleness, and patience bearing with one another in love."[1]

He speaks of building up the Body into a mature family that is not blown around by every wind of doctrine. As children of light, we must protect each other by "speaking the truth in love."[2]

Unity is God's dream for his family. A disunited church draws no one inward. We, therefore, must learn to do that which we are never taught and is seldom addressed. As a new believer, I learned that the truth will set me free and that the Scriptures are the standard for truth. But no one ever taught me how to speak the truth to another person in a gentle, loving manner.

Truth is not a weapon; it is not an instrument of retaliation or a mechanism for being proved right. When a brother or sister is living counter to that which they profess, those who love them must confront them humbly for their benefit and on behalf of the entire family of God.[3]

Drive-by confrontation is, in my opinion, as bad as whatever sins are being confronted. It has no place in the Kingdom! If you haven't been on your knees asking God to prepare your own heart, as well as theirs, you should stay put until you do. If you don't plan to be there for them as they forsake their sin, you have no right to speak. If your words are not filtered and heard through the gentleness of the Holy Spirit, you will have lost a friend and they may even pull away from their faith.

There is a precarious balance in exercising truth and love, but it is critical for the flourishing of God's Kingdom.

---

[1] Eph. 4:2 [2] Eph. 4:15 [3] 2 Cor. 2:4

Submit to One Another

"Submit to one another out of reverence for Christ." Ephesians 5:21 (NIV)

Submission isn't exactly a cherished ideal in our culture. The emphasis is more about having authority and dominance over each other. All the more reason to take this admonition seriously and ponder its meaning. Submission is intended to be the essence of our walk with Christ. It is the posture of a servant. The tone of this command to the modern ear is not a happy tune. In our highly individualistic culture, we resist being under the authority of anyone. Even as believers, we are generally willing to defer only to God. I *know what is best for me,* we say. But the end of the verse tells us why we should submit … "*out of reverence for Christ.*"

God set up the authority-submission principle because He is a God of order, not chaos. This passage is God's desire and intent for us to respect His ordained authority. In vs. 22-23, we see the *ever-popular* call for wives to submit to their husbands. But this is followed by the command for a husband to love his wife as Christ loved the Church. How did He love the church? Sacrificially! It has nothing to do with being smarter, better, or more capable. Israel was the bride of God; the church is the bride of Christ, and the wife is the image of the Church.

Her willing submission to her husband balances and should reflect the sacrificial leadership of her husband in caring for his bride.

My wife influences everything I do, down to the clothes I wear, the way I cut my hair, and my schedule. Her influence on me is immense. I listen because she doesn't rebel or try to usurp the role I was given. It is not a competition and her willing submission makes me more intent to be the man God wants me to be. Jesus, who was God, submitted to His parents who were not.[1] Children are to submit to their parents.[2] As citizens, we are to submit to the authority of our government,[3] the whole created order is subject to Jesus Christ,[4] and Jesus is subject to His Father.[5] What is misogynistic about that?

When we first moved to Washington, D.C., in 1980, I willingly submitted myself under the leadership of Doug Coe because I wanted to know Jesus better and be a true disciple. It was not a task; it was a joyful choice because I knew I could trust him. Submission is not what most people think. If you want to grow as a man or woman in Christ, this principle must be embraced.

---

[1]Luke 2:51   [2]Eph. 6:1   [3]Rom. 13:1, 5   [4]1 Cor. 15:27   [5]1 Cor. 15:28

215

Give Away Your Gifts to One Another

"As each one of us has received a special gift, employ it in serving one another as good stewards of the manifold blessing of God." 1 Peter 4:10

Everything that God gives to us or does in our lives is meant to be recycled and given to others. Everyone who has a relationship with Jesus has been given at least one spiritual gift.[1] Your gifts are essential for the Body of Christ to function properly and should be used to the maximum.[2] There is a difference in gifts and talents, although both are given for the benefit of others. Talents are the result of genetics and training. They are given to people regardless of their beliefs. Spiritual gifts are endowed by the Holy Spirit to followers of Jesus.

There is much debate about how many spiritual gifts there are. Most are listed in Romans 12, 1 Corinthians 12, and Ephesians 4, but several others are scattered in other parts of Scripture. For instance, Paul says celibacy is a gift for certain people.[3] The most common are teaching, giving, faith, mercy, exhortation (encouragement) service, and wisdom. But there are gifts of prophesy, tongues, healing, administration, and others. Whether a gift or a talent, it is meant to be shared.

I have seen gifts wasted or used selfishly, but far more often, I have seen people use their gifts in ways that have literally brought me to my knees. During my mother's last hours on earth, she was cared for by a young woman from Hospice. She had a beautiful voice and during my mother's last moments, she asked her to sing song after song, mostly hymns. My mother literally died with a smile on her face. I flew immediately down to Charlotte from D.C. and the young woman waited almost four hours for me to arrive so she could sit with me and recount my mother's last hours. What a gift! That same day my friend, Jerry Leachman, helped me book my ticket, and to my surprise showed up in the seat beside me on the plane. He stayed with me until I was at my mother's house, greeted family members, then flew back to D.C. Those are gifts you never forget.

Whatever your gift or talent, its value is in its use for the benefit of others and the building up of the Body of Christ. Without your gift, we all suffer and with it, we are better and stronger.

---

[1] 1 Cor. 12:6–7   [2] Rom. 12:6–8   [3] 1 Cor. 7:7

Don't Slander One Another

"Brothers do not slander one another. Anyone who speaks against his brother or judges him, speaks against the law and judges it." James 4:11

Did you know that you can slander a brother or sister just by a look? A roll of the eyes, shaking of the head, or even a sarcastic chuckle is enough to put yourself in the position of judge and jury. Done in their presence, and especially in their *absence,* shows disregard for them as a person and is usually is based on faulty or spotty evidence. Whatever the case, slander or gossip is hurtful and divisive and has no place within the family of God. This is how the Psalmist puts it: "Whoever slanders his neighbor secretly I will destroy. Whoever has a haughty look and an arrogant heart I will not endure."[1] All through the Scriptures, it is evident that God hates slander, malice, and gossip!

What if someone commits a sin against a person you know. Let's say they confess their failure to God and ask forgiveness of those they have wronged. They never commit this sin again and try to go on with their life. But you decide that you want them to keep paying and you do everything possible to denigrate them to everyone you know. You have basically defined their entire life by this one careless act. All the good and positive things they have done and will do are being sublimated to a sin that happened ten, twenty or, thirty years ago. Whatever their sin was, it is forgiven by God and even those who were sinned against, but you have decided to bash them further and encourage others to do the same. I believe the Scripture teaches that this is anything but righteous indignation. The forgiven person will never again answer for that sin and the one who keeps it alive will stand before God and give account. He is looking God in the eye and saying His verdict is not satisfactory.

Slander and gossip are serious sins in the eyes of God. They may be more socially acceptable and minor in the eyes of the world, but they are a death-blow to the fabric of unity, and love of Jesus. Look at the "one another" passages we have been considering for the past two weeks … Love, bearing each other's burdens, serving, being devoted, comforting one another, etc. How can slander and gossip fit in this kind of family?

Confess Your Sins to One Another

"Therefore, confess your sins to one another and pray for one another that you may be healed. The prayer of a righteous man is powerful and effective."
James 5:16

The natural impulse that we all have when we sin is to cover it up. We may blame our mother or father, minimize it, or say it never happened, but those denials and excuses will not help us grow and heal. They keep us cowering in the shadows always wondering when someone will discover that which we have tried to keep hidden. This prevents us from prospering.[1]

We are constantly told that we should create an image or persona that will impress people. Branding has nothing whosoever to do with vulnerability and honesty. It is an attempt to connect you with an image of invulnerability and entitlement. Many people spend a lifetime building a portrait of themselves that their spouse and children would never recognize.

Confession is an agreement. It is concurring with God's diagnosis of sin. It is being vulnerable at the highest level … an unvarnished admission that we have missed the mark and need forgiveness. Failing to confess is disagreement with God concerning our offense. It puts a wall between God and us just as in a family. A child ignores the rules of your home. You know she is guilty, but she will not admit it. You still love her deeply, but your fellowship is damaged until a confession is made. Then you forgive and move on. God does the same.[2]

Why does James insist that we confess our sins to another person? (He is obviously not saying to everyone). I suggest a couple of primary reasons. It is relatively easy to confess to God because He knows anyway. When we humble ourselves, push aside the façade, and admit to a trusted friend or two that we have feet of clay just like everyone else, a great burden is lifted. We no longer have to pretend, and we have the opportunity to experience unconditional love from those whom we have honored with the truth. Additionally, confession to a trusted few creates a certain level of accountability. It alerts those few to watch your back and protect you at that point of weakness or vulnerability. Judgment must be put aside, and when that happens we become one in a deeper way than ever before.

---

[1]Prov. 28:13   [2]1 John 1:9

Extend Hospitality to One Another

"Be hospitable to one another without complaint. As each one has received a special gift, employ it in serving one another as good stewards of the manifold grace of God." 1 Peter 4:9–10

The hospitality of sharing food and lodging is a requirement in Jewish Law. Strangers and even enemies are to receive the same cordiality that is given to members of the household. All outsiders are considered sent by God, and therefore deserving every kindness. Welcoming others to a meal is considered a privilege from God while dining alone is a disappointment.

Imagine Mary, when she learned that she would bear a son, traveling to see Elizabeth in the hill country of Judea and staying three months. It would be a privilege, not an imposition.[1] Jesus does not speak directly about hospitality because it is a *given* in that culture. However, we see him affirm a prostitute for anointing His feet with oil and rebuking Simon, the Pharisee, for his lack of even offering the traditional basin and towel upon His arrival.[2]

I have seen believers build large ornate homes with every detail designed to impress. They would say the home belongs to the Lord and yet few are ever even invited in except family. A home is more than a comfortable place to reside and raise kids.

It is a place to enjoy the fellowship of friends; it is a unique opportunity to make those that enter feel loved and appreciated. Sadly, many homes are designed as a showplace ... a tribute to the tasteful elegance and financial success of its owners.

By contrast, we have very close friends in Atlanta who own a beautiful home, but everything in it reflects a welcoming spirit of comfort and care to everyone who enters. I have stayed there more nights than I can count and always leave a better person than when I entered. The focus is never the home or its owners, but on the guests. Beautiful antique silverware handed down from generations is used at every meal. My wife once asked why she used her priceless sterling silver place settings for regular daily meals. Her response was classic: "Lamb, who could ever be more special than anyone comes through this front door." This is true hospitality and it is to Robert and Nell Watt a simple expression of love and care ... a ministry of *open arms* to all who walk through its doors. Many who have entered this home could tell the same story.

---

[1] Luke 1:39–40   [2] Luke 7:36–50

Fellowship with One Another

"Beloved, let us love one another for love is from God and everyone who loves is born of God and knows God." 1 John 4:7

When Jewish people greet one another, they say "Shalom." It is much more than a simple greeting of *peace.* It literally means, *nothing missing, nothing broken.* It is a term of wholeness meant to reflect concern for the internal spiritual and relational welfare of the hearer. Our greetings seem very shallow by comparison ... *"How are you?" we ask, not really looking for an answer. What's up? Also requiring a mindless response,* or just" *Hey"* or *"Hi."* Shalom is much warmer and evokes a deep sense of fellowship.

Believers use the word "fellowship" for basically any get-together. We even build an attachment to the sanctuary and call it "Fellowship Hall." After all, how can you have fellowship without a hall to have it in? Jesus spends more than three years with twelve men on a virtual camping trip and I dare say the conversations were about things that really mattered. If you travel within the villages of the countries in Africa, you will see men squatting beside a fire, like baseball catchers, talking for hours. They don't speak of investments or the new car they bought, nor do they gossip and one-up each other. The talk will always be about family and relationships. They are miles ahead of the Western World in terms of a caring fellowship.

Who can you call at three in the morning and share your greatest pain or deepest hope? With whom have you developed a level of trust through the years that will love you enough to confront you about harmful behavior? Have you built and nurtured a growing relationship with a few friends that will go to the mat for each other? Real fellowship is not just chit-chat or watching the ballgame together with beer and chips. One man told me he had been in a Bible study for eleven years with a group and not once had anyone asked him about his relationship with his wife. He said, "I have been unhappily married for over twenty years." How can that happen? It's wonderful to laugh and have fun together, but at some point, we must enter each other's lives. At age fifty-nine, my uncle choked to death one night at a dinner party while everyone at the table laughed and drank never realizing until too late that it was a heart attack. For me, it is a very sorrowful but fitting image of the lack of awareness many of us have of the desperate unspoken cried all around us.

Encouraging our Children

"Train up a child in the way he should go; and when he is old, he will not depart from it." Proverbs 22:6 (KJV)

Good and loving parents unknowingly mislead their children by telling them something that sounds very positive, upbeat and deeply affirming, but will almost guarantee heartache in the long run. It goes something like this: "Honey, reach for the stars; there is nothing in life that you cannot achieve if you really want it bad enough. You can be anything you want to be." These positive, *can do* words may be a momentary adrenalin shot for the child, but it will hurt them eventually because you are in effect telling the child that they can control their own destiny. It is like saying. "If you really want something with all your heart, you can have it whether God wants it for you or not."

For me to tell a 160-pound high school football player that his dream of being a linebacker in the NFL is just a matter of wanting it badly enough is guaranteed disappointment. Sure, we can point to Abe Lincoln becoming President without even a high school diploma, or Spud Webb who played in the NBA at five foot six, but these are one in a million. Wouldn't it be more positive and loving to help the child identify his gifts and talents and look at his dreams in light of how God had made him?

In the Proverbs passage above, it appears to be a direct command and if obeyed, is an absolute promise. Parents often suffer great guilt and remorse when, after gallant and consistent efforts to read the right books and teach the right things, the child still goes into the *far country*, sometimes never to return. But Proverbs is a book of general truths and not necessarily meant as cookie-cutter commands with absolute promises. They are not like a recipe for perfect pancakes.

The Hebrew rendering is "train up a child in *his own* skin."

The phrase is a Hebrew idiom referring to a child's specific personality and singular traits. The "way," therefore, does not refer to an exact path of whatever child-rearing book you read, but to the specific characteristics of each child. As parents, we study our children, learn their gifts, proclivities and natural talents, and then build God's principles into their uniqueness.

Truth is never negotiable, but the application of truth can take different forms in different people. Adolf Hitler, in his youth, was a very gifted painter. What if he had been encouraged to develop that gift and share it with the world rather than what he did? Why not encourage that which will lead to the thriving of a child's natural and spiritual gifts?

There's No One You Can't Learn From

"But we were gentle among you like a nursing mother taking care of her own children." 1 Thessalonians 2:7 (ESV)

If you sit quietly beside a stream or take a long walk down a dirt road, you will often receive a thought from God that has been patiently waiting to be heard. If you listen carefully, He may walk you back through decisions you have made that have brought you to the place in life where you now reside.

Decisions we make do take us along circuitous roads and over troublesome waters as well as cherished memories of the best of times. But I have found that the relationships I have developed along the way, have sculpted much of my life. God seems to have initiated learning experiences, both good and bad from the people I have encountered. I have found that I can learn from every person I meet regardless of their pedigree or the lack thereof. The homeless guy on the street that I buy a hamburger for and talk with on the park bench, has something to teach me. The janitor who mops the floors and cleans the bathrooms tells me how thankful he is to have a job that allows him to provide for his family. His gratefulness challenges me. The multi-millionaire who tearfully tells me he would give it all up just to have his estranged son give him a hug. This engenders a grateful heart for the closeness I enjoy with my three sons. Every encounter we have in life is either an affirmation, a caution, a rebuke, or an education that Harvard cannot give.

God is intensely interested in the relationships that we have and how they are nurtured. I know this because there are somewhere around sixty Scriptures in the New Testament that speak to the matter of how we treat "one another." The most prominent and repeated "one another" is the *action* of loving one another. Love is a verb that is not passive; it is not a feeling that comes and goes; it is *willing the best for another.* It's not an *air kiss at a cocktail party* kind of love, but one that is willing to risk entering the dark and painful recesses of another's life.

God uses relationships to help sculpt and refine our lives. Sometimes little more than a simple word of kindness, an understanding nod, or a compassionate touch at the right time can change everything.

We often look for the great theological nugget that will be our breakthrough, but most of them come in the simplest of ways from those who we would never expect. In the next couple of weeks, I want to remind us of some well-known "one another" passages that can help knit us together.

Things that Are Non-Negotiable

"What we have seen and heard we proclaim to you also, so that you too may have fellowship with us; and indeed, our fellowship is with the Father and His Son, Jesus."
1 John 1:3

Have you ever wondered why the early disciples in the first century had such a powerful influence? They faced Jews who still hated Jesus, and to the west, the Greek and Roman world largely worshipped pagan deities. At every turn, their message of redemption was opposed and resented. They were sometimes beaten, put in prisons, and constantly ridiculed and humiliated. The platitudes and religious clichés of today wouldn't do. They had to be real and have a message with power behind it. It also had to be demonstrated in the disciple's lives.[1]

Often, when I hear someone deliver a message, I wonder if the truth they speak is from their own experience or something they read or heard in a talk. We have all been guilty of hearing something we feel is profound and passing it along without critiquing it against Scripture and testing it out. I spent the first few years after coming to Christ exporting biblical ideas I had heard but weren't a reality in my own life. I wanted to learn so I absorbed everything I could, but I didn't *own* it. It was years before I began to speak from a place of intimate knowledge.

John says the words he and his brothers proclaim is not simply warmed-over ideas from a book or a sermon. They spoke what they knew for certain. It was not mere words, but an internal reality being built inside of them. Their message had power because it was true, tested, and real. It rang with the authority and power of the Holy Spirit and people listened and responded.

If you could ask the Samaritan woman to speak at your church, she would tell about that day when Jesus sat beside her at the well, asked for a drink of water and all that resulted from those moments with Him.[2] If you asked Nicodemus, he would tell how he nervously came by night to ask questions of Jesus and how that led to his conversion and which came at a great personal cost.[3] Those who encountered Jesus would tell their story because that is what "they had seen and heard."

What do you know for certain? What is non-negotiable in your life? Write it down and share that. God will bless it and it will have power and impact. Study and learn, but speak what you know … what you own, and it will be heard. When you do, God will give you more truth to stand on. Speak of what you know for sure.

---

[1] 1 Thess. 1:5   [2] John 4:7–38   [3] John 3:1–21

Desperate Efforts to Be in Control

"Remember the former things long past, for I am God and there is no other;
I am God and there is no one like Me. Declaring the end from the beginning, and
from ancient times things which have not been done, saying My purpose will be
established, and I will accomplish my good pleasure.'" Isaiah 46:9–10

It doesn't matter what gender, nationality, ethnic group, or social status you occupy; you want to be in control. You want to control your spouse, your children's choices, your style of life, and even your destiny. Control is the gold ring!

But consider the things you have no power to control ... your birth, your parents, your gender, the color of your eyes, and whether you will even be alive for the next five minutes. We try desperately to manipulate circumstances that we feel will determine the outcome that we want. Genetic engineers are madly seeking to control a baby's gender and even manipulate genes to the point where a prospective parent can choose movie star looks, great athletic prowess or an operatic voice. So, the great race is on to become God ... Master of the Universe. If you think this is far-fetched, you haven't seen anything yet.

God speaks through Isaiah saying, *just in case you are thinking you can be Me ... remember, I am God and you will never be Me. I was here in the beginning and I will be here in the end, and my purpose will be established regardless of your plans.* Have you ever wondered what God sounds like when He laughs? Just tell Him what all your plans are!

Just look around at the atrocities in God's world that we have caused by seeking control ... concentration camps, slavery, sex trafficking, chemical euphoria, the build-up of nuclear arms, greed, and oppression. On and on it goes; all are attempts for us to get what we want by control. Yet God upholds the world by the word of His power with a loving heart full of grace and truth.[1]

One reason why people resist giving their life to Christ is the fear of losing control. The truth is, you lost that the moment you were conceived. You're not in control of anything! You can't guarantee the lights will come on when you flip the switch. You can't be absolutely certain the floor will hold you when you walk in your house, or that the car will stop when you hit the brakes. What's really in that box of cornflakes? You're at the mercy of the people at the Kellogg factory. It's all a crapshoot unless you yield yourself to the One who controls time, space and eternity.

---

[1] Heb. 1:3

Recruit or Send?

Some years ago, I was asked by a college in New York City to develop a student initiative to get top-level International students to come there to study They had internationals attending but could not get them to return to their home after graduation and apply the things they learned. I felt that recruiting them was not the way to go. Instead, why not go to the natural leadership of different countries, pitch the value of the College's curriculum and great professors to them and have them nominate and send students to the school. That way the country's leaders would have a vested interest in a student's progress, stay in touch, and offer a path of opportunity to come back home and ply their trade.

In the Scripture, this is the kind of thing you see. Paul sends Timothy to Corinth, to Thessalonica, and the Philippi to work with the people and be available to them.[1] Paul would often ask them to accept Timothy just as they would accept him. It's a fantastic model. The fellowship of men and woman that I have worked with for over forty years think that way. You can't be everywhere and the community of believers in cities all over the world need encouragement. Why not send a like-minded friend to spend a few days with those you care about?

I have three sons. I never felt that I Susan and I could raise them by ourselves. We wanted them to gain insights and perspective from close fronds whom we trusted. They had gifts and experiences that we didn't have. We often did the same with the children of our friends. We had people live in our home for many years. They helped our kids as much as we did.

We live in a very unilateral culture where we are expected to call all the shots and close every deal. They did it differently in the first century. They sent trusted friends to sit at the feet of those of whom they had great respect for.

My oldest son, Josh, is a college professor. As I write this, he, Anna and their four children have recently arrived in the Czech Republic where he will teach in a University in Prague for two years. In Nashville, he has linked arms with a group of men that have been together now for many years to encourage spiritual growth. They have walked with him and his family every step of the way. They have the idea that they and others are sending Josh and Anna to Prague and that their family will give themselves to care for the city on behalf of the whole group. Most of us just decide what we will do and then tell everyone. Josh wanted the decision to be in accord with not only his wife and children but with these brothers and their church. They were sent. That is a biblical way of thinking!

---

[1] 1 Cor. 4:17; 1 Thess. 3:2; Phil. 2:19

Practical Idolatry

"Of what value is an idol carved by a craftsman? Or an image that teaches lies? For the one who makes it trusts in his own creation; he makes idols that cannot speak." Habakkuk 2:18 (NIV)

If you ask people which of the 10 commandments are the most violated, they will generally say, lying, coveting, theft, and taking God's name in vain. Seldom does idolatry even get into the top eight. How many people do you know who carve idols in their spare time for their personal worship?

What is idolatry? A simple definition is *when we take temporal things and treat them as ultimate things.* If we really looked at it seriously, idolatry would top the list of the most violated of God's commandments. Anything that we hold to be of ultimate value and act in the light of it. We all know that money is often an idol; a girlfriend or boyfriend can have inordinate prominence in our life; a house, a boat, a sport, a career; all these things qualify. There is nothing wrong with any of them in and of themselves, but when they begin to dominate our thoughts and priorities, they can occupy the place that was intended for God.

Have you ever wondered why the Great Commandment is so total ... so comprehensive? Love God with *all* your heart, *all* your mind, *all* your strength.[1] How can you give God *all* of your love? What about other people and the dreams and goals you have that occupy such a prominent place in your life? Idolatry places them before your love for God. But we don't want *that*, so we seek to maintain their importance and love God as well. It won't work. God wants *all* your love. If you give it *all* to Him, He will do as He did when He fed the 5,000 with five loaves and two fish. He didn't try to give a crumb to everyone; He took the little boy's lunch, blessed it, fed everyone and they ate until they were satisfied. There were even with twelve baskets leftover.

When you give all your love to Him, He purifies it, gives it back to you so that you have enough love for everyone you will ever meet. And those things like career, athletics, money, and ambition will begin to take an appropriate place in your life. When temporal, transient things become ultimate things, this is idolatry. God demands all our love because He deserves it. He will multiply that which is given to Him and return it. Love for anything that begins and ends with you, rather than with God *through* you, is like giving someone a stale donut.

---

[1] Matt. 22:36–40

You Want Me to Go Where?

Have you ever disliked someone so intensely that you would honestly be a little disappointed if you heard they had completely changed and were now following Jesus? What if Charles Manson or Osama Bin Laden had trusted Jesus before they died and were now in heaven? Would you be glad or be a little disgusted? Something in us demands justice for others who have lived atrocious lives and we feel that their redemption would have allowed them to live a perverted life and still go to heaven. This is the issue for the Prophet Jonah in the book of Jonah. We know his story from childhood, but there is a side road we should travel that can help us learn from his mistakes.

Jonah was a prophet who lived during the reign of Jeroboam II, the Northern Kingdom's most powerful King. One day God spoke to Jonah and gave him a mission to go to Nineveh, the capital city of Assyria five hundred miles to the east. He was to tell the people there they must repent of their evil ways and turn to the Lord. It was not an unusual assignment for a prophet, but Jonah knew two things with which he could not make peace. He knew that because of Israel's continual rebellion, Amos and Hosea had both prophesied that God was going to use the Assyrians as an instrument of punishment against Israel, his people.[1] Any loyal Jew would have been horrified at the thought. But to Jonah, it was even more egregious because the Northern Kingdom was his

homeland, and he would be preaching God's salvation to the Ninevites who would, in 722 BC invade Samaria, kill his kinsmen and take thousands of hostages.

So, Jonah takes off; he boards a ship and goes in the opposite direction fleeing from God.[2] A deadly storm ensues, and the crew believes God's anger has been aroused. Awakened from his sleep below deck, he comes up and confesses that the storm is because of his disobedience to God and that their only hope is to get rid of him. They oblige by tossing him into the raging sea and God sends a great fish who swallows him. Jonah stays in the fish's belly for 3 days and 3 nights until he is finally vomited up on shore.

Jonah does finally go to Nineveh and many repent, including the King. They even made restitution to all who they had wronged. But Jonah was not happy for them, he was dejected. He even wanted to die. What if God told you to leave the comforts of your home and go to the most despicable people you know and tell them of God's love. What if you knew these people in a few years would start World War III and invade America, killing friends and family that you dearly love?

This is the dilemma Jonah faced. God loves all people; He even loves those we despise and against whom we harbor resentment. Do you love and have concern for all the people God cares about or do you pick and choose?

---

[1] Amos 5:27; Hosea 11:5   [2] Jonah 1:3

Eyes on the Street

"Be of sober spirit, be on the alert. Your adversary, the devil prowls around like a roaring lion seeking someone to devour." 1 Peter 5:8–11

In the 1960s when concerns about crime in the urban cities of America was at its peak, a phrase was coined, *Eyes on the Street*. It was a plea to neighborhoods in the inter-city to take the blinders off, go off *cruise control* and become the eyes and ears of police to help stop crime. It wasn't enough, but it was a start.

We spend much of our life on *cruise control*. We become so accustomed to things we see, hear and do that we become oblivious to what's going on around us. "How are y'all doing'? She says to an acquaintance at the grocery store, "We're fine; how are you and Bob doing?" ... "Just fine; we'd love to have you over for dinner." That'd be great, "Well, take care." ... "You too" That is southern cruise control. We do it every day; we speak without communicating, look without seeing, and hear without listening, and we would croak if they actually showed up. Bless their hearts!

We pray the Lord's Prayer with no conscious thought about it. We ask the blessing at meals because we have been taught to. We have become so numb to the things around us that they become invisible. A friend of mine visited a family in Atlanta for two days and shaved off half his mustache the first night before bed. They had breakfast and spent hours talking and the half mustache was not detected until he pointed it out. Cruise control!

Peter, in this passage, warns us that we cannot live a life with Jesus Christ and do it without staying alert. There is an enemy out there who is like a roaring lion looking for someone to destroy. A prowling lion is a predator! It's not a joke. We have turned a real, personality in the universe, into a cartoon character in a red jumpsuit with a pitchfork. That is exactly the way he wants us to see him. We put our lives on cruise control and miss all the road signs. Maybe Peter, as he writes this is remembering being told to stay alert and watch and pray as Jesus spent those last hours with His Father in Gethsemane. Maybe Peter remembers how he and the others fell asleep three times and what it cost him.

Our adversary, Satan is subtle. He doesn't advertise; he doesn't call ahead and say he's coming. He does everything the opposite of what you would expect. We don't need to be paranoid, but we must know his strategies and know how to stand firm. He is powerful, but ... "Greater is He that is in you than he who is in the world."[1] Keep your eyes on the street!

---

[1] John 4:4

Passing Along Spiritual Disciplines

After spending most the first decade of my adult life on a treadmill of "you must, you should" rules and laws, I was introduced to grace. I had read about it and thought I understood it, but I had no clue as to how it worked in a person's life. I was an athlete and I had learned that you could fix any deficiency with practice and sheer determination. If I was having trouble with my timing on a post pattern, I asked my receivers to work with me after practice. I did it until the ball started going where I wanted it to go. I thought this discipline would translate into my walk with Jesus. If I had lustful thoughts, I made rules for myself, but before long I was worse off than when I started. When I was erratic with quiet times, I asked a friend to call me every morning before he went to work and ask if I had done it. Sometimes, I went just through the motions so he wouldn't bless me out.

I lived this way for several years. I practiced it, like pumping weights, but to no avail. I have never been comfortable with what is called *spiritual disciplines*. They resonated with the early church fathers as a foundational aid to living a Christian life. They vary in number from twelve to eighteen, depending on the source, but the term spiritual discipline, nor the list, is in the Scriptures. I believe in the

principles, just not the way they are stated. Life in Christ is a free-flowing intimate friendship. It involves disciplines, but the moment you present a list of *disciplines*, you are talking about a system that overrides the relationship rather than springing *from* the relationship. Calling them *disciplines* conjures up all my failed attempts to create godliness by guts and determination. It is a religious term, not a relational term.

When you consider prayer, study, fellowship, and worship as *disciplines*, it feels like law again. Certainly, issues like fasting, solitude, meditation, and even confession require discipline. But, I believe these efforts to grow come less from *practice and diligence* than by seeking an atmosphere where they can be seen flowing through people. My love for the Scriptures came not by trying harder, but by seeing the confidence and wisdom it created in godly people. I saw the way their eyes lit up as he spoke of God's Word and I wanted it too.

Paul said, "Follow me as follow Christ."[1] We say, "Don't do as I do; do as I say." But had you hung out with Paul; his spiritual DNA would be all over you. You'd see how he lived and loved, and you'd want it too. In the next 5 days, let's look at a few principles that I have not already addressed in another context.

---

[1] 1 Cor. 11:1

Prayer and Bible Study

What would you think about someone who never studied the Bible and who never prayed? These are the basic pillars of knowing God. How could someone have the audacity to say they were believers and never open a Bible or talked to God? Well, meet the twelve apostles of Jesus. They possessed no Bible during their entire lifetime. The New Testament was in the process of being written and the Tanakh, or Old Testament Scriptures were kept in the Temple and not available for private consumption.

The disciples never prayed in terms of prayer as we know it. They had learned from the Pharisees who recited very ornate, flowery prayers designed to impress. They had no sense of being able to approach God in a personal manner as a Father well into a year and a half of their sojourn with Jesus. We know this because as they followed Him before sunrise one morning and observed the intimacy with which he addressed the Father.[1] They finally made the connection between the character, wisdom, and compassion of their Rabbi and the personal times He was alone with His Father. It was this reality that prompted them to say, "Lord, teach us to pray."[2] In essence, they were saying, *"Lord we have noticed your intimacy with God, and we know that it has something to do with the time you spend alone with Him each morning. We want that! Will you teach us to pray so we can be like you?"* The same thing happened with his wisdom and insight. They knew it came from the Scriptures.

This is the answer to the question all of us have about motivating our children or someone we are discipling. How do I get them to pray and read the Scriptures and other important materials that will help them grow? What will motivate them? Some try intimidation ... some use fear, and others use Law. I know a woman who gave her children a dollar for every verse they memorized. But, how did Jesus get His men to pray? He just kept doing it Himself! We have not one record of Jesus ever lecturing his men about praying or knowing the Scripture. Not a word! He thought and answered everything by the Word, and He knew that the Spirit of God would, at some point, put it together for them. I cringe when I think of times I worked so hard to get others to study or pray, then suddenly realize I was so busy trying to convince them, I wasn't even doing it myself.

There is a world of difference in a child being told he should pray and read the Bible verses the child seeing you do it yourself humbly and without fanfare. One day they will ask, and their curiosity and the example you have set will never be forgotten.

---

[1]Mark 1:36–36   [2]Luke 11:1–4

Solitude

"Jesus went out to a mountainside to pray and spent the night praying to God. When morning came, he called his disciples to him." Luke 6:12–13 (NIV)

Blaise Pascal died at the age of thirty-nine. He was a man of deep faith and is responsible for much of our basic understanding and development of Physics and the laws of probability. Before he died, he pulled together fragments of his private thoughts that were later published in a book called *Pensée's*. One of his thoughts is, "All of man's misfortune comes from one thing, which is not knowing how to sit quietly in a room." He asserts that we fear the silence of existence and we dread boredom. Therefore, we choose aimless distractions and run from the problems of our emotions into false comforts we have created.

Solitude is not easy for most of us. Pascal wrote these thoughts over 350 years ago and yet they are even more relevant now than when he wrote them. Twenty-first-century people have no clue how to be alone and most have no desire. There are too many texts to answer, tweets to make, and games to play. There are too many songs to hear, videos to watch and apps to download. Solitude involves no phone or electronics … in fact, no distractions at all. Many of us would claim we don't have the time. Others would worry about boredom and a host of other excuses.

Socrates said, "the unexamined life is not worth living." I would agree, but also add that *a life that was never really lived is not worth examining.* The most fascinating people I've met are those who take uninterrupted time to think, to pray and re-examine their relationships, their attitudes and decisions. Depth and character come from time alone with God in a private place.

We live in a climate of massive change, astounding innovation, unlimited possibilities. We are stressed out, terminally busy, and unsure about the future. Our leadership is fractured, and the political alienation has bubbled over into the private sector. Amid this turmoil, there has never been a time when quiet and thoughtful self-examination is more needed.

Our idea of heaven would be something like Hawaii or Tahiti, but God seems to love the desert. His people are desert people. There they must live in complete dependence on Him. In the desert, they hear His voice when He speaks, and they know His thoughts. Solitude creates this kind of atmosphere.

Don't allow the clamor of obligations and allure of what's around the next corner to cause you to miss the desert moments of quiet in a secret place.

Simplicity

"And make it your ambition to lead a quiet life and attend to your own business and work with your hands, just as we commanded you." 1 Thessalonians 4:11 (NIV)

"It's complicated," he said when I asked him about how he and his fiancée were doing. It was the same answer I received the week before by another guy who failed to show up for a lunch appointment. Complicated? How can being in love with your fiancé and having lunch with someone be complicated? It's the *go-to* answer for every relationship that is broken, every sin that is committed, and every life that is out of sync. It is the answer we give so we won't have to explain the underlying problem and it means absolutely nothing. It's the modern version of "it's none of your business and you wouldn't understand anyway."

God created us and gave us everything necessary for a life of joy and fulfillment. He certainly hasn't complicated it. He didn't pollute the air and water; it wasn't He who was never satisfied with the created order. He didn't stimulate animosity between nations, races, friends, and spouses. In fact, it was He who showed us how to live in harmony, love, and contentment.

Why does marriage become so complicated? It wasn't that way when we were dating. It only became complicated when other factors entered that don't belong there; a third party, a hidden expectation, a selfish desire, an unforgiving heart. These and more are factors that complicate a union that is based on two simple promises: to *love* and be *faithful* to one another.

To speak of simplicity in the complicated, overindulged society we have created is like extolling the virtues of Nutri-System to the animal kingdom. Everyone says they were the happiest when they started out and lived in a tiny apartment and ate Raman Noodles. Why? Because they had nothing but God and each other. The people in the Penthouse down the street had everything *but* that. Life was simple because we had none of the *stuff* that everyone told us would uncomplicate our lives.

I don't believe the answer is to isolate, but I do feel that we must first clear out some of the clutter that dominates our time, our thoughts and our energy. We must draw some boundaries by deciding what is hindering us from maximizing our relationship with God and one another. Only a few things really matter in life and none of them have to do with gadgets. Ask God to give you the desire to take the emotional journey back to your beginnings.

Praise and Worship

"Let everything that has breath praise the Lord." Psalm 150:6

The most neglected part of being alone with God is the expression of worship and praise. The easiest thing we do is ask for things. Praise and adoration for who God is requires a much more intimate posture. I have struggled with this through much of my adult life. I have learned from friends along the way and am much more at peace with this now, but I wasted many years failing to understand that God wanted me to simply *sit in His lap.*

My church experience was basically non-existent growing up. After I met Jesus, I attended churches that were heavy on teaching but light on worship. What I was exposed to in the way of praise was the high drama, breathy praise songs that seemed to me more about the musicians than about God. It seemed like a show and I just couldn't get into it. I knew praise and worship were very important to God and I wanted to experience it. Gradually, Susan and I attended some very praise-oriented gatherings and were moved by what we experienced. More and more we began to see and experience authentic worship.

In the Book of Acts, we see one of the great values of praise and adoration. Peter and John had been brought

in for questioning. Peter gives a magnificent retort to their accusations. They again hit the street and tell the truth and are immediately commanded to cease preaching *in Jesus name.*[1] They return to the other disciples and report the Sanhedrin's threats. What did they do? Whine? Run and hide? They immediately begin to praise God in verse 24. They praise Him for His creation, for the power of His words through David, for the opposition that raged against them. Finally, five verses later they mention the threat of the Jewish leaders. They never ask God to take it away. They say, "Lord, *consider* their threats and enable your servants to speak your word with great boldness."[2] Why did they not seek protection? Why do they appear unafraid? Here is what praise does: Their first thought was to remind God and themselves of His power, His creative nature, and His track record throughout history. By the time they finished praising God, the threat of these authorities was *peanuts. It was nothing! Give us boldness to declare your truth anyway!* Praise reorients your mind and heart so that you realize Who is in charge and that opposition to Him is like a gnat on an elephant's back.

---

[1] Acts 4:18–20   [2] Acts 4:24

Superintendents of the Earth

"The earth is the Lord's, and everything in it, the world, and all who live in it."
Psalm 24:1 (NIV)

Who created the ground you stand upon? Why was it created? How will it be preserved? When God created the world, He gave the first man a charge to care for that which he had been given to richly enjoy.[1] Adam was to be superintendent of the earth; a steward who would maintain it in a manner befitting its creator. It was neither intended as a punishment or a suggestion.

If you gave a car to your son or daughter, you would probably relish the look on their face as they saw it. You might say something like, "I have only two demands: one is that you obey the law and two is that you take care of the car." It is an extremely generous gift, and for your kids to ignore your two requests would be blatant arrogance. It's pretty simple: God has given us time, which is irretrievable, a world with unlimited resources. With that he gave us the creative energy to use the raw materials He created to enhance our lives. He entrusts it into our care. If we abuse it, we will have to live with the consequences.

Generally, the only time you hear stewardship mentioned is on Stewardship Sunday regarding your pledge for the year. It was never meant as a duty, but a privilege and was designed by God for the benefit and blessing of the giver.[2] The Jews always paid for the maintenance of the Temple through a tax. Across Europe today a mandatory tax is taken from your paycheck for the State Church. As believers, everything we have belongs to God and we freely give back to Him as He has blessed us and touched our hearts.

We are stewards of our children also. They are not really ours; they belong to God and He allows us to nurture, instruct and encourage them until they are returned to Him. I am weary of every concern about the environment being tagged as liberal. If you are not passionate about the purity and beauty of the earth, air, and water that God created you don't understand the Scriptures and the heart of God. I know some of it is political and there is big money to be made there, but that's true of anything.

We are stewards of the earth and if ever anyone should be an environmentalist it should be those who love God. Read the parable of the Vineyard. A landowner entrusted his servants with its care and expected a good return on his investment.[3]

Everything we have is a trust given by God. What kind of return are you prepared to give back to God for His trust in you?

---

[1]Acts 20:35   [2]Ps. 127:3   [3]Matt. 21:33–46

The Fruit of the Spirit

"But the fruit of the Spirit is love, joy, peace, forbearance, kindness, goodness, faithfulness, gentleness, and self-control. Against such things, there is no law."
Galatians 5:22–23

As well as I can remember when I gave my life to Jesus I thought that was all there was to it. I did know that some things had to change, I just didn't realize the extent. I began to read in the gospels every day, attended a Bible study each week and my love for God began to increase. Still, I had no real notion that God wanted to create in me the visible results of His Spirit living within me. I was a couple of years into college before I heard about the fruit of the Spirit. I had been praying for God to give me more love, more patience, more gentleness, and self-control. I assumed that the fruit of the Spirit was something I had to produce rather than the Spirit producing those qualities in me.

As I grew, I realized that my prayers for self-control and patience were fruitless (pardon the pun). If I had the Holy Spirit in me, I had the fruit of the Spirit also. They came in together. The problem was that I was blocking the way. My attempts to produce what only God can produce was getting in the way and gumming up the works. I began to learn that I had to yield my impatience, my lack of self-control and my discontent to the Holy Spirit. As my awareness of these deficits in me surfaced, I began to listen first and then speak. I became aware of the hard edges in my life and over time became open to the kind of gentleness Jesus displayed.

It is a journey, and I have miles to go, but I do know now that it is not up to me. These characteristics can easily become a self-improvement program if we're not careful. To the degree that we step out of the way, God will release these characteristics of His Spirit in us.

If the fruit is allowed to grow in us, we will begin to reflect what Jesus is like to a hurting world. *The Fruit of the Spirit is the character of Jesus*. It is what you see of Him as you read the gospels. It is what the Jewish leaders recognized in Peter and John when they saw their boldness and knew that even as uneducated and untrained men, they had been with Jesus.[1] In the next nine days let's look briefly at the nine fruit of the Spirit.

---

[1]Acts 4:13

The Fruit of the Spirit is Love

"Dear friends, let us love one another, for love comes from God. Everyone who loves has been born of God and knows God. Whoever does not love does not know God, because God is love." 1 John 4:7–8 (NIV)

It is the cornerstone of every thought God thinks, everything God does, and every reason God does it. The Scripture says that *love* is God's definition of Himself.[1] So, Love is not simply a warm giddy feeling or a deeply felt sentiment; love is a *Person*. If God is Love and you and I hold Him at bay or shut Him out of our lives, how can we then give or receive real love? A Diva sings her newest hit on stage in front of millions and shouts "I love you" to her adoring fans. She doesn't know us, but she loves us. It's a nice thought but we know that it has more to do with her hope that we love *her* enough to help her music climb the charts.

No word in the English language is thrown around more carelessly than *love*. But at the same time, no word is so pregnant with meaning and substance when it comes from within the deepest part of us. Can someone experience and express the true essence of love without knowing God? They certainly can experience the intense emotion, the sense of well-being. But if God is love and when there is no connection with Him, how can the fullness of that Divine gift be known by that person. First Corinthians

Thirteen has become a *go-to* wedding passage over the years but is not only a pure definition of love but a pure description of Jesus. The bottom line of this chapter is that no matter how gifted, spiritually-minded, generous, or sacrificial a person is capable of being if he does not possess love, he is a lot of noise. Paul then goes on to express the character of love which is found in Jesus.

Love is inexorably woven within the fabric of the Father, the Son, and the Holy Spirit. Without God's dramatic demonstration of love through His Son, the world knows nothing of love except for the emotional by-products that come from an "electric" feeling. This is why love is the fruit of the Spirit and comes with the Spirit when He enters the human heart. I believe that mankind can experience a *shadow* or *a faint reflection* of love. But to expect the Author of love to fully bestow that fruit on those who want only the gift without the Giver would violate His own character.

Imagine the depth of the love of a Father and a Son in full agreement that the cross was the only hope for you and me. Imagine that same love transferred into the heart all who believe.

---

[1] 1 John 4:8, 16

The Fruit of the Spirit is Joy

"But the angel said to them, 'Do not be afraid; for behold, I bring you good news of great joy which will be for all the people." Luke 2:10

Joy is not a word I ever used as a kid and for that matter, a word I ever heard used except at Christmas. It didn't seem like a very manly word and I can't imagine telling my teammates about the *joy it gave me to complete a pass or hit a line drive!* I'm not sure I ever even thought about the word until I was in my late twenties. I have always been an upbeat, easy-going person; I love to laugh and play practical jokes, so I suppose I considered that kind of happiness as one and the same with joy. It was when I finally took a serious look at this encounter of the Angel and the shepherds that I discovered it was far more than a sweet story we read to the children on Christmas Eve.

Happiness is a word we use in time of great euphoria, but as we all discover, it can flip in the opposite direction without warning and with even greater force. A pay raise, a good grade on an exam, or a new car can produce a level of happiness, but it always fades into a distant memory as time goes by. Happiness can be produced temporarily by a positive result. Joy is an internal endowment that builds and nurtures the soul. Happiness depends on circumstances, good or bad. Joy is the *fruit* that overrides circumstances and becomes an internal reality.

The Jewish shepherds in the fields were and are today traditionally eleven to thirteen-year-old kids, both male and female. For the Angel Gabriel to speak of "good news of a great joy" was an announcement second to none in human history. The "good news," of course was that the long-awaited Messiah had finally come and the "great joy" was that the solution to mankind's unsolvable problem of sin was at hand. And the best news to these lowly, marginalized shepherds was the words, "for all people." As lowly outcasts, invisible to the world, they were finally included and given a place at the table!

The joy introduced on that hillside is the same joy that comes with the Holy Spirit when He enters the life of a believer. His presence must be nurtured by trust and obedience. When it is, it will override and outdistance any affliction and negative circumstance. This is the beauty of joy; it cannot be overcome by bad news.

The Fruit of the Spirit is Peace

"May the God of hope fill you with all joy and peace as you trust in him, so that you may overflow with hope by the power of the Holy Spirit." Romans 15:13 (NIV)

While digging around in your attic, you uncover an oddly shaped container. To your amazement, a genie appears and gives you one wish. Most would probably ask to win the Mega Lottery. Others might wish for perfect health or fame and celebrity, but peace would probably not make the top ten. I find that fascinating because if we possess complete peace, we would also possess contentment. We wouldn't care if we won the lottery or if we were well known or anonymous, and peace would even override poor health. Peace eliminates longing for all the things we don't have and celebrates all that we have been given.[1] On the other side, stress and anxiety come from fear, guilt, and dissatisfaction. So, we seek temporary relief through pills, alcohol, sex, and numerous forms of entertainment.

After Jesus was crucified, the disciples scattered like a covey of quail and later huddled together in fear with every knock at the door. Jesus appears to them and each time He greets them with "peace be with you."[2] They didn't care about money, their golf handicap, or a house in the country; they had lost their Rabbi, their friend, their Lord and feared that death was moments away.

For a believer, peace is not something that comes from somewhere else. The fruit of the Spirit came within you when the Holy Spirit came. What activates the peace Jesus left with all His disciples? I want to suggest a few things that I am seeking to learn. First, complete trust that God is in control and that whatever the cutting edge in your life is, it doesn't depend on you. Secondly, is there any sense of guilt that exists in me that I have not confessed and released? Guilt always trains you to allow the mistakes of the past to hamper the fruit of the Spirit that resides in you. Finally, have you accepted any definition of who you are other than God's definition? Who you are in Christ is not about your behavior ... bad or good. Your identity is about your value to God as a person. Peace will never be available without truth.

You don't need a Genie. Get alone, breathe deeply and spend quiet moments expecting God presence. Ask God to release the Spirit of peace within you. Do it regularly.

---

[1]Phil. 4:12 [2]John 20:19

The Fruit of the Spirit is Patience

"The end of a matter is better than its beginning, and patience is better than pride."
Ecclesiastes 7:8 (NIV)

We usually plead for patience when our spouse goes off on us and we are trying not to be defensive. Most of the time we want patience because we are fighting the tide of immediate gratification that permeates our culture. When is this *great* stock I purchased going to finally get moving? When are these golf lessons going to kick in and why is God taking so long to answer my prayers?

Tolstoy said, "The two most powerful warriors are patience and time." Almost three thousand years prior, Solomon mused that the end of a matter is better than the beginning. What causes that is time and patience. The best wine is that which is aged over time. Jesus, in His first miracle at Cana, compressed time and not only turned brackish water into wine but into superbly aged wine. That is what we all want. We want a level of quality immediately that can only develop over time. Patience means learning the value of *waiting*. Growing up, I wanted everything immediately. I want to throw a football more accurately, hit a baseball farther, and shoot a basketball better than anyone. "You've got to be patient; it takes time to develop your skills," I was told. They said that about everything! I felt at times like I was spending my whole life just waiting.

One day I read what the writer of Hebrews said about laying aside every weight that could hinder us and run the race that is before us.[1] Later, I read those who *wait* on the Lord will renew their strength and fly like eagles and the endurance they build will not let them become tired and quit.[2] I began to realize that learning to wait patiently is the thing that reveals our faith in God's timing. The Old Testament prophets were astounding in their determination to be patient even in the worst of difficulties. Job demonstrated patience in the face of horrific tragedy.[3] His loss was so great and his faithfulness so strong that I have a hard time even relating to him.

I have learned that trials are God's way to perfect our patience. Jesus is our great model. "Who for the joy set before Him, He endured the cross."[4] He knew what was coming. He endured literal hell patiently waiting because He was able to look past the pain and see only the joy that would be His when His work on earth was completed.

---

[1]Heb. 12:1   [2]Isa. 40:31   [3]James 5:11   [4]Heb. 12:2

The Fruit of the Spirit is Kindness

"'Though the mountains be shaken and the hills be removed, yet my unfailing love for you will not be shaken nor my covenant of peace be removed,' says the Lord, who has compassion on you.'" Isaiah 54:10 (NIV)

Kindness is another attribute that I seldom considered growing up. It wasn't something my coaches would emphasize in practice or before a game. Kindness was your grandmother and the "Good Fairy." Being a recipient of kindness from many people over the years was something that I was late in recognizing. As an adult, I have become eternally grateful for these kindnesses that I had overlooked. I was of a generation where we were taught to be tough, unemotional, and walk with a big stick. Today I have a keen dislike for the macho, tough-guy persona. It has nothing to do with giftedness or ability and everything to do with false image and values. Real winners don't have to sell themselves beat their chest like that.

As I have grown older, being kind to people has become one of my greatest desires. It is not a "woman thing," as I once thought; it is an attribute echoed throughout the Scripture. It wasn't only love that initiated God's determination to pursue mankind and bring Him home; it was the kindness of His nature.

When I first met Jesus the Young Life Leader, Mal McSwain, gave me a little booklet to read called "Quiet Time." What I remember most was the statement that went like this: *It is one thing that the Creator of the Universe would allow a mere man to spend personal time with Him, but quite another that He deeply desires that kind of intimacy.* The kindness of God is in His anticipation of sitting alone with you and me. His love is what makes that kind of relationship possible and His kindness is that He longs for it.

When I see a random act of kindness on the street, I am touched and challenged. Once, my wife once returned from the grocery store in a terrible snow blizzard. She brought a strange man with her whose car had been disabled and was on the side of the road. She fed him and gave him a bed for the night. I was moved and my love for her increased by that single act. I would take kindheartedness over talent and giftedness any day. A kind person exudes grace and compassion and will build bridges rather than walls. The journey is as important as the end result.

It is always the simplest things that make the biggest difference ... letting a car enter from a side street, courtesy and a caring smile to the person behind the counter. Kindness shows the heart of God. It is a supreme act that says to someone, "You have great value to God and therefore to me."

The Fruit of the Spirit is Goodness

"Remember, Lord, your great mercy and love, for they are from of old. Do not remember the sins of my youth and my rebellious ways; according to your love remember me, for you, Lord, are good." Psalm 25:6–7 (NIV)

A young Pharisee came to Jesus one day and asked a question that, as a student of the Law, he would have already known. "Good Teacher, what must I do to inherit eternal life?"[1] We know from the other accounts that this young man was rich, which in Pharisaic teaching kept him in God's favor. We also know that he was young, had a position of leadership and was very religious. And yet, despite appearing to have it all, Mark's gospel says that he wasn't there to trick or embarrass Jesus. The man "knelt at Jesus' feet, a sign of great respect."[2] He asks Jesus a question was given a common Rabbinic response. "Why do you call me good? Only God is good." In other words, *if you are willing to say that I am good are you also willing to say that I am God?* There seems to have been a realization in the man that though he appeared to have it made, he knew there was a hole in his heart.

What is real goodness? The Scripture says, "all of our goodness (thinks that are self-produced) is like filthy rags before the Lord."[3] Paul says that *no one is good ... not even one!*[4] I have met many wonderful people from all over the world ... winsome people, kind and caring, but I have learned that a person's self-initiated goodness can be the very obstacle that is blocking true fellowship with God? If you are a good person, why do you need God? Jesus tells us: No one is good except God ... therefore any goodness that is self-propelled is but a nice gesture. The money you gave the ministry or the old lady you gave up your seat to on the subway will be appreciated, but God sees it as a substitute for knowing Him. When it is initiated by and through Him, your goodness will be of a different sort ... lasting and redemptive.

We want our children and grandchildren to be good so we teach them right from wrong, but it can't be simply keeping the rules. Good moral behavior is not enough. It is the character built inside a person by the Holy Spirit and not by anything we can produce.[5] Teach your children who Jesus is and how He thinks, and they will radiate the goodness of God effortlessly. It is an endowment by and from God through you to the world.

---

[1]Matt. 18:18–30   [2]Mark 10:17   [3]Isa. 64:6   [4]Rom. 3:20   [5]2 Pet. 1:3

The Fruit of the Spirit is Faithfulness

"Many claim to have unfailing love, but a faithful person who can find?"
Proverbs 20:6 (NIV)

This is one of the most endearing by-products of the Holy Spirit's energizing life in us. Every day, promises are made and seldom kept. Years ago I came to the place that when someone told me they would do this or that, I always made a secondary plan because I knew the chances were great that they would not do as they promised. They were, I'm sure well-intentioned, but not faithful.

Few things create greater security in a relationship than someone who you can count on. If they say they will do something it is as good as done. The opposite creates the greatest insecurity in the relationship. In the parable of the talents, Jesus tells of a wealthy *Lord* who leaves three assistants in charge of taking care of his money while he is away. These guys knew the character and values of their *Lord* and the first two invest and trade, accordingly, making a hundred percent profit for him. The third was driven by fear, which led him to bury the money and make sure he didn't lose it. The *Lord* returns and to the first two, he says, "Well done, good and faithful servant! You have been faithful with a few things; I will put you in charge of many things. Come and share your master's happiness." Is there any believer who doesn't want to hear these words when they stand before God one day? The third is scolded and punished. He could not be trusted.[1]

This is not complicated, but it is inconvenient. It means that *come hell or high water* you will honor what you have said even if it costs you dearly. In the emotion of the moment, it is easy to be the hero who boldly says, "Just leave it to me," but often the boldest of promises become broken promises. Unfaithfulness can label you forever. It cannot be done by a personal desire to ingratiate yourself to someone. This is why faithfulness must be generated continually by the Spirit of God. Get out of the way; put personal agendas aside and be led by the Spirit. Never make promises unless you will see them through, regardless of the personal cost to you. If you are faithful, God will always entrust more responsibility to you down the road. *"Many claim to have unfailing love, but a faithful person who can find?"*

---

[1]Matt. 25:21, 23

The Fruit of the Spirit is Gentleness

"Let your gentle spirit be known to all men. The Lord is near." Philippians 4:5

The ancient Rabbis rejoiced over the idea that the coming Messiah would be a *Conquering King* who would free the Jews from bondage. But they struggled over passages in Isaiah 53 that spoke of the "Coming One" as a *Suffering Servant* and the idea of His being "the Lamb of God that takes away the sins of the world." This seemed to them contradictory and some Rabbis even believed that two different Messiah's would come.

Gentleness, or meekness, is not generally a characteristic that fits with a great and mighty King. But, we see that it is in His gentleness that we observe His might and splendor. I have known many gentle and kind women, and a lesser number of men, who have the qualities of gentleness. But those men whose life exemplifies gentleness appear, by far, more impressive than the macho type. I shared something deeply personal with an older man whom I greatly admired and as I did tears began to come and I was embarrassed. He put his hand on my shoulder and said, "Neb, a man who won't let himself cry isn't much of a man." A softened heart is what God uses and a hard heart is of no use at all.

Isaiah alludes to the greatness of God as *the gently flowing waters of a stream.*[1] Solomon says *gentle words exert great power.*[2] We see the tenderness of God as He "gently leads those who are nursing their young."[3] God displays Himself "not only in wind and fire and earthquake but, also, in a whisper."[4] Jesus displays the same care as "the Good Shepherd"[5] and Paul follows His lead in treating those under his care "like a mother caring for her little children."[6] This kind of gentleness is everywhere in Scripture.

It is not easy for men who have been taught differently their whole life to desire a gentle response. But, unlearning the inappropriate response is part of growing and making room for the truth. On a practical level, gentleness is far more easily heard than harshness. When someone talks down to me and is legalistic and demanding like he's the Grand Pooh-Bah and I'm an errand boy, my tendency is to walk out of the room. Even a reprimand, which is sometimes needed, can be done gently but firmly. I have found that the louder people yell and pound on the table (or pulpit), the greater the chance that they are unsure of their own words. We tend to advertise our weakness. Gentleness is an attribute to be coveted.

---

[1] Isa. 8:6   [2] Prov. 15:1; 25:15   [3] Isa. 40:11   [4] 1 Kings 19:11–13
[5] John 10:11   [6] 1 Thess. 2:7

The Fruit of the Spirit is Self-Control

"Like a city whose walls are broken through is a person who lacks self–control."
Proverbs 25:28 (NIV)

This is the last of the nine fruit of the Spirit but being listed last, in no way, means it is the *runt of the litter*. It is what most of us struggle with more often than any other. We look around us and see scant signs of patience, gentleness, kindness and even love in people we know. In some, it seems more effortless than in others. But, none of us exudes self-control in all areas. We usually think of controlling our anger, jealousy, lust, selfishness, bitterness, and our tongue. The Scripture speaks specifically to each of these, and all of us go down on most of them.

The self-control of which the Scriptures speak is not a *grit your teeth and count to ten* admonition. It is much deeper than that; it's the fruit of the Spirit that God wants to energize and empower in us. All nine expressions of the fruit of the Spirit are a graphic picture of the Person of Jesus.

The quandary of all philosophy has to do with the "self." What do I do about me?" Confucius said we must "control ourselves." Same as the Bible, right? Not at all. You have no natural power to control your lust, self-centeredness, your tendency toward greed, or your raw emotions. Only a supernatural act of God in our heart can *conquer* these natural responses. So, self-control is not about controlling yourself; it is the self under the control of the Holy Spirit. Sure, discipline matters. Someone reams you out … the natural response is to defend yourself and fire back. But, if God has convinced you that it's His glory that is at stake and that "a gentle response turns back wrath,"[1] you may well see an epiphany in the other party. This is how Jesus responds and He wants us to be like Him, but it will not happen by discipline alone. There are certain practical ways to control greed like giving more and focusing on people rather than stuff. There are ways to control lust by guarding what you expose yourself to. But the question you must ask yourself is this: Do you want your responses of control to be a synthetic self-improvement program or a genuine response from the heart?

Who controls your actions? You or the Holy Spirit? The acid test is not in how you force yourself to respond under pressure, but in how you *spontaneously* respond. God can change our natural reactions to supernatural reactions if you yield to Him.

---

[1]Prov. 15:1

To Know One is to Know All

"But Jesus on his part did not entrust himself to them, because he knew all people and needed no one to bear witness about man, for he himself knew what was in man" John 2:24–25 (ESV)

Every human being was created in God's image. That does not mean that we are all magically like God or that He looks like us. But when He breathed life into that first man, He breathed in all the potential to be like God, in character and perspective. Every newborn baby has the same basic biological and emotional needs. Differences in personality development, as the child grows, becomes apparent. His thinking, his views life, death, pain, are sculpted by his parents, school, friends and other outside influences. But as youth morphs into adulthood, as unique and different as he may appear, his internal need to be loved, valued, and to know his purpose is universal.

We know that God wants us to be His vessel to share His love with others, but often we feel self-conscious and awkward; we generally fumble every opportunity to connect with people on a deeper level. Jesus never had that problem. He knew how to go straight to the heart. It wasn't just because He was God; it was because He knew the hearts of men and women. You and I don't have the ability to know someone's heart, but if you know another person deeply, you can, in a real sense, know all people.

During World War II, Albert Speer was in Hitler's inner circle in the Third Reich. An architect by training, he was suddenly appointed by Hitler as Minister of Armaments of which he had no knowledge whatsoever. To educate himself in the field of arms, he disassembled an entire "Panzer Tank," reasoning that if he could understand its functioning he would have a basic knowledge of all weaponry. It is true that "the mysteries of the ocean are found in one drop of water." To know one person deeply is to fundamentally know all people.

Every man I have ever met struggles with the same issues: a wrong relationship with God, their spouse and children, the opposite sex, and money. Anyone you sit with for coffee is dealing with one or more of these at any given time. When you know this going in, you already have a point of identity because you realize they are dealing with the same issues as you. How many times have you muttered to yourself, *nobody understands me*? But your issue is common to everyone. If you will take a risk to share your heart with someone, and really listen to them, when you go your separate ways you will both say to yourselves, "Finally, someone who understands my world!"

Navigation

"If you wander off the road to the right or the left, you will hear his voice behind you saying, 'Here is the road. Follow it.'" Isaiah 30:21 (GNT)

I love this image that God paints through the prophet Isaiah. In the newer cars these days there is a radar mechanism that senses when you wander into another lane or drive to close to the shoulder of the road. A continuous beep will sound to get your attention or wake you up to get you back on track. The radar is programmed to keep you from potential disaster.

God seems to be saying that He is attentive in watching His beloved as they journey through life. He is not like a highway patrolman lurking behind the trees hoping to catch us speeding. He watches lovingly and intently, not to prevent our choices or even our mistakes, but to guide us back on course and avert *needless* harm.

Our three boys were adventurous children. They loved exploring and experiencing new things. We lived in North Arlington, Virginia, just outside Washington, D.C. We gave them parameters, but otherwise, allowed them a wide range so they could just be kids. There were times when they lost my tools in the woods behind our house, trampled the flowers in

a neighbor's yard, and snuck out to meet their friends late on a weekend night. We made them replace some of the tools, go to the neighbors to apologize and make amends with the irate neighbors. We were the GPS for keeping our children on track. God teaches us and we teach them until they are capable of making the right decisions.

Susan and I were never helicopter parents who hovered over our kids fearful they would skin a knee or cut their chin. If you don't allow your kids freedom to fail, and make mistakes, they will be doing some version of the same bad decision twenty years later. We did monitor activities that could put them in harm's way. It is a precarious balance, and God must give you wisdom for when to say no. In our experience, the "no" times arose when we felt they were either testing our resolve or unaware of the gravity of what they were asking.

You and I are just an older version of our children ... with diversions that are a little more sophisticated and powerful, that cause us to veer off the path. If we desire His guidance, we will often hear a soft voice that says, "Here is the road, follow it."

The Strategy of Our Enemy

"Now the serpent was more crafty than any of the wild animals the Lord God had made." Genesis 3:1 (NIV)

The Scripture says that the devil spends much of his time commuting back and forth between earth and heaven to accuse God's friends.[1] In fact, Satan once told God that the only reason people liked Him was that He did things for them. God spoke of His friend Job as a faithful man and Satan countered by saying that he loved God because he was rich and had a great family. *Just let affliction creep in and he will wilt like a lettuce leaf,* the devil assured God. So, they made a wager. God said that the devil could tempt Job in any manner except he could not kill him. God asserted that Job would remain faithful no matter what.[2]

So goes the story of Job and his patience and faithfulness despite losing his family, his wealth, his position, and his health. These are the types of people that Satan messes with. People constantly say the devil is trying to get me. He is usually portrayed as a cartoon character with a pitchfork in a red jumpsuit, nor some evil, hideous, Gargoyle that makes people vomit as their head spins around. He is neither of those caricatures, but a very real power and influence in the universe.

Our other two enemies are the *world* and the *flesh*. Everyone is afraid of Satan, but they flirt with and are enticed by the world and the flesh. So great is this infatuation with the ways of the world and the lure of the flesh that Satan only has the need to personally focus on those like Job who cause him heartburn. Why would Satan be threatened by a person who thinks of nothing all day except shopping for expensive clothes, obsessing over their body, and ways to impress their friends? Why would he attack someone who looks at pornography, dreams of their next conquest, or spends every waking moment seeking new ways to make more money. Both have disqualified themselves already.

I believe that Satan's mantra is something like this: *allow those who are shooting blanks to continue to fire at will.* Why bother a sleeping Pit Bull by poking him with a stick. Satan has no need to bother with most of us; the world and the flesh have already rendered us ineffective. He will concentrate on the Jobs of the world who take God seriously ... who love and desire to be like Him. I don't minimize Satan's influence, but I fear that the world and the flesh have given Satan much more leisure time.

---

[1]Rev. 12:7–12   [2]Job 1:6–12; 2:1–6

Welcome Temptations as Friends

"When all kinds of trials and temptations crowd into your lives my brothers, don't resent them as intruders, but welcome them as friends. Realize that they come to test your faith and to produce in you the quality of endurance. But let the process go on until that endurance is fully developed and you will find that you have become men of mature character, men of integrity with no weak spots."
James 1:2–4 (Phillips)

When, as a new believer, I first read this passage in this great Phillips Translation, I closed it, tossed it aside and muttered, "This James character is a fruit cake." I couldn't believe what I was reading. I had paid no attention to temptation for eighteen years; I give my life to Jesus and temptation becomes the nemesis that is trying to take me down. Then, I read that I should embrace temptations as a friend and not resent them.

When my head stopped spinning, I discussed it with Mal McSwain, the Young Life leader who introduced me to Jesus. He explained that if you always face weak opponents in sports events, you never improve or become stronger. Temptation is like a strong opponent that pushes you to reach deeper and will produce endurance and character. That encouraged me, and I began to see that God allows temptation to help me grow up.

The world's agenda flies in the face of that which honors God and fulfills his purposes. When you and I walk into that world with the intent to live by *His life in us*, there will be immediate conflict. Some temptations are easy to detect, but many are very subtle and often appear to be true and, therefore, not a temptation.

There was a time when I would lead a small group study or speak at some gathering several days of the week. I would also teach studies that I would develop on biblical subjects and teach several nights a week, then fly out on the weekend to speak at a retreat or a conference. Not once did I consider those requests as temptations until my close brothers, Robby Rowan and Blake Rymer, confronted me. They asked me how I could to be a good husband and father when I was seldom home. I was stepping over my family to help other people and it was hypocritical.

This was many years ago and was the first time anyone ever challenged me about what I considered "my work." They said, "Your work is your family!" No one ever tells you that you're attending too many Bible studies or helping people too much, but those things can keep you farther from God than almost anything else. The subtle temptation to choose the needs of others as more important than your family echoes the words of Oswald Chambers ... "the greatest enemy of Christ is Christian work."

How Jesus Faced Temptation

"And behold the heavens were opened and He saw the Spirit of God descending as a dove and lighting on Him; and behold a voice out of the heavens said, this is my beloved Son in whom I am well pleased." Matthew 3:16–17

No one has ever faced the level of temptation that Jesus faced. As God's Son, His glory was hidden for thirty-three years. With the abuse and taunting Jesus received at the hands of Jewish leaders, a snap of His fingers could have initiated a miracle so stupendous and irrefutable that all would have been convinced of His Messiahship. But, He resisted the temptation and stripped Himself of His rights as God's equal.[1] His desire was to be received by faith, not by drama. Throughout His life He resisted temptations. In the end, He knew He could have saved Himself from the cross[2] but, His love for us and His unwavering obedience to His Father only strengthened His resolve.

How could He resist constant temptation? I believe the answer is found at His Baptism in the Jordon River. When the Glory of God came down and the voice of God said, "This is my Son in whom I am well pleased;" for whose primary benefit were those words? Was it John or the crowd watching on the bank? Possibly, but I think those words were primarily for Jesus' benefit because of what was to happen immediately after the baptism. He will fast for 40 days and do hand to hand combat with Satan.

He had to be fully convinced of who He was and how the Father felt about Him to resist Satan. CS Lewis said, "It is better to remind than to instruct." The Father wanted to remind Jesus that He was pleased with Him. God's favor didn't rest on Jesus because of any accomplishment. He hadn't begun His ministry. Mary was "highly favored" by God as a young girl,[3] not for works she had done, but because of the *person* she was.

Temptations can never be conquered until we understand who we are. As His redeemed child, His view of you is always a 10 on a 1-10 scale. Your performance may not be pleasing to Him at times, but your *person* is *always* pleasing.

So, you're alone on a business trip, having dinner at the end of the day. Your eyes meet with those of a very attractive person across the room. *No one will know; after all, I'm just a pitiful sinner anyway," you reason. "I'm not perfect!"* But, what if you were convinced that God's sees you as righteous, forgiven, cleansed, holy and acceptable … one with whom He is *pleased?* Why wouldn't you be more apt to walk away based on who you are? What you believe about yourself directly impacts how you live.

---

[1]Phil. 2:6–11   [2]Matt. 26:53   [3]Luke 1:28

Confidence in the Conflict

"You will not have to fight this battle. Take up your positions; stand firm and see the deliverance the Lord will give you. Judah and Jerusalem. Do not be afraid; do not be discouraged. Go out to face them tomorrow, and the Lord will be with you."
2 Chronicles 20:17 (NIV)

The context of this great passage is that King Jehoshaphat has been told that a vast army is moving against him. In fact, a group of nations had joined together to fight him. The King immediately calls the people to fast and pray. He tells God they have no power to stop this assault, but that their eyes are only on Him. God tells him to go out and face the enemy, unafraid and in the knowledge that the Lord will stand with him. Jehoshaphat fell on his face and praised God and then told the people to trust God and they *will* see victory. Along the way to the place of the battle, they sang praises to God. The King knew that God inhabits the praise of His people.[1] Confidence began to build until the people were focused not on the enemy, but on the nature of God. When you are anchored in God's heart there is no reason, whatsoever, to think that victory is not forthcoming.

Paul said, "We are *more than conquerors* through Him who loved us."[2] The difference in a conqueror and a *more than a conqueror* is that a conqueror must fight the battle to determine if he has conquered; a *more than conqueror* knows he has won before the battle is ever fought. This was King Jehoshaphat.

As followers of Jesus, we do not fight in hope of a victory, we are fighting *from* victory. As *more than conquerors*, we have reason to declare victory ahead of time. God has defeated Satan and all the powers of darkness. This is the meaning of the cross. God is not punching it out with Satan as a fierce competitor. Nonsense! Satan is a created being who fell from grace.[3] He is no competition for God at all. He exists only as a training ground for believers who will reign with Him forever.

God's intent was that those He created would destroy the powers of darkness by overcoming evil with good. But, man forfeited that ability because he sinned. Jesus became flesh and defeated the powers of darkness on the cross, and then handed the keys of His personal victory to us.

Be aware, but don't fear the powers of darkness. If we trust God as Jehoshaphat did, we can walk into any circumstance with confidence and know that God has gone before us.

---

[1] Ps. 22:3   [2] Rom. 8:37   [3] Isa. 14:13–15

The Full Counsel of the Scriptures

"For I have not shunned to declare unto you all the counsel of God."
Acts 20:27 (KJV)

You can take the Word of God, and if you are willing to isolate passages and disconnect them from their context, you can make a case for almost anything. It will be misleading and, at best, only partially true. It would, in no way, reflect the intent of the Author.

When our need to be right eclipses our desire for truth, we often build our case with bits and pieces that do not belong together. Politicians do it; you and I do it, and *all* the news media does it, taking sound bites and using only that which affirms the narrative they want. Being right and adjudicating our own bias has become an accepted way to get what you want.

Ministers do it all the time. When they are teaching a section of Scripture and they run into a passage that conflicts with their denominational or theological position, they often skip or gloss over it. Even great men of God like Dwight L. Moody injected his own bias, preaching that it was a sin for men to wear ruffled shirts. Billy Sunday said it was a sin for women to chew gum. These are personal preferences, not biblical commands.

When you see something in the Bible that appears to be saying this or that, if you want the true intent of God, you must trace that idea through the entirety of Scripture. If it is contradicted elsewhere, there is a problem. God does not contradict Himself. Therefore, you are not seeing this issue in the context which it was given. Jesus heals a man who is demon-possessed and cannot speak. The multitudes are leaning toward the fact that He may really be the Messiah. The Pharisees are backed into a corner; they must either agree or come up with something credible to refute it. Their answer is to assert that Jesus does miracles by the power of Satan. It was an egregious accusation and deeply offends Jesus. Later in the chapter, He says there will be no forgiveness for this kind of blasphemy.[1]

For centuries people have agonized over the fear that in a moment of rage, they may have committed the unforgivable sin. But in context, and seeing the full counsel of Scripture, this was a *generational statement.* Four times in this passage Jesus refers to "this generation."[2] It is not a universal sin that you or I can commit but pertains to those Jewish leaders who He knew would never repent. Throughout the Scriptures, Jesus affirms eternal security: "I give them eternal life, and *no one* shall pluck them out of my hand."[3] "If we confess our sins, He is faithful and just to *forgive us* our sins and cleanse us from all unrighteousness.[4] Always consult the *full counsel* of the Word.

---

[1]Matt. 12:22–37   [2]Matt. 12:39, 41, 42, 45   [3]John 10:28   [4]1 John 1:9

251

"Que Será, Será"?

Joshua 1:6–11

It was the title of a very popular song introduced by Doris Day in 1956. It begins like this: "When I was just a little girl, I asked my mother what will I be? Will I be pretty, will I be rich? Here's what she said to me ... *Que será, será*, whatever will be will be, the future's not ours to see, *Que será, será*." It was one of those catchy tunes I remember my mother singing around the house when I was a little boy. Great song, but not so great a philosophy.

After the death of Moses, Joshua leads the children of Israel towards the land that God had promised them. Spies had been sent out to survey the land that they were to possess. The spies return saying the land truly *is* a land flowing with milk and honey, meaning great abundance. But standing between them is a formidable enemy who was well-trained and powerful. The spies felt like "grasshoppers" compared to what they saw.[1] The assurance of God's guidance and protection is a powerful promise in the Scripture. God tells them to be strong and courageous because He has promised to their forefathers that every place their foot will step in this land is their inheritance.

How many times have you heard people say, or said yourself, "if it is meant to be, it will be; if not, it won't." This sounds very accepting and compliant with whatever happens. But, the "whatever" perspective is only in the *gospel according to Uncle Sam*. The Scripture is "living and active."[2] We depend on God to work through us, but that does not mean we are to be passive. God promised an abundant land for His children to live in and prosper. He also promised that he would be with them every step of the way, instructing them to meditate on His Word day and night and they would then prosper.[3]

God has a destiny for you, but to passively say *Que será, será* and wait around until something happens is not His intent. You and I *must step into* the promises of God just as the Israelites had to go and possess the land God promised them. He does want us to prosper, but the primary way is not the bankrolls, boats and private jets the TV preachers brag about, but internal prosperity that takes us to a whole new level of living ... a place where we tap into an eternal unlimited Kingdom. The promises of God will not happen by saying, "whatever" to everything. Israel had to obey God, meditate on His Word and move forward in His strength to take Jericho.[3] To meditate on God's Word *rewires* your mind to understand when and how to move forward into the future He has prepared for you.

---

[1] Num. 13:32–33   [2] Heb. 4:12   [3] Josh. 1:9–11

Your Philosophy of Life

"It all accords with my own earnest wishes and hopes, which are that I should never be in any way ashamed, but that now, as always, I should honour Christ with the utmost boldness by the way I live, whether that means I am to face death or to go on living. For living to me means simply 'Christ', and if I die I should merely gain more of him." Philippians 1:20–21 (Phillips)

When you are at lunch, playing golf, at a cocktail party, or shopping with friends, has anyone ever asked you what your philosophy of life is? That is a question that few have ever been asked, and yet, the answer to that question is the motivating factor that creates your perspective, drives your relationships, and influences your decisions in life.

I think it is fair to say that the above statement Paul made to the Church at Philippi was his personal philosophy. The German Bible translates it very succinctly, "Christ is my life, death is my gain." Insecurity is something with which we all struggle to some degree. Paul seems to have brought that plane in for a landing because he says, *"my life is wrapped up in a Person. If my enemies let me live, then living to me is Christ. If they kill me, death will give me even greater access to Him."* But what if they let him live and persecute him continually? Paul received forty lashes five times, was beaten with rods three times, was stoned, shipwrecked three times and was in the ocean for a day and a night.[1] He was persecuted from all sides and his attitude was that he counted it a privilege to suffer for Christ's sake. Ironically, the most joy-filled books in the Bible are Paul's "Prison Epistles,"

Ephesians, Philippians, Colossians, and Philemon. Each was written while he was locked up in Rome.[2]

If you let Paul live, He will be happy; if you kill him, he will be happy and if you persecute him, he will consider it a privilege to suffer for Christ's sake. How does an enemy hold any power over a man like that? He was just a man, but because of his perspective, he was untouchable.

Whatever you might say is your philosophy of life, it must be adequate for life, death, and affliction. Otherwise, you will never know true security. You will live in fear of death, be shaken by the eventualities in life, and you will compromise to avoid persecution. Jesus bridged each of these things and if He lives in you and me, we can know this kind of peace at every level.

---

[1] 2 Cor. 11:24–31   [2] Acts 28:16–21

A Fair and Accurate Assumption

"And love your neighbor as yourself." Matthew 22:39

It is called the great commandment, but over fourteen hundred years before Jesus spoke these words, Moses gave this command to Israel that is called the "schema," and is the centerpiece for Jewish life. It is not really two different commandments because one cannot really exist without the other. How can you say you love God and not love those who God loves?[1] If God is love, and the essence of love flows from Him, how can you really love your neighbor unless you love Him?

Loving your neighbor as you love yourself gives definition to the command of how we love others rather than leaving it for us to define. How do I love and take care of myself? I always make sure I have the fundamentals of life … food, clothing, shelter, transportation, etc. I make sure I am comfortable, stay healthy and look presentable. We all do it without even thinking twice.

When Jesus said these words to a young Pharisee, he was asked, "who is my neighbor?" Jesus tells the story of the *Good Samaritan.* One of the great debates of that day was the weight each of God's commands carried. Most agreed that loving God was the greatest, but the second was an issue of intense debate. Rabbi Shammai, the most conservative of the seven Pharisaic schools of thought, believed that keeping the Sabbath was the greatest. Purity and several other commands came well before loving your neighbor. The young Pharisee wants Jesus to enter the debate and Jesus affirms the command that comes from Leviticus.[2] It specifically defines what loving your neighbor as yourself means. It speaks of respecting the property of others, being generous with the poor and the outsider, and never defrauding anyone financially. Moses concludes with extending forgiveness and never holding a grudge.

The truth is, if you don't love yourself as God loved you, your neighbor is in big trouble. We have all known angry and insecure people who seem to stay on the defensive. Do you enjoy their company? Probably not, because they lash out in anger without provocation and carry a negative perspective. They hate themselves and that hatred spills over into every relationship. If, on the other hand, you appreciate how God made you and have a grateful heart, you will tend to treat others in a like manner.

---

[1] 1 John 4:20   [2] Lev. 19:9–11

Living in the Moment?

"For what is a man profited, if he shall gain the whole world, and lose his own soul?"
Matthew 16:26 (KJV)

"Live in the moment" is a popular mantra these days. Many of the popular sayings and clichés are fairly thin perspectives about life, but this one has merit. You can't read the gospels and fail to notice how focused Jesus was with everyone He encountered. He did live in the moment; He gave himself fully to people. I feel certain that if you had been around Him in a crowd of people, as his eyes moved from person to person, you would have felt that He was speaking directly to you. The man who discipled and mentored me was like that. He knew people from literally every country in the world and if you asked any of them about their relationship with him, they would say he was one of their closest friends. He had a unique gift of making you feel that you were the most important person he knew.

This thing of multitasking and doing each task well is a myth. Studies have shown that to do anything with excellence, it cannot be done in concert with several other things. Everything will suffer. You can't stay in the moment and multi-task.

There is a big difference in living *in* the moment and living *for* the moment. When you live *for* any moment in time, you are almost always disappointed because that moment can never live up to your expectations. The Scripture teaches that we are to enjoy and revel in the gift of every moment, but the bigger picture is to live your life in the light of eternity. Our time on this earth is like a snap of your fingers compared to what God has in store for those who love Him.[1] Why would you trade everlasting joy for more productivity right now?

No one likes to think about death, but your perspective of it will shape the way you live. Mickey Mantle, my childhood idol, and a Hall of Fame baseball player had the tools to be the greatest player ever, but he lived only *for* the moment. He said in an interview, "If I'd known I would live this long, I would have taken better care of myself." Too late. He thought about death, but instead of being like a bright star in the universe[2] he took an Epicurean route: "Eat, drink, and be merry for tomorrow we die."

Our life on earth is a dress rehearsal for the big event which will last as long as the heavens. Live in the moment, focus on everyone you meet, apply your gifts to every task, but remember the words of James: "Yet you do not even know what tomorrow will bring. What is your life? For you are a mist that appears for a little while and then vanishes."[3] Live now but look toward eternity and your life will be a fragrance to everyone you meet.[4]

---

[1] 1 Cor. 2:9   [2] Phil. 2:15   [3] James 4:14   [4] 2 Cor. 2:15

The Speck and the Plank

"Why do you look at the speck that is in your brother's eye, but do not notice the log that is in your own eye? Or how can you say to your brother, 'Let me take the speck out of your eye,' and behold, the log is in your own eye? You hypocrite, first take the log out of your own eye, and then you will see clearly to take the speck out of your brother's eye." Matthew 7:3–5

Jesus had just said, "Judge not lest you be judged." This does not mean that you fail to call sin or destructive behavior what it is. You are not to judge a person's intent or motive because you cannot know that. By saying that you know the intent behind an action is to put yourself in the place of God, our ultimate judge. No one likes a hypocrite and, yet, we all fall into that category at some point. If, as a father, a grandfather, or a friend and brother, I must be antiseptically pure in order to help someone I love to get back on track, it will never happen.

The Scripture tells us to be ready to reprove, rebuke, and exhort people who are living in error.[1] Who will ever help them if not us? The issue is concerning the attitude with which it is to be done. My motive for bringing something to a friend's attention is known only by me. I must be sure it is for his good and not any vendetta or sense of satisfaction I might receive from it. I may never be pure enough to point out something in another, but my motive for doing it must be pure.

If you saw a friend damaging his marriage or his relationship with his children, and you knew he is playing with fire, wouldn't you care enough to try to save him from that possibility?[2] Paul instructs the Galatian church that those who are spiritual should gently restore such a person.[3] In other words, it should be one who can do this with a great sense of humility and one who would take no pleasure in doing it.

Loving one another is not always comfortable and cuddly. It can be the most difficult thing you ever do. To reach the desired outcome, pray for God's direction and guidance. Pray also for the hearts of the other person to be receptive and non-defensive. All discipline is for the intent to reclaim, rather than to cast out.

---

[1] 2 Tim. 4:2   [2] Jude 22–23   [3] Gal. 6:1

Salvation by Formula

"If you confess with your mouth, Jesus as Lord, and believe in your heart that God raised Him from the dead, you will be saved." Romans 10:9

I did not grow up in a *spit and polish*, paint by numbers, kind of home. Meals were not served at the same time every day and as early as eight or nine years old, I got up early, made my own breakfast and got myself to school. Not necessarily the prescribed formula for family living, but I liked the minimal structure. Later, I went to Alabama on a football scholarship and everything we did was highly structured. Coach Bryant left nothing to chance, and it was a big adjustment. As my faith began to grow, I became involved in a church, went to Bible studies, and got around people who I respected and thought would challenge me. The church was just like my football world ... very structured, very precise, and, I thought ... a bit legalistic.

I remember being in a class where a man taught how to share your faith. Everything was programmed perfectly, and the specific steps in the presentation were outlined. I had, by that time, read the New Testament enough to ask where these steps came from. He seemed offended and never really answered my question. From then on, I heard many of these formula type solutions I couldn't find in the Bible. When a person's heart is touched by the Spirit of God, it is because the person was drawn, not coerced.[1] There are resources like the "Four Spiritual Laws" or "The Roman Road" that are helpful, but no such steps are outlined in the Scriptures.

A thief hung on a cross beside Jesus and reprimanded another man saying Jesus did not deserve the cross. He said to Jesus, "Remember me when you come into your kingdom." Jesus responded, "Today you will be with me in paradise." No four steps or special sinner's prayers ... just simple trust.[2]

One of my favorite little books is "Children's Letters to God." It came out over forty years ago, but it is priceless. My favorite letter to God is also the shortest. An eight-year-old simply wrote, *Dear God ... Count me in ... Your friend, Herbie.* That simple prayer from the heart is enough to take a person from death to life! I mean no disrespect to all the formulas, but they are man's marketing ideas for presenting Jesus. Dr. Richard Halverson once told me, "Allow God to be as original with others as he has been with you."

[1] John 6:44   [2] Luke 23:39–43

Breaking Through Tunnel Vision

"See then that you walk circumspectly, not as fools but as wise."
Ephesians 5:15 (KJV)

My grandfather was an ophthalmologist. When I was about seven, I asked him what tunnel vision was. He told me to make an "OK" sign with my thumb and forefinger, and then curve the other three fingers to make a cylinder. "Now close one eye and look through the tube you've made and tell me what you see." I told him I could see straight ahead but not to each side. "That's tunnel vision," he said. "Just be thankful you can see from side to side."

As I grew up and began my friendship with God, I learned that this lack of peripheral vision is not simply physical, but a spiritual malady deeply woven within the church. Paul tells us we must walk *circumspectly*.[1] It's a King James word we seldom use anymore. It opens the boundaries and lets you see around you.

If we know what we believe and why we believe it, then what frightens us so much about hearing another perspective? If we approach life with humility, listening and learning as we go, it should strengthen, not weaken our faith. Most of us engage meaningfully with less than four or five people per week. They are generally from the same socio-economic level, same church, and fundamentally the same spiritual and political beliefs. If we travel abroad our usual contact is with the hotel clerk, the waiters, and taxicab drivers. We see the sights, eat in nice restaurants, and fly home never having any meaningful interaction with the locals. I hear people speak of Muslims in fearful and often caustic tones, and yet, most have never known or had a conversation with one.

Most Americans are very apprehensive about China because of what they see on TV news. But the growth of the Church of Jesus Christ in China is the fastest on the planet. The second is in Iran, mostly among young people.

Tunnel vision comes from fear usually caused by lack of exposure. We socialize with the same people who all have similar backgrounds, think alike, live in the same area, etc. We seldom take a risk to step out of our comfort zone and build relationships with people who are culturally different from us. It doesn't take God for people who are exactly alike to love one another. But what if you reached out, took a chance, and invited people to dinner with whom you think you have nothing in common. You might be surprised, and you might learn more from them than you have from all your other friends put together. Take a chance!

[1] Eph. 5:15–17

Learning to Trust the Invisible

"Jesus said to her, (Martha) did I not say to you that if you believe you will see the glory of God?" John 11:40

One of the great temptations Jesus faced during His three and a half years of public ministry was to do *a dog and pony show* for the skeptical Pharisees to prove He was really the Messiah. These "signs," as John called them in his gospel, were miracles that Jesus performed on a daily basis but the Pharisees wanted Him to perform *on-demand,* but He refused.

Human nature always wants to see observable, measurable, tangible evidence of things we are asked to believe. "Prove it," we always say. "Show me and then I will believe." Jesus' response is always, "No, you believe me because of Who I am, and then you will see." In other words, learn to trust the invisible things of God based solely on His Person and His track record.

This is what is happening in the encounter between Jesus and Martha, the sister of Lazarus. She had seen Jesus heal people and knew He could prevent death, but was uncertain about His ability to actually *overcome* death. He wants her to believe in Him as the *Resurrection and the Life,* and the proof of that will be in the raising of Lazarus. However, He wants her to believe before she has visible evidence of such. "If you believe, you will see,"

are His words to her and to every person down through the centuries. *Faith always comes before knowledge.* The invisible always precedes the visible ... otherwise, it's not faith. Jesus agreed with His Father that leaving the comforts of heaven and living among men for thirty-three uncomfortable, misunderstood and often gut-wrenching years was the only solution to redeem the world, but Jesus had to trust Him completely.

God's Word is worthy of trust. When He speaks, He delivers. If He tells you to walk down the darkened path, you don't necessarily know what lurks in the shadows. But, if He says "Walk" there is no need for light because He is the light that shines in the darkness.[1]

That which you and I see with our physical eyes is almost never a true reflection of that which we can count on; it's a mirage. Getting to the top of the pyramid and grasping the gold ring looks satisfying, but it never is. It always disappoints. Trust in the invisible things that God promises, and you will never be disappointed. The visible is temporary; it will never accompany you into eternity. The invisible is your transportation there!

---

[1] John 1:5

Selling Out for Methods

"Trust in the Lord with all your heart and do not lean not on your own understanding. In all your ways acknowledge Him, and He will make your paths straight." Proverbs 3:5–6

Have you noticed that in the Bible there is no methodology? You can't find any "Four Secrets to Happiness" or "Six Keys for a Successful Marriage." The answers are in there, but they are purposely not listed like a "quick and simple" recipe for what ails you. What we do see are principles that reflect Gods mind.

I have loved golf since I was about twelve. I played many times with a man who mentored and challenged my thinking for almost forty-four years. He loved golf too and was even more competitive than I was. Instead of betting money he always wanted to wager a verse of Scripture per hole. For every hole he won, at the end of the round, he gave you a verse to memorize. I felt I was a better golfer, but somehow, he seemed to beat me more than half the time. We were at a meeting in Chicago and a few of us slipped out to play eighteen holes one afternoon. He wanted to bet an *hour* per hole. He played hard and I was two holes down with two holes to play. I asked for double or nothing and he beat me. I owed him four hours of anything he wanted me to do. I figured I would be washing his car or raking leaves when we got back to D.C., but he handed me a little book called *Power through Prayer* by E. M. Bounds. He said, "Neb, this will be the

best bet you ever lost!" I want you to get up a 4 am, read this booklet; it will take about an hour. The second hour I want you to pray, the third hour read it again, and then pray again during the fourth hour."

He was right; those four hours changed everything for me. I learned to really pray; to cry out to God and to listen intently. There was something in that booklet that really challenged my thinking. E. M. Bounds said, "Men are searching for better methods, but God is searching for better men." We always are looking for jiffy ways to do things. The western mind always wants *steps,* but the thrust of the Scriptures, written by and to middle eastern Hebrews, is a story that opens principles that will change your heart and develop your character.

How-To books are big sellers because they give us a recipe to follow, but life is not like that. Methods tend to eliminate trust. Why rely on God? I have the formula. Life is not a computer program; that's why it rains when you save enough to finally go on that trip to Hawaii or why your neighbor brings over a hot apple pie after you just began your long overdue diet. Life is a constant bevy of contrary and unpredictable things that can only be navigated by the eternal principles that God has graciously given.

Acceptance without Expectation

"Christ loved the church and gave himself up for her . . . so that he might present the church to himself in splendor, without spot or wrinkle or any such thing, that she might be holy and without blemish." Ephesians 5:25, 27 (ESV)

I have learned through the years that if I read the Scriptures with any motive other than an unconditional desire to grow and flourish, I am misusing a precious gift. The Scriptures can be used as a gun to shoot someone down. It can be used to win; to humiliate and attack someone. I know of a situation where someone committed a grievous sin and repented of it, asking forgiveness of all involved, and it never happened again. Yet, one person who had no direct involvement in the matter continually quoted the old testament passage about the "sins of the father" being passed on the third and fourth generation.[1] This person went around town gossiping and saying "sins of the father ... sins of the father" to anyone who would listen. It was used as a hammer to try to wound someone and define their entire life by that one sin that had been confessed and forgiven. In my opinion, what this person did with gossip and misusing the Scripture was worse than the sin committed by the offender.

Susan and I have had many conversations over the years about how to help our children, and now grandchildren, to flourish. That is God's intent for all of us. At the point when you plant flowers in the ground, your greatest hope is in the flourishing of that seedling into a beautiful burst of color. How do we give our spouse, children, and friends the freedom to move forward and not put them under some legalistic obligation? How do we accept them and allow them space to bloom, and even to fail, without laying any of our expectations on them? The only way I know is to do what Jesus did. He loved the church despite her blemishes. He allowed her to fail. He accepted her back like the Father of the Prodigal Son, running down the road with open arms.

I used to think my wife was a pushover when it came to our sons. I was tougher on them when they misbehaved than she. But I have had to learn that it was not permissive parenting on her part. It was unconditional love because instead of making a big deal about their bad behavior, she showed them another way that was positive and accomplished the same thing with far less tears.

There are consequences for our choices in life, but what you never see is God throwing up His hands in disgust and walking away.[2] He desires ... but doesn't expect. He longs for ... but doesn't coerce. He has a destiny for us ... but he doesn't force it on us.

---

[1] Exod. 34:7 [2] Rom. 5:8

The Value of One

"Are not two sparrows sold for a penny? And not one of them will fall to the ground apart from your Father. But even the hairs of your head are all numbered."
Matthew 10: 29–30 (ESV)

I remember seeing a bumper sticker that said, "If you ever think that no one knows you're alive, just miss a few car payments." Sometimes we do feel alone in a crowded world. Everyone is moving at a frantic pace and we often pass each other like ships in the night. One of my big questions as a kid was how can God hear my prayers when millions are trying to get his attention at the same time? I still wonder about that!

An even greater collision of thought is the tension between the agenda of God and the value of the individual. Many believe that if God's plan is to reconcile the world to Himself, we need to get on board and not waste a minute.[1] The quest to fulfill the Great Commission should take precedence over every other issue in life.[2] While I concur wholeheartedly with God's desire to redeem mankind, I know that as you go from point A to point B in this mission, there are wounded people along the way. There are marital struggles, issues of depression, loneliness, addictions and broken relationships within the rank of those who march in the mission. Do we run over or past the hurting to get to the agenda or do we value the *many* over the *one*?

All I know is that most big movements with lofty goals of winning the world tend to glide past many people along the way. God's agenda *is* people. Massive, sweeping plans to do something great for God often ignores those who languish within its ranks. When the agenda trumps the individual, we are denying the very message we propagate to a lost world. "Come unto me, all you who are weary and heavy laden, and I will give you rest" is an invitation to the unredeemed and the redeemed.

In the amazing movie, "Saving Private Ryan," a squad of men was sent behind enemy lines to bring home one man whose three brothers had already been killed. There was griping in the ranks by the men. They had mothers who wanted them home as well. The theme surfaced: *how much is one man's life worth?* The goal was to win the war, but General Marshall understood that ignoring the pain of a mother who had just lost three sons would be exactly the kind of tyranny we were fighting against.

There was a time in the early years when I neglected the needs of a lonely wife to get to "God's Agenda." Some close friends helped me realize that *she was God's agenda* and everything else was secondary. I learned that if it's not working at home; it's not working anywhere else either. It's simply … showtime!

---

[1]2 Cor. 5:19   [2]Matt. 28:19

Thomas the Doubter?

"Unless I see the nail marks in his hands and put my finger where the nails were, and put my hand into his side, I will not believe." John 20:25 (NIV)

Putting labels on people is unfair and unethical. It is unfair because it pigeonholes people and puts them in an inescapable box that time won't even change. It is unethical because it's like gossip; it's never the full truth. We do it all the time: A British accent connotes intelligence and a southern accent means you're Forrest Gump. A hoodie means you're dangerous, while pinstriped suit means you're reputable. In the Scriptures, we see Abraham as the man of faith, Job as a man of patience, Moses as a leader. These labels are true, but only tell part of their story. Jacob cheated his brother, David sent a man to certain death to cover his sin, and Peter denied even knowing Jesus. So, there is much more to these men that their label suggests. What if you were caught cheating on an exam in high school? Would you want that to be your identity for the rest of your life? What if you drank too much at a fraternity party? Would you mind being considered a drunk twenty years later? No one is the total equivalent of something they once said or did. Labels marginalize the person or group and relegate their entire life to a moment in time.

Thomas gets a bum rap. He did doubt that it was the risen Jesus that stood before him, but the others were only a day or so ahead of him. They had all scattered like a covey of quail and hid, trembling in fear. When Jesus and the twelve were in Perea, outside the Sanhedrin's jurisdiction, Jesus received word that Lazarus was ill. All the disciples were against Him going to Bethany except Thomas.[1] Had Jesus *not* gone, we may have never known Him as *The Resurrection and the Life.*

Jesus explained to the twelve that He will not be with them much longer. They now know where He is going, and they know how to get there. Each of them stood silent, acting as if they understood and yet did not have a clue. It was Thomas who had the courage to tell Jesus that *"we have no idea where you are going and haven't a clue how we can get there."* It was his boldness and honesty that caused Jesus to give arguably the greatest statement ever made. "I am the way, the truth, and the life. No man comes to the Father except by me."[2] Thomas became a great missionary in India and was martyred in 72 AD.

We are always more than the way we are perceived. Never define people, describe them. A description introduces them into the relationship, and they can see the person for themselves without prejudice. It builds a bridge rather than a wall.

---

[1]John 11:5–8, 16 [2]John 14:6

Losing Our Voice

"What good will it be for someone to gain the whole world, yet forfeit their soul?"
Matthew 16:26 (NIV)

Jesus wants His disciples to be "a light on a hill", "the salt of the earth," and a "fragrance of life" to the world. It is for this reason that we read passages warning us not to link ourselves with people that would negate that which we say we believe. Being "unequally yoked" is often cited when a believer is planning to marry a non-believer or a business partnership that espouses a completely different value system.

As I write these thoughts, I have a concern that cuts even deeper than the above. Our country is currently facing the most divisive and potentially catastrophic affront since the Civil War. The viciousness and hatred between liberals and conservatives have become so neurotic, *on both sides,* that genuine healing in our nation may take generations unless people of faith take the lead. Lifelong friends and families are alienated over political issues … imagine that … a political or social position taking precedent over a marital covenant. Father and sons, mothers and daughters determined to insist on the rightness of their position over the relationship with their family and close friends.

I remember watching the Watergate Hearings as a young man. Democrats and Republicans eventually set aside their political differences and dug for the truth without partisanship. Woodward and Bernstein, the Washington Post reporters who broke the story, were as different as night and day. One was liberal, one conservative; one was a WASP the other was a Jew; one was a good writer, the other was just average, and they didn't particularly like each other, but they worked together for the truth.

Today it is all about winning! The truth has become a side issue of much less importance. Many of our leaders seek personal career security and only incidentally seek the good of the country. Real courage, it seems, has "left the building." Where are the people of God? We have taken sides rather than being catalysts, called by God to be "ministers of reconciliation."[1] We are selling out for *issues* over *character* and in the process, we are losing our voice. Evangelicals are already seen as the *hysterical fringe.* People of faith are only acknowledged because of our vote. They are unimpressed, and the unredeemed will use our belligerent attitudes as another reason to turn away from God. Why be like us? Our influence is being diminished by the hatred in our voices. We must be reconcilers, not avengers. "The world will know us by our love,"[2] not by our political position.

---

[1] 2 Cor. 5:18   [2] John 13:35

Wishing and Hoping

"Do not let your heart envy sinners, but live in the fear of the Lord always. Surely there is a future, and your hope will not be cut off." Proverbs 23:17–18

Do you ever feel like the child standing in front of the window of life, faced pressed against the pane wishing you could have everything the neighborhood kids had? The poet, Ralph Waldo Emerson wrote, "Every ship seems romantic except the one on which I sail." It is easy to develop an envy perspective when you look around. Comparing ourselves to others is a natural, but unhealthy, response that can either cause you to retreat or to fabricate gifts and abilities that you don't have.

I have known people who were single and wanted desperately to be married and married people who desperately wanted to be single. I have known poor people who wanted to be rich and some very wealthy people who would leave it all and become poor if their son or daughter would only give them a hug.

When we envy the lives of others or resent our own, it cuts off the creative flow that God wants us to experience in our lives. It is discontentment at its core and usually ends up being a mirage. When you look behind the curtain, the great Wizard that awed us is just a little old man.

When I was a kid, like most of us, I wanted to be like the celebrities I saw in the movies. Through the years I have had the opportunity to meet some of those kinds of people. Talk about disappointment! Most were completely self-absorbed, insecure, and lived in constant fear that their star power would vanish any minute. Many who lived in the public eye eventually drift into seclusion as they fall out of favor, forgotten and alone.

What we fail to realize is that if they knew the One that you know, they would stand in awe and would gladly trade places with you in a heartbeat! God wants us to be confident people: not self-confident, but people who hold their heads high, their backs straight and with no apologies for who we are. You can walk in a room, fling open the drapes and scatter the darkness.

What would it be like to admire a talent or a possession of someone and be happy for them without wishing it was yours? What value is walking around feeling like you have been shortchanged and wishing you were someone else? Make a habit of thanking God continuously for what He has given you.

"Let your roots grow down into Him, and let your lives be built on him. Then your faith will grow strong in the truth you were taught, and you will overflow with thankfulness."[1]

---

[1] Col. 2:7

Life Choices Based on Disappointment

"Weeping may tarry for the night, but joy comes with the morning"
Psalm 30:5 (ESV)

For a serious follower of Christ, the guiding standard and mandate for all of life is God's revelation to mankind contained in the Scriptures. Our standard is not our feelings; it's not based on the opinions of others, and just because something works, it does not mean it is true. God chose to reveal His heart, His mind, and His emotions through faithful men whom He appointed to pen the Scriptures. Our view of the world, our philosophy of life must be based on revelation from the heart of God rather than on the disappointments we have suffered.

When I left graduate school, I was asked to start Young Life in Huntsville, Alabama. This is a remarkably effective worldwide ministry with teenagers. I quickly met many who became lifelong friends. One young sophomore just couldn't get enough; he was hungry to learn and grow. Over the next three high school years and on into college, I discipled him, and he became a volunteer leader with Young Life. I moved to Washington, D.C., but kept in close touch. I had such high hopes for him and his leadership abilities. Gradually he dropped out of sight and I learned that he had basically given up on his faith. His father had become ill and he prayed confidently for his healing but to no avail. Apparently, bitterness and disappointment reshaped his view of God.

Disappointment is a harsh mistress. It beckons to us, whispering words of doubt and unfairness. It causes us to ask the unanswerable questions of "Why" rather than "to what end."

John the Baptist, according to Jesus was "the greatest man ever born of woman."[1] John was a front-line warrior, confident and fearless. But he had confronted Herod Antipas about his marriage to his brother's divorced wife which was against Jewish law. As a result, John is rotting in prison, unable to continue his work. He begins to doubt, wondering if he could possibly have tapped the wrong man. Why was he in jail? Why was he shut down in the prime of his life and ministry? Jesus sends word to him about all the good that is happening, a coded way of saying, "John, you did not make a mistake." It seems that Jesus wants John to change his focus on what is not happening to what is.

Disappointment comes from accenting the unfinished, rather than the finished ... the negative, rather than the positive. Base your hope in Jesus and His unchanging truth. Focus on what has happened rather than what has not. The human mind will never be able to plumb the depths of the ways of God.

---

[1] Matt. 11:11

When Lifestyle Dictates Beliefs

"Whether you turn to the right or to the left, your ears will hear a voice behind you, saying, 'This is the way; walk in it.'" Isaiah 30:21 (NIV)

If your son or daughter, grandchild or good friend asked you what you believe about God, what drove your decision to live your life as you do, and what you think about heaven and hell, what would you say? Would your answer be based on careful thought and study of the Scripture over the years or would it be a collage of random and disconnected ideas from various sources? Many believers who honestly love God have allowed their theology to be deeply influenced by their culture and by their chosen lifestyle.

Some years ago, a friend met Christ at a Promise Keepers Conference. He had been a very loose living guy who was in the Advertising business. After we met several times, I encouraged him to get involved with a good church. Always a heavy smoker and drinker, he asked me if he would have to quit. I said, "That's a matter between you and God,." He said he thought a very fine Baptist Church nearby where his sister attended would probably be his choice. Two weeks later, I heard he had joined another church. He told me the deciding factor was the hard line the Baptist Church took on his recreational issues and the fact that it was a non-issue at the church he joined. The problem for me wasn't the smoking and drinking; it was the fact that his lifestyle rather than his desire to grow was what drove his decision.

Why do so many celebrities join the Church of Scientology? As long as they keep sending checks, the church looks the other way concerning their morality. Their morality and lifestyle hold sway over their theology.

I respect people who are seekers; those who may struggle with the Deity of Christ, the authority of the Scripture, or the reality of heaven and hell. The fact that they are chasing it down and willing to learn in an atmosphere where they are well in the minority is, to me, very positive. When they discover the truth, they become the powerful instruments of God because it wasn't handed to them; they dug in and uncovered the truth.

Who is whispering in your ear and which way is the voice telling you to walk? We can't make Biblical principles line up with a lifestyle of our choosing and with which we feel comfortable; it has to be the other way around. God's truth is always the standard and our choices must spring from that.

Show Me Your Numbers

"But it is not this way with you, but the one who is the greatest among you must become like the youngest and the leader like the servant." Luke 22:26

It's no secret that in America, we determine worth by statistical data. Sports franchises have such sophisticated computer analysis of athletes that watching the athlete perform is almost secondary to studying his statistics. We determine success in business in much the same way. We often vote based on the polling and data that crossed our screens.

What is disconcerting is that we also find ways to assign value to people based on a set of measurements. If what I do, and my level of production defines my value as a person then I am on a treadmill where my only possibility of contentment is to run faster than you so I will get a higher rating. Imagine how you would feel if your *performance* as a spouse, a parent, a grandparent, and a believer was fed into a computer program, analyzed, rated and published for all to see. We would be outraged because we know you can't attach a measurable gauge on matters of the heart.

After three years of ministry, if you tried to put Jesus' accomplishments into the hopper, how would He rate? Relatively few believed He was the Son of God and those closest to Him weren't convinced until after He was resurrected. Even His miracles were said by the Pharisees to be done by the power of Satan.[1] You cannot measure the things in life that really matter. Who loves God and their spouse the most? Who has the most peace? The great commandment is the purpose of life. Why isn't its evangelism or Bible study? Maybe it is so that we can't measure who is winning. Only God can know the level of our love!

I think the reason we go for the tangible evidence of spirituality is because of our deep sense of insecurity. If you want to see real insecurity, take away our ability to measure or control what we do either personally or in the church. We'd go nuts because we have been taught to compete and to base our worth on how our performance compares with others could be more debilitating. It is not like the old joke about the bear chasing us and all I must do is outrun you rather than the bear. Jesus never pitted one disciple against another. When they argued about who was the greatest, Jesus said: "you must become the least and the servant." How can you measure that?

---

[1] Matt. 12:24

Justice, Mercy, and Humility

"He has told you, O man, what is good; and what does the Lord require of you?
But to do justice, to love kindness, and to walk humbly with your God."
Micah 6:8

You know this verse, but have you ever wondered why God listed these three principles in the same breath? At first glance, justice and mercy seem contradictory and the third, humility, seems out of place. Someone crashed into the front of my car a few months ago in the Walmart parking lot while I was inside. It was a hit and run and the two witnesses could not get the license number. I expected the police to bring them to justice. When I reported the incident to my insurance carrier, and they said I was liable for the five-hundred-dollar deductible. I argued that a crime of that nature was tantamount to vandalism and that the deductible should be waived. I wanted *justice*; they said, "No."

Mercy is one of the most attractive attributes of God. It is a stunningly gracious decision not to prosecute a sin that is well deserved. It is the winsome touch of a rescuing hand to a drowning humanity. God understands the pull of the world on us; He knows that we will stumble and just as a parent wants their child to flourish, God's mercy is there to redeem rather than to condemn us. Mercy is not a weakness in God, it reveals strength. Sin is offensive to God and when He shows mercy, it is like Him taking a kick to the head, embracing us, and saying *I love you*.

A woman is brought before Jesus and thrown down naked in the dust. The Jewish leaders charged her with adultery.[1] It is a trap. Adultery was punishable by stoning, but earlier that year Rome had abolished the Jews' right to enact capital punishment. They have Jesus cornered. If He says, "Stone her," he breaks Jewish law and cannot be the Messiah. If he says, "Let her go," he will be arrested by the Romans. Jesus turns the question of sin back on the accusers and says, "He who has never sinned throw the first stone." They realized that Jesus knew their motives for this whole escapade.

After they left, Jesus asks if anyone condemned her. She says, "no one," and He says, "neither do I condemn you; go and sin no more." He did not exonerate her sin; He pardoned it by His mercy. He knew she had been set up. He also knew that loneliness and pain had made her vulnerable. He is merciful.

Justice and mercy are inseparable. Justice without mercy is legalism. Mercy without justice is sentimentality. For you and me to be merciful we must humble ourselves. If I seek acclaim for a wrong that I have righted it glorifies me and is self-serving. True mercy is done quietly and without desire for recognition.

---

[1] John 8:1–11

Priscilla and Aquila

"Two are better than one, because they have a good return for their labor, if either of them falls down, one can help the other up." Ecclesiastes 4:9–10 (NIV)

Children think in pictures. Adults can think conceptually but are more comfortable picturing an idea. The Jewish Rabbis spoke continually in parables, and Jesus did the same. Only a few of the parables He taught were original. They had been told for generations, but Jesus would put a different spin on the parable to illustrate the truth He was teaching.

We all struggle to be more of what God desires in our marriages, and the Scriptures give us principles to guide us. But if you're like me, you need to see *a picture* of what a healthy marriage looks like. I was raised in a broken home, so I never observed a healthy marriage. In my teen years, I finally got to see a marriage that truly honored God. Mal and Wanda McSwain, whom I had met through Young Life, had a relationship to aspire to. I have known them for over fifty years, and it's hard to think of one without thinking of the other. They have worked with high school kids who were *off the rails* like me for over 60 years and have continued to stay linked with thousands well into adulthood.

Priscilla and Aquila were like that. They were Jews who had lived in Italy until Claudius kicked all Jews out of Rome. They settled in Corinth and set up shop in the marketplace making and selling tents. Soon they met the Apostle Paul who also had skills in tentmaking. They became fast friends and Paul lived in their home for eighteen months while teaching and developing the church there. Corinth had been re-founded as a colony by Julius Caesar and became a port for sailors.[1] There was a Temple of Aphrodite, the goddess of sex and fertility. It was said that there were 1,000 prostitutes in the temple overlooking the city. It was in this atmosphere that Priscilla and Aquila locked arms with Paul, determined to communicate and model the love of Jesus. Paul later sailed to Syria and Priscilla and Aquila accompanied him.

This young couple had, no doubt, grown immensely during the year and a half living under the same roof with Paul. From what he later writes to the Corinthians, the house church they had started was thriving.[2] Paul was devoted to this great couple.[3]

Paul was single; he was called to a unique mission that could never have flourished had he married. But I can't help but think that after observing the marriage of Priscilla and Aquila up close, he would have learned much from seeing two people, hopelessly in love, and who gave their lives in the service of others.

---

[1] Acts 18:1–4   [2] 1 Cor. 16:19   [3] 2 Tim. 4:19

A True Vision or a Good Idea?

"Then the Lord answered me and said, 'Record the vision and inscribe it on tablets, that the one who reads it may run. For the vision is yet for the appointed time; it hastens toward the goal and will not fail. Though it tarries, wait for it; for it will certainly come and not delay.'" Habakkuk 2:23

I have spent a good part of my life listening to various entrepreneurial-minded people tell me about a vision they have for different things. Some are very exciting and seem to be carried forward by a wind that is not of human invention. It seems to have a life of its own and does not need to be marketed ... only guided. On the other hand, I have heard elaborate schemes that are ornately illustrated like an architectural rendering with color-coded projections. They mean well, but it usually turns out to be a good idea from a person rather than a vision from God.

How do you tell the difference? All I know is that it seems that the "good ideas" concocted by people either lose momentum and die or their efforts to make it work or are so stressful that they soon turn to something else. But I've seen others ... like a young man I know well who always had a heart for the poor and disenfranchised. He hurt for them and one day walked into an inner-city project and asked the leaders about their needs. That set in motion a city galvanized around a vision enlisting hundreds of volunteers to rehab dozens of houses, a school, a church and literally changed the face of an urban community. This

was a vision from God and the young man had the guts to follow it.

I know another man and woman named Dois and Shirley Rosser in Virginia who turned their considerable wealth into a vision to use his skills as a businessman to develop a world-wide ministry to build churches, and training centers by the thousands in developing countries. I have seen it firsthand, and believe me, it is a vision from God.

The greatest visionary I have ever seen was Doug Coe, whom I have mentioned several times. I worked with him for forty-four years until his death in 2017. A man with a vision for the world, Doug loved everything God loved. He was a unique man as he didn't ride his own private "hobby horse," traveling all over the world asking the national leadership what was on their heart for their country. He would listen, then enlist others to stand with them. He did not want to run it or take charge; he simply *blew on the flames that were already smoldering*. He never tried to bring his vision under any particular umbrella. His only concern was that Jesus was at the center and that the credit and glory were God's alone. This the difference in a vision and a good idea.

Influence and Impact

"For our gospel did not come to you in word only, but also in power and in the Holy Spirit, and with full conviction; just as you know what kind of men we proved to be among you for your sake." 1 Thessalonians 1:5

Consider this simple question: What is the influence of the institutional church in the world today? But in your answer, don't give numbers of people attending, don't cite the budget for the coming year, and don't consider the programs or classes that are operating. Now, what is the influence of your church in the community? The point is not to make you feel bad, but to show that we tend to assign value based on a faulty measurement. None of the things I asked you *not* to include in your answer are necessarily related to the level of influence the church is having … they simply *appear* to be a good criterion.

The early church of the first century thrived within a firestorm of opposition because their faith had to be mature enough to live within the eye of that storm. There were no tricks or sleight of hand; no athletes coming to give talks, no pizzas being served to the young people, and no special lighting and music to create an atmosphere more conducive for worship. It was the reality of the truth and the presence of the Holy Spirit that moved them out of their comfort zones. They were an integral part of each other.[1]

I believe the difference in the early church and the 21st-century church is that the first-century believers created a *culture* around the principles of truth that they had learned. Earlier, on Days 156-165 we considered ten specific principles that Jesus taught His disciples. These principles were taught to me when I was a young believer, but I learned and practiced them within the context of a community of people who affirmed my growth as well as yielded a level of loving accountability. If you teach principles and biblical mandates in a vacuum, and without the empowering of the Holy Spirit, it will be sterile information without power. It will be like planting a garden in the desert where no one lives.

God wants a place to rest in the midst of His people. Principles without the presence of God's Spirit will wither. We have often settled for a doctrine without building a relationship in which to develop the truths we learn. Classes, projects, and activities in themselves will not make an impact in our fellowship or in our cities; they just look good! Transformation comes when the truth is learned and practiced within the context of a loving community.

---

[1]Acts 2:42–46

What is the Bible Really About?

"The Word of the Lord is living and active and sharper than any two–edged sword."
Hebrews 4:12

The Bible is the most misunderstood book ever written. Year after year, it is at the top of the bestseller list and yet, it gathers dust in most homes. Its wisdom, comfort, and life-giving power to all who believe are mostly ignored except in times of crisis. Interestingly, the word *Bible* does not even appear in the Bible. It is referred to as *the Scriptures* and the *Word of God,* and Jews refer to it as *the Text.*

The Bible tells us of a God who is hidden until we meet Him for the first time, and from that moment on He reveals Himself and how He thinks as we turn each page. From Genesis to Revelation, this book graphically shows us a God who not only loves the world He created, but constantly demonstrates that love by his patience, compassion, and forgiving heart. He is a God who pursues his people, no matter how disobedient and self-absorbed they become.

The Bible is not just a book, it is a *place* where we meet this extravagant lover face-to-face, and in the process, we meet ourselves, who we haven't really known until we meet Him. The Bible is your story! You will not only see yourself in the lives of the men and women of its pages, but you will experience the same fears and doubts, joys and sorrows as they do. This book is universal. It can be taken into any culture, at any time, in the history of man and have the same effect on the human heart.

Its sixty-six books were written over a period of sixteen hundred years by over forty different authors from twelve different countries, and yet, retains one constant theme: God's plan to reconcile the world back to Himself! It has survived intellectual and physical attacks along with constant criticism and abuse from every quarter. Yet the attackers eventually die off, and the Bible lives on with resurgent power to change every heart that believes.

The Bible is God's love letter to his children, but it is not a magical book or a lucky charm. Reading it won't guarantee you a new job, pay off your back taxes, or heal you from cancer. It is the basis of all truth and deserves to be the foundation of all of life. Without it, all morality, direction, and reason go up in smoke. If there is no standard, everyone is left to his own definition of good and bad, right and wrong, and values become optional.

Religion or Life

"For I tell you unless your righteousness exceeds that of the scribes and Pharisees, you will never enter the kingdom of heaven." Matthew 5:20

This may seem like an odd pairing, but I believe it is the central issue of the New Testament. The apostle Paul looks like he is continually facing off against the Jewish leaders and the Roman Empire. In the Old Testament, the wars and conflicts look as if they were nation against nation, people fighting people. Jesus faces off with the religious leaders, and it appears that they are His enemy, but the enemy is never people.

John 3:16 has been called the theme of the Bible. "For God so loved the *world*, that he gave his only begotten Son ..." When you read the Old Testament and see the battles and conflicts, God is righteous,[1] but that doesn't mean He hated the unrighteous. Jesus never hated Rome and never hated those who persecuted Him and eventually put Him to death. From the cross, Jesus asked His Father to forgive them.[2] The enemy is an *attitude* of independence. Evil actions stem from that attitude.

Religion has always been the greatest enemy of life. Jesus came that we might have *abundant life*.[3] Religion creates a barrier between us and life. The Jewish leaders were extremely religious. Rules were more important than people. They even invented Oral Laws, often called "Hedge Laws"

to supposedly form a barrier of protection around the Law of Moses. But these man-made laws became an inescapable burden on the people. Religious performance became everything, and "Life" that offered freedom and liberty was considered a license to sin.

Jesus is "Life." He came offering Sabbath rest[4] and the enjoyment of God's presence. The Pharisees' perspective was to *force* people to be righteous and penalize them if they weren't. Jesus asks only for their love and trust.[5] The religious seek to please God by flawless behavior, biblical knowledge, and constant activity. This leads to frustration because you never know if you've done enough.

How do you recognize truth when you hear it? I believe it comes from the awareness of a personal need. The prostitutes and tax collectors in the gospels always recognized Jesus as the Truth, and they ran to Him. Even the demons knew life when they saw it. But religion insulates you from the awareness of a personal need. Those who recognize Jesus are those who are most aware of their own wretchedness. Jesus loved all people, even the arrogance of the religious that hung Him on the cross.

---

[1] Jer. 9:24   [2] Luke 23:34   [3] John 10:10   [4] Heb. 4:9   [5] Matt. 9:23

The Answer Isn't Out There Somewhere

2 Kings 4:1–7

There is a fascinating story in the Old Testament about a woman whose husband was a Prophet. He dies and leaves her with a consuming debt. She has no ability to pay her creditors and they even demand her sons as collateral until the debt is paid. You can imagine the panic and fear that sets in. She doesn't know where to get a job to sustain her family much less pay these people what her husband owed them.

The woman has a choice, as we all do in times of duress. She can fake it, paint on a big smile, say "Praise the Lord," and act as if everything is wonderful. Or, she can admit she has a huge problem and ask for help. "I don't want to be a nuisance and bother people with my problem," she could have said. But isn't that what the family of faith is all about? We shoulder one another's burdens and stand together. Yes, but it takes vulnerability to admit you are flat broke. And to her credit, she does. She takes image and concern for what her neighbors may think out of the equation and goes to the Prophet, Elisha. "What can I do for you?" He asks. And before she can answer he asks her, "What do you have in your house?" She doesn't know it, but his question is the answer to her need. She tells him that she has no possessions but remembers a jar of oil she kept in the kitchen. He tells her, and her sons, to go throughout the neighborhood and collect every pot they can find and bring them back to the house.

If the neighbors ever wondered how she was doing, they now know. The neighbors always know more about you than you think. But the widow doesn't care; she does what Elisha says and now has a house full of empty pots. He tells her to close the door behind her. Why? I think he was telling her to quit. Stop analyzing and trying to fit a square peg in a round hole. *Trust God, dear lady, and realize that the jar of oil you have is far more than you will ever need. It represents your redemption.*

Oil in the Scripture symbolizes the Holy Spirit whom she had taken for granted when she said she had nothing left. It's easy to do because we are always looking for visible results.

The Prophet tells her to pour the oil in the pots, and like the bread and fish that Jesus gave to the five thousand, the oil continued to flow until all of the pots were full. He tells her to sell the oil and it will be enough to pay her debts and provide her living. A simple story with a powerful reminder that no believer, regardless of their loss, is ever without resources.

Willingness to Risk

"When you dig a well, you might fall in. When you demolish an old wall, you could be bitten by a snake." Ecclesiastes 10:8 (NLT)

No one ever deepens their faith and matures without taking some uncomfortable risks. Growth is never static; you can't push "pause" or "save" on your relationship with Christ and return at a convenient time to take up where you left off. Everything in life that happens moves you closer to God or farther away. If Jesus lives in you, you can't go on a vacation from Him and return to find that everything in the relationship is the same. Jesus is the same as is His love for you, but you lose the *cutting edge* on the relationship and you miss out on blessings that God wants to give you. If you are an athlete and slack off for a week or two you will lose your edge, your timing, your quickness. You can regain it, but it will take time. When you re-engage with God you won't be able to simply take up where you left off.

How do we grow and mature? The typical answers are to study, pray, have fellowship, etc. But if you long to deepen your faith, you must be willing to risk ... to develop some attitudes and take some actions that are not button-down, tidy, and neat. You'll have to get dirty. You'll have to learn to love the unlovely, become an extravagant giver, show kindness to the arrogant, and be patient with those whose point of view makes you want to vomit.

Every believer says they want to be Christ-like, but few ever consider what it will cost. Jesus spent regular time with people we cross the street to avoid. He went into the homes of despicable people and ate meals with Pharisees whose spiritual and political views were the antithesis of His. He lived simply, He gave all His time to people, and when He spoke harshly, it was directly to his enemies, and never behind their backs. He gave no concern to His image and "made Himself of no reputation."[1]

Still want to be like Jesus? I believe the way to start a real faith walk is to ask God to lead you to a few people who are ethnically, religiously, and politically different than you. Build a friendship, take them to lunch, have them to dinner and when it feels right, ask them to tell their story and listen to the heart of each person.

Don't see it as a project, but a lifestyle. Nobody wants to be your experiment. If you are sincere you will deepen your understanding of God and you will learn from your new friend in ways that would never happen in a Bible study in a comfortable home with chips and dip. To grow we must stretch; to stretch will mean risk, and when you risk you will see God's power on display.

---

[1] Phil. 2:7–10

God's People . . . Our People

"I will call them my people, which were not my people; and call her my loved one who is not my loved one" Romans 9:25 (NIV)

Hosea was a Jewish prophet who God commanded to marry a prostitute named Gomer. This is obviously not a principle we are to follow but a picture of Israel's spiritual adultery. They had been the bride of God,[1] then strayed and found other lovers blindly betraying the purpose for which they were created. Gomer and Hosea had three children and God gave them names that paint a picture of how His people had rejected Him. In Hosea 2:9, which Paul cites here in Romans, it says that one of those sons was named "Not My People" to reflect the fact that God's people had been cut off from Him because of their arrogance.

That prophecy was soon fulfilled when the ten tribes in the Northern Kingdom, Israel, were taken into captivity by Assyria. The point Paul is making is that the same prophecy is being fulfilled again in his day by the Jew's rejection of Jesus. By their choice, they had become "not His people." The Gentiles were not His people to begin with, but after the Jews soundly rejected Jesus, He turned His attention to the Gentiles, and they *became* His people. The good news is that many of God's beloved Jews will return to Him one day and become His people once again.

This verse touches me in a profound way. I grew up in Charlotte, North Carolina. We were a white, Protestant, middle-class family.

We were not racist in any respect that I can recall, but there was no social interaction with people of color. You could say that black people, Jews, Muslims, Hispanics, and other ethnic groups were not really *our people*. When I was in High School integration was initiated and I began to meet a few black kids my age. By the time I was a senior, I had become close friends with a wonderful guy named Jimmie Kirkpatrick. He was the best running back I ever saw, and we began a lifelong friendship. He and many others of color became "my people." I became friends along the way with many African Americans as well as Muslims, Buddhists and others whom, until I met Jesus, I would never have called "my people." God loves His creation and calls them "His people." What right or reason would I have to call them anything else? Paul's plea in Romans is for the church in Rome to accept and respect the Jews and Gentiles equally.

I've come to believe that anyone who God loves, and anything Gods cares about, deserves my love and compassion as well.

---

[1] Isa. 54:5; Hosea 2:7; Ezek. 16:32–34

Where Do the Poor Fit in Your Theology?

"If you pour yourself out for the hungry and satisfy the desire of the afflicted, then shall your light rise in the darkness and your gloom be as the noonday.
Isaiah 58:10 (ESV)

There are more than two thousand verses in the Bible concerning God's compassion for the poor. Throughout my college years, I never once heard a sermon, a Bible study, or remember any conversation concerning our responsibility to the poor and oppressed. I attended some very good churches and listened to some riveting speakers, but never once did anyone speak of the poor. Then I met a man named Tom Skinner. He had been the head of The Harlem Lords, a vicious New York gang in the early sixties. He met Jesus and became one of the most articulate and powerful speakers in the country. He had a prolific grasp of the Scriptures and a deep love and concern for the disenfranchised of the world. I felt compelled to talk to him, so I wrote him a letter not really expecting an answer. To my surprise, he wrote me back and we set up a meeting in Atlanta after he addressed a large conference. For three hours, I asked question after question, and I left feeling like I had met a modern-day prophet. We later became friends.

I look back on my college years with great appreciation for the people I met and the opportunities I had. But I was puzzled and a little angry at how it was possible for over two thousand verses to never find their way into a sermon or Bible study I attended. I later learned that evangelicals tended to lean away from matters that they considered "the social gospel." They felt that presenting salvation to the lost was the main, and in some cases, the only responsibility of believers. I could not reconcile that attitude with what I was seeing in the Scriptures. I read books like *The Autobiography of Malcolm X* and gained an understanding of what being locked out of the system can do to a person. I met others along the way like Bill Millikan, the founder of "Communities and Schools." He became another hero of mine as he helped me see that the radical call to the *least of these* was fully compatible with my desire to follow Jesus. Throughout my life, I have always believed in the centrality of Jesus, the inerrancy of Scripture, and with it, the God-appointed command to love mercy, do justice and walk humbly before God.[1] Justice demands that we care for "the least of these," not as a token measure, but with our whole heart.

I run into people regularly who love God. They are good and kind but don't seem to share His love for the disenfranchised of the world.[2] I would be lying if I told you I understood that, but maybe they are like I was before I was shown the true heart of God.

---

[1]Mic. 6:8 [2]Matt. 25:40–45

Accountability

"Brothers, if anyone is caught in any transgression, you who are spiritual should restore him in a spirit of gentleness. Keep watch on yourself, lest you too be tempted. Bear one another's burdens, and so fulfill the law of Christ."
Galatians 6:1–5 (ESV)

Some thirty to forty years ago, the idea of believers being accountable to one another hit the top of the charts, particularly among young people. To *reprove, rebuke, and exhort* has always been a well-known command of God, though generally ignored by the church.[1] However, in the seventies, eighties, and into the nineties, it became somewhat of a "Christian trend." Everywhere you looked young people were getting into "accountability groups." I believe strongly in small clusters of folks locking arms and encouraging, challenging, and at times confronting one another to honor God in their lives. My concern was that when accountability becomes the primary purpose of the gathering, it can easily degenerate into an attack group with each person looking for flaws in the others and nailing them. I don't believe this is the best way to build healthy relationships. I have been in very close relationships with a few men for the last forty-five years. Our only agenda has been to help each other grow in our intimacy with God, our families and one another. We have also looked for ways to help each other better utilize our individual gifts and to do, with excellence, that which God has called us to. Along with that, we confessed our sins to one another,

and as we grew closer there were times we had to confront unhealthy behavior in each other. So, accountability is part of our commitment, but not the primary purpose of walking together.

There is something almost magical about believers who really love one another but avoid becoming a clique that makes others feel left out. For instance, if you have a secure relationship with a few close companions, you don't have to cling together at a party or a gathering. You remind each other to spread out and make others feel welcome and included. If you cling together, others will feel marginalized and you will be seen as an exclusive clique.

Exercising authority in another person's life is best served when it is a request by that person. Authority should be given, not taken. If I ask you to help me with an area of my life and later you ask me some hard questions around it, how can I be offended? I asked you to hold me accountable. If you want to grow, someone other than your spouse, who is not as emotionally connected, can be an invaluable asset to help you smooth the rough edges in your life. The only question is, are you willing to be that humble.

---

[1] 2 Tim. 4:2

People are Basically Good . . . or Not!

"None is righteous, no, not one; no one understands; no one seeks for God. All have turned aside; together they have become worthless; no one does good, not even one." Romans 3:10–12 (ESV)

For some reason, this is a hard pill for many to swallow, particularly in this current *politically correct* environment. As a culture, we have become super-sensitive and must almost tiptoe around each other trying to avoid the growing list of offenses. There seems to be an effort afoot to lock people of faith into a worldview that is counter to God's values. Words of comfort and compassion in the Scriptures are welcomed, but anything God stands against, short of murder, is written off as insensitive and intolerant. Any inference that heaven won't be populated by all the people they feel should automatically be there is considered narrow and judgmental. The issue centers on the assertion that people are born basically *good*. In modern psychology, you find that it echoes views like that of L. Ron Hubbard, the founder of Scientology. He said; "Man is basically good, but man can act badly."

The Bible says man is born without God's life in Him. God is good; if I am born apart from His life, where lies my capacity to be good? Sure, you can be nice and generous, etc., but the goodness of the heart comes *only* from God. That's why the Scripture says we can't trust our heart; it is desperately wicked.[1] Do you remember as a teenager, in the back of a car when, in the heat of passion, you were sure you were in love? But years later you say, "What was I thinking?" You weren't ... your heart deceived you.

I don't know why it hurts people's feelings to hear that man is at his core not good. If we're honest and look deep within, we would say, *I don't know why God would want anything to do with me*. If our hearts are basically good, all things being equal, we will always do that which is right. If I am bad, the inequities of society are the cause, not me. A thief would say *I stole because the system is corrupt, and I couldn't get a job*. It is a way to shift personal responsibility to a faceless, nameless culture.

Do you lock your door at night? Do you use passwords on personal accounts? Why? You *know* why! To admit our inability to be who and what we want to be is not an insult to humanity. It is an invitation. Jesus said to a lawyer, "Why do you call me good? No one is good but God."[2] He is saying, *if you are willing to say I'm good are you also willing to say I am God?* It means we need a Savior and His presence will create in us the goodness we were designed to have.

---

[1]Mark 10:17–18   [2]Rom. 3:10–12

Standing Against the North Wind

"Whatever happens, conduct yourselves in a manner worthy of the gospel of Christ. Then, whether I come to see you or only hear about you in my absence, I will know that you stand firm in one spirit, contending as one man for the faith of the gospel . . ." Philippians 1:27 (NIV)

Regardless of where you stand politically, economically, socially, or where you are along the road spiritually, there is a strong north wind blowing in our land. Our economy is not as strong as the politicians would have us believe. The stock market looks like it is booming, but much of that is smoke and mirrors. We still accumulate debt at two million dollars per minute. Politically, there has never been greater division and hatred on both sides of the aisle than presently. Spiritually, you see big crowds at some of the mega-churches, but that had little to do with depth and maturity. No matter how positive we want to be, the reality is that the north wind is picking up steam. As followers of Jesus, we must be able to utilize every spiritual asset available to stand strong.

This is not a doomsday prediction, but to take a Pollyanna, "it will all work out fine" approach is like an ostrich who puts his head in the sand and thinks, "if I don't see it, it's not there." We are warned all through the Scripture that we must stand firm and strong against whatever the world throws at us.

Earlier, I wrote some daily thoughts on the Scripture's admonition about *walking* with God in several different ways. We are also told to *stand firm*, anchored by our faith in God's unwavering love and care.[1] This involves a *lifestyle* of daily spiritual preparation so that we don't simply grit our teeth and brace for it but are prepared and take it in stride confidently.

Paul writes to the Philippians from a Roman prison to remind them to "stand firm in one spirit."[2] This means it is not a solitary, *me against the world* admonition. We are part of a family of believers who stand together, united by one faith and the belief that God stands with us and goes before us. Paul also says we must "stand against the schemes of the devil."[3] As I mentioned earlier, his focus is not on those who are already captured by the *world* and the *flesh*. They are no threat to him; only those who *stand* against his schemes will prosper. God told Ezekiel that He was looking for someone to *stand in the gap*. Who will be that advocate or catalyst? Who will be the mortar between the bricks?[4]

In the next few days, we'll look at what it takes to stand firm.

---

[1] 1 Cor. 16:13   [2] Phil. 2:27   [3] Eph. 6:11   [4] Ezek. 22:30

281

Stand Firm in the Faith

"Be on your guard, stand firm in the faith; be men of courage; be strong. Do everything in love." 1 Corinthians 16:13 (NIV)

When you read the words, "Be on your guard," what comes to mind? A sentry at his post? A platoon of soldiers walking cautiously through a minefield. Whatever your first thought was, if it doesn't coalesce or affirm what the rest of the Scripture says about the way we approach life, it doesn't mean what you think. The fruit of the spirit is peace, joy, love, gentleness, kindness, etc.[1] As the Good Shepherd, Jesus feeds, loves, leads, and protects His sheep. Paul tells us to walk in the light; to walk in love, wisdom, and gratitude. How does a paranoid person do that? There *are* forces at work that want to counter everything you and I believe, but being on your guard does *not* mean being suspicious of everyone you meet and considering everything in life as a minefield. What a horrible way to live.

Instead, don't be naïve or cavalier, just be aware. Don't think the devil is hiding behind every tree or be defensive if someone's theology doesn't line up perfectly with yours. Satan is not omnipresent like God. He can only be one place at a time. He does have help, but they don't possess his power. For someone to think he or she must be on guard like a soldier on patrol is just about as arrogant as anyone could be.

Out of millions of believers, you think Satan is spending all his time and energy just on you?

Stand firm in your faith means be consistent in what you know is from God. Many give talks and write books, but what do you know for certain that is non-negotiable? Be courageous because it takes courage to stand firm and not waver when your friends think you are nuts. Smile, don't be defensive, laugh with them and keep standing firm in your faith.

Some years ago, Susan and I hosted about a dozen couples from different states at the National Prayer Breakfast in Washington, D.C. On the third night, we invited them to dinner at our home and had a wonderful time with everyone. A week later I received a scathing letter from a man from South Carolina for serving wine to the guests in our home. He said he was appalled and angry that a man of God would serve alcohol. I called him to apologize for offending him, but he blasted me even more, saying I was "a wolf in sheep's clothing." He said he was simply "standing firm in his faith." I am sorry I offended him, and I accept his position. I do wish that he had thought to read the rest of the verse: "Do everything in love."

---

[1]Gal. 5:22

Stand Firm in One Spirit

"Whatever happens, conduct yourselves in a manner worthy of the gospel of Christ. Then, whether I come and see you or only hear about you in my absence, I will know that you stand firm in one Spirit, striving together as one for the faith of the gospel." Philippians 1:27 (NIV)

No matter what happens, live worthy of the One whom you follow, says Paul. *And if I am here with you or simply receive news about you, I will know that you are standing together, speaking and living as one honoring the Savior.*

Our greatest problem in the Body of Christ is not that we agree on very little, but that we can't love each other in spite of it. That is why there are thousands of denominations out there. "Standing firm in one spirit" and "striving together" is like wearing a tuxedo with flip flops. Paul knew this would be our Achilles Heel; that's why he speaks of unity so much. Nothing you read in the Scriptures will work without people being of one spirit. Think of how ridiculous it is to spend so much money and time trying to lure the world into our churches only for them to discover that they have been invited into a food fight. There is liberty in our brother and sisterhood. Many do not understand that although we must stand firm on the basic principles of Scripture, we have the liberty of different strategies to get there. The man who was angry that I served wine to my guests (from yesterday's thoughts) has a perfect right to abstain. But he does not have a right

to decide that for the other eighteen people at our house. In fact, he doesn't have to right to break fellowship over it and neither do I. The reason is that if the world sees that we can't even agree on something that is not even an absolute in Scripture, why would they want to add the church to their mounting list of headaches? We must have something to call people into and continuing disunity isn't it!

We should agree on the essential precepts of God's Word, but there are non-essentials that we can and should give each other room to grow. Even if a belief is questionable, no one gets it right all at once. We must allow people to hear from God and own their faith. To shame them is to drive them into the shadows.

I can think of places I have been where I could absolutely tell you that people are standing fast and standing in unity because I know them close-up as well as from a distance. Becoming one is what gets the attention of the non-believing world, not being right. If we don't agree on an issue, we work through it together. We give each other the latitude to grow and allow God to speak.

D

Stand Against the Schemes of the Enemy

"Put on the full armor of God so that you can take your stand against the Devil's schemes." Ephesians 6:11 (NIV)

Most people there is evil in the world. The debate is more about the source of evil. Is it flaws in human nature or is there an actual evil personality in the universe behind it all. The Bible says that Satan is a fallen angel who rebelled against God and who not only propagates evil but who *is* evil personified.[1] To see him as a cute little red-suited cartoon character with a pitchfork or as a hideous monster who makes people's head spin around is inaccurate and it distracts us from his real persona.

The verse above continues to say that the armor of God is not physical weapons because it is not a physical enemy with which we contend. In this passage, Paul speaks of the helmet of salvation, the breastplate of righteousness, the belt of truth and so on. Our fight is with unseen powers and domains so we can't beat them up! We must first understand what we are up against and how this brazen enemy of peace and contentment operates. Whatever we think his scheme to mess with us is … we're probably wrong! The Bible says that Satan is the craftiest of any creature.[2] His character is seen in the names he is called: *Deceiver, Hinderer, Angel of light, Tempter.* Satan means *adversary.*

One thing we know: our enemy is crafty and he will not try to disable us in any textbook manner. He does not advertise; he moves in secret, in the shadows. Have you ever received a message on your computer that malware is present? The company that sends that announcement claims they can solve the problem. But much of the time they are actually the ones who will *install* the malware if give them access. Why would the devil present himself as the problem when he could appear to be the solution? Our fight is not usually hand-to-hand combat. Our adversary simply observes what we are already doing and joins us. If I am lazy, why try to get me to rob a bank? Why not affirm me by telling me I should relax more?

I was at a men's conference and we had a man speak that I had known for many years. Senator Harold Hughes from Iowa was a big, powerful man who had a voice that you would swear God must sound like. Deep and resonate, he asked the men this question: "If you saw Satan face to face what do you think he would look like?" Four hundred men sat silent. "He would be the most beautiful thing you ever saw in your life and you would give your soul to possess him." That's the main scheme. Everything about him is attractive; every enticement looks legit … foolproof … essential … perfect … and that's why we must always *stand firm.*

---

[1] Isa. 14:13–15 [2] Gen. 3:1

Standing in the Gap

"I looked for someone among them who would build up the wall and stand before me in the gap on behalf of the land so I would not have to destroy it, but I found no one." Ezekiel 22:30 (NIV)

Just about every book you read and every movie you watch that touches you deeply is about people who "stand in the gap" on someone else's behalf. *Saving Private Ryan* was just such a movie where a platoon of men went behind enemy lines to find and bring home a single soldier. Seeing someone put their own safety aside to defend another evokes an emotion deep within us.

The ultimate bridge across the gap was in God sending His own Son to connect the breach between man and God. To stand in the gap means to intercede between two or more parties. "Intercede come from two Latin words, *inter* meaning "between" and *ced* which means "go." An intercessor is a "go-Between." Then, Ezekiel writes, "to build up the wall ..." Bricks or stones used in building a wall must have mortar to bind them together? The mortar is the "go-between" that makes the wall stable. This is what God is looking for.

Often the word *intercessor* is used in sermons to mean those who stand in the gap for others in prayer. That is certainly true, but that is not all of it. Just as the mortar strengthens and gives stability to the wall, it can become vulnerable where the mortar is chipped and weakened over time. The sad part of this verse is that in God's search for someone to stand as a "go-between" to present Jesus as the bridge to God, He finds no one.

What could a man or woman in the marketplace do to stand in the gap on behalf of the Kingdom of God? We don't need more *Christian* lawyers, doctors, teachers, businessmen, and athletes. We need more than that! We need people in the marketplace who will impact their profession at its core. It's not about simply being an employee who doesn't gossip or pad his expense account and refuses to listen to dirty jokes. It means representing God's integrity, respecting people, and becoming catalysts for change. The works of Satan in the marketplace are such things as inequity, injustice, greed, divisiveness, sexism, and lack of integrity. Stand in the gap where the mortar is chipping away and become so good at your job that you become irreplaceable. Those people earn the right to speak prophetically to the *powers that be* about issues that need correcting.

Owning Your Faith

"When Christ, who is our life, is revealed, then you also will be revealed with Him in glory." Colossians 3:4

When I was on Young Life staff just out of college, all staff were required to complete six semesters of study at the Young Life Institute in Colorado Springs. Summer after summer I studied under some top seminary professors in the country. One Saturday, two other staff guys and I went into town for lunch and later to Baskin-Robbins for a milkshake. The girl who served us wore a beautiful silver cross and one of my friends asked her if it had any special meaning. She stopped scooping ice cream, looked in his eyes and said, "Yes, it's my life." What a great answer! I loved the fact that she didn't give a theological response, but *who she was* in relation to *the cross she wore*.

I met Jesus just before my senior year in high school. I became intensely interested and wanted to learn more about my new faith. But looking back on my college years, though I became very active and was known as a "Christian Athlete," my faith was a mixture of articles I read, talks I heard, and Bible Studies I attended. I was serious about my faith, but I became the latest book I read and when I spoke at gatherings, anything beyond my personal story was borrowed from other people I admired. In other words, it took years before I finally began to *own* my faith.

I find this the norm among believers even twenty or thirty years down the road. They love God; they know verses of Scripture and have read all the recommended *flavor of the month* Christian books. Yet, something is often missing. It is not really theirs. They couldn't say, "It's my life," as the ice cream girl said.

If you are ever in Israel and can speak with young children who are observant Jews, do it! Ask them to describe God, they will say things like, "He's my Shepherd, my Living Water, my Rock, my Shelter." If you ask almost believer in the west, he or she will give a theological answer … "God is just, merciful, omnipresent, omniscient, etc. These are correct, but the Jewish kid's words paint a picture or image: a rock, a shepherd, living water. The theological descriptions are correct but are words and concepts that seldom reach the heart. The Jewish kids use the personal pronoun "my" to describe God. It is intimacy and ownership. We teach in a way that accents what we *know* as the important connection to God. A Rabbi wants his student's hearts to be touched. Then, learning becomes part of his personal story.

Do you own your faith? Is Jesus your life or something added to what you already have going? Thomas' doubt was not solved by intellect. When he saw the truth, he said, "*My* Lord and *my* God." It was personal; it was ownership.

Build Your Brokenness into Your Story

When we lived in New York City, I was encouraged by a very fine agent to attend a seminar called "Story" by Robert McKee. He is the guru of Hollywood scriptwriters and though I don't write screenplays, she convinced me that the three-day workshop about crafting stories would be beneficial. The amazing seminar got my attention right away. McKee said that biographies and autobiographies are marketed as true and candid but they're all fiction! They leave out the affairs, the depression, the addiction with pornography, or the resentment toward a family member, etc.

I think he was right. If you are trying to market yourself, there are certain things you do not include. If you create a biographical piece about yourself, you never include that you abused your wife or your father was in the KKK or that you cheated on the S.A.T. Unflattering things seldom make the cut, therefore the picture that is painted is a fictional version of who you are.

There is only one avenue in life where your liabilities are what qualify you for membership. There is no level of sin that can grow and prosper in a person that cannot be covered by the grace that God offers.[1] Nothing we ever do could surprise or disgust God. He is never flustered or shocked.

Why would he be if He knows when we rise up and when we sit down and knows all of our thoughts?[2] Our secrets and our failures are the very things that make us candidates for a relationship with Almighty God. If you and I were good, if we were sufficient in ourselves to merit a friendship with God we wouldn't need a Savior. In fact, we would never even sense the need for one.

We are all different people; we come from different backgrounds, cultures and different places in life. What connects us is not our victories, our strengths, or our abilities; what links us together are our flaws. We relate to one another at the point of our greatest weaknesses. How many of us can relate with a Phi Beta Kappa, a CEO of a large company, or a Hall of Fame athlete? But when a guy talks about his grandkids and gets choked up, I understand that perfectly. When someone makes a stupid blunder or drops the ball on a task he promised to complete, I get that ... I've been there ... done that!

Broken people, those who walk with a limp like Jacob (and me), help others most and show the power of God when they build that brokenness into their story. Our weakness is what draws us to God and is the place where our lives connect.

---

[1] Rom. 5:20 [2] Ps. 139:1–2

Pursue Those Rejected by Others

"Religion that is pure and undefiled before God, the Father, is this: to visit orphans and widows in their affliction, and to keep oneself unstained from the world."
James 1:27 (ESV)

When we see Scriptures like this concerning widows and orphans, or when Jesus speaks of "the least of these" in Matthew 25,[1] we think of the poor and disenfranchised as indeed we should. But if you study Jesus' life, you see an aggressive concern and love for *all* those who are marginalized in society. It is clear to me that "the least of these" includes those who live in the shadows ... those who may have financial means, but have been mentally or physically challenged, emotionally wounded, or those who simply lack the social skills to relate easily.

When I see an advertisement on TV and the smiling self-satisfied actor hops in his beautiful new convertible with his girlfriend and the voiceover says, "Affordable at $39,995," I think, *Affordable to who?* What do those words sound like to a single mother making minimum wage as she realizes any dream she ever had has gone up in smoke. Will she grow old just trying to hang on? Does God care about this? If He does, where do you and I, who say we want to be like Jesus, fit into this equation?

Jesus told the Pharisees, "I desire compassion, not sacrifice."[2] For us to drive across town with a group from our church and help clean up an urban neighborhood makes us feel good, but it's not the issue. God is searching for "a heart that is completely His."[3] How can that compassion toward the forgotten, the socially inept, and the disabled become a natural extension of the way we think rather than simply a project.

After college, I worked with teenagers, and as they gave their life to Jesus, we met with them in small groups to help them learn and grow. Most wanted to know how to explain their faith to family and friends. "Keep your mouth shut," I would usually say. "Go home and clean up your room without being asked, wash your parent's cars, cut the grass and don't complain. At school eat lunch with the kids who eat alone because they have no friends. Learn the names of students you never paid any attention to; befriend them and listen to their story. Soon, they will ask *you what makes you tick!*"

Thinking like Jesus is not about the big things; it's about the mundane everyday things we seldom even consider. A simple compliment to someone could be the only positive thing that person has heard in months ... a smile, a pat on the back, a hug. I believe this is one way to think like Jesus.

---

[1]Matt. 25:40   [2]Matt. 9:13   [3]2 Chron. 16:9

Faithfulness:
Is God Involved or Not?

"His master said to him, 'Well done, good and faithful servant! You have been
faithful over a little; I will set you over much. Enter into the joy of your master.'"
Matthew 25:21 (ESV)

While I was working at a college in New York City I had many conversations with students about their career goals and hopes for the future. They were extremely intelligent and astute, but for most, their career dreams included a starting salary in the six-figure range and a company car. Most of these kids were believers and from good families from across the country. We had just gone through the 2008 financial meltdown and Wall Street brokers were trying to get jobs a Starbucks. Still, their dream never faded. One day a group of us went to a coffee shop on 6th Avenue and I asked them if they had ever considered going with the intent to serve people in the workplace and lay the results at God's feet. We had a great discussion and I remember being stunned that these students had never really considered the idea of trusting God and being servants in a corporate venue.

I asked for thoughts on this verse: "A faithful man will abound with blessings, but whoever hastens to be rich will not go unpunished."[1] They sat silent. We have failed to help people see the value of a towel and a basin as opposed to fantasizing about a corner office and a key to the executive restroom.

There is nothing wrong with ambition and wanting to succeed, but that's not the problem. Everything you hear and see all day long is about zooming to the top and getting what you want. Where are the voices that teach and remind people that if you make it your aim to serve those around you, God will reward faithfulness in the little things and move you onward.

In the church and in many homes, children are taught about a relationship with God but there seems to be little mention about building the Kingdom in the marketplace. I paraphrase what one student in New York said that day: *My church and my parents taught me to read my Bible and pray daily, abstain from sex before marriage, stand strong against abortion and homosexuality, join a good church, and vote Republican.* But what about half of your sixteen waking hours daily? The implication of this teaching is to trust God in all the social and personal issues, but concerning your career, you have to make it happen!

No one ever explains that if you go into the workplace as a faithful servant, doing what no one else is willing to do, you will eventually become known as a trustworthy, proactive, loyal employee. What employer do you know who wouldn't kill to have someone like that? *Faithful with little will be trusted with much.*[2]

---

[1]Prov. 28:20   [2]Luke 16:10

289

Defensiveness

"With all humility and gentleness, with patience, showing tolerance for one another in love . . ." Ephesians 4:2

Defensiveness is a battle where the winner ultimately becomes the loser. It is an effort to be right regardless of the personal cost and potential damage to the relationship.

When we are threatened, we usually shoot back by denying what is said and then shifting the blame to the accuser. This insatiable need to *win* is a product of the flesh. We want to be right all the time ... not just some of the time. The roots of this response go back to Adam and Eve. When they eat the forbidden fruit, God confronts Adam and asks him why. "The woman *you* gave me," Adam responds. *It's not my fault, Lord, it's yours.* Then God asks Eve what she had done. "The serpent deceived me," she sheepishly replies. *Blame him! I was just window shopping, he tricked me into going into the store!*

I have struggled with this demon much of my life. I've wrestled with God and He's always won. That is why I "walk with a limp." When you wrestle with God and finally admit he is right, you become the beneficiary of His victory.[3]

Defensiveness can alter a friendship forever. It can also change how you are perceived. If you become a person who always has to win and be right, people will intentionally or subconsciously avoid being around you. It is just not worth the energy to always be in a debate with someone.

Jesus was attacked constantly. Even in refuting the erroneous teaching of the Pharisees, He never was defensive. In His trial, they tried to throw the book at Him, but He refused to defend Himself. He taught His disciples to turn the other cheek, don't resist one who is evil.[2] Peter said that when Jesus was hated He did not return hate.[3] He taught His disciples to take the *offensive*, the opposite of what their emotions dictated. "Pray for your enemies and do good to those who abuse you."[4]

Defensiveness cannot thrive in the presence of vulnerability. To confess your sins, humble yourself, and forgive someone requires an openness to being wrong. True humility chases away defensiveness. No one is ever *always* right. Learn to say things like, "That's a good point," or "that's worth considering." It will save a lot of needless heartaches and will build a humble spirit in you.

---

[1]Prov. 15:1   [2]Matt. 5:39   [3]1 Pet. 2:23   [4]Matt. 5:43–45

Interconnectedness

"We sent Timothy, who is our brother and co–worker in God's service in spreading the gospel of Christ, to strengthen and encourage you in your faith."
1 Thessalonians 3:2 (NIV)

The tendency of people is to think of themselves in a stand-alone, solitary manner. Men certainly display that characteristic more than women, but we all lean toward autonomy. After all, the heart of sin is independence, the desire to self-govern.

When you and I come to Jesus Christ in brokenness, we are essentially saying, *Lord, I've tried to do my own thing in life, and my own thing isn't working. I have failed. I need you and I need a family of brothers and sisters to walk beside me and help me.* We were never meant to be solitary people. Paul uses the metaphor of the human body to illustrate this. The eyes, the hands, the feet, the ears, all need each other and cannot work the way they are designed if they don't work together in harmony.[1] As believers, we cannot function properly apart from one another. We cannot afford to pass like ships in the night. If our common goal is to glorify God, we can't fully do it apart from each other.

The interconnectedness we have as a family is more than theoretical; it's practical. My friend Tom Skinner used to say, "If I ask you how you are treating your wife, you can't say it's none of my business. You are my brother and she is my sister, and I have every right to ask how my brother is treating my sister."

One of the most important things I learned from the men and women I have worked with over the years is that our connection is based purely on our common relationship with Jesus. It not based on what church, political party, or doctrinal tradition we each endorse; our commonality is Jesus. That means that if you and I are brothers, we have access to each other's gifts, influence, and relationships. Paul would often send Timothy to a city and write in advance asking them to treat Timothy as they would treat him.[2] Many times, when I have traveled to other countries, a friend will write ahead and ask his friends there to greet and meet with me on his behalf. I can't tell you the times I've stayed in the homes of strangers and left as lifelong friends because we shared a common friendship. Susan and I have had the same privilege to extend hospitality to scores of *friends of friends* over the years and we have been the beneficiaries.

The world is big, but when you see it as an interconnected family it shrinks. If you think about *people* and *places* rather than *things* and *commodities,* life becomes a great adventure.

---

[1] 1 Cor. 12:15–31   [2] 1 Cor. 4:17; Phil. 2:19–24

Truth Doesn't Come in Versions

"Be diligent to present yourself to God as a workman who does not need to be ashamed, accurately handling the word of truth." 2 Timothy 2:15 (NASB 1977)

All of us want security; we want good security systems that protect our homes, our cars, and our money. Multiple types of insurance make us feel more immune to the storms of life. But, in reality, the only security we have is the *truth*. Everything God says is true. You can count on it. But instead of resting the full weight of our concerns on that immutable reality we try to amend and create versions of the truth that will guarantee failure over time. As followers of Jesus shouldn't we speak the truth in a manner that is clear, accurate, and resistant to misunderstanding?

My wife's parents were married for fifty-five years. Sarah always made sure that John had an ample serving of his favorite vegetable at least three times a week. This continued for forty-four years until one-night John said, in frustration "Sarah, must I eat this god-awful broccoli every other night?" He had always hated the green stuff, but he never communicated it to her, and she thought he just couldn't get enough.

We have heard expressions of faith that are repeated in a rote-like manner, year after year, and they frequently become an overused, and often erroneous Christian cliché. For instance, "winning someone to Christ" is a common mantra in the *evangelical world* and yet the expression clearly assumes that it is up to us. If we don't "win" people, they will be doomed and it will be our fault. Nothing could be farther from the truth. To assume that we can do anything to change the heart of another is arrogance at the highest level. That is the job of the Holy Spirit.[1] We can give them information, but we cannot give them revelation. I resist the idea of one person, who God created, being seen as a project to be completed, or a *scalp* to be hung on the wall.

The term "evangelical" has become prominent, mainly because today's media uses it as a more stepped-up, aggressive version of an ordinary *Christian*. The term is nowhere in the Bible and is derived from the Greek word *Evangelion* meaning "gospel" or "good news." The *Evangel* was simply a bringer of Good News. Is there any *version* of a man or woman who loves and follows Jesus who would not fit that notion? We continue to create qualifying adjectives to precede the word Christian because we intuitively know it has lost its meaning. Why use words that confuse and divide us rather than accurately express our faith?

---

[1] John 6:44

Telling the Story

"But sanctify Christ as Lord in your hearts, always being ready to make a defense to everyone who asks you to give an account for the hope that is in you, yet with gentleness and reverence." 1 Peter 3:15

If I eat at a great restaurant, I will tell people about it. If I read an exceptional book, I will encourage others to read it as well. If I have experienced the extravagance of God, the joy of knowing that the past is finished and gone and that I am a new creation, why would I want to keep that secret?

We have created levels of spiritual veracity by placing words like *Bible-believing, born again, charismatic,* or *evangelical* in front of the word *Christian* as if it places one on a higher or more serious level. No divisions like this exist in the Scriptures. A person was either "in Christ" or lingering on the outside. There were no second-class levels, no new and improved varieties.

Peter clearly tells us that the focus of our lives should be intimacy with Jesus. As a natural by-product of that intimacy, we grow in our knowledge and understanding of Him to the point that when we are asked what makes us tick, we give *a gentle and respectful answer.* I believe this is evangelism at its essence. It doesn't preclude going "into all the world,"[1] but the thrust of sharing your faith is centripetal, which draws people inward, rather than centrifugal, which thrusts people outward.

No man or woman can "win" someone to Christ. The Holy Spirit must draw them in.[2] No one can even "lead" another to Jesus. You can point the way, give a convincing argument to a person, be patient and loving, but you cannot take a person from death to life. That is God's prerogative. As my friend and mentor, Doug Coe used to say, "A fountain is a place people come to drink when they are thirsty. You never see the fountain running through town trying to find thirsty people." Real evangelism is when we focus on being a fountain of living water where the lost and lonely can come to refresh their soul.

The best form of evangelism is to *lift up* Christ.[3] He does not need to be branded or marketed in any way. He does not need a public relations firm or a slick way to get His message out. He *is* the Message, and He stands on His own. When people see the invisible God become visible in a man or woman they will be irresistibly drawn toward the light and run from the darkness.

---

[1] John 28:19   [2] John 6:65   [3] John 12:32

Are We Hearing and Being Heard?

"He who has ears to hear, let him hear." Matthew 11:15 (ESV)

I bought a poster in the early seventies in Sausalito, just across the San Francisco Bay. It said more than words could ever convey. The scene was a typical church service on Sunday morning. The picture was taken from behind a minister standing at His pulpit holding forth. Facing him was the congregation of mostly middle age and older, very stone-faced people who looked like deer caught in the headlights. On the front row sat a man with long hair, beard and sandals in a long white robe (obviously Jesus) sound asleep with a copy of the *Village Voice* in His lap.

About that time, I had read a survey by the National Council of Churches saying *that if two-thirds of the pews were removed from the New England churches they would never be missed*. I was a young believer, naïve spiritually, but from what I had observed the poster was a sad but fitting metaphor of the way we are seen by the world. Do you ever wonder why with all the relational skills and creative avenues of communication available to us, we still can't convey the truth? Obviously, we're part of the problem. To a watching world, we don't seem much different than them.

I believe much of our problem is the language we use. A word may be meaningful to you, but the people you are communicating to may only understand that word in light of their own experience. To you, the term "Christian" may be synonymous with Jesus, but not to ninety percent of the world. You can talk to a Muslim all day about Jesus but talking about Christianity will end the conversation. Why? Too much baggage to unpack!

"Christianity" is a made-up word and "Christian" appears only once in 1 Peter,[1] and twice in the Acts,[2] but never as it is used today (The Christian record company, Christian movies or Jack and Sally become Christians). The followers of Jesus did not call themselves Christians. The word was coined by Jesus' enemies. He never uttered the word, nor did Paul, John, or the other disciples. Jesus Christ and Christianity are miles apart. Arnold Toynbee said back in the 1950s that "Twentieth-century man has not rejected Christ; only a poor caricature of Him." People are rejecting an "enterprise" not a Person and most have confused the two.

Why does this matter? I want to suggest a couple of reasons in tomorrow's thoughts that may be helpful as you think through this. I want to be a good communicator; I want people to know the truth, and I never want to use words or phrases that do not convey what I intended.

---

[1] 1 Pet. 4:13   [2] Acts 11:26; 26:28

Our Language is Confusing

"Our Bible study group is praying that the Jewish kids in school will become Christians." The sentiment of concern is great, but there is nothing in the Bible that even hints at such a notion. Paul was converted after an encounter with God on the Damascus Road. He was a Jew and remained a Jew. He never once referred to himself as a Christian. He met Jesus, the Messiah, and became a true Jew, a completed Jew.

What we have missed is that Jesus did not come to start a new religion called Christianity (this idea appears nowhere in the Bible). Jesus came to call the world to himself. If you believe the Scripture, there is no such thing as the Christian religion. You and I were never called to become Christians. That is an idea concocted by people who may have had good intentions but has misled people for centuries. If you introduced a friend to me and wanted me to know what a devoted believer she is, would you simply say, "This is Emily: she's a Christian?" Probably not! You might say, "She's a *born-again* Christian (as if there was another kind) or you might say any number of qualifiers like *evangelical, Bible-believing, Charismatic, serious, or fired up Christian.*

The point is that when we must qualify a word with another word it means that the word you are qualifying has no ability to convey what you are saying. So, we have now created numerous versions or types of "Christians" and none accurately reflect the Person of Jesus. We have dumbed down the term *Christian* so much that it means only what the hearer has learned by experiences they may have had. Sometimes it may even conjure up very negative memories. Why would we continue to use a word that has no power to communicate?

Have you considered the importance of the name "Jesus?" The Scripture says, by no other NAME can a person be saved.[1] At one point Jesus' disciples were ordered by the authorities never again to preach in that NAME. It wasn't preaching they objected to; it was preaching in that NAME.[2] With a paralytic, they said, "In the Name of Jesus of Nazareth stand up and walk."[3] When Jesus returns every knee will bow and every tongue will confess the NAME Jesus .[4] Once you substitute something else for the NAME of Jesus, you diminish who He is. A friend used to say, "If Jesus and Christian are the same why wouldn't you end your prayers with, *in the name of Christianity, Amen?"* Christianity did *not die for us on a cross, Jesus did. There is power in that NAME.*

---

[1]Acts 4:12   [2]Acts 4:18   [3]Acts 3:3–6   [4]Phil. 2:10–11

Lining up Truth with Our Agenda

"You will always have the poor among you, but you will not always have me."
John 12:8 (NIV)

This statement was made by Jesus at the home of Lazarus whom He had recently raised from the dead. A dinner was given in Jesus' honor and His disciples were also in attendance. Mary, Lazarus' sister, took about a pint of pure nard (a fragrant oil) and poured it on Jesus' feet. Its monetary value was about one year's wages. Then Mary wiped His feet with her hair. Judas, who held the money bag for the group, was outraged by the extravagance of this act. He was angered by this warm, affectionate gesture of Mary, not because he cared about helping the needy, but because he wanted access to the funds for himself.

Jesus' response may well have been what sealed Judas' decision to betray Him. Jesus responds saying that they will always have the poor but He would be with them for less than a week. It is quite easy to turn Jesus' response into a "legitimate" reason to excuse myself from any responsibility to the poor. It would go like this: "There are so many people in the world who live in poverty that no matter what we do, it is like trying to fill a bucket with a hole in the bottom … etc." But that is not at all what Jesus is saying. He quotes Moses who spoke firmly about never hardening your heart to the poor because they would always be in your land. Every Jew would have been familiar with Moses' command to "Open wide your hand to your brother, to the needy and the poor."[1] Jesus is saying that what Mary did for Him shows that she understands that He will soon be crucified and is anointing Him for burial while there is time. The poor will always be here and you will have the privilege, as God's representatives on earth, to care for them just as He would.

Living with an open hand is the essence of following Jesus. His hand was always open to the poor and disenfranchised. In my own experience, without exception, those whom I have heard try to build a case that people are poor because it's their own fault are always wealthy, self-absorbed believers who think if they give 10% the rest is their money to spend on themselves. The Scriptures are replete with commands, not suggestions, concerning opening our hearts and wallets to the poor. King Solomon said these harrowing words many years before Jesus, "He who shut his ears to the cry of the poor will also cry out and not be answered."[2] God's heart throbs for the poor!

---

[1] Deut. 15:7–11   [2] Prov. 21:13

A Subtle Addiction

"You diligently study the Scriptures because by them you possess eternal life. These are the Scriptures that testify about Me, yet you refuse to come to Me to have life." John 5:39 (NIV)

We are all aware of addiction to alcohol, opioids, gambling, sex, shopping, and a host of other dependencies. But Jesus taps an area that believers seldom, if ever, list as an unhealthy or dangerous addiction. He is at one of the large festivals in Jerusalem, probably Passover. After healing a paralytic at the Pool of Bethesda on the Sabbath, Jesus is verbally attacked by the Jewish leaders who want to kill Him. He has consistently broken their "fence" or "Oral Laws" which were not God's laws, but man's. There is a confrontation in John 5 and Jesus presents His case that He was sent by the Father and is His Son. He basically says, *You guys scour the Scriptures as if it is some magical charm that will give you favor with God. You memorize it, beat the people over the head with it, add your own laws to it, and everything you read in it points to the One who now stands before you. You are addicted to words that you don't even believe!*

Some people are actually addicted to words. Some are writers, poets, or simply "wordsmiths" whose greatest joy is weaving together sentences or verses that will evoke a particular emotion. You have probably heard a minister, or public speaker, who appears to be in love with the sound of his own voice. It is very easy to fall in love with the gift rather than the Giver. It's easy to have a great affection for powerful passages in Scripture and to memorize and collect them like rare stamps but to never internalize their meaning. The Bible can become an end in itself rather than a means to know and understand God.

I once spoke at a gathering with a former Miss America. During a Q&A she was asked why she always carried her Bible with her. "She said, "I feel like it is my personal good luck charm." The Scripture was never intended to be a magic wand. I have actually seen Bible studies lure people away from the reality of Jesus. It becomes an intellectual exercise rather than an encounter with the living God. You can scour the Scriptures, like the Pharisees, and never see what Paul saw ... "Jesus *is* life.[1]

The Bible is God's Word, but the Bible is *not* God. My goal is not to know more verses than anybody else; it is to know the One who wrote those verses. Any addiction, even a good one, can lure you to a place where the good can become the enemy of the best.

---

[1]Col. 3:4

World Vision

"For God so loved the world . . ." John 3:16

Most of us spend our days trying to make a living, caring for our family, and being involved in our church and community. How in the world can we take the time and energy to develop a vision for the world? It seems so overwhelming that it is seldom spoken of except on *Missionary Sunday*. You have seen the documentaries on TV of the feeding camps in developing countries, and the malnourished children with flies covering their little faces. It is heartbreaking, and at that moment you want to do something. You may send a check and may even be moved to sign up for a Mission Trip. But usually, after the emotion of the moment subsides, the phone will ring, there'll be a problem at work, or the dog will start limping and you rush her to the Vet. Your heart was moved to care in a specific way, but the issues of life drown it out.

Before I met those who would become life-long companions in Washington, D.C., I rarely even thought about much beyond my consuming work with high school kids. Doug Coe invited me to begin coming up there regularly in 1974 and spend time with the men and women who were not thinking as myopically as I was. Every person I met seemed to have an incredible story of what God was doing in different countries.

I began to meet people from around the globe, hear their stories, and their dreams for their nation. When my family and I finally moved to the D.C. area in 1980 I became involved in various meetings and gatherings that were sometimes overwhelming in terms of the things I heard. We would meet at *Fellowship House*, a huge home just off Embassy Row, often gathering in "The Map Room." One by one people walked up to a wall-sized map and put a pin on a country. They might talk about a man or woman there or a small group that wanted God to impact their people. Others would mention someone they had met from there and we would pray for these people. We would ask God to show us how we could come along beside them, help lift their burden and encourage them.

As I began praying for people from all over the world I developed a love for them and the things they cared about. This led to trips to many countries over the years to spend time with them and meet their friends. It was and continues to be, a revolutionary influence in my life. You may not be able to go yourself, but you can love the world by the power of the Holy Spirit in prayer. Learning a name or writing a letter may be the way God will open a door. God can build in you a vision for the world.

Loyalty: God's Faithfulness to His Children

"Know therefore that the Lord your God, He is God, the faithful God, who keeps His covenant and His lovingkindness to a thousandth generation with those who love Him and keep His commandments." Deuteronomy 7:9

Second, only to His unending love, God's faithfulness and loyalty to His children is one of the most enduring attributes of all. You can get a sense of God's loyalty to us by observing animals and even fish. It is said that an Octopus will lay large amounts of eggs and will not even eat or leave the area while guarding them. A study was done in Monterrey, California of a deep-sea Octopus who guarded her young for four and a half years. Anyone who has hiked or hunted in open country knows you never get between a mama bear and her cubs. Any mother, human or animal, has a natural instinct of loyalty and protection of her young.

Imagine the faithfulness of a God who, even after we are grown, never leaves us to fend for ourselves but jealously protects and provides for us until we are with Him in Heaven. Do you remember the autonomy and freedom you felt when you first were allowed to ride your bike anywhere you wanted? It was liberating! The world was your oyster and you could go anywhere you wanted without restriction. But as the day wears on and the shadows lengthen, you suddenly realize the streets and buildings are unfamiliar; you are hungry and discover that you have a flat tire and darkness is approaching. Strangely, the autonomy you felt as you peddled away that June afternoon from everything that was comfortable and familiar lost its luster. It is usurped by uncertainty and a tinge of fear as you notice a group of rough-looking guys staring at you from across the street. You suddenly realize that autonomy carries a price. Who will be there for you?

Paul asks, *who can separate us for the love of Christ ... will it be trouble, hardship, persecution, or a flat tire on a rough side of town?*[1] Then he says, "I have become absolutely convinced that neither death nor life, neither messenger from heaven nor monarch of earth, neither what happened today nor what happens tomorrow, neither a power from on high nor a power from below, nor anything else in God's whole world has any power to separate us from the love of God in Christ Jesus our Lord."[2]

What a blank check of complete loyalty God has toward us. What else do I need? Earthly parents can do just so much and cannot be everywhere at once, but not so with God. Wherever we go, He goes with us. His faithfulness and loyalty never wavers.

---

[1]Rom. 8:35   [2]Rom. 8:38–39 (Phillips)

Faithfulness: Our Loyalty to God

"I delight in loyalty rather than sacrifice and the knowledge of God rather than burnt offerings." Hosea 6:6

Faithfulness to God is not about *making a list and checking it twice,* evaluating our behavior day by day like a nervous accountant trying to balance the books. Loyalty or faithfulness is a response of love and gratitude that will begin to surface naturally as we become more intimate with God. Loyalty is a way of thinking that develops into a style of life. If you must think about it or tie a string around your finger to remember, you don't get it. Loyalty to the God who gave you life, and sustains it, is not meant to be checked off on *a To-Do List*. It is not a contrived response, but a natural one that flows out of gratefulness. A man who must remind himself to tell his wife he loves her and thank her for a delicious meal is self-absorbed and arrogant. He never had to remind himself to eat dinner!

In yesterday's passage (Deut. 7:9) about God's loyalty to us, it goes on to say that those who *hate* Him will be repaid without delay. Hate is a tough word. People may say they don't believe in God but you rarely hear someone say they hate God unless they face a dramatic loss and are under duress. But what is the opposite of love? Hate is the obvious answer, but in light of this verse, *apathy* would probably fit better. Will God be faithful

to those who couldn't care less and are oblivious to His compassion? What if you and I mess up and are unfaithful? "If we are faithless, He remains faithful. He cannot deny Himself."[1]

In a seminar, a lady asked me if one of my son's told me he was gay would I still love and accept him. "Absolutely," I answered. "Even if you don't agree with his lifestyle?" she said. "That's not the issue," I responded. "I will love him for the rest of my life, no matter what he does or doesn't do!" I know parents who have suffered untold pain as a result of the actions of their kids. Some have disowned their children. I don't understand that.

The same parent who would disown a child for having an abortion is usually the parent who routinely exceeds the speed limit, pads his expense reports, and hides income from the IRS. *Not the same*, you say. Yes, it is. It's an attitude of disloyalty to God that pushes truth aside the same way they feel the child did. The severity is not the point. We would never question that a man beating and injuring his wife was a horrible sin, but we often give each other a pass on gossip that can also destroy someone. It is the same thing because it is a perspective. Loyalty is seeing everything in life as God sees it.

---

[1] 2 Tim. 2:13

Loyalty and Faithfulness to Others

"A wicked messenger falls into adversity, but a faithful envoy brings healing."
Proverbs 13:17

The words *loyalty* and *faithfulness* are used interchangeably many times, but the core of their meaning is different. *Loyalty* is derived from the Old French word *loial,* which was often used in a legal sense. Faithfulness carries more the idea of an inward sincerity that goes beyond a required pledge. If you work for a company they may require some sort of loyalty pledge. Marketing people want us to have loyalty to their brand. When we think of faithfulness it is an enduring commitment of the heart, not simply because we must, but because of the devotion that compels us.

If you are married you made a vow of faithfulness to your spouse "for better or worse, for richer or poorer, in sickness or in health until you are parted by death." Almost six-thousand-two-hundred marriages break that vow every day. King Solomon asks a penetrating question, "Many a man claims to have unfailing love, but a faithful man who can find?"[1] This is not only about marriages but the way we think in terms of all relationships. Woody Allen was on to something when he said, "Eighty percent of life is just showing up." Think of how many times we have been told by someone that they will do this or that and it is never done. When you do find one who is faithful to follow through you have found a rare person who will soon be trusted by many, simply because he *shows up.*

We spend millions trying to teach believers ways to evangelize the world, and it is generally nullified by an action on our part that makes them roll their eyes. If you and I will simply be faithful in serving people, never gossiping, and simply following through with what we have said, the most caustic non-believer you know will eventually be open to anything you wish to tell him because you have earned the right to be heard.

Being faithful stands in such stark contrast to what the secular world sees every day that it will often create curiosity as to what makes you tick. Sharing your faith is not about trying to prove how old the earth is or enumerating all of the things you are against; it is about the difference they see in your treatment of people, how you do business, and how you deal with affliction. Are you the same person in a storm as in fair weather? Being faithful not only says who you are, but whose you are.

---

[1]Prov. 20:6

A Dangerous Loyalty

"Bear with each other and forgive one another if any of you has a grievance against someone. Forgive as the Lord forgave you." Colossians 3:13 (NIV)

There is a type of loyalty that can be dangerous. It's called *tribal loyalty*. At its base, it is harmless and can become a kind of gathering point for like-minded people. But if it is uncontrolled it can become like *kudzu* and literally engulf a group of people. Tribal loyalty can be denominational, political, theological, or social. Most of us are members of either a mainline or independent denomination. Most of us lean toward a specific political position, have a particular theological stance as well as strong opinions on social issues. There is nothing wrong with any of those until our passion and loyalty for our group and its position demonizes the others and causes us to lose our perspective. We are commanded, first and foremost, to love God and one another ... No exceptions![1]

I grew up in an Episcopal Church. My participation was minimal as a kid, but I do remember the fervor and loyalty that the congregation exhibited to that denomination. I've seen the same loyalty and pride in Baptists, Methodists, Presbyterians, and Catholic Churches. I've also been in churches where people seemed more passionate for the denomination and the minister than for Jesus. "I was born a Baptist and I'll die a Baptist," a neighbor once said to me. There is a big difference in loving your church and denomination and allowing blind loyalty to overrule faithfulness to God. It becomes *tribal loyalty* and will alienate you from other believers.

Today, because of the *political tribalism* that exists, we may well see people of opposing views literally take to the streets against one another. I have heard all the reasons why each side accuses the other of destroying our democracy. But while our words of hatred echo across the abyss, our childish banter is dividing families and life-long friendships, many of which may never recover. I pray that our spiritual leaders will stop taking sides and defending indefensible behavior and be men and women who step in the breach as agents of reconciliation.[2] If we are not spiritually mature enough to reason together with people of a different view, and still accept and love them, we are frauds. And no matter what we may say, truth is far too often replaced by personal opinion.

If we can't disagree without writing each other off and trying to recruit God to our side, we disqualify ourselves from having a voice that will be heard by anyone except our own choir. It is a *dangerous loyalty* because any loyalty to a group must always be, by comparison, incidental to our loyalty to God and His truth.

---

[1]Mark 12:30–31   [2]2 Cor. 5:11–2

A Biblical Conundrum . . . *Kind of* . . .

"Wives submit to your husbands as to the Lord. For the husband is head of the wife as Christ is head of the church, His body of which He is the Savior."
Ephesians 5:22–23 (NIV)

In our culture, we have a very conflicted relationship with authority. As a young believer, I first heard this verse quoted at a church service in Tuscaloosa, Alabama. It didn't really pertain to me at the time because I was single, but in the next few years, I heard it more and more. I was convinced from the beginning of my walk with Jesus that the Scriptures were the real thing. Yet there were many passages I didn't understand and this was one of them. The red flag to me was that the verse is clearly directed to women, but over the years the only people I ever heard beat this drum were men. Was this a control thing? I didn't know. The second instance came a couple of years later and confused me even more. I was listening to a talk by a popular woman Bible teacher. She quoted this passage and spoke of a recent night when she came home from a long drive, bone-tired, and looked forward to soaking in a hot bath. A couple of minutes after she slid in the tub, her husband walks in and orders her to get out of the tub because he needed something. She pleaded in vain for just five minutes more, then she said she "joyfully submitted" to her husband's demand. I couldn't believe it. What kind of jerk of a husband would do that, and why would this intelligent woman believe that this selfish demand was what the verse meant?

Susan and I had a couple over for dinner the first year we were married. In the middle of dinner, the man ordered his wife to get up and go get him some more iced tea. She dutifully hopped up and he turned to me and said proudly, "I have an obedient wife; she does what I tell her!" I thought … *I have a dog just like that.*

Today, I've learned that you never judge something based on its abuse. Men must love their wife as Jesus loved the church.[1] I didn't see the love of Jesus in those two examples and I understand women's ambivalence toward this passage given its misuse. Seldom do we quote the previous verse: "Submit *to one another* out of reverence for Christ." Marriage is the process of giving up legitimate rights for the good of the other. If both insist on their rights, harmony is impossible. If covered in love and allowed sufficient input from the woman, she can trust her husband confidently. To bicker over who is in charge is ludicrous. Jesus gladly submitted to death on my behalf. Why would I have a problem submitting to that kind of love? If you must compete … serve her more than she serves you! You may hear her say, "I trust you for the decision, as you trust God for the outcome."

[1]Eph. 5:25

303

Tempting God

"Jesus answered him, it is also written, do not put the Lord your God to the test."
Matthew 4:7 (NIV)

How does a person test or tempt God? The above passage is taken from Jesus' temptations when He stood face to face with Satan on a mountain after fasting for forty days. Satan is trying to get Jesus to do things in His own strength without relying on His Father. His third try was to get Jesus to do a swan dive off the Temple in Jerusalem. It was to prove His identity as the Son of God knowing that He will be caught by angels. Jesus quotes Deuteronomy saying, you shall not tempt God.[1]

To tempt God is to, in a sense, demand from Him three forms of ID rather than to trust His character. It is tantamount to the worst insult you could think of. I heard a story from a close and reliable friend that illustrates this. Bobby Bowden was one of the great college football coaches of all time and a genuine follower of Jesus. I met him several times and have great respect for him as a person as well as a coach. Toward the end of his career, he was supposedly courted heavily by a major university to be their new head coach. As the story goes, he agreed to an interview. Around the table with the Athletic Director, President, and several key alumni, he was given a quiz. What would be

done in this or that situation in a critical game? Here is a man who had won well over three hundred games. He gets up, thanks them for their time, and says, "I don't have to do this," and walks out of the room.

Though hardly comparable with testing God, it does catch the absurdity of a great coach like Bowden having to audition for a bunch of suits. God doesn't need to prove anything to anybody. It is an assault on His character. To question His reliability is to push Him to violate His commands. We often do this by *telling a little white lie* or by reasoning, "I know living together is wrong, but everyone is doing it and we live in a different world today." When we push the line, we are seeking a dumbed-down version of the truth. We want God to meet our expectations, and "if He really is a God of love, He will." That's tempting God.

The Jewish leaders were always questioning Jesus' identity and continually asking Him to show a "sign" to validate Himself. He had done everything except give them an autographed picture of His Father and they still refused to believe. It's like saying, "I know who you are, but that's just not good enough."

---

[1]Deut. 6:16

Making it Real

"They said to Him, the things about Jesus the Nazarene who was a prophet, mighty in deed and word in the sight of God and all the people." Luke 24:19

The context of this passage is after Jesus' resurrection as He joins two men walking on a road leading to a little village of Emmaus. Cleopas and another man are discussing all that had happened in Jerusalem. Jesus joins them on the walk but they do not recognize Him. Along the way, He asks questions pretending He knows nothing of what has happened. They tell Him about this *Jesus* and their description is that He was "a prophet mighty in *deed* and *word* in the sight of God and all the people." The order of those two words is not a mistake. The normal way we would say those two *words* is always, "word and deed," rather than the reverse.

Biblically, words flow from deeds, not the other way around. We reverse the order in conversation because we have been programmed in our culture to believe words and information are the keys to communication. The ancient Jews valued deeds first; words were simply explanations of the deed. If every believer in your city could not speak for a week, would anyone meet Jesus? We rely on words and information so heavily that the *way we live* becomes almost optional.

I have a close friend named Keith Tyner who lives in Indiana. He is a remarkable guy who runs his own business but carves out a tremendous amount of time for his family and for people. When there is a hurricane or almost any kind of disaster, Keith will drop everything, gather a team of people and take off in his RV. Many in his city and around the country have felt his impact in their lives.

He called me one day and said he, his wife, and son were driving to Raleigh North Carolina to talk to a family about God. That's a thirteen hundred mile round trip! He had met a man through his work who was a scientist and an atheist. His teenage daughters had followed suit. They met in the man's home one night and I drove to Raleigh the next day to meet him for lunch. Keith was upbeat but confessed that he doubted much positive ground had been gained. "Are you kidding?" I said. "You left your home and work, spent a lot of money on gas and hotels to drive thirteen hundred miles for a conversation because you cared about that man and his daughters. There is not a person that guy knows who would do that for a stranger, let alone a good friend!" The words Keith said were incidental to what he, his wife and son did. The words simply identified the heart of the deed. Keith recently flew to Montana to take a lonely man he knew to lunch on his 70th birthday. These acts of love eclipse the spoken word.

Chasing the Truth

"Instead, speaking the truth in love, we will in all things grow up into Him who is the Head, that is Christ." Ephesians 4:15 (NIV)

I don't know about you, but I have always had a curious mind. I never walk in a home or a business that I don't wonder what kind of people live or work there. I am curious about what makes people tick ... what caused them to choose their profession? How did they meet their spouse and what first attracted them to each other? I am fascinated by the circumstances of their spiritual journey. It's not just being nosey; I find that the more I understand about people, the more I understand about God. Every person is as different as a snowflake and each has a story to tell that illustrates how uniquely God works in each life.

When we think of pursuing the truth, we envision digging into the Scriptures, reading good books, and attending Bible studies. But there is another side of *chasing the truth* that is profoundly important. To pursue truth is also to study, understand, and come to a prayerful conclusion about *the other side of the argument*.

When you hear people passionately argue their position on issues facing us as believers or even as a nation, those voices are often so loud and zealous that they give no opportunity for response. It becomes a matter of who can yell the loudest. We certainly see it on the political front, but even more disturbing is the discord on matters of truth among believers. Winning and being right often eclipses our mandate to *be humble, gentle, and patient with one another in love.*[1] We cannot thoughtfully listen, understand, and fairly consider an opposing view in a chaotic atmosphere and at a fever pitch.

To actively listen is to make sure we understand what is being said and respond respectfully. This puts the narrative on a higher plane. What we often forget, as we passionately make our arguments, is that the secular world is still watching closely to see if we can be as loving within the marketplace as we are on Sunday morning at eleven.

No matter how important an issue is to us we can never allow our love for each other to be subordinated to that issue. If we convinced the whole world to agree with us, but in doing so are alienated from one another, we would have accomplished nothing.[2] When the dust settles and we have won our battle, they will look at us and say, "They are always such kind and thoughtful people ... until you disagree with them."

---

[1]Eph. 4:2   [2]Mark 8:36

The Gambler in Everyone

"But those who hope in the Lord will renew their strength. They will soar on wings like eagles; they will run and not grow weary; they will walk and not be faint."
Isaiah 40:31 (NIV)

A question I often ask people is, "What are you betting on?" I usually get a puzzled look until I explain. Everyone is a gambler; some of us may bet more conservatively than others, but we are all heavily counting on a payoff in one way or another. An atheist is betting his life that hell doesn't exist and he is free to make his own heaven here and now. A Muslim is betting eternity that his strict adherence to the Koran's teaching will earn him a place in heaven.

The gambler in us shows up in everyday life issues as well. A high school student works hard to make the grades to get into a prestigious college. She wants a high paying job so she can earn lots of money and be financially independent. The gamble is that this kind of future will make her life happy and content. I meet people constantly who are gambling on their own goodness to please God. On and on it goes as we bet against the house and hope that we will be the one to beat the odds and hit the jackpot.

The Scripture does not speak of "luck" and it categorically leans against man's efforts to earn his way to contentment and happiness. It does, however, speak of *hope*; not the kind where a student with a 750 SAT score and a "D" average *hopes* to be accepted at Harvard. In the Scripture, hope is not an expression of uncertainty or better odds than normal, it is the confident expectation of things to come. Another student with 1400 on the ACT, and first in her class, is *hoping* to be accepted at Harvard. The same word is used, but the *reason* for her *hope* is different.

We worry about our country and *hope* for a leadership that will honor God and keep us safe and prosperous, but Paul says, "The hope for the nations is Christ in you."[1] Why? God cannot fail and when our *hope* is the Christ living in us, it is not a gamble, but a sure thing. "God takes great *pleasure* in those who fear Him and who have *hope* in his unfailing love."[2] Solomon says, "the *hope* of the righteous brings *joy*, but the expectation of the wicked will perish."[3] When a person buys lottery tickets and waits for the numbers to be posted, the dominant emotion is *anxiety* rather than an expectation of joy when his numbers hit. God says our hope produces *joy* as we wait. Many people wait anxiously throughout life because they are betting on false hopes. God guarantees the result. What are you betting on?

---

[1]Col. 1:27   [2]Ps. 147:11   [3]Prov. 10:28

Something to Hang Your Hat On

"So that you may know the exact truth about the things you have been taught."
Luke 1:4

I had to buy a new computer not long ago. I didn't want to, and I couldn't afford it, but I couldn't finish this book without one, plus I had some other projects pending. I picked one out and the sales guy asked me if I wanted to purchase a two-year warranty. Really? If this elite computer company can't stand by something this expensive for two years, why would I even want it? As advanced as we have become, is there anything that we can really hang our hat on that is guaranteed to do what it says?

When Luke begins writing his gospel account, he gives his readers an unlimited guarantee. He says he is writing so that they may know the *exact* truth. This guarantee is not for two years, or two thousand years, but throughout eternity. The teachings of Scripture will never go out of date or be surpassed by something more modern and more relevant. There is a lifetime warranty that will never break or go out of style.

The word *doctrine* makes many people uneasy because it conjures up someone wagging his legalistic finger in your face. It's not! Doctrine is simply a position or principle. Churches have doctrines; there are political doctrines such as the *Monroe Doctrine*. Paul had strong words for anyone attempting to alter God's Word: "But even if we or an angel from heaven, should preach to you a gospel contrary to what we have preached to you, let him be eternally condemned!"[1] Altering God's Word is a serious offense because it tampers with our lifetime warranty.

Where I have seen the greatest abuse on the matter of doctrine is when it becomes the ultimate goal. Information doesn't change people, the Holy Spirit does. The Scriptures tell a story of God's redemptive plan and the circuitous route He takes as He works with ordinary, fallible people to accomplish His plan. Woven through this amazing story are principles that help us separate truth from error, good from bad, better from best. But the relationship with God and with people is the centerpiece. You don't run over or walk by people who are not quite there on a certain doctrine. I believe in strong doctrine, but if I have the choice to show compassion to someone who is hurting or preach to them, I will choose compassion. If someone is hungry, they need food first because they cannot hear your gospel over a growling stomach. The doctrines of God's Word are something you can hang your hat on, but we don't run over people in order to make our point because people *are* the point.

---

[1] Gal. 1:8

Biblical Truth and Personal Experience

"We have received . . . the Spirit who is from God, that we might know the things that have been freely given to us by God." 1 Corinthians 2:12

After seventy years in captivity, King Cyrus of Persia allowed the Jews to return to their homeland. Only about two-hundred thousand left at that point and settled in the northwest corner of Israel, which was called the "Land of the Twelve" or Judah. These were somber, serious Jews who lived by the letter of the law and thought of themselves as superior to others. Years later, many remaining Jews migrated back to Israel and settled in the southeastern area known as Galilee. These were very gregarious people who loved God and would worship by dancing before the Lord and raising their hands in praise. They wanted to experience God in the deepest way and believed that faith is not simply knowing the truth, but how a person lives in relation to what they know. The two groups were not an easy mix; they avoided each other as much as possible.

Today there is an uneasy marriage between biblical truth and personal experience. It shouldn't be an either/or proposition. If the truth you learn from the Scripture does not become part of your experience it is simply an intellectual exercise. On the other hand, an experience is not what gives validity to biblical truth. Truth is reality, but what gives it meaning is when that truth comes alive in our daily experience.

We have all heard stories about people hearing God's voice or seeing Jesus' face in a cloud or a piece of toast. "God told me to do this or that" is common. Is it real or imagined? I can't be the judge of those matters and would never argue with someone who told me of a similar experience as long as it didn't contradict the Scripture. God can work in ways we have never imagined, but they will never be contrary to what He has already said. Before Jesus came, God spoke through the Prophets at different times and in many different ways, but now it is through His Son.[1] In fact, John says in Revelation that Jesus is The Word of God.[2]

The ancient Jews believed God first touched the heart and that the mind would follow. Experiences with God that moved a person profoundly would create a hunger for that person to know the truth more deeply. In the West, we focus on learning, knowing, memorizing truth and assuming it will soon work its way down into the heart. The Judeans lined up closer to that perspective. Both have merit but they must line up with the truth of Scripture.

---

[1] Heb. 1:1–2   [2] Rev. 19:13

Who Will You Follow?

"The crucible for silver and the furnace for gold, but man is tested by the praise he receives." Proverbs 27:21 (author's paraphrase)

Do you want someone to disciple you ... to take you on a deeper journey with God ... someone to whom you are willing to give some authority in your life? If you are, then pray for someone who has been through pain and suffering and whose faith in God has remained unshaken ... someone who "walks with a limp." This is the one to listen to; this is the one at whose feet you should sit.

When you find someone who has come through the fires and continues on ... this is a person to learn from. If pain and failure do not drive you into God's presence, success will never do it. Dick Woodward was a Pastor in Williamsburg, Virginia for many years. At the height of a great teaching ministry, Dick contracted what was thought to be Multiple Sclerosis only to find years later that is was the wrong diagnosis. He was confined to a wheelchair, and eventually bedridden for years until his death in 2014. Dick never complained, never became bitter, and never asked the proverbial question, "Why me?" He became a quadriplegic and though he was unable to write, he authored books and study guides verbally through a computer while lying in his bed. He spoke to Governor's Prayer Breakfasts and other gatherings right from his bed via satellite. He often said that this disease was the best thing that ever happened to him.

I would visit him whenever I was in Williamsburg and once asked him how he could stay so positive after what he had suffered. I never forgot his answer. He said, "The greater issue in life is what you do with success and praise, not how you handle suffering. Had I continued at the pace I was going I would never have known God as I have come to know Him. It is the affirmation I receive from what I have been allowed to do from this bed that is the greatest danger." Wow! That was not what I expected to hear, but it gave me a new thought, and years later I ran across this verse in Proverbs that says, "a man is tested by the praise he receives." I doubt Dick would have come to the place where he recognized that the real test is not how you deal with affliction, but how you deal with acclaim. Here is the kind of man at whose feet I would sit any day.

Don't waste time listening to those who offer snappy little Christian clichés, untested and untried. Find someone who has come through the fires, but who also knows how to handle the praise given him or her after they have come through it.

An Echo of God's Presence

Forty-five years ago, I met a man in Washington, D.C., who is, in my mind, an echo of God's presence. Howard Peck, or HP as he prefers to be called, is not a speaker, a teacher, or someone whom you would invite to a cocktail party, but he has made an indelible mark on us all. He is in his late seventies now, lives in a VA facility and spends the little money he has buying stamps to send weekly letters to 50-60 of his "family" to encourage us.

Employment secured for him by friends over the years has often ended in bruised relationships as HP may, after a few days, decide to tell the owner how to better run his company. He knows every inch of D.C., chauffeuring the Washington elite in limousines to places like the Kennedy Center. The awkward disconnect comes when he fails to return to pick them up.

Howard is the prototype of the character played by Bill Murray in the movie, *What About Bob?* However, those of us who have known him over the years, especially Doug Holladay, Jim Hiskey, and John Yates could write a better screenplay from actual happenings. Once on Christmas Eve he stealthily slipped onto the stage at the Kennedy Center and maneuvered his way into the ensemble performing "The Messiah" until they finally gave him the hook. There are dozens of true stories like this but there is a deeper story that should encourage you.

All attempts over the years to get Howard the help he needs have ended with frustration and the facilities everyone hoped would offer a solution have even thrown their hands up in despair. Howard has a high IQ, but the absence of basic social graces makes the high-powered world of Washington, D.C., an awkward *bedfellow*.

But we all have learned that Howard is a barometer of our relationship with Jesus. He is a test that reminds us who Jesus is and the unconventional ways He walks among us. He is that "angel unaware," who comes among us for a purpose. He used to carry around a grocery bag of loose potato chips, half-eaten sandwiches and oil-stained notebook paper on which he had written Bible verses. Every week those barely legible handwritten letters still arrive in the mail filled with his favorite verses and quotes of encouragement. Howard is not simply a dangling participle of humanity; he is the voice of the Prophets whose clarion call reminds us that to reject one who does not fit our synthetic profile, is the same as rejecting Jesus.

Howard loves the Scriptures and he loves people. He is a faithful man … maybe the most faithful man I know. I have little doubt that one day those of us who have been graced by his friendship will stand before God and hear the words, "As you responded to Howard Peck, you have responded to Me."

Interacting with God's Word

"Study to shew thyself approved unto God, a workman that needeth not to be ashamed, rightly dividing the word of truth." 2 Timothy 2:15 (KJV)

If you asked me to tell you about my wife and children you would be horrified if I said, *'I'm sorry, but I don't know much about those people."* If the average believer knew as little about his profession as he knows about the Scriptures he would be walking around outside Costco holding a "Will Work for Food" sign. Most believers know random bits and pieces, but relatively little about the context of stories they love or how they fit into the big story.

Most of us have either been put to sleep or terminally confused by some teachers and ministers. I never understood why certain words were used in church. The words *study* and *school* never really connected for me. Looking back to my school years studying didn't really evoke any great sense of nostalgia. So, why would we send kids to school all week, where they long for the weekend and then send them to something called Sunday *School?* Call it *Happy Hour or Hippity Hop to Jesus* ... anything but school. We train kids to dislike things simply because they associate the name with something negative or unappealing.

Delving deeper into the meaning and context of a passage means real *interaction* with the story and the message. I don't think of *studying* the life of Jesus any more than I try to *study* my family, as if they are a frog in biology class. I interact with them naturally, in a variety of circumstances, both good and bad. The more I am around them, the more I know them, and understand their heart. Why wouldn't I do the same with the Scriptures?

I am fascinated by the truth and by the realization that never again will I be at the mercy of whoever steps to the podium to preach. The goal is to really own your faith, to know what and why you believe, and to be able to say with the Psalmist that God's words are "more desirable than gold and sweeter than honey,"[1] and really mean it! To "be ready to give an answer for the hope you have" comes by interacting with the Scriptures by desire, rather than out of responsibility.[2]

Remember this is a Jewish book. It is written as a story. Within the story is a glimpse into the mind and heart of God. There is much to learn, but there is also much to feel and experience as you slip on sandals and walk the dusty roads of God's creation with people much like you. Every emotion you ever felt is found in the people in the story. They laugh, they cry, they doubt, they sin, and the limp along together. Step into the story!

---

[1] Ps. 19:10   [2] 2 Pet. 3:15

Questions

"Then the Lord God said to the woman, 'What is this you have done?'"
Genesis 3:13 (NIV)

It's the best way to start a conversation, the least defensive way to respond to an accusation or sarcastic remark, and the surest way to take a conversation to a deeper level. We all know that Jesus used questions to answer questions, but long before Jesus was born, the ancient Rabbis had developed answering questions with questions as an art form. Socrates is said to have used this with his students and today it is called, "The Socratic Method." But even before this, one of God's first recorded words to Adam and Eve was after they ate of the fruit, became aware of the nakedness, and hid from God. God said, "Where are you?" When God asks a question, He is not looking for information. He knew where they were. He doesn't accuse; He allows them to recognize and own what they did and confess it.

A woman in a tourist group was shopping in Jerusalem and came to a store where an old Jewish man sat on a stool in front surrounded by paintings. They were of landscapes and beautiful vistas and the woman asked the bearded man which of the pictures was his favorite. He responded in typical Jewish fashion, "Madam, are you married?" "Yes," she answered. "Do you have children? She looked at him quizzically and said, "Yes, I have two sons and two daughters." The old man asked, "Which is your favorite?" No mere *answer* could have made such a salient point.

Sometimes answering with a question can be a simple tactic of avoidance, but I have found in my teaching that it is a profound way to get people to think more clearly and deeply. We all tend to *own* what we help to create. If you participate in renovating your house with a professional you will feel far more personal affirmation when someone tells you how nice it looks. When questions help you uncover the answer you are looking for you will be much more committed to moving forward.

Sometimes a question can make you rethink something you have done. My senior year at Alabama we played Oklahoma in the Bluebonnet Bowl. I had a date after the game with a girl from the University of Houston. The team was given tickets to a big dinner and concert by a well-known band. A huge bottle of champagne sat in the middle of each table. My date began mindlessly sipping and sipping, and by the end of the evening, after she threw up on me, I took her home in a cab. I told the story a year later to Mal, the man who had introduced me to Jesus, and laughed as I described it. His response was simply, "Do you feel that you were helpful to her that night?" I never forgot the question and I never let it happen again.

Flip-Flop Value System

"There is a way which seems right to a man, but its end is the way of death.
Proverbs 14:12

With what we seem to witness every day in terms of companies, and even the government being hacked with sensitive information being stolen, it reminded me of a "What If" talk I gave to a group of high school kids many years ago. "What if a couple of guys, bored with life and yearning for excitement want to create some turmoil in their town?"

Let's say it is "Black Friday," the day after Thanksgiving when huge discounts are available that early Christmas shoppers can take advantage of great deals on just about everything. Let's say these young guys somehow break into a big retail store and change the prices on everything from toasters to computers to televisions. A seventy-inch flat-screen would be priced at $49.95 and baseball glove at $949.00 and so on. When the door opened and people flooded in, you can imagine the hysteria as people discovered the bogus pricing. Items of minor value sold for exorbitant prices and electronics and living room sets were selling for peanuts! If you were the manager or the owner of the store, what would you do?

If we look at our culture from God's perspective, this is a pretty accurate picture of what He sees when He looks at a world where the price tags have all been swapped; values have been mixed-up and traded. Things of little or no eternal value are highly touted, and essentials of life are virtually ignored on the shelves.

When I was a couple of years out of college, a movie came out called The Poseidon Adventure. It was later re-made in 2005. It is about a cruise ship that was hit by a gigantic rogue wave and literally flipped upside down. Those who survived were now standing on the ceiling. Everything that was up was now down and what was down was now up. The movie is about a small group of passengers who try to make the circuitous journey *upward* to the *bottom* of the ship to hopefully be rescued.

Is this not a fitting picture of us? Because the world has introduced values that we have come to covet, the ship has inverted and that which we are told will lead us to life is taking us in the wrong direction. The insidiousness of this is that we don't even realize that what we believe is taking us up is really taking us down. *"There is a way that seems right to man, but it will end in death," says King Solomon.* What we think is up is down and what we think is optional, or lacks value, is the way to life.

The Kingdom of God

"Repent, for the kingdom of heaven is at hand." Matthew 4:17 (ESV)

This is the message Jesus spoke at the beginning of His public ministry and it remained the theme of His earthly sojourn.[1] The Kingdom of God (or Heaven) is mentioned some fifty times and mostly from Jesus' teaching. What is it? Matthew gives us a word picture from the teaching of Jesus. It is like a mustard seed, it's like yeast, a buried treasure, a merchant searching for fine pearls, and a big net cast into the sea.[2] From these images, we see the Kingdom as starting small but growing rapidly, deep and wide and expanding as it grows. It has inestimable worth like a buried treasure or a pearl found by a merchant, and it has the ability to gather multitudes like a great fishing net.

This Kingdom is like no other. The cost of admission is faith and obedience to its King.[3] The Kingdom is for the *poor in spirit,* full of those who recognize their own spiritual poverty;[4] it is for the humble and child-like.[4] The Kingdom is a mystery,[5] because it is the opposite of all human expectations.[6]

The disturbing thing is that the growth of the Kingdom of God can be hindered by division. "A kingdom divided against itself cannot stand."[7] You and I can have the evangelistic fervor of a hurricane, but God cannot honor division. To reach out to the world but be alienated from your neighbor is a mockery.

You and I are called to be Ambassadors representing the Kingdom of Heaven.[8] This is the ministry of every believer. What is the role of an ambassador? He must thoroughly understand the heart of the King in order to accurately represent Him. He must learn the mind of the King so that His thoughts and perspective are never compromised. An Ambassador never reinterprets or adds his own twist to the orders of the King.

Any Ambassador must be completely loyal to the King and care for every person in the Kingdom as the King would. A loyal Ambassador does not show partiality to any one sector of the Kingdom. He never considers one group as inferior to another because this violates the heart and the intent of the King.

There is more about this great Kingdom that is present among us but not yet fully revealed. It is very near,[9] and here is the kicker … This kingdom is absolutely assured of the final victory over evil.[10] And *that* is really good news!

---

[1]Matt. 4:17   [2]Matt. 13:31–33; 44–48   [3]Matt. 5:19; 7:21   [4]Matt.5:3; 18:3–4;
[5]Matt. 13:11   [6]Matt. 20:1–16   [7]Matt. 12:25   [8]2 Cor. 5:20
[9]Matt. 3:2; 4:17; 10:7   [10]Matt. 13:30, 41, 47–50

A Broken Heart for a Broken World

"When He approached Jerusalem, He saw the city and wept over it." Luke 19:41

My youngest son, David, is an EMT. He has seen and experienced things that no one should have to see and experience. When I've asked him how he is able to do it he says that you must focus on the task in front of you and put your personal emotions aside. But he also confided, that after the adrenaline subsides and you lie in your bed at night, it can cover you like a thick cloud. Physicians have to step aside from their feeling and emotions, but I can't imagine doing that.

Apparently, Jesus, in His humanity, made no attempt to separate Himself from people's suffering and pain. Standing in front of Lazarus' tomb He wept and was apparently not the least bit embarrassed to show his emotions. Luke, the only Gentile of the gospel writers, tells us that after His triumphal entry Jesus entered Jerusalem and tears filled His eyes and streamed down His face. This was after throngs of Jews had said, "Hosanna, blessed is He who comes in the name of the Lord." But Jesus knew the shallowness of those chants. The Jewish leaders, as well as the disciples, believed what they saw but Jesus knew their proclamation was false and, indeed, in five days the same crowd would be yelling, "Crucify Him!"

The next few verses tell us why He wept. The Jews had rejected Him in favor of their "traditions." It was killing the multitudes, but they had become accustomed to living by law, and though grace held much appeal they had become too comfortable to take a risk. Jesus shed bitter tears for them because He knew what they were facing at the hands of the Romans in 70 AD. He knew 1.1 million Jewish men, women and children would be viciously cut down by the Roman siege of Jerusalem. It broke his heart.

Do you ever pray for your city? Would Jesus be encouraged if he came to your community? Are you heart-broken about broken people? Do you know any of the key people who are believers in various divisions of labor? (Legal, Medical, Education, Political, Business, etc.) What if you stopped by and saw one or two of these people every week and simply asked how you might pray for them and their work? Professional people are bombarded with requests and complaints daily, but rarely does someone come by and ask how they can be helpful and supportive.

If we continue to be as divided and oblivious to God's truths as we presently are, we will see the world change before our eyes. Look at the fields … they are ripe unto harvest. Pray for laborers and allow God to show your city to you through His eyes.[1]

---

[1]John 4:35–36

What's Wrong with Us?

"Faithful are the wounds of a friend; profuse are the kisses of an enemy."
Proverbs 27:6 (ESV)

Let's face it, many Bible studies and prayer groups tend to avoid confrontation. We learn Scripture, we pray for physical needs, and may even discuss minor differences, but seldom do we discuss why we are not having a greater impact on the world.

There is a difference between critical thinking and being critical. Today's Scripture is saying that if you are questioned or corrected by a friend, realize that it will be helpful to you in the long run and that it was risky for that person to speak up. Conversely, an enemy will "kiss up" to you because he has an agenda . . . he wants something.

Many years ago, a group of us in Washington, D.C., had a chance to meet with Consumer Advocate Ralph Nader. In the 60's he took on the automobile industry concerning safety issues. He won the case and an all-out assault on him by GM ensued to try to discredit him personally. They found nothing but a dedicated man of great integrity. A friend asked him to talk to us on the subject, "What's Wrong with Us?" ("us" meaning the Body of Christ). Nader was less than anxious to do this, and initially told us he felt ill-equipped to offer any critique of people of faith. He spoke of growing up in the Methodist church in Connecticut and his encounters with people of faith along the way. His comments were very instructive. He simply talked about how the business and political world looks at ardent believers and some of the reactions along the way from believers that puzzled him.

The Scripture is filled with admonitions to believers to help one another grow and avoid sin but there are times when a friend who knows you well, but who may not be a believer, could be a great resource. During an average week you are with people at your place of business, other people at church, maybe a few others with whom you go out to eat, play golf, tennis, or cards. Each group of people probably sees you differently. Why not ask one or two from each group how they generally view the faith community? Sure, it's a risk for you and them, but to continue on shooting blanks in term of drawing people toward Jesus is a greater risk. Imagine believers doing this across your city. It could be instructive and humbling in areas that we, in the body of Christ, would never see. A non-believer may not be able to give you the answer, but they can sure help you assess the problem. They watch you every day and they have opinions. Why not ask God to test your heart and mind with some unlikely people?[1]

---

[1]Ps. 26:2

Listen Intently and Be Consistent

"My dear brothers and sisters, take note of this: Everyone should be quick to listen, slow to speak and slow to become angry." James 1:19 (NIV)

This is a fundamental principle of human relationships. Notice that James does not say "be *careful* or remember to listen," but uses the word "*quick*." Be in a hurry to listen! With most of us, the opposite is true; we are in a hurry to talk, to have our opinion heard. This "quick draw" approach is particularly true as believers seek to apply biblical truth to political and social issues. Back in the late nineties, a great fervor arose over Disney's policy of hiring gays. Many ministers and Christian groups called for a boycott of Disney properties. Others joined the fray until it was discovered that Microsoft had the same basic hiring policy as Disney. As this came to light, the issue lost steam, and basically went away. I wonder why. To boycott Microsoft would be catastrophic for businesses as well as personally. It would be extremely inconvenient and the cost would devastate the average person. It's easy to be indignant when we have nothing on the line, but when it will cost us we realize we should have investigated before becoming so irate.

James warns us to be quick to listen. That means looking at every side of an issue, get all the facts, consider the implications, take it before the Lord and act accordingly. Many of the hot button issues have far-reaching implications. This is why James says we should be *in a hurry to listen and be slow to speak.*

Imagine a twelve or thirteen-year-old girl hearing from an angel that she would be the mother of the Messiah. She didn't go into a tailspin and panic, she "pondered these things in her heart."[1] Think of the accusations hurled at Jesus for three and a half years and He never became defensive. Quick to listen … slow to speak … slow to anger.

If God's family is going to be taken seriously rather than thought of as the lunatic fringe we must learn how to listen, to carefully consider the entire issue including the opposing position and give a gentle and respectful response. We must learn how to frame an argument without attacking the integrity of the other side. If we allow emotions to carry the day, we will continue to shoot from the hip, and there will be carnage on both sides. What often happens when we are quick to speak and quick to judgment is that even if we win, we lose.

[1]Luke 2:19

Self-Expression or God's Intention

"Beloved, now are we the sons of God, and it doth not yet appear what we shall be: but we know that, when he shall appear, we shall be like him; for we shall see him as he is." 1 John 3:2 (KJV)

Jean-Jacques Rousseau was a Swiss philosopher, writer, and composer who had great influence during the Enlightenment period of the 18th century. He believed that man was basically good but had been corrupted by society. He believed that creative self-expression would lead people to a more productive life.

Without realizing it, the Western world bought into this idea that self-expression is the fixer of what ails you. We see people expressing themselves creatively every day in the way they dress, the way they cut their hair, in elaborate tattoos, body piercing, dance, art, and dozens of other ways that shout, "I want to be significant … I want to matter … I want to be unique."

I understand; we all want to feel special. My concern is when it takes some superficial adornment to make us feel that way. You are, in the mind of God, the hottest commodity in the universe. The clothes, the nose ring, the funky haircut or the uncomfortable trendy high heels do not make you *more* unique. Just as you are, you are the best expression of what God can do! What makes us try to enhance ourselves is that we have allowed the culture to define what beauty looks like or what is cool, and we have

allowed the marketing world to tell us what is *in* and what is *out*.

The issue for one who loves God is to discover and recognize God's *intent*. When we learn who we are and why we are here and let self-expression flow naturally from that understanding, we will experience completeness and contentment. When we leave to go out, we say, "How do I look?" But if they wrinkle up their nose we become insecure because it challenges our attempt to express ourselves. Even though we liked what we saw in the mirror, we now have doubts because of one opinion. But you, as a living being, are the unique expression of God Himself, and every truth you learn and believe along the way deepens that reality.

The J. B. Phillips translation really nails it as John begins his gospel this way: "At the beginning God expressed himself. That personal expression, that word, was with God, and was God, and he existed with God from the beginning."[1] Jesus Christ was the self-expression of God and now He lives in you. There is no way to improve on that. Wear what you enjoy, create beauty as you see it, but never allow those things to define you. You are God's personal expression of everything He intended.

---

[1] John 1:1–3 (Phillips)

"Give Me Your Christ, but . . ."

"See to it that you are not misled; for many will come in My Name, saying, 'I am He,' and 'the time is near.' Do not go after them." Luke 21:8

A frequent comment I hear from people who are *standing at the door* yet are hesitant to knock goes something like this, *"I believe Jesus was the Son of God and I believe He died for me, but almost every Christian I know is someone I don't enjoy being around and I certainly don't want to be like them."* They often go on to say, "They all talk alike, they huddle in exclusive cliques, they are super critical of the behavior of others, and are intolerant with ideas or thoughts that don't line up with their own. If following Jesus means I have to be like them, I'll pass."

That's a valid statement, and it's unfortunate that it must be said. Many believers create standards that are more personal preferences than biblical admonitions. To be told that a true believer should belong to a certain political party or vote for a specific candidate is not a command from God, but a personal choice. To say that a godly parent would not let their children Trick or Treat on Halloween or go to a movie or dance, or that you and your spouse can't enjoy a glass of wine, is imposing personal preference and calling it a biblical command. There may be a better choice, but it is *your* standard, not God's. We must know the difference, or we will continually put people under law, and it will repel the world rather than draw them in.

Manmade taboos, such as these, only display our spiritual ignorance and distract seekers from seeing the real Christ. The minute we try to tie Jesus to the Republican Party or a particular denomination, we have moved away from biblical truth. When we wrap the American flag around Jesus and claim they are one and the same, we are swinging on a rotten vine. God loves the world. We don't define righteousness by a person's political or social views, their voting preference, or their nationality or color, but by the character that comes from a redeemed heart.

Gandhi was a young lawyer in England who was interested in Jesus and tried to attend a tent meeting to hear about Him. He was turned away because of the color of his skin. He always revered Jesus but could not get past the lack of resemblance between Jesus and His followers. Gandhi's statement, "Give me your Christ, but spare me your Christians," is both a call and a warning. It is a call for believers to reconsider how well we reflect the light of the authentic Christ, and it is a warning that a watching world can tell the difference.

A Gentle Answer on Tough Issues

"A gentle answer turns away wrath, but a harsh word stirs up anger. The tongue of the wise makes knowledge acceptable." Proverbs 15:1–2

This verse is often quoted using only the first six words and does not convey the full thrust of the passage. In fact, the second part of the verse explains the first. A gentle answer to an accusatory or sarcastic remark is a form of meekness. It is not a weak position as some might think, it is power under control. The one who is being attacked has the ability to be even nastier, louder, and more offensive but chooses to give a gentle answer. This will soften and turn away the contempt of the accuser. The second half of the verse tells us that this kind of wise response is what makes the perspective you bring acceptable.

Few times in our nation's history have these truths been more apropos than now. There are clashes on social, political, and personal issues that are dividing good people because we do not know how to respond with a gentle answer. We have our position, we are armed with our Bible verses, but rather than speaking the truth in love and being respectful, we use these verses like weapons to blow away those who disagree. The paradox of this kind of behavior is that we are ignoring biblical principles trying to shut others down who are espousing unbiblical principles!

Homosexuality is a hot button issue. The Bible does say that a gay lifestyle is a sin. Paul says the unrighteous (those who are not right with God) will not inherit the kingdom of God. He then lists nine types of sin that fall in the category.[1] It includes adultery, drunkards, thieves, the greedy and homosexuality. Yet, we don't march or hold up signs about adultery, idolatry or greed. Heterosexual promiscuity is no less a sin than homosexual behavior. Scripture says both are an offense to God, but we decide that adultery is a *purer* form of sin. I don't understand the sexual attraction to another man, but if I am consumed with greed, it doesn't make me more honorable than a man or woman attracted to the same sex. Jesus spoke far more against greed than he even did about adultery.

The point is that none of us have the right to denigrate a gay person and single his sin out as more grievous than gossip or cheating in business. The Church has been shameful in our treatment of homosexuals. No gay person will go to hell because they are gay any more than you or I will go to heaven because we are heterosexual. A person winds up separated from God because he *did not trust Christ, not because of bad behavior.*[2]

We need to learn to approach people and issues with meekness.[3] As we do, it will communicate where words fail.

---

[1] 1 Cor. 6:9–10   [2] John 14:6   [3] 1 Pet. 3:15; Gal. 6:1

A Gentle Answer on Tough Issues (2)

"A gentle answer turns away wrath, but a harsh word stirs up anger. The tongue of the wise makes knowledge acceptable." Proverbs 15:1–2

This passage that we looked at yesterday strongly applies to another deeply emotional issue facing our nation. It may be the most volatile issue we face. Since 1973 the Supreme Court ruled that a woman has a right to have an abortion if she so chooses. The issue has been at the center of debate for over forty years and is now at its summit.

It is not my intent to argue the issue here but to encourage you, as believers, to carefully consider how you address those with whom you disagree. What we constantly hear at every rally, debate or march is intense and hurtful rhetoric that demeans not only those to whom the vitriol is aimed but also the one who speaks. It is true of both sides, but my concern here is how we as believers stand for what is true and right but do it in a manner that "turns away anger" and open the door for creative dialogue.

I remember years ago seeing picketing at abortion clinics where there were many believers holding signs with words like "murderer" and "Burn in Hell" while screaming at young women who tried to enter the clinic. There were some who were not there to attack but to offer alternatives and who were kind and loving. This would be the group that Jesus would champion. I know that because there is not one instance in which he ever yelled at or degraded anyone.

I have been in church services, and once at a funeral last year, when the minister thought it would be a great opportunity to get a shot in about abortion ... leaving the bewildered family of the dead man wondering where that came from. I believe in the sanctity of life, but I also know that in any group of people, at a dinner party, at church, or around the water cooler at work, there is someone and probably several there who have had an abortion. They have endured this secret shame for ten, twenty, thirty or more years living with a level of guilt that I cannot imagine. They have confessed their sin to God and are forgiven, but many of us who say that forgiveness is the cornerstone of our faith have not allowed them to experience it. Every time the subject comes up in a movie, on the news, or even casually at a coffee shop, we force them to feel the pain again and again. I believe we should never speak on this matter without also reminding people of God's loving forgiveness.

We may well see a reversal by the Supreme Court soon. The battle may be won, but if we continue to marginalize those women who have stumbled, many of whom were scared young girls from poor communities, we may find that we have lost the support of God along the way.

Legalism: Fear of Freedom

"All things are lawful for me but not all things are profitable. All things are lawful for me, but I will not be mastered by anything." 1 Corinthians 6:12

An elder in a large church asked me to meet him for lunch. He wanted to talk about grace. When he brought it up I assumed he wanted to make sure I was fully on board with the principle. His church was highly regarded as a very grace-oriented body. To my surprise, he said, "I have always believed in the grace of God, but I am convinced that we are going overboard in our emphasis. I believe people will take advantage of their freedom and run wild ... grace must have boundaries." What do you think?

I was a bit stunned, realizing that he had little understanding of grace. The moment you put fences or boundaries around it, you have reverted back to law. If a man or woman is predisposed to do something immoral no level of fear, pleading, and no restrictions you try to erect will be strong enough to stop them. The constraints must come from within. As a follower of Jesus, I am free to do what I want to do, but the love of Christ constrains me, and therefore, what I want to do is honor Him with my life. Grace is not about what we are not supposed to do; it is all about who we want to be. Paul was saying something similar in this verse. I am free to do anything, but some things are unhealthy and won't help me become the man I want to be, so I choose not to engage in those things.

When I worked in the Empire State Building, I took some college students to a floor near the top that was being renovated. As we looked at the scene below, I told them that they were *free* to jump if they wanted to, but the moment their feet leave that window they were no longer free. They now are prisoners to a law called gravity that will smush them like a bug on 34th Street.

God did not have to send His Son to us. He was under no obligation. He did it because He wanted to. That's grace! Many are very fearful of freedom; they don't want the Holy Spirit to guide them. They want a list of rules of what they can and cannot do. It makes them feel secure, but they are never free. They are robots. You will never be free to stay unless you are free to run. Legalism hates the thought of liberty. If you live by the law, you have no need for Jesus, all you need is a rule book and a checklist. Do's and don'ts will not change a heart; they can only give the appearance of change. We were set free by Christ, never to be burdened again by the yoke of slavery.[1] Enjoy your freedom in Christ and use it to help others do the same.

---

[1] Gal. 5:1

Defining Moments

"As he neared Damascus on his journey, suddenly a light from heaven flashed around him." Acts 9:3 (NIV)

In each of our lives, there are those moments that in some way define our direction or initiate a significant change in us. They are moments that cannot be manufactured or controlled. They are part of our story. The apostle Paul would certainly have said that his Damascus Road experience would have set the tone of his entire life. We all have critical experiences such as these sculpt our lives and form our story.

I have had several defining moments but none more powerful than the first time I personally witnessed God's grace and power of healing. During my freshman year I had become involved with the Fellowship of Christian Athletes, and out of this evolved a prayer group with some of my teammates. A man named Wales Goebel spoke at an FCA meeting and challenged us to use our influence on campus to make a visible impact.

Soon after that, we were at practice, and across another field, we saw a crowd gather where the freshman defense was having drills with the Varsity offense. We saw an ambulance pull up, and I discovered that Don Greeley from Northern Virginia had suffered a serious head injury. When we finished practice word came down that Don was in critical condition and in a coma. His brain was swelling and the next 48 hours would be critical to his survival. Our little group of teammates instinctively went to our knees to pray for Don. When we finished most of the team had taken a knee as well ... Guys like Kenny Stabler and others, who were not known to have much spiritual interest but who realized the gravity of the situation, knelt with us. A young assistant coach suggested that we have an around the clock prayer vigil for the 48 crucial hours. Team members signed up every hour for the next two days. We began to realize that this may answer the challenge given to us by Wales Goebel at the FCA meeting. Throughout this time, some of the older guys saw this as a natural opportunity to share Jesus with team members. The receptiveness was staggering!

Don came out of the coma three days later with Coach Bryant sitting beside his bed. He recovered and many players gave their lives to Christ, including Don. The word spread across the state and many of us were asked to come and tell the story.

This was the first time I saw the power of God. I had only read and heard about it. It was a defining moment in my life and many others have followed. Take some time and identify the defining moments in your life. Then share them with people you love.

Insecurity: The Thief of Confidence

"Do not be anxious about anything, but in every situation, by prayer and petition, with thanksgiving, present your requests to God. And the peace of God, which transcends all understanding, will guard your hearts and your minds in Christ Jesus." Philippians 4:6–7 (NIV)

As you well know, there are many obstacles that can throw sand in the gears of an otherwise placid and productive life. Some suffer ill health and all its ramifications; some feel strangled with more responsibilities than anyone should have to bear. Some struggle with pride, greed, addictions, but with few exceptions, most men struggle with a subtle form of insecurity. Women seem to have less insecurity than men, possibly because of the macho role that has been thrust upon us.

Psychologist and Psychiatrists will break insecurity into categories such as social anxiety, failure, rejection, a childhood trauma, etc. I am sure all of these are correct, but the insecurity I have seen is never more visible in a man than when is he unable to *fix* something that is broken or erratic. His wife begins to cry, he asks her what is wrong ... but she won't say. She doesn't know why, and we men are too dense to let it wind down gradually. We are fearful that it relates to something we have done, and we can't rest until we *fix it*.

The second kind of insecurity is when we see something that we can't define. We are built to want to mentally and emotionally file everything in the right place. If we can't define it ... we can't file it. Everything must have a label and a definition because if I can't specifically identify something, I have no control over it ... and I must have control!

Finally, in order to feel secure, men need to be able to measure everything. At the end of each day or task, we need to be able to see where the hole is that we dug. We want visible evidence that something worthwhile happened. To be assured that we will see the results down the road just won't do it.

If we can't fix it, define it, or measure it we are like a downhill skier without snow. We are anxious and bewildered, unable to be fully present. Things are left hanging and we feel incomplete.

In the next few days, I want to take each of these a little deeper. It's not okay to just say," this is just the way I am." God never intended for us to be anything but confident, relaxed, and at peace. These insecurities create in us the opposite effect.

Insecurity: When We Can't Fix It

If something is broken, whether it is a relationship, a promise or a simple misunderstanding, men always think they should try to fix it. My wife says its pride because anyone who thinks they are the final solution to a whatever ails you is vicariously trying to play God. I think she's on to something.

Men have been taught that we validate ourselves by swooping in like a superhero and solving difficult problems just in time to save the day. It is part of the macho persona that we have created in our culture. Even on the smallest of issues, I sometimes find myself giving advice that was unsolicited. I am realizing more and more that though my intentions are simply to be helpful, I cannot fight all the battles for all the people all the time.

I can't stand to see division among people. If I see two people fighting, my mentality is to break up the fight. If I see a nasty argument heating up I don't usually get involved, but everything in me wants to get them to kiss and make up. The problem is that you can't fix alienation with a quick solution because it usually has roots that go much deeper than the present argument.

Moses was a fixer. One day he saw an Egyptian beating a Hebrew. He came to the rescue of his brethren, killed the Egyptian, and buried him thinking no one would know. The next day he saw two Hebrews fighting and he tried to fix it and stop the aggressor. One of the men asked, "Will you kill me like you killed the Egyptian?" Moses knew had been found out, and it led to the Pharaoh trying to kill him. This forced Moses to flee the country.[1] His loyalty for his people was commendable, but God can show us when to intervene and when to stand down.

If we try to solve all our children's problems they'll never learn to trust God. As I write this there was a huge scandal where parents were paying to give their kids a leg up in getting into certain elite colleges. One celebrity couple paid $500,000 for their daughters to get in USC, and one of their daughters had no interest in even going to school. From what I read, it has caused a rift in the marriage, and the daughters are now alienated from their parents.

The greatest thing we can learn in life is how to trust God. That cannot happen when we are always intervening. It may be done in love, but it is a reckless love that will never allow the object of that love to grow up. It's a hard lesson to learn, but any insecurity that is allowed to continue can cause irreparable damage.

---

[1]Gen. 2:11–14

Insecurity: When We Can't Define It

Have you ever considered why we all have the same go-to questions when we meet someone at a party or social gathering? The default question will be some form of "What do you do?" This is partially because it's a safe question, not too personal but it gives us the knowledge of where to mentally file the person. Women are far more comfortable diving into a conversation than men. They will learn where the other woman got her purse, her outfit, who does her hair, and how many kids she has within a few minutes.

Men want to know what category the other person fits in because it feels uncomfortable not to know. When we think about the person we intuitively want to think of him, or her, in a specific slot. It is really about control! We don't know how we feel about someone if we can't place him in our invisible file cabinet.

I have worked in a ministry to people in public life for over forty years. The people I work with are like-minded friends around the world whose common ground is our relationship with Jesus Christ. It's not what we do, where we attend church, or where we stand politically; we are related by a shared love for God as His children. It's not an organization but a fellowship of friends with no desire to be labeled or recognized but to simply engage with and be part of the worldwide family of believers. The hardest thing about the work we do is trying to explain it. People are trained to think institutionally, but we are trying to be a non-institutional "family" of friends in the deepest sense. The moment you put a tag or label on your work or ministry you seal yourself off from others. Why didn't Jesus name His group of disciples or his "new movement?" His mission was people ... of all kinds. He could be with a Jew, a Samaritan, a Roman officer, a Pharisee or a Phoenician woman, and they all spoke freely with Him. In my work, for instance, I must be able to bridge the gap among those with whom I flatly disagree. It has nothing to do with politics and everything to do with loving and caring for people.

Labels and definitions tend to separate us. It is insecurity that lures us to hide behind them. When I meet with a young man or woman who wants to start a ministry with athletes, businessmen, or high school kids, I always wonder why the first word on their yellow pad is a name or logo to identify their ministry. Why not just do what you are called to do? Why not let your ministry be defined by the compassion and love you have for the people?

Once you define something you can control it. The early church could not be controlled. They were a family held together, not by a membership, but by the Spirit of God. They were unstoppable!

Insecurity:
When We Can't Measure It

Possibly the greatest confidence breaker for most of us is when there is no mechanism by which we can calculate or measure what we have done and accomplished. In my work, I may spend many long hours with someone, or a group of people, trying to help them sort through a relational problem. I may never have any tangible evidence that those hours I spent were helpful. That I was there for them may be deeply appreciated, but there is generally no way I can measure how far the line was moved and what positive progress was made. I have to believe that when you are faithful and lack a personal agenda, asking nothing in return, it may have some effect ... but I may not know for years.

God says that His Word will never return void to Him.[1] That is a huge promise that I rely on. You can spend years caring for someone and just when you think they have had a breakthrough, they go backward. Was it a waste of time? I don't think so, although I have had many disappointments over the years.

Normally, when you go into a conflict, you learn whether you won or lost after it's over. Paul said, "we are more than conquerors through Him who loved us."[2] The difference in a conqueror and a *more* than a conqueror is that a conqueror doesn't know he has won until he *has* won, but a more than conqueror knows he has won before the battle is ever fought.

Whatever is done under God's direction must be done with no expectation of any tangible reward. The reward is an internal one that cannot be measured. It took me a long time to learn that. I have known people addicted to drugs or alcohol and their spouse may have to hang in there for years before there is real progress. You can't measure the important things is life, but the insecurity drives us crazy. That's where your confidence that God is at work must take over. We are obsessed with charts and digital readouts and we decide the validation of everything based on numbers. Those charts can never tell the story of a human heart.

"I love my wife more than you love yours," he says. How so? "She has a bigger diamond, a nicer car, a more luxurious home." These are, no doubt, more of a measurement of money than of love. Statistics are great for sports and banks, but in human relationships they are meaningless.

---

[1] Isa. 55:11   [2] Rom. 8:37

Words that Frighten Believers

"After this, I looked, and there before me was a great multitude that no one could count, from every nation, tribe, people and language, standing before the throne and before the Lamb." Revelation 7:9–10 (NIV)

There are few words that strike more fear into the hearts of most believers than *diversity* and *tolerance.* The reason for this is that both words have been kidnapped by the world's system and now appear to signify the opposite of their true meaning.

There is little doubt that in our society there is an effort to secularize many of those deeply felt traditions and practices that have been a sacred part of our lives. "Merry Christmas" versus "Happy Holidays" has crossed swords for many years. I will always be a Merry Christmas guy, but I'm also aware that most of us who fight for that phrase will spend most of December in stores buying stuff, decorating inside and outside and attending parties that have nothing to do with the real meaning of Christmas.

Diversity is the biblical companion of unity. Unity without diversity will end up as a private, exclusive club that only certain people can get in. Faith in Jesus Christ spreads its arms wide to all who will come. It is not exclusive, but inclusive. Yes, it requires faith, but you can't see or judge who has it and who doesn't. It is a matter of the heart and it is available to all living beings because we all have one. Because the LGBTQ community's mantra is about *diversity* we have this idea that to use that word is to compromise the Scripture. But a biblical principle is always valid no matter who tries to commandeer it with another meaning.

Tolerance is much the same. It does not mean compromising our values or dumbing down our faith. If you love classical music do you force your teenagers to like it also? If your daughter wants to date a person of color do you lock her in her room until she is twenty-one? My middle son, Jonathan, worked for six years at American University in Washington, D.C., for the former Muslim Ambassador from Pakistan to the United Kingdom. He traveled with him, worked on two books with him, and remains very close to him years later. They worked together on reconciliation issues between followers of Jesus, Jews, and Muslims. Jonathan, who is a follower of Jesus, gained much from this learned and compassionate man and has developed a great understanding and appreciation for the Muslim people.

Diversity is what you see every time you look at the sky, consider the complexities of the human body, or look at the uniqueness of a snowflake. Jesus practiced *tolerance*, even with those He disagreed with the most. To embrace differences does not mean to agree with everyone. To embrace is to say, "we may not agree on everything, but I love you anyway."

Broken Hearts and Crushed Spirits

"The Lord is near to the brokenhearted and saves those who are crushed in spirit."
Psalm 34:18

Have you ever had a broken heart? I hope you have to think back a long way. Almost everyone reading this will have suffered something so disappointing and painful that you may have used that term to describe it. Who can say what actually qualifies as a broken heart? It usually is associated with extreme sorrow or grief that feels so devastating that actual physical pain is experienced.

I remember driving on the beltway around D.C. one day and on the news came a report that a man and his two sons were deer hunting in Maryland. The Father shot at what he thought was a deer only to discover that he had accidentally shot his son. His other son immediately ran through the woods toward the car to get help and then heard the sickening sound of another gunshot. I have three sons and I couldn't imagine the abject horror that father must have felt as he realized what he had done. His heart was broken, but the hopelessness he surely must have felt when he instinctively turned the rifle on himself was more than a broken heart. The end of this verse refers to a "crushed spirit." A broken heart may mend, but a crushed spirit can cause one to lose hope.

God's specialty is staying close to the brokenhearted and saving the crushed in spirit. In a moment of tragedy, our reason can become unhinged, but I wish so much that the boy's father had known that God can restore a crushed spirit. I wish he'd had enough clarity to see the double heartbreak that his wife and their other son would have to endure. I still think of them from time to time and pray for their continued healing.

The Samaritan woman Jesus encountered by the well had a crushed spirit. She had been married five times; a couple of her husbands may have died prematurely, which was common in those days. Under the liberal interpretation of Jewish law, other husbands may have divorced her even for the most trivial of reasons. There is a good possibility she was abandoned because she was barren. She was now living with a man, and Jesus knew she was a woman with a crushed spirit who had lost all hope.

You may be living with a broken heart as you read this. It may be from a betrayal, the death of a loved one or a lifelong dream that you may feel was stolen from you. Whatever it is, please give that broken heart and crushed spirit to God and remember these words: *"He heals the brokenhearted and bandages their wounds. He counts the stars and assigns each a name. Our Lord is great, with limitless strength. We will never comprehend what he knows and does. God puts the fallen on their feet again."*[1]

---

[1] Ps. 147:2–6

Passion

"His word is in my heart like a fire, a fire shut up in my bones. I am weary of holding it in, indeed I cannot." Jeremiah 20:9 (NIV)

When we lived in New York City, Susan dragged me to Filene's Basement one Saturday morning. Their flagship store in Boston had been famous since opening in 1911 because of the incredible bargains. We went to the New York store and it was a moment in time that I will never forget. We got there just as it opened. When the doors parted, women bolted in, knocking over displays and nearly trampling over slower shoppers. I watched in disbelief as they charged the bridal gowns that were dramatically reduced. Several women wanted the same wedding dress and pulled and tugged at it until they fell on the floor cussing and yelling at each other, tearing the dress into shreds. I had heard about catfights but had never seen one up close. It was unlike any experience I ever had.

Later, as we rode home on the subway, I remember thinking how similar this was to be watching a game in Yankee Stadium, minus the fighting and bridal gowns. The passion was about the same as Filene's and I couldn't remember anything like that excitement and enthusiasm in any church that I had ever been in!

Passion is a strong and intense emotional feeling. It is mostly associated with lust and intense desire for someone in a physical sense, but passion can be positive and creative as well. We call the week of Jesus' walk to the cross "Passion Week." He wasn't excited about suffering and dying, but His desire and determination to accomplish the reason He came was so fervent and powerful that it looked past the natural human fear and dread of a Roman cross.

Physically, passion can drive you in unhealthy directions. But if passion is channeled in the right direction and is controlled by the Spirit of God, it can become an unquenchable partnership to a hurting world.

Jeremiah complained to God about the treatment he was receiving from the unbelievers. He felt that the ridicule he received was due to his prophetic voice on God's behalf. It was a complaint, but then he says that the truth he knows burned within him like a fire shut up in his bones. It drives him.[1] Martin Luther said, "Here I stand; I can do no other." Passion for the truth drove him. Paul said "Woe to me if I do not preach the gospel.[2]

Passion is not foaming at the mouth and being obnoxious; it is a deep well of certainty in your soul that cannot be contained.

---

[1] Jer. 20:7–12   [2] 1 Cor. 9:16

The Ultimate Wedding

"Then I will take you for My people, and I will be your God; and you shall know that I am the Lord your God, who brought you out from under the burdens of the Egyptians." Exodus 6:7

Marriage is the most sacred thing you will ever do. It is not just a piece of paper; it is a holy covenant, the merging of two hearts into one. God promised the Hebrews that he would take them from under the yolk of the Egyptians and free them from slavery. He said, "I will redeem you with an outstretched arm."[1] Picture the prodigal son coming home and his father running to him with his arms outstretched. Then God says, "I will take you to be my people."[2] The word "take" is the Hebrew phrase for marriage. Isaac *took* Rebecca to be his wife. Jeremiah said, "You loved me like a bride."[3] Isaiah says, "your maker is your husband."[4] We see this image throughout the Old Testament.

On Mount Sinai, this great wedding had all the elements of a Jewish wedding today. There a *Chuppah*, which is a canopy under which the bride and groom stand. It is a covering that symbolizes God's protection. The Scripture says God covered the mountain with a cloud as the people stood at its base. There was a *Mikvah*, or purification bath, where the bride bathed and was cleansed or set apart to be holy. Moses has the people wash their clothes but not to climb the mountain or to touch it.[5]

In a Jewish wedding, there is a *Ketubah* or marital contract. Unlike the vows we make, it is a written contract. The contract between God and His people was the two stone tablets written by the finger of God. A ring is a symbol of the marital covenant, but God said the sign of the covenant of our relationship was the *Sabbath*. Finally, the vows between the bride and groom were the commandments of God promising provision and protection.

As believers, we must reclaim this great love affair of a bride with her husband. What went wrong? While God was with Moses on the mountain, the Hebrews were having an affair ... at the wedding no less! Later, Moses sees the golden calf the people had made and smashed the tablets into pieces.[6]

God's marriage to His people is no joke. People who think that if you love each other, why not just live together; marriage is just a formality, a piece of paper. No, it's not! It is a critically important covenant which God takes very seriously. The Holy Scripture is the story of two marriages ... two sacred covenants. They should never be taken lightly.

---

[1]Exod. 6:6 [2]Gen. 24:67 [3]Jer. 2:2 [4]Isa. 54:5 [5]Exod. 19:12, 14 [6]Exod. 32:19

Glorifying God

"Everyone who is called by my name, whom I created for my glory, whom I formed and made." Isaiah 43:7 (NIV)

"The Bible says God made mankind for His glory and that He demands our worship. Why would I follow a God who had an ego bigger than Mount Everest? If I had an ego like that you would say it was a sin." This was a comment from a college student after a talk I made to a group at NYU. I understood her confusion because, to the untutored ear, being created for God's glory seems contrary to the humility Jesus displayed and preached.

When people invite others to their home they receive compliments from their guests about how beautiful, warm and inviting it is. The owners thank them and receive full credit even though they never hammered the first nail. "Yes," you say, "But they told the builder what they wanted and paid money to get it." Where did they get the money? "They earned it." How did they earn it? "They studied and got a degree ..." You can see where this is going?

You trace everything backward and you come to the baseline of either God creating everything as the Scripture claims, or it was *time* plus *matter* plus *chance*. To look at the complexity of the human body and believe we simply climbed out of the primordial slime is ludicrous. To imagine the precision of the earth and planets moving around the sun did not involve an intelligent mind is a greater level of faith than to believe that God created it.

God has no needs! Everything He does in creation is for our benefit. Even for us to acknowledge this, by our praise and worship, is the most natural response we could have. That He wants us to put His glory on display is not because He needs it, but because we need it. What He has done for us is a supreme act of humility, not ego. He sent His only Son to pay for what He did not owe by dying on a Roman cross in order to make His people, who did not deserve it, free. The truth is, if I believe that I accomplished my own life, I then should be expected to be responsible for everything that happens, both painful and even catastrophic. Why then, when a loved one is rushed to the emergency room, do I not call out in agony to other people for mercy ... or better yet, to myself?

It is in acknowledging God's glory that our purpose for living makes sense. When I aim away from my own glory and give glory to Him, something happens to me internally. Jesus said a play-actor (hypocrite) steals glory that belongs to God.[1] Giving God glory is the certainty that I know who I am, and I know who He is, and I am in sync with the purpose for which I was created.

---

[1]Matt. 6:1–8

Keeping the Bigger Picture in Mind

"And this is the plan: At the right time he will bring everything together under the authority of Christ—everything in heaven and on earth." Ephesians. 1:10 (NLT)

After the Persian army defeated the Babylonians, King Cyrus released the Jews to return to their homeland and rebuild the Temple and their city of Jerusalem. Some 250,000 Jews returned and slowly began the work. After years of toil, and what seemed like a snail's pace to the workers, God sent two prophets to encourage them. One of them was Zechariah. The workers began to feel, as we often do, that the enormity of the task was so great, and they had progressed so slowly, that they began to lose heart. Zechariah gave them hope by helping them to see the big picture. He told them that one day this very entrance into the great city would be lined with people and that the Messiah would ride down through this sea of humanity on a donkey. This would announce that He was the long-awaited salvation of His people. It was enough encouragement that they stepped into a higher gear simply by the reminder that their small part in the larger picture would be so monumental that it would shake the world's foundation.[1]

Whether you are a fan of Tiger Wood or not, unless you have been living on a different planet, you have heard about the remarkable comeback he has made from twenty-two injuries he endured since 1997. Knee and back injuries cost him years when he was in his prime, and at times could not even get out of bed. The thought that he would even be able to swing a golf club again was doubtful. Recovery from spinal fusion, enabling him to compete at the professional level, was unthinkable. The inches of progress he was trying to make would have capsized most people's will to continue, but not Tiger. Little by little, he kept the big picture in mind while moving as slowly as molasses in winter. Out of nowhere, he wins the Tour Championship in 2018 and no one could believe it. Then in April of 2019, He wins His fifth Masters, a feat that was beyond the imagination of anyone who has known extreme pain and understands golf.

When you look at your life, it is easy to feel defeated by how slow you are progressing, but this is a cross country "walk," not a sprint. Focus on the big picture and, inch by inch, progress will be made. It will be critical in completing the final picture.[2]

---

[1] Zech. 9:9   [2] 1 Tim. 4:15

334

Relax

"Be still and know that I am God." Psalm 46:10 (NIV)

This short verse is a favorite among many believers. It is easy to remember, easy to recite, and it applies to everyone. I am indebted to my friend, Keith Tyner, who showed me that "Be still" can also be translated "Relax." It gave me a wider perspective on a familiar passage. Visualize this: "Relax and know that I am God." Can you think of a time when you felt the most relaxed and free from cares and burdens? You will probably think of a vacation, lying in a hammock on a beautiful beach with an umbrella beverage nearby and only the sound of the waves crashing on the shore. It might be the feeling of autonomy when you graduated and moved into a career or when you paid off the mortgage and were finally debt-free.

Whatever your most relaxing time was, imagine living that way even in the midst of concerns and responsibilities, confidently knowing that because God is at work out in front of you, you can relax. This does not mean passivity; it does not mean an absence of determination, discipline or exacting labor. The result of hard work is usually exhaustion, but much

of that fatigue is due to the uncertainty that our efforts will be rewarded or appreciated. But what if you knew and believed this: "For I am the Lord your God who takes hold of your right hand and says to you, "Do not fear; I will help you."[1]

A wonderful friend, visiting from Africa, once made a very profound statement to a friend of mine. He said, "I have learned the secret of working rested." This is what Sabbath rest is all about. God works in us while we are at rest. You may be caring for a patient, arguing a case in court, selling a product, teaching your students, or framing a house, but to know that God is at work within you produces a level of confidence that overcomes stress and angst.

When you collapse in a hammock, listen to the ocean as you breathe in the salty air, the stress begins to drain away. The issues you had back home are still there, but they are not having the same impact on you as before because you are in a state of rest. This is the state that God wants His children to be in all the time. "Relax and know that I am God."

---

[1] Isa. 41:13

Love on Steroids

"Greater love has no one than this, that one lay down his life for his friends."
John 15:13

Most people have heard the story of Chuck Colson's involvement in the Watergate scandal, his imprisonment, and conversion to Jesus Christ. You know of his tireless work in the prison systems in the United States as well as in countries around the world. But you may not know a back story that Chuck used to refer to as, "the act of love that broke me."

Doug Coe had gone to meet with Colson at the request of Tom Phillips, a mutual friend in Boston. Colson and Doug became fast friends and Doug began to disciple him. He called three close friends to gather around Chuck, knowing that he would need tremendous support as the Watergate hearings heated up. Congressman Al Quie of Minnesota, Congressman Graham Purcell of Texas, and Senator Harold Hughes of Iowa were asked to have an initial meeting to hear about Colson's story. It was a dramatic coming together of men from different political persuasions but each who loved Jesus.

The five met faithfully until Colson was convicted and sentenced to prison down in Alabama. The group visited and called, encouraging him to stay positive. During one month, his mother died, his son was arrested for drugs, and he was disbarred from ever practicing law again. The group continued to meet and pray. Al Quie discovered an obscure statute still on the Alabama law books where *in cases of severe duress, one man can serve a prison term for another.* After discussing this with his family and the group, Al stepped forward. The group came to Chuck and told him the Judge had agreed that Al could leave Congress and serve the remainder of Chuck's prison term so that he could be with his family.

I heard Chuck tell this story many times and he always said that it was this selfless act of sacrificial love that broke him. As it turned out, Judge Gisel commuted the rest of his sentence and he was allowed to go home. I knew each of the men involved and, at this writing, only Al Quie is still living. But anyone who knew Colson or any of the others will attest to the fact that this great act of love was the impetus of much of what God accomplished through Prison Fellowship over these many years.

This was not a publicity stunt. Each of the men in the group were willing to do the same. It was known by no one until Colson shared it several years later.

Getting What We Want

"Do not be deceived: God cannot be mocked. A man reaps what he sows."
Galatians 6:7 (NIV)

Do the ends justify the means? Does a good outcome excuse any wrongs committed while trying to secure it? It is a question that goes all the way back to the sixteenth century and has become a characteristic in today's society. If I want a specific job and feel that I am well suited for it, I lie on my resume in order to escort myself to the front of the line. If I get the job, I feel justified because "It's a dog eat dog world" and you must be aggressive if you want to get anywhere. That is the essential argument that is becoming more and more common, even among believers.

When you look at it on the surface, any person who wants their life to reflect the character of Jesus would never say yes to such a question. It would be basically the same as saying that in order to help prostitutes come to faith it justifies using their services to do it. Of course, those who champion this point of view are much more subtle than this, but it is ethically and morally the same. Manipulation of the truth in order to get what you want for any reason is mocking God and is a dead end.

King David had sex with Uriah's wife and to hide his sin he sent Uriah to the front lines so he would be killed. He believed that the end justified the means. Jacob deceived his father and cheated his brother out of the birthright for the same reason. Both men later prospered, but not before paying a great price and having to humble themselves before God. We see people claw their way up the ladder in business and politics citing the great things they can do once they get in a position of authority. The problem is that when they finally get there the lies and compromising that propelled them forward often causes them to forget why they started. Is driving a stolen car more satisfying than saving, sacrificing and finally buying it free and clear?

The bottom line for believers is this: When we manipulate our way to any goal and are willing to lie and deceive to get there, we are simply saying to God, "I don't trust you! I don't believe you can take me where I want to go and furthermore, I am afraid this may not be your will, but it is mine, so I am moving ahead." Sometimes we fail to understand that getting to the top of the ladder to do great things is irrelevant to God. If you are not making a difference where you are, how can you make a difference where you aren't? To sacrifice character for a position, or whatever you perceive to be the *gold ring,* is the same as mocking God. Everything about walking with Jesus Christ is about *trust.*

Four Critical Questions

"The two disciples heard him speak and they followed Jesus. Turning around, Jesus saw them following and asked, 'What do you want?'" John 1:37–38 (NIV)

John the Baptist is in the desert with two of his disciples and Jesus walks by. John says, *See that man? You are looking at the Lamb of God. He's the One whom you have heard about your whole life. He will take away the sins of the world.* The two men follow Him. Jesus turns and asks, "What do you want?"

As believers, we know that God will supply all our needs,[1] but I have found that what people *want* is a window into their true character. A young man asked me to help him get a youth ministry job at a local church. He spoke enthusiastically about his "calling" to help young people. Six months later he quit and took a job as an accountant. We had lunch and I pressed him about what had happened to his "calling" to work with kids. He confessed that the ministry job was because nothing else was available at the time." It had nothing to do with a calling. If a person will be brutally honest about what they want, you will soon discover *who* they are.

In the next four days, I want to offer four questions that I believe will be helpful in getting to the core issues of character. The first is this: Will you settle once and for all … *How much is enough?* People concoct multiple reasons to stockpile money and to keep adding to the pile. There is nothing wrong with saving, but *how much is enough?* I have heard many say, "I want to give more to the work of God, and I will do that as soon as I get my financial house in order." But I have never heard someone say they got there. Why? Because they never defined *how much is enough.* They kept extending the boundaries to build "bigger barns."[2] It's not just a money question. When the kids are grown, how much of a house do we really need? How important is our image? How many more years will I give away time that I can never retrieve, in order to duplicate what I already have?

Larry Sitton, a good friend who is retired now, was a very fine attorney in a large law firm in his city. The billable hours that were required stole time from his family and his faith. As he grew spiritually he wanted to be involved in things that made a difference in people's lives, but he just didn't have the time. After prayer with his family and a few close friends, he walked into a partners meeting and told them that he wanted to invest more time with his family and in growing spiritually. He asked for his hours to be cut and for his salary to be reduced commensurate with the time he took off. He did this for many years and remained an excellent lawyer making a big difference in many people's lives. All of this was because he asked: "How much is enough?"

---

[1] Phil. 4:19 [2] Luke 12:13–21

Critical Questions, part 2

"Humble yourselves in the presence of the Lord and He will exalt you." James 4:10

The second question is this: *Will I seek to distinguish myself among people or will I humble myself before God?* Most of us don't think of it in these exact terms, but the classic struggle is how do I utilize the gifts and talents I have been given and display a genuine sense of humility at the same time? If my abilities are applauded by people, am I to be a shrinking violet and act embarrassed when my talent or gifts are appreciated? Of course not! If you have a beautiful voice and people applaud and praise you for it, consider it as a gift to them. For people to acknowledge it is the same as saying "Thanks for sharing this great gift with us."

In one sense, humility is a choice and, in another sense, it is not possible apart from the Spirit of God within us. Humility will seldom be our first thought in response to acclamation. We all want to be loved, appreciated and recognized. When God replaces our heart of stone with a heart of flesh the way we think about adulation changes.[1] The affirmation still feels good, but the knowledge that you use the talents God gave you for His glory and to enhance the lives of others is beyond measure.

Every human being wrestles with ego. If we could solve every problem in the universe, there would still be the problem of *what to do with me.* This is what philosophy, since the time of Socrates, has been trying to answer. All religions struggle with what to do with the human *self.* Jesus said to "Deny yourself."[2] Be unresponsive to the tendencies to exalt and promote yourself. No one is born humble. We all want the applause, recognition, and honor for our achievements.[2] If you study humility in Scripture you find that it is a *choice* rather than a state of being. The new heart God created within us offers the capability to deflect the glory from ourselves, but it's not on autopilot. We choose to defer to the One who gave us the gift. "Humble yourself."[3] Don't make the mistake of asking God to humble you. You don't want that!

An athlete I admired growing up was Bobby Richardson, the second baseman for the New York Yankees during their dynasty of the '50s and early '60s. I remember when he was honored at Yankee Stadium when he retired. He made a brief but gracious speech, and at the end simply said, "To God be the glory." No verbose sermonette … just a simple statement that communicated his entire perspective about his career and his life. It's a decision and an act of grace. Will your success be all about you or about God who lives within you?

---

[1]Ezek. 36:26   [2]Matt. 16:24   [3]1 Pet. 5:6

Critical Questions, part 3

"For everything there is a season, and a time for every matter under heaven . . ."
Ecclesiastes 3:1–8 (ESV)

The third critical question is this: *Will I become a person of balance or a person of extremes?* By balance I am not talking about being in the middle of the road or living in a neutral zone; I am talking about a level of stability that can only come from exposing yourself to the full counsel of God rather than selected bits and pieces.[1] Let's face it, most of us are rabbit chasers, trend hoppers, or fad grabbers. We get every book by every flavor of the month *spiritual expert* that comes along. We pass along "news" making the rounds at the coffee shops, Bible studies, and fellowship halls ... happily jumping on board. We tend to bounce from one extreme to another. James speaks of being tossed back and forth like a wave on the ocean and the instability that results.[2] A ballast on a sailboat is what provides stability and balance. Without it, we are at the mercy of whoever steps to the microphone.

Back in the 1990s a huge issue erupted that caused havoc and hysteria and maligned a highly respected company. A rumor was started in New York, New Jersey, and Philadelphia that Proctor and Gamble were a satanic company that gave a large amount of their profits to The Church of Satan. It all started with a logo on the boxes of products that portrayed a crescent moon with thirteen stars around it. The rumors began and calls came in by the thousands to Proctor and Gamble by people saying they would never again use their products. P&G had to spend a small fortune on lawyers to defend their reputation. A court case ensued and culminated in a twenty-million-dollar settlement against another a company with strong spiritual underpinnings and competitors of P&G. It was a slanderous attempt by distributors of the company to beat the competition. Thousands of churches had jumped on the bandwagon simply based on a rumor.

There is symmetry and harmony in life that God wants his children to step into, but we must stay focused. We can't pick and choose our favorite verses and still be stable and balanced. Jesus was perfectly balanced. He was never a religious nut as were his enemies; He never dabbled with fads or obsessed on the issues of the times. If you and I chase after issues and trends we will become unbalanced and unattractive to the watching world. But if we are solely focused on Jesus we will be perfectly in sync.

Tossed like a wave or balanced? ... A question worthy to consider.

---

[1] Acts 2:27   [2] James 1:6–8

Critical Questions, part 4

"Two are better than one, because they have a good return for their labor: If either of them falls down, one can help the other up. But pity anyone who falls and has no one to help them up." Ecclesiastes 4: 9–12 (NIV)

The fourth question is this: *Will I walk through life as a solitary man or woman, or walk within the context of a few like-minded companions?* My parent's generation was largely taught that life is a solo journey except for your spouse and children. Everything was to be held close to the vest. Strength and determination were the daily mantras; problems were not discussed outside the home and emotions were kept to a minimum, especially for men. My first twenty years were lived in the shadow of that kind of perspective until I met a very unique woman from Atlanta, who everyone called "Elvis." She became a surrogate mother to me and she gently, but determinedly, made me open up and be unafraid of vulnerability. She is in her mid-90s now and remains to me … pure oxygen!

In 1974 I met Doug Coe in Washington, D.C. He challenged me to ask God for a core of like-minded men to walk alongside in our common journey with Jesus. Blake Rymer, Robby Rowan, and Larry Nicastro became those guys, and we began a lifelong friendship. Larry is in heaven and I live in a different state from Robby and Blake, but the relationship always remains. I have learned much walking with these men and could tell you many stories of how God used them in my life.

There was a reason the early church prospered despite obsessive attempts to wipe them out and crush their mission. They were men and women who *walked with a limp.* They were like three-legged dogs who leaned on each other for encouragement, understanding, and accountability. Had they set out as *lone rangers* and sought to be superstars they would have failed. We make Paul a great white knight vanquishing the pagan world out in front of the others, but he never saw himself that way. He had men with him like Paul, Silas, Timothy and others who saw themselves, not as individuals engaged in a conquest, but a true cadre of companions who would move together or not at all. You see this clearly after Jesus was resurrected. He told his disciples on three occasions to meet him in Galilee, but each time they failed to go.[1] As you study the story you begin to see that it was because of Thomas. He was holding them back with his doubts, and they would not leave without their brother! I love that! It is that spirit that held them together and kept the Roman Empire up late at night trying to figure out how to stop them. "A three-stranded cord is not easily broken"[2]

---

[1]Luke 24:6; Mark 14:27–28; Matt. 28:10   [2]Eccles. 9:12

Waiting: Our Default Position

"But they that wait upon the Lord shall renew their strength; they shall mount up with wings as eagles; they shall run, and not be weary, and they shall walk, and not faint." Isaiah 40:31 (KJV)

If there is anything people don't like to do it's waiting. We're waiting to go, waiting to return, waiting to get in, waiting to get out, waiting to begin and waiting to finish. *Good things come to those who wait,* we are told, but it seems like all we do is wait. Now Isaiah tells us to *wait* on the Lord. He goes on to say that waiting will renew our strength and we will fly like eagles and run without getting tired and walk without tapping out.

God knows us better than we know ourselves. He knows how we think, what makes us happy and sad; He knows our strengths and weaknesses, and what motivates or crushes us. When He looks over the landscape, His eyes are always searching for someone with a good heart.[1] He focuses in on that person who has been *waiting*, whose strength has been renewed and who is *ready*. He matches the gifts of that person with someone who yearns for the very thing he or she possesses. When He leads them to each other, he "strongly supports" the *waiting person* and directs him to those who are in need.

A man named Phillip was waiting one day and God told him to get up and start walking south down the desert road between Jerusalem and Gaza. Meanwhile, an Ethiopian eunuch, the treasurer of an Ethiopian Queen, was in his chariot frustrated as he read a passage in Isaiah about the coming of the Messiah. God told Phillip that the chariot was just up the road. The two met and the Ethiopian asked Phillip to explain what Isaiah was saying. Phillip explained, and the man's life was never the same! What if Phillip had charged out on his own timing to find someone to witness to? Had the Eunuch not just returned from a church gathering Jerusalem, he may not have been receptive. But God knew that his time in Jerusalem had piqued his interest. He put Phillip on a collision course with a man desperate for answers.

We come up with great innovative ideas. They are good ideas, but they may not be God's ideas. Waiting on God is not passive. It is about God's timing. I have seen zealous people go out like car salesmen who think it is up to them. They appear proactive and ready to shake the world, but they will often run over people whose hearts have not been prepared. Jesus did not respond to needs … He responded to the Father. If you go around trying to meet needs you will never leave your neighborhood. Why not wait on the Lord and when He says "Go" it will be perfect timing.

---

[1] Acts 8:26–40

Against the Grain

"Don't let the world around you squeeze you into its own mould, but let God re-mould your minds from within." Romans 12:2 (Phillips)

As I have mentioned before, everything concerning an ongoing companionship with Jesus Christ is counterintuitive. Whatever way you and I would attempt to solve a problem, build a coalition of like-minded friends or work toward a consensus with those who oppose us, God's counsel would generally be the exact opposite. Without a renewed mind that sees life through the lens of faith, we are simply running in circles, pooling our collective ignorance. God's mind works against the grain.

As an athlete, I was taught that regardless of the opponent or adversary, you out-think him, out-quick him, go around him, or run over him, but you never give in to him ... you never quit. That is the nature of an athletic contest. I thought it would transfer to my faith as I stepped into the murky waters of a world where I was overmatched and underequipped.

I went to an FCA Conference and an All-Pro Linebacker talked about taking Satan by the throat and putting him on the ground. So, I went back and tried it and got creamed. Every natural athletic instinct I knew failed me in spiritual warfare. I couldn't out-think, outrun, or overpower temptations. I couldn't wrestle pride or selfishness to the floor. The more I tried the worse it got. I finally met a man

named Tom Skinner who told me a simple, but oh so profound truth. He said I should quit trying! I said, "I'll never quit; it's not in my DNA." Tom said, "Well if you don't, it's just a matter of time before you will sink without a trace!" He said, "Neb, you have the King of Kings living in you; what can you do that He can't do better than you? This whole life is about giving up the fight and giving in to Him." Then, he said something that has become a mantra to me, "Life is *Christ in you, living His own life through you, without any help or assistance from you!*"

In the 1940s until the mid-60s ministers and evangelists used to talk of *yielding* yourself to Christ. To yield is to *surrender*, to *give up*, to transfer title to God. But somewhere in the mid-60s, the verbiage changed. "Commit yourself to Christ." Semantics you say! No, it is two different things. Yielding means my life is no longer my own. Everything is His. But the *commitment faith* that I was exposed to early on means that I decide to commit when and how much. For many, it morphed into attaching Jesus like a bumper sticker to the life I was already living.

God calls us to a life that cuts across the grain. Bonhoeffer said, "When Christ calls a man. He bids him come and die."

A Different Way to Memorize Scripture

"Let the word of Christ richly dwell within you." Colossians 3:16

As far back as I can remember, this passage has been used to underline how the Scriptures should be taught ... "line upon line, precept upon precept." The idea of verse by verse expository teaching comes from this idea. However, the context of the passage is a mocking response to Isaiah's repetitive teaching. It is how you might teach your children. It was *not* meant as instruction on how to study the Bible.

Repetition and memorization were essential in ancient times because there was no printing press until the sixteenth century. Repetition is still a good way to learn. Apparently, Isaiah offended people by the simplicity of the way he taught. The simple truth has always been offensive to the elite.

Word by word and line upon line study may be essential for seminary students and teachers, but for the person in the marketplace, it can become not only monotonous but also misleading. I like expository preaching by articulate, creative people, but I have heard some that transported me into the third stage of anesthesia.

What if you begin to approach the Bible book by book? Not only will you begin to understand the thrust, the content and the author's intent, but you will inadvertently memorize passages by exposure and repetition. I've used memory systems and they are fine, but years ago I stumbled over a way that works best for me.

Take the epistles—they are letters to various churches from the Apostle Paul and others. When you receive a letter, you don't read a few words or a sentence and put it aside for the next day. You read the entire letter. That was the writer's intent. Why would we read Paul's letters any differently? Philippians contains four chapters; each takes about fifteen minutes to read. We read letters from loved ones again and again. What if you were to read the entire letter every day for thirty days? You will begin to understand the context, the essence, and the intent of the author. As a bonus, you will be amazed how much of it you have unintentionally memorized. Your confidence will mount, and you will find that as you read other epistles in the same manner, you will see principles and precepts merge together into one harmonious blend of God's unchanging truth.

The Way That Exceeds All Others

"I will show you a still more excellent way" 1 Corinthians 12:31 (ESV)

If you think your church is having problems, consider for a minute what the Apostle Paul had to deal with. He had founded the church in Corinth in the early 40s AD along with Priscilla and Aquila. His initial converts were street people who were tough, poor and uncouth. Corinth was the largest city in Greece and was a strategic seaport for trade. By 51 AD when he writes his first letter to the Corinthians, there was a sizable cluster of believers in the church, but it was covered in problems. There was partisanship among the leaders who had split into factions;[1] there was incest,[2] prostitution,[3] lawsuits,[4] idolatry, chaos in worship services,[5] and denials of the resurrection of the body[6] to name a few. It was a train wreck in slow motion!

This toxic atmosphere and the weakness of the local leaders were allowing the gifts of the Spirit to be sources of ego and pride among the people. Image and physical appearance were at a premium among the elite. Wealth was displayed shamelessly, with clothing and personal attractiveness being highly regarded. The *rock stars* of the day were public speakers, highly trained in rhetorical skills who could charge huge sums and hold a crowd spellbound for hours. Into this curious mix came

Paul, not a physically attractive person, living hand to mouth and renting a small dirty hovel on the street where he made tents to earn money to live. Many scholars believe that his affliction was his eyes. He may well have contracted a severe case of conjunctivitis which made his eyes red, swollen and weepy looking. Imagine being this man; godly and educated but untrained in the flashy tradition of the Greco-Roman world, trying to tell of the love of Jesus.

In the first 11 chapters, Paul deals with many of the problems of the Corinthian church. In Chapter 12, he sums it all up by saying that of all the gifts they may possess and take pride in, there is "a still more excellent way." It is love! It was simply a word of affection to the people that had more to do with physical pleasure than anything else. So, Paul breaks down that more excellent way in Chapter 13. He begins by saying, *"If I speak in the tongues of men and angels and have not love, I am just a lot of noise."* He defines love in the most prolific ways imaginable. I don't believe he was thinking in theological concepts as he writes; He was describing Jesus. God is love and love is the power of life. Love is a Person. Read it. It will show you a more excellent way.

---

[1] 1 Cor. 1:10–4:21; 16:10–18   [2] 1 Cor. 5:1–13   [3] 1 Cor. 6:12–21
[4] 1 Cor. 6:1–11   [5] 1 Cor. 8:1–11:1   [6] 1 Cor. 15:1–58

Even If There Wasn't A God . . .

"If anyone says, 'I love God,' and hates his brother, he is a liar." 1 John 4:20 (ESV)

If there wasn't a God, we could still meet every Sunday morning in a beautiful building with comfortable seats in a warm inviting atmosphere. We could still sing hymns, listen to inspiring messages, sip coffee and hug each other in Fellowship Hall. We could still help the less fortunate by giving our worn-out sofas and mattresses to Good Will. We could still stand together in solidarity and march, if necessary, against the social ills of society. We could do just about everything we are presently doing if there wasn't a God ... except for one thing. We couldn't love, which enable us to embrace and seek to understand those who were different from us.

But there *is* a God and because of His power in us, we can do the one thing we couldn't do without Him. For people of the same basic socio-economic background, political persuasion, and the same social interests, to love one another is easy. It is when I am commanded to love and honor people who are different from me, in every way, that I am at a loss apart from the power of Jesus.

Jesus began a revolution with vagabonds, thieves, men who always smelled like fish, and at least two who carried a deep resentment toward one another. Peter was a zealot; he was an anti-Rome activist who carried a concealed weapon and used it when Jesus was arrested. He hated the system and resented those Jews who were complacent about their lot in life and who had knuckled under to the Romans. Jesus had already chosen Simon Peter when He walked up to Matthew at his tax booth and said: "Follow Me." From a Rabbi to a Jew, that means, "I see in you a man who can be *like* Me." We know of no response from Matthew because he would have been stunned. He worked for Rome and collected taxes from Jews traveling the busy Via Mares trade route that runs just outside the Capernaum. Rome taxed everything ... roads entering and leaving the city, bridges, goods bought and sold, harbor taxes, carts and even the animal that pulled it. Matthew would have been very wealthy but deeply hated by fellow Jews, and disrespected by his Roman employers.

That Jesus chose two men who were opposites was not an accident. He wasn't trying to put together a mutual admiration group. He wanted the world to see what can happen when people who are completely different learn to love and accept each other. I have no doubt that Jesus pulled the two aside a few times to remind them of that. The world wants to see people with differences do what people with differences cannot do apart from the miraculous healing power of Christ. Loving those just like us does not require God and shows the world nothing.

Surrendering Power to Express Love

"Your attitude should be the same as that of Christ Jesus: Who being in the very nature of God did not consider equality with God a thing to be grasped."
Philippians 2:5–8 (NIV)

There is a principle that is fundamental to the dynamics of human relationships. The one who is the least interested has the most power. Who of us hasn't watched the news as reporters scurry down the halls of the courthouse or the Capitol trying desperately to get a quote for their story? But the lawyer, the defendant, or the congressman has no intention of giving a comment. You go to buy a car and immediately one catches your eye, but you act uninterested and continue to walk around as though you are just window shopping. The moment you show that you are in love with a particular car, the power shifts from you to the salesman. In a marital relationship, the wife desperately tried to hold the marriage together but the husband couldn't care less. Who has the power? The husband does; but as he clings to his power, he is expressing the least love.

Love diminishes a person's ability to maintain power. When you love deeply the desire to dominate and have supremacy over someone weakens. This is why I have never been able to understand these power grabs in marriages that are supposedly centered in Christ. I have never even had a serious discussion with my wife about being the head honcho. If love drives the train, it overcomes any desire to always run the show. If you want to compete for the head of the table compete in giving honor to one another.[1] Why would your goal be to grasp control anyway? Why wouldn't you try to be the greatest servant of your spouse? A similar argument is the idiotic debates over whether the tithe should come out of your net or gross income. If that is your concern, you have missed the essence of giving. Giving is primarily meant to bless you, not who or what you give to. Would you pray that your surgeon operates from his net or gross ability?

Jesus relinquished all that made Him God's equal and consented to be a servant. Love always does that. Everyone was amazed that Jesus spoke with such authority.[2] He gave up power but had enormous authority because authority comes from sacrificial love. Any power Jesus displayed in his miracles came not from Him, but from His Father.[3] People like Martin Luther King, Gandhi and Mother Teresa had no power but had great authority. They wielded no weapons and had no armies, only a deep love for people. To the degree that we give up the quest for power, we can fully express love and speak with authority.

---

[1] Rom. 12:10   [2] Mark 1:22   [3] John 14:10

347

Recovering Your Spiritual Passion

"Restore to me the joy of Your salvation and sustain me with a willing spirit."
Psalm 51:12

There are many reasons why we lose our spiritual cutting edge. I am by nature a very upbeat person and in the past the combination of my personality and spiritual immaturity caused me to brush aside spiritual dryness without knowing it was there. As I grew in my relationship with God and exposed myself to people who could help me grow, I began to pinpoint tendencies that pulled me off course.

I was always busy. I have a lot of energy and being sedentary is very uncomfortable for me. In college I had to learn to balance intense football practices, meetings and film study with a rigorous academic schedule, and active involvement of speaking, small groups and, of course, dating. I often found that I was *drinking from an empty cup*. I was so busy that I was giving out far more than I was taking in. It made me spiritually sick. I went through the motions, but there was no life there. Proverbs says, "Hope deferred makes the heart sick."[1] Any number of things can jar your hope and cause you to think that the desert you are living in is as good as it is going to get.

I wanted to give to others out of the overflow of what God is doing in me. I learned that we lose our passion by trying to please people, and by doing things out of obligation rather than out of love and desire. It took me a long time to learn to say "No." To say yes to everything is as arrogant as it gets because the unspoken thought is *It will all fall apart unless I do it!*

Susan and I have had to learn that we must put the oxygen mask on ourselves first so we will be able to help others. When you hit those dry spots and just don't want to pray or study or do much of anything, try to switch it up a bit. Get alone and listen to some beautiful music, take long walks … stop trying to get yourself back on course. If you could do it, you would have already done it! Get alone and let God speak to your heart. He is always trying to get our attention, but we often drown him out with our cell phones and devices so that we don't hear the way Elijah, Isaiah, and Jeremiah heard from Him. It has nothing to do with geography or the time we live in, it has to do with being available in solitude. Notice where these guys were when you read, "And God said to Elijah …" He was alone, in solitude, quiet, available to hear. God said, "I will pour water on the thirsty land, and streams on the dry ground; I will pour out my Spirit."[2]

---

[1] Prov. 13:12   [2] Isa. 44:3

Exposure

"I have given them your word and the world has hated them, for they are not of the world any more than I am of the world." John 17:14 (NIV)

America is geographically composed of dozens of large cities that offer a wide range of social and cultural opportunities, as well as a population of diverse people from multicultural backgrounds. But, most countries are clustered with small to medium-size cities, towns, and hamlets where people are born, raise their families and never leave. In these smaller cities, people tend to gravitate to the familiar, the comfortable and the traditional. They live in the same part of town, attend the same churches, eat at the same restaurants, shop in the same stores and share the same theological, socio-economic and political views. It is a very natural way of life because there is a predictable, amiable, and comfortable lifestyle to which they are accustomed. But, what if a person wanted to share in the authentic life of the Jesus of the Scripture? What if the principles and thoughts I have suggested in these daily readings resonated within people living in these kinds of cities and towns?

Realistically, there are two ways to go. We can either make Jesus one of us or we can allow God to make us like Him. Few would consciously choose the former and, yet, the latter cannot happen unless there is an intentional path forward. I have lived in places like I just described and there are wonderful people there, many of whom want to expand their worldview without compromising their faith, but they don't know how.

Ingrown faith will always lack the challenge of hearing and seeing a variety of perspectives because we tend to avoid the unfamiliar. I believe exposure is the greatest way a believer can begin to see people as God sees them. You don't have to go around the world; it can be done right where you live. It must be intentional; it won't happen by accident. We have drawn great divisions in our culture. We demonize and avoid people who are not like us or with whom our views differ. Sadly, there is nothing about that way of thinking that is biblical.

Jesus made his headquarters in Capernaum which was a crossroads where travelers for other nations constantly rubbed shoulders with local Jews. Not once does Jesus avoid, criticize or even differentiate one group from another. Not once does He shy away from exposing His disciples to anything. Security in who you are and what you believe never necessitates avoidance of different points of view. Tomorrow we will look at some practical ways to be in, but not of the world.

Exposure (2)

Years ago, a friend and I talked about ways to expose some of the people in our city to folks they would never ordinarily have contact with. We pulled together a group of men to meet weekly; half of them were white and the other half black and all were from fairly diverse backgrounds. None of the white men had ever even had a meaningful conversation with a person of color. We had each man tell their personal story in the next few months. One week a black man who was the head of the NAACP chapter in the area told of his experience in Viet Nam and the racial horrors he had experienced throughout his life. A white surgeon in the group pulled me aside afterward and, fighting back tears, told me he had never heard anything like that in his life. He just shook his head and said over and over, "I had no idea." It wasn't his fault, but for fifty years no one had ever exposed him to someone other than those same people in his church and social circle.

Have you ever had a real conversation with a Muslim? When you travel on vacation or business to another country, have you ever talked to any of the locals and asked them about their family, how they became a waiter, hotel clerk or a tour guide? I still keep up with a cab driver I met in Turkey in 1985 and we have a great friendship. Why are we so afraid to watch anything other than one news channel? Where did we get the idea that Democrats are all socialists and are mostly secular? Why are Republicans all labeled intolerant and insensitive concerning the plight of the poor? These types of questions must be addressed if we are serious about discipleship. Jesus didn't talk like we do; He didn't think about divisions in people and groups as we do. The only division in the Scripture is whether a person is "in Christ" or "outside of Christ," and we don't get to decide. Every other division in life is constructed and maintained by people who have sought to marginalize those who are not like them.

Following Jesus means taking risks. "Greater love has no man than this, that he would lay down his life for his friend."[1] If we won't be patient with a friend who is not in line with our theology or politics ... we would certainly not die for him!

If we have studied to show ourselves approved unto God, we will never have to be embarrassed or afraid of a dissenting opinion.[2] If we can't expose ourselves to a variety of positions and people trying to understand their arguments, it's likely because we aren't sure what we believe. How can we introduce Jesus to the world if we don't go where the people of the world congregate and try to understand the way they think? *Exposure in the right way will drive you into the Scripture rather than pull you away.*

---

[1] John 15:13   [2] 2 Tim. 2:15

The Supreme Value of Women

"Reward her for all she has done. Let her deeds publicly declare her praise."
Proverbs 31:31 (NLT)

Whenever I hear statements about the treatment of women, I usually feel two strong emotions. When they use words like *oppressed, unappreciated, undervalued, and subordinated* by men, I feel embarrassment and shame because it's true. Any reasonable person who takes an unbiased look at history, the wage index, social profiling and the general labeling of women as sex objects have no grounds for disagreement. But, when I hear some of the radical feminists' assertions that God is anti-feminist and that the Bible reflects His diminished view of women, I know that knowledge of the Scriptures and the character of God is well above their pay grade. Random verses were cherry-picked out of context and conclusions were built on partial information.

When you open the Bible, you are stepping into an alien world. Nothing any westerner has ever experienced or considered is the same as the world of the Middle East. It is an ancient culture of desert people where survival was primary and because of that reality, there was the need to build a family to share the load. Women were critical to that need. By necessity, men did the heavy lifting and women cared for the children, cooked and made the dwelling inhabitable. A Patriarchal society flourished and women had minimal value.

However, from day one, the Scripture affirmed that women bore the stamp of His image and were created equal.[1]

During Jesus' ministry, it was a group of women who provided for His financial needs.[2] Some have asserted that only men were disciples, but the Bible tells of seven different women who "sat at Jesus' feet." This is a Jewish way of saying they were His *disciples*. Women were the first to see Jesus after His resurrection. His compassion in allowing a prostitute to anoint Him with oil and wipe his feet with her hair will be, according to Jesus, told across the universe for the rest of time.[3] No religion on earth gives more respect to women than Jesus does.

To believe there isn't a God devalues women completely because there is no place for value to come from. There is no point of reference for worth. If there is no God, who gets to define value? God's respect and honor of women echoes throughout the Scriptures.

---

[1]Gen. 1:27; 5:1–2   [2]Luke 8:1–3   [3]Matt. 26:12–13

351

Anger with God

"The Lord said, 'Do you have good reason to be angry?'" Jonah 4:4

Recently, I asked a group of men and women if they ever got angry with God? I waited in silence for someone to break the ice. Some shifted nervously, two avoided eye contact and finally, one brave soul said, "I know it's wrong, and I know it shows my immaturity, but I get angry at God all the time." I noticed her husband nudge her disapprovingly with his knee, but instead of stopping she said, "No, Jim, I won't shut-up; this has been bothering me for a long time and I want to talk about it." Another woman said, "Good for you!" So, the discussion began with a couple of us assuring her that it is okay to express anger toward God. He can handle it. An elderly couple bristled a little, but the discussion was lively and very positive.

In the Psalms, David complains often to God.[1] What you also notice is that these squabbles always ended in praise. David just needed to ventilate. God understands anger and He lets you tear into Him and air it out! When He had to turn His back on His own Son as he hung on a cross, He shook the earth with a tremendous quake. Do you think He wasn't angry at the price it cost Him to destroy the power of sin?

Throughout Scripture, we see verses like "don't let the sun go down on your anger."[2] Paul *assumes* that anger will occur, toward each other and toward God, but it shouldn't linger. I have seen people so grieved by a sudden loss that they have said they *hated* God for "what He took from them." God gets that! He also knows that those words and feelings of hatred spring from the other end of the emotional scale. Hate comes out of the love they feel was stolen. Some of the gentlest people I know can become the angriest when the object of their love is threatened. Nine different times in the gospels Jesus *yelled.* The translators soften it by saying He, "spoke in a loud voice." No, he yelled! When he wept over Lazarus' death, it says "He was deeply moved." It wasn't just sadness; it was *anger.* The word means *bellowed or snorted like a bull.* He was angry at death![3] God never intended for us to die. It was sin that gave birth to death.[4]

At times I've been angry over Susan's many years of intense pain since a car crash in 1997. But confidence in a relationship enables the level of honesty. We don't fight with strangers over and over; what's the point? We fight with those we love because we feel secure in their love. When the meeting ended, I hugged the lady and said, "You and God must *really* be great friends."

---

[1] Ps. 13:1–6; 35:17–18; 42:9–11   [2] Eph. 4:26   [3] John 11:33   [4] Rom. 5:12

The Only Attraction

"And I, if I am lifted up from the earth, will draw all men to Myself." John 12:32

I think it was my junior year in college; I was part of a group of students promoting a series of speakers we wanted to come to the campus and talk about matters of living out our faith in the university setting. I was asked to pick up the speaker for the initial gathering. I had heard of Dr. Elton Trueblood and knew he had written many books but had never met him. I picked him up at the airport and during the conversation, I felt that I should prepare him in case the turnout wasn't what we had hoped. I was in the middle of my rambling explanation of all of the conflicting things that might keep some students away when he patted me on the knee and said, "Son those whom God intended to be there will be there ... the hardest meeting to get Christians to come to is one where Jesus Christ is the only attraction."

I think I nodded or made some sound of agreement even though I didn't really understand. It was the next morning when I took him back to the airport after a very successful night that I asked him what he meant. He explained that Jesus has been so misrepresented over the years that in order to get people to listen to a message about faith we must have special music, serve pizzas, and have Miss America or a sports star to draw a crowd. I don't remember the whole conversation but the line that has

never left me was this: "If people ever saw the authentic Jesus of the gospels, anything extra would simply be an unneeded distraction."

Thirty years later, I was speaking at the funeral of a dear friend who died in a plane crash and I met Ravi Zacharias, who gave his eulogy after mine. I have great respect for him and during our conversation, he said something very similar to Dr. Trueblood. We talked about the seeming lack of impact that believers were having in this country and he said, "Neb, always remember that what you win them with you will win them to." In other words, he was saying that if it is the music or sports celebrity that brings people in and gets them excited, that will often be what wins them over rather than Christ and it will not last. I told him that Dr. Trueblood had said basically the same thing to me thirty years prior. It was, during the loss of a close friend, that this affirmation of always keeping Jesus as the focal point came crashing through.

The matters that press in on us today are important, but to allow an issue to overshadow or in any way distract from the focus being purely on Jesus is to miss the boat. Jesus told His disciples that *if He was lifted up and seen as the resurrected Christ, the power to draw all people inward was absolutely certain.*

A Walk Through the Christmas Story

"Let Earth Receive Her King"
(A suggestion: Read the Christmas Story from December 12–25)

I have placed these events leading up to the birth of Jesus near the end of these daily thoughts so that you can leave the particular day you are reading for two weeks prior to Christmas and then continue where you left off afterward.

Christmas is the most joyful and highly anticipated time of the year. Unfortunately, traditions have been created and embellished concerning the time and circumstances of Jesus' birth. First-century, Middle Eastern, life has been compromised and re-sculpted to fit our western understanding of life, and in the process has distanced Jesus from His culture. Our manger scenes with wise men and shepherds huddled around the baby Jesus while cattle and sheep stand placidly look at snow-covered landscape is a far cry from the biblical and historical realities. Though we are limited by space I wanted to give you the flavor of what the birth of the Savior and the days preceding and following it would have looked like in Middle Eastern culture.

We all know the Christmas story of Jesus' birth. Often, because of its familiarity and because it is so buried under western symbols and understanding, Jesus has been lifted out of the culture of His birth. During this time of year, we become so caught up in the commercial side of Christmas that we pay little attention to the events that occurred apart from the traditional story. My hope is to give you a little of the flavor of what was going on during those eventful days that changed the world.

A Family Album

"The record of the genealogy of Jesus the Messiah, the Son of David, the son of Abraham." Matthew 1:1

When you were first introduced to the New Testament, I can almost guarantee that you skipped the first seventeen verses of Matthew's Gospel and Luke 3:23-37. Without the background and context, it's like reading the phone book. But hang on for a few minutes and you'll see why the things that Matthew and Luke describe here sets the tone for the most revolutionary event in human history.

Since the time of Abraham, the people of God have stressed the importance of understanding their uniqueness. Knowing their heritage and background gave them a deep sense of pride as well as courage during difficult times. Roots were important because Israel's faith is deeply embedded in history. Therefore, knowledge of beginnings is central to biblical thought. To an ancient Jew, reading these genealogies was like browsing through a family album. This is one of the reasons why the destruction of the Temple in 70 AD was so traumatic. In addition to the loss of over a million lives, all the genealogy records were stored there and were destroyed in that fire, losing all that precious information forever.

Matthew is a Jew writing to Jews and Luke is a Gentile who is writing to Gentiles, specifically to Greeks. Luke shows in his genealogy that Jesus is a descendant of the House of David and, therefore, qualifies to be the Messiah.[1] Matthew, on the other hand, lists Joseph's line proving that he could not have been Jesus' father. Matthew also breaks with Jewish protocol by listing five women; a very un-Jewish thing to do. He lists Tamar, a Jew; Ruth a Moabite, a non-Jew who later converted; Rahab, a prostitute; Bathsheba, a wealthy adulteress, and Mary a peasant girl who found favor with God. Why? Matthew is saying that the dawning of a new age has come where there will be no more, *we and they; us and them.* Everyone will be on equal footing before God ... rich and poor, Jew and Gentile, male and female, saints and sinners. All are equal in the eyes of God and all are invited to know Him and experience His love and forgiveness.

This cuts across everything Jews had been taught. The Messiah will reach out to the poor and disinherited; He will turn to the Gentiles after the Jews reject Him and woman will be seen forevermore as "party of the first part." A new day has come!

---

[1] Luke 3:23–37

The Announcement of the Messenger

Luke 1:5–25

Zacharias was a priest. He and his wife Elizabeth were a couple who loved God deeply and had lived exemplary lives. They had dreamed of a family, but Elizabeth was unable to bear children. It was devastating for them both and for her an extreme embarrassment. The ancient Jews had a belief that is not uncommon even today among certain church groups. It is a "cause and effect" mentality that assumes some afflictions in life are a direct result of past actions that have displeased or offended God. Elizabeth's infertility was considered by Jews to be a great tragedy. Moreover, there was the stigma that strongly suggested that either she was not loved by her husband or that her barrenness was the consequence of some secret sin that God was punishing.[1] Elizabeth would probably have lived in shame since her mid-teens because of her inability to bear children. This is important to know because this is an early Jewish picture of God. It was pure myth, but it shaped their world view and enhanced the belief that if you ever get out of line God will exact a harsh punishment upon you. Many churches teach this, and it is a perspective absent from grace and does nothing to accurately convey a true picture of God's redeeming love. It will create nothing but angst and bitterness over the long run.

Priests drew *lots* for the most prominent duties in the Temple. Zacharias drew the lot which entitled him to enter the Temple and burn the incense on the altar. This was a big deal and a large crowd stood outside and prayed that God would be pleased.[2]

The angel Gabriel appears beside the altar and tells Zacharias that his prayers have been answered. Elizabeth would bear a son who would prepare the way for the Messiah. The Jews believed Gabriel to be the greatest of all God's angels. For him to appear to Zacharias was a huge honor. Elizabeth was well beyond childbearing age and though Zacharias was a godly man, he had never been tested at this level and did not believe the angel.

This critical scene sounds the beginning notes of God's redemptive call to all humanity. We clearly see how victimized Zacharias was by faulty tradition. It kept him from seeing the truth. It is easy to become wed to that which we have become accustomed when it comes from those we deem to be a "credible source." It can be a time-honored denominational perspective, or simply something taught to us by a loved one. Zacharias was a respected senior priest, but he had bought into a tradition that was untrue and had obviously taught others the same.

---

[1]Gen. 30:1–2   [2]Luke 1:10

A Young Girl Receives Unprecedented News

Luke 1:26–38

A young girl encounters Gabriel, the same angel who had spoken to Zacharias, and is told incredible news. Imagine that you are twelve or thirteen and a messenger of God tells you that you are pregnant by the Holy Spirit and will give birth to the coming Messiah which you have heard about all your life. How could you even process that? By Jewish law, a girl was eligible for marriage at twelve years plus a day and usually married within a year after their first menstrual period. The male must be eighteen. Mary was already engaged to Joseph and a contract called a *Ketubah* is signed by the groom where he pledges a certain amount of money to the bride. This engagement contract was tantamount to marriage and could be broken only by a bill of divorcement. Imagine the drama for this young girl. She is pregnant with the Messiah; how can she possibly help her fiancé understand this?

She needs counsel so she journeys for or five days from Galilee to the hill country of Judea. The moment she enters the home of her cousin, Elizabeth, the child in Elizabeth's womb leaps for joy at the presence of the Savior in their midst. Elizabeth exclaims, *"Why am I so favored that the mother of God has come to visit me"?*[1] She is an elderly woman, six months pregnant and Mary is a young girl who will stay with her for three months until just before Elizabeth's baby is born. Mary immediately gives a song of praise for what is happening. *"My soul glorifies the Lord and my spirit rejoices in God my Savior."*[2]

Take a minute and imagine the conversations these two must have had. How can we be a mother worthy of these sons? How can we raise and educate them properly? And the immediate question of Mary … How do I tell Joseph? What will he do?

Mary departs in the last days before her cousin gives birth to John the Baptist. Despite their many conversations, Mary's throat begins to tighten as she gets closer to home and the inevitable confrontation with her fiancé. She will have to trust God in at least three ways: First, for His protection as her pregnancy becomes more obvious. The penalty for pregnancy outside of marriage was death by stoning. Secondly, for the reaction of the community and thirdly, for the reaction of her fiancé.

This would be difficult under any circumstances, but she remembers that God had not interacted with His people in over 400 years. This was the Intertestamental period between the Old and New Testaments where no one had verbally heard from God or even an angel in four centuries. Now Zacharias and Mary hear words from Gabriel that will revolutionize the entire human race.

---

[1]Luke 1:43   [2]Luke 1:47

An Amazing Young Man

Matthew 1:18–25

Not wanting to prolong the agony, Mary goes to her fiancé soon after arriving from Judea. "Joey, we have to talk." Joseph's first words after her revelation were probably, "You're what?" Imagine being this young man. This is devastating news on a human level. Joseph is a young man of 18 or 19. He loves God and knows that throughout Israel's history God has given commands and directed people in ways that would seem ridiculous from a human perspective. He may have thought of the unorthodox manner of victory that God engineered with Joshua over Jericho. He may have remembered God sending a shepherd like Moses, who had a stuttering problem, to confront the Pharaoh of Egypt and demand the release of God's people. So, Joseph was not ignorant of God's unconventional ways.

There was something else he knew. He knew Mary since her birth in the small community where they grew up. He knew her parents and how she was raised to love and fear God. He knew her character and he knew there was no way she would ever give herself to a man to whom she was not married. He knew that it took sexual intimacy to produce a pregnancy. He also understood the Mosaic Law and that stoning was the penalty for this offense. He knows she is innocent, and because of this certainty he ignores the law and decides to quietly pull out of the contractual marital agreement to save her from public humiliation because "he was a *just* man."[1] Justice was always defined as equal application under the law. But God uses this young man to override justice with mercy and compassion redefining what justice is. It becomes compassion for the mistreated, the needy and the hurting.[2] His only aim was to protect this innocent girl.

It wasn't easy! The next verse says that after he *considered* (the divorce option) the angel Gabriel came and confirmed to him what he already believed about Mary. The word *considered* can mean that he pondered or thought it through, but it can also mean he slammed his fist on the table or threw a chair across the room, which is more likely. He was hurting for his bride to be.

This passage is seldom spoken of but shows what a hero this young man was. For anyone falsely accused he is the standard for mercy, compassion, and believing the best against all opposition.

---

[1] Luke 1:19   [2] Deut. 22:23–24

359

The Context Around Jesus' Birth

Luke 2:1–7

Elizabeth had given birth to John the Baptist approximately six months earlier as Mary and Joseph approached the final weeks of her pregnancy. A decree went out from Quirinius, Governor of Syria, concerning taxation and the census. It was to take effect incrementally throughout the regions of Palestine somewhere between 6 and 7 BC. As a descendant of David, Joseph was required to return to Bethlehem. Also, of the House of David, Mary goes with him as his wife but was not required to register. He obviously took her because of the nearness of her time of delivery, but also to protect her from local repercussions of her pregnancy. When viewed from a human perspective, the couple came to Bethlehem together out of necessity. But from the divine perspective, God was acting providentially to bring them to the place where Micah had prophesied the Messiah would be born.[1]

The trip of 85 or more miles would have taken the young couple four to five days and they are certain to have traveled in the company of others. It would have been too dangerous to travel alone. The journey would have been hard for Mary and, despite our images of her riding on a donkey, only the very wealthy could have afforded a donkey.

The time of year would most probably have been in late August or September. The roads were impassable in winter and Rome wanted to be certain of a successful turnout. The spring is not likely because this is the time of the Passover Feast, Pentecost, and Feast of Tabernacles which was mandatory for all men 12 and over. Late spring and summer would be harvest time and, also unsuitable. Therefore, the most reasonable window would be in late summer to early fall after the harvest.

Mary and Joseph arrive at night at a home, not an Inn as we know it. Homes would often rent a space in one part of the house to travelers. It was called a *Kataluma*. Houses in the area were usually built into the side of a hill with an area underneath adjoining the house where sheep and goats would be kept out of harm's way. There had been no cattle in that area for many years.

This would have been where Mary and Joseph slept. We assume that she gave birth that night, but the Scripture says, *"while they were there, the days were completed for her to give birth."*[2] It could have been a week or more. The important thing to know is that everything happened as God had designed it. This is where the Christmas story begins ...

---

[1]Mic. 5:2–5   [2]Luke 2:6

The Uncluttered Faith of the Young

Consider what has happened to this young couple within the past nine months: Mary has been told by the greatest of all angels that she, who had never known a man, was pregnant with the seed of God Almighty, and that through the birth canal of her womb would come the Messiah who would save His people.

Mary knew the Scriptures and would not have been surprised that the Messiah would come in the normal manner of birth but through a virgin.[1] For seven hundred years, since the time of Isaiah, every young girl would have dreamed that she might be the one. The one prophecy that would have caused her to think she would not qualify was Micah's prophesy that said the Messiah would be born in Judea and she lived in Galilee. Now, here she is at the point of giving birth, having just arrived with her husband in a little town called Bethlehem of Judea.

We have seen three encounters so far with the Angel Gabriel. The first was with Zacharias, who does not believe him because Elizabeth was well beyond child-bearing age. He was a mature, devout man with much experience, but could not believe that which had never previously happened. Next, Gabriel comes to Mary saying that she had found favor with God and will bear His Son. Her reaction was *not* doubt, but *astonishment* because of her virginity. She answers, "I belong to the Lord body and soul. Let it happen as you say."[2] A 12-year-old believes the *impossible,* and a priest of many years cannot believe even the *improbable.* The third encounter with Gabriel was as he affirmed in a dream to Joseph what Mary had told him. It is obvious that he had believed that Mary had never been with a man, but still wrestled with how to help with the consequences she would face in the community. When Joseph awoke, he immediately let go of his fears and married Mary as the angel commanded.

What can we learn here? First, God does not have to meet the specifications or parameters of what we think is reasonable. He never has. Secondly, we must realize how we have limited the voice of young people. They must wait until an age we ascribe to have a legitimate voice. A young girl of twelve and a boy of eighteen made a faith leap that a senior priest could not make. Paul told Timothy to allow no one to intimidate him because of his youth.[3] We often silence a beautiful source of uncluttered wisdom. Listen carefully to your kids. They haven't had time to have allowed disappointment with life to make them cynical.

---

[1]Isa. 7:14   [2]Luke 1:38   [3]1 Tim. 4:12

Unto Us A Child is Born . . . A Son is Given

Luke 2:6–7

Joseph, Jesus' stepfather, was from this little village of Bethlehem so he would have known many people there. Many would have shared in his and Mary's joy when the baby was born. Some have defied historical records and said it never happened. Some have said he grew up to become a great Rabbi. Others said he was a prophet. But consider the following, even as we look at the first moments that he came into the world: He was born in Bethlehem, which literally means *House of Bread*. Who was Jesus? The *Bread of Life*. So, he was born in a bakery ... a house of bread. Where was he laid after his birth? A manger was not a feeding trough, but a *water trough* usually carved out of stone. Since there were no cattle, there was no straw. The manger would have probably been lined with soft animal skins. Who was this Child? He was the *Living Water*. Coincidence? I don't think so. If most historians are correct in their assertion that He was born in early to mid-September, we have another interesting possibility. If you count backward nine months you arrive at the previous December. This is the celebration of what today is called Hanukkah or Festival of Lights. Who was this child? The *Light of the World*.

Luke says he was wrapped in *cloths* and laid in the manger. Many scholars point to the fact that the "cloths" were the same kind that was wrapped around the deceased as their body was anointed with spices for burial. Before you think of how morbid that would be, consider what Jesus will later say that His reason for being born was to die.[1] It was His destiny. No other person on earth was born to die except Jesus. Was that statement of His identity being made with the winding cloths? (There is another reason for this simple *sign of "cloths"* that would identify Him which we will discuss tomorrow.)

There was nothing ordinary about this birth, yet the simplicity and utter humility of all its circumstances are both staggering and refreshing. This child would be a man for all people ... of every race, gender and nationality. He will identify with the wretched of the earth; He will refuse all honors and ignore any and all efforts to make Him King. From this simple setting where He took His first breath until He breathes His last breath on a Roman cross and was buried in a borrowed tomb, He was, and is, God of all creation.

---

[1]John 12:27; Heb. 2:9–18

The Greatest News to the Lowliest People

"In the same region, there were some shepherds staying out in the fields and keeping watch over their flock by night." Luke 2:8

You probably already know that shepherds were not exactly at the top of the food chain in Jesus' days. They had a reputation as scoundrels who would steal you blind if given the chance. They were survivors who took on a thankless job caring for the assets of other people. The Babylonian Talmud lists shepherds as a profession you should never allow your children to undertake. Because "their profession is a profession of robbers." The kids were the shepherds and once she or he began to shepherd the flock, none of the sheep would respond to any other voice. This is why Jesus said, "My sheep know my voice."[1]

Shepherd kids were considered a necessary nuisance. They were not respected and had no upward social mobility. How fitting that God, who made and loves all His creation, chose these reprobates to be the first to hear the news of Jesus' birth. Why not the most respected in the region ... a prosperous, educated man who was deemed a great leader of the people ... the kind who are elders and leaders

of the people? If this doesn't tell you something about the nature and priorities of God, you are not listening. The greatest announcement ever made was not given to Kings, Presidents, or Captains of Industry, but to the lowliest people on the planet.

When believers speak of being "godly men or women" it never seems to include entrusting anything of real value to those of low esteem. We will see a similar act by God after Jesus' death and resurrection. The first people to see the resurrected Christ are women, who in that culture were not considered a credible source. Yet God chose them just as He chose those lowly kids out in the fields.

These young kids sat around a fire after a long day of finding grass and water for the sheep, but now the real task began. They would have to be on their guard because nightfall was the time when predators roam. Suddenly, in the dark of night, the silence was broken and a blinding light along with a chorus of the Heavenly Hosts singing praises terrified them.

---

[1] John 10:27

Good News of a Great Joy

Luke 2:9–12

The Glory of God surrounded these young shepherds and they must have thought the world was coming to an end. Remember, no one except Zacharias, Mary, and Joseph had heard anything directly from God in the over four hundred years. Between the end of the Old Testament and the beginning of the events surrounding the birth of Jesus nothing like this had ever happened.

The Glory of God was not just a bright light. It had appeared in the Old Testament to Moses from a burning bush,[1] then on Mount Sinai when he was given the Law.[2] It resided in the Tabernacle in the wilderness,[3] and then in Solomon's Temple after it was dedicated.[4] Now, this same Glory is surrounding these lowly shepherds while Gabriel tells them not to be afraid. He brings "good news of a great joy and that it would be for all people."[5]

Be those shepherds for a moment. What good and joyous news have you ever heard? You lead sequestered lives without hope or encouragement. But what would get your attention is the phrase, "good news of a great joy for all people?" *All* means that this good news was for them too. How so? They have never been included in anything good. He tells them that the Messiah they had heard about their whole life had come, and before you can say, *"that should be really nice for all the rich*

people," Gabriel tells them where to find Him and the *sign* that will validate it.

The sign was the swaddling clothes. Wealthy people would wrap their baby in beautiful linens. But the Messiah would be in simple cloths used by people without means. What would make them get someone to look after the sheep while they travel over the ridge to see the Savior? They would know that His family was of humble means and they would feel welcome there.

An elder of a large church once asked me how they could get more people of color in their church. I told him that his church made the decision to exclude them when they built their church in the wealthiest, whitest part of town. "Why would black people leave the community where they live, work, and have relationships to suddenly run over to your church on Sunday?" God did not say to these shepherds, *"Come to my palace on the hill. I'll have My driver pick you up."* Instead, He left the comforts of heaven and came to *all* people where they were. If the shepherds had thought for a moment that they were going to a palatial palace to ask to see the baby King, they would never have left the hillside. They had to feel like He really came for all people. That's what you see when you read the Christmas story.

---

[1]Exod. 3 [2]Exod. 19—20 [3]Exod. 25–40 [4]Exod. 40 [5]Luke 2:12

The Favor of God

"Glory to God in the highest and on earth, peace to men on whom His favor rests."
Luke 2:13–14 (NIV)

Since I was a small boy I heard these words every Christmas in song and story. And, like all of us, I felt the comfort and nostalgia of this wonderful season. It was many years later when the meaning of those words found their mark and changed everything for me. I never realized the connection between experiencing peace and pleasing God ... experiencing His favor. My immediate response was that if the price of peace was that I had to be pleasing to God, I had better get cracking. I doubled down on my quiet times, I tried to give more, I taught more Bible studies and tried to be more patient and kinder. There were two problems. First, I was never sure when I had improved enough to please God. Secondly, the more I worked at trying to earn God's favor, the less peace I had. I was worn out, and frustrated.

Finally, through a friend, I began to see that being in God's favor had nothing to do with my efforts on His behalf; it was a matter of seeing myself through God's eyes. This was what the angel was saying to those lowly shepherds and to all of God's people. They had defined themselves by the way other's saw them. They were considered liars, deceivers and scoundrels and they had begun to see themselves that way as well. Peace was a stranger to them because they had never seen themselves as God saw them. They were living unnaturally!

Consider how you and I, even as followers of Jesus, define ourselves with much help from the religious community. We are "rotten sinners saved by grace." That was true until we met Christ. We still sin, but we cannot be defined as sinners! If so, we must delete dozens of Scriptures that say the opposite. Paul said, "we are the righteousness of God,"[1] "we are possessors of peace,"[2] "we are holy and without blame,"[3] we are "God's possession,"[4] and we are a "friend of Jesus."[5] I have found about fifty of these kinds of affirmations in the Scriptures. The point is, we are not still defined as sinners. We still sin sometimes, but *what we do is not who we are!* The Scripture defines all believers as *Saints.*[6] We were saved by grace, but we are no longer sinners. We are Saints who sometimes sin. The worse thing about me is that I still sin, but why would I define my whole life by the worst thing about me? It is this truth that believers need more than the air we breathe. We are people in whom the Spirit of God lives. We must understand that we can never be at peace until we accept who we are as defined by God, and not by the world.

---

[1]Rom. 1:17; 3:21–26   [2]Acts 10:36   [3]1 Cor. 3:17   [4]2 Tim. 2:19
[5]John 15:15   [6]Eph. 1:1; Phil. 1:1

The Favor of God: The Practical Side

What difference would it make to those young shepherds, and to us, in seeing ourselves as God sees us? Insecurity is one of man's greatest problems. We don't like who we are; we are always wondering and worrying what others think of us, and we try to cover our pain with a kind of synthetic image or branding we create for ourselves. You and I were born without the life of God in us. It was a condition, not an action. As we grew up, that condition was reflected in the way we lived. When we met Jesus, the condition we inherited from birth was broken and we became a new creation.[1] We still sin but we don't have to because the power of sin has been broken by Jesus' death on the cross. When He cried out, "It is finished" that's what he was talking about; sin had been defeated.[2] However, our flesh still pulls us and unfortunately, sometimes we give in.

We have a new identity. Those shepherds no longer have any reason to believe those who define them as a worthless nuisance to society, and you and I have no reason to apologize to the world by creating a false image. God has put His stamp of approval on us and we can hold our head high and live out our destiny with no regrets. This is where peace comes from.

What about temptation? We all face it every day. Let's say you are on the road for your job. You finish your day and plan to eat a meal in the hotel restaurant and hit the sack. But as you order, your eyes meet with an attractive person sitting at the bar. You are alone in a city where no one knows you. A striking possibility for the flesh. What goes through your mind? If you think of yourself as just a "dirty sinner saved by grace," why wouldn't you reason to yourself that "nobody's perfect … I am a sinner, and this is a one-time thing." But if you saw yourself as God sees you your self-talk might go like this … *I am the righteousness of God; I am a brother of Christ, and in me dwells God's Spirit. As enticing as this may be to my flesh, it's not who I am … I'm outta here!*

This is not a trick or a technique … it is a way of thinking governed by how you define yourself. If you consider yourself a sinner, why wouldn't you feel free to sin? A thief steals; a liar lies, but a friend of God is one who walks with God … all the time.

Peace is not the absence of conflict; it is knowing who you are and that God's favor rests on you all the time … not because you deserve it, but because you are His.

---

[1] 2 Cor. 5:17   [2] John 19:30

An Enemy Lurking in the Distance

We pause to meet a man who will, directly and indirectly, have a great impact on Jesus' ministry. He was called Herod the Great, mainly because of his prowess as a builder. His distrust concerning his position and power made him a seditious killer as well. He was a complicated man; an Arab by birth, a Jew by conversion, a Greek culturally, and a Roman politically.

Paranoia ruled his life. He slaughtered anyone and everyone for even the slightest offense. He married 10 women, three of whom he had executed. At least 3 of his sons were executed because of rumors concerning their alleged unfaithfulness or perceived desire to take his throne. He Executed 45 of 70 Sanhedrin members and stole their land and money to secure his position and authority. Early in his reign, he becomes jealous of the young Chief Priest who has been appointed. He invites him to his palace in Jericho, encourages him to take a dip in the swimming pool, and has him drowned.

His relationship with the Jews was difficult. He was never accepted as a true Jew. They hated him because he was sadistic and ruthless. He was committed to the pagan values of Greek Hellenism which flew soundly in the face of Jewish law and tradition. Sadducees (the priests) hated him

because he had severely curtailed their influence and power. The Pharisees (the lawyers) hated him because he ignored God's Law.

Fearful that no one would mourn on the day of his death, he ordered prominent families to be herded into the Hippodrome and slaughtered so that there would be weeping in the land. Fortunately, his wife intervened after his death and freed the families. Herod lost almost every semblance of sanity during his later years. He lived a bloodthirsty and pathetic existence until his agonizing death in Jericho of a disease akin to syphilis.

The paranoia that Herod displayed throughout his reign makes its final appearance as he meets and tries to trick travelers from the east who come to honor the Christ-child. He will murder hundreds of children under two in order to protect his position from an infant baby.

It's important to understand Herod because his attempt to have Jesus eliminated will cause Mary and Joseph to move to Egypt until after his death. Also, his three sons will come after him and one of them, Herod Antipas, Tetrarch of Galilee, will play a vital role before and after Jesus is arrested and tried.

Like father, like son; Herod created a legacy of hatred.

Visitors from Afar

Extremely prominent in our celebration of Jesus' birth is the men who traveled some seven hundred miles from Babylon to honor the Child born in Bethlehem. We see pictures of three kings on camels bringing their gifts to Jesus lying in the manger. They were not kings, and most scholars believe that there would have been a large entourage. In our Western Christmas lore, we assume that the Magi immediately appeared at the manger and worshipped Jesus. But we know for certain that when they arrived, Jesus had already been taken to Jerusalem to be presented at the Temple and purified.[1] This, by Jewish law, was 40 days after the birth. Also, the Magi, as well as Herod, describe Jesus as "the child" not the baby.[2] In fact, Herod's reason for commanding that all children in the district, two years and under, be killed comes by their calculations that He was somewhere near that age when the Magi entered Bethlehem.[3] When they arrive, Jesus and His family were in a home of friends in the village.

Who were these men and why did they come such a distance? They were not Jews, but worshipers of Zoroaster, a pagan god. These "Wise Men" were astrologers, men of natural science who sometimes interpreted dreams. They were men of wisdom and were primarily advisors to the King because of their keen insight concerning political issues of the day.

These men of astrology would have known from Old Testament writings, particularly in the Book of Daniel, that a star would appear in the east at a certain time which Daniel identifies. They studied the movement and position of the stars and saw a star that appeared to be hovering. It was different and it moved from east to west. I believe it was the *Shechinah Glory of God;* the same Glory that appeared to the shepherds in the fields.

The Magi enter Jerusalem asking where they might find the *boy* who was born "King of the Jews." Word reaches Herod and he summons Jewish leaders and asks about the prophecies concerning the coming of the Messiah. He then arranges a meeting with the Magi at his Palace. When he hears the phrase "King of the Jews" he begins to hyperventilate. The Magi were unaware that Rome had recently given that title to Herod. He lies to them saying he also wishes to worship the Christ-Child.[4]

The magi depart for Bethlehem promising to return and tell Herod the Child's location. After they travel on to Bethlehem and visit the Christ child, God protects them by instructing them to return home by another route. But there is still a question we must answer: *Why would pagan Magi leave their families and travel seven hundred miles to bring gifts and pay homage to a Jewish Messiah?*

---

[1]Luke 2:22–39   [2]Matt. 2:8–9   [3]Matt. 2:16   [4]Matt. 2:1–4

A Key Player in the Story

One of the most courageous and fascinating people of all history is a young man named Daniel. He lived five hundred years before Christ and authored a book in the Old Testament that zeros in on the time of the Savior's birth. So impressive was he that a ruthless pagan king recognized his proficiency in many disciplines and made him a chamberlain in the royal court.

King Nebuchadnezzar had invaded Jerusalem three times taking large numbers of Jews each time and in 586 BC he burns Solomon's Temple to the ground. Daniel had been taken in the second wave but maintained his faithfulness to God, refusing to eat the non-kosher food and existing on legumes and water. He prospered even better than the others. The Babylonians changed his name seeking to make him forsake his Jewish heritage, but it never fazed him. He was very handsome and was already a scholar in his late teens.

One night the king had a dream and awoke in a cold sweat. He called together his advisors, wise men who gave him counsel. He commands them to tell him the meaning of the dream but will not tell them what the dream was. Their failure to perform meant execution. Daniel prays and God tells him the dream and its meaning. He goes to the king, tells him the meaning of the dream and, thereby, saves his "wise men" from execution. Word of Daniel's wisdom makes him a folk hero. The wise men who come bearing gifts were direct descendants of the men whose lives Daniel saved. Most of the Book of Daniel is written in Aramaic so it would have been easy reading for these advisors. Their gratefulness and desire to come and see the King of the Jews would have known no bounds because Jesus was in Daniels line.

We know that Joseph and Mary were poor. We also know that because of Herod's intent to kill Jesus, they would have to move to Egypt until Herod died. How would they live?

Magi, or wise men, came from the east with gifts of gold, frankincense, and myrrh for Jesus, who was a descendant of Daniel, the unrecognized hero of the Christmas story.

God cares about all his children. He knew Mary and Joseph would be forced to leave their country to escape the wrath of Herod without any real means of support. He planned for their financial needs 500 years earlier. He used unlikely people who didn't even know Him, but who understood that without Daniel's faithfulness their descendants would have been executed and *they* would never have been born. I believe that is why the Magi came seven hundred miles bearing gifts for the King of the Jews.

The family escaped to Egypt where they stayed until Herod died. After that, they return to Nazareth where Jesus will stay until He begins His earthly ministry at age thirty.

The Death and Resurrection of Christ

(A suggestion: Begin these readings about 16 days prior to Easter)

To most people, the Easter season appears each year as an almost unexpected guest. Except for Palm Sunday, the weekend prior, and chocolate eggs and bunnies covering the stores most would scarcely know of its arrival.

I want to take a sixteen-day break from our daily readings and focus on the intrigue and suspense of what was really going on behind the scenes during the last week of Jesus' earthly ministry. I want to walk with you in Jewish sandals into Jerusalem as Jesus was arrested, tried and sentenced to death. We will walk into the drama of His corrupt trial, His bone-chilling crucifixion and His glorious resurrection three days later, which is the centerpiece of our faith. We will also look briefly at those forty days before he ascended back to His father.

This is a story most of us know only in part. We have limited space here, but hopefully, in these next sixteen days leading to Easter, we can fill in some blanks and gain a deeper appreciation of this unprecedented drama that changed the world.

Easter: Beyond Bunnies and Eggs

Year in and year out, no celebration in America compares with Christmas. It is the baseline measurement for the year's success in most commercial businesses. Office parties, shopping, eggnog, lighted trees, Santa Claus and turkey with all the trimmings dominates the landscape for the entire month of December. But in the Scriptures, there are only a handful of chapters by the gospel writers about the events surrounding Jesus' birth. By contrast, the events leading to Christ's death and resurrection occupy a major portion of the gospels. Christmas and Easter are inexorably connected; they cannot be isolated from each other.

The coming of the Messiah was anxiously anticipated by God's people for over seven hundred years. Families sat in candlelit rooms listening to their elders talk of the coming of the Messiah. When He finally came, the multitudes failed to recognize Him because of the deceptive and erroneous teaching of the Jewish leaders. He was loved by many, hated by most. When He was born to peasant teenagers in Bethlehem, His birth was hardly noticed. When He was crucified the foundations of the earth shook and regardless of the attempts of many to disprove His resurrection, its reality only grows in intensity as the years go by.

The Death and Resurrection of Jesus is a drama that few fully understand. But it is through the uncovering of the *back-door* events leading to His death that we gain a deeper appreciation and are drawn into the story. *Were You There When They Crucified My Lord?* This is far more than the word of a moving hymn.; it is undeniably true. We were there. The same selfish, independent attitudes that existed in those who watched in the shadows are present in us today. The same ambivalence, and hatred that was in the crowd who yelled "Crucify Him" is the essential nature resident in all of us until we meet Him.

Let's take a walk in Jewish sandals through the back streets, secret meetings and carefully coordinated efforts of the Jewish leaders to trap Jesus and take His life. We will see that even as His enemies celebrated His death, with mocking voices yelling "We won" as His bloodied head dropped forward on the cross, a bigger voice that first Easter Morning said, "No, you lost." It was the voice of a Father with a broken heart for the humiliation of His Son, but now re-united He looked proudly at what that Son had accomplished.

For the next fifteen days will take a closer look at what transpired leading to the cross and Resurrection of Jesus on that first Easter morning. It has nothing to do with colored eggs and bunnies and everything to do with our destiny.

Born to Die

"And what shall I say, 'Father save me from this hour?' No, it was for this very reason that I came to this hour." John 12:27 (NIV)

Jesus Christ is the only person ever to be born as the result of His own choice. The rest of us are conceived and born because of the choice of others. Jesus and His Father chose the time, place, and manner of His death. It had been decided from the moment Adam and Eve sinned. His birth, mission, death, and resurrection were foretold by the prophets in very specific ways. Jesus was born in the shadow of the cross. He was born to die.[1] He knew it, and John the Baptist knew it before His ministry began. In the desert, John points to Jesus and says, "the Lamb of God who takes away the sins of the world."[2]

As His disciples begin to follow Him they have no understanding of His death being the solution to the problem of mankind. They think death must be avoided at all costs. After Peter says, "You are the Christ, the Son of the Living God," at Caesarea Philippi, Jesus tells them he is going to be crucified and Peter passionately objects.[3] He had no clue that to circumvent the cross would destroy Jesus' purpose of coming. Jesus will tell the twelve numerous times that He will die but even in His last hours, it will fly right over their heads. They think just like we think. You don't win by *losing*; you win by *winning*! They saw death as a failure; Jesus saw His death as the only road to victory. We think submission is weakness, but to God, it's the pathway to authority.

The way to really understand these events that lead to the cross is to realize that two perspectives are always at work. There is the intent of the Jewish leaders who are threatened by Jesus and want to be rid of him so they can preserve their power base. Then, there is God's intent to walk Jesus toward the cross, but for a completely different purpose.

Satan is also a player. Through the Jewish Leaders, he engineers Jesus' death, yet it is by His death that Satan will be defeated. Keep this in mind as you read.

Many Jews and non-believing Gentiles think Jesus failed in His mission. They consider it *"Close, but no cigar."* From a human standpoint, He fell short, but if you know that the plan was always the cross, you also understand that God engineered His son's death. Satan, the Jewish leaders, and the Romans were simply *bit* players who accomplished exactly what God had always planned.

---

[1] John 12:27   [2] John 1:29   [3] Matt. 16:16

The Storm Clouds Gather

"What are we accomplishing? they asked. Here is this man performing many miraculous signs. If we let Him go on like this everyone will believe in Him and the Romans will come and take away both our place and our nation."
John 11:47–48 (NIV)

The Jewish leaders wanted to be rid of Jesus since He first cleansed the Temple at the outset of His Ministry. Annas had been High Priest until he was deposed by the Romans five years earlier. They inserted Caiaphas, his son-in-law, but to the Jewish people, Annas was still High Priest though he no longer had the duties of the office. He and his family found a way to make money by scamming peasants who came to the Jewish festivals with animals to sacrifice. The Pharisees called it "the bazaar of the sons of Annas." Jesus' actions in the temple made Him their enemy. His fame grew, as did His list of *adversaries*. They hated Him for several reasons: He called God "Father." In Judaism, the eldest son was considered equal to his father. It was considered blasphemous! They resented His claims, detested His lack of respect for their *oral traditions* and He posed a threat to their power base. They loved the spotlight, but the people were intrigued by Him. It drove their animosity to the point that they asserted that His miracles were performed by Satan's power.[1] When Jesus raises Lazarus from the dead, it was the last straw for the Jewish leaders. They gathered together to plot His death. At the meeting, Caiaphas makes an astounding statement, unaware of its prophetic impact. He bellows, "You know nothing at all. You do not realize that it is better for you that one man dies for the people than that the whole nation perish."[2] From that day on the storm clouds gathered to end Jesus' life.[3]

There was a problem. They had to be careful not to incite the multitudes who followed Him. Rome allowed the Sanhedrin to continue to exist only if the Jews were kept peaceful. This is why they did not take Jesus by force. But also, God oversaw His plan. Jesus must die in Jerusalem and He must be crucified. Earlier that year the Romans had rescinded the Jews authority to enact capital punishment. Typically, they would have stoned Him. As Jesus and the twelve make the last trip to Jerusalem, the leaders will try to trip Jesus up so He would lose the support of the people.

Notice that Jesus never fights back. As corrupt and vicious as these people were, He still loved them. That kind of love is beyond human capacity. It comes only through the power of God.

---

[1]Matt. 12:22–28   [2]John 11:49–51   [3]John 11:53

Jesus' Last Journey to Jerusalem

"Hosanna (God save us) to the Son of David; Blessed is He who comes in the Name of the Lord; Hosanna in the highest." Matthew 21:9 (NIV)

As Jesus and His disciples make their way toward Jerusalem, Jesus sits them down and tells them that this will be the end of His ministry on earth. He explains that He will be condemned by the Jewish leadership and turned over to the Romans to be mocked, beaten and crucified. Then, He will be raised from the dead.[1] Can you imagine being a disciple and hearing this from a man who you watched heal hundreds of people and who had just raised a man who had been dead four days? *How could anyone take Jesus' life? Why would they do it? We won't allow it!* Jesus and the twelve arrived in Bethany on Friday afternoon, the eighth of *Nisan* (March 31, 30 AD). This is six days before the Passover and one week before His crucifixion.[2] This would be the fourth Passover Jesus has attended during His ministry. The Chief Priests and Pharisees want to seize Him now![3] They want nothing to do with a religious trial during Passover. Yet, Jesus will be crucified on Friday, the fifteenth of Nisan (April 7th), the exact time the *lamb* will be sacrificed in the Temple. This is not coincidental as we'll see.

Zachariah prophesied that the Messiah would enter Jerusalem on a young donkey that had never been ridden.[4] An interesting footnote: After the Jews were released by King Cyrus in Babylon to return and rebuild the Temple and the walls in Jerusalem, they became lethargic during their years of laboring there. It was Zachariah that God sent to encourage the workers. He told them to *take heart* because one day the Messiah would ride a donkey along this very wall that they were currently re-building.

Jesus begins His ride through the city. The crowds were huge as Passover approached. The disciples drape their garments over the donkey's back and the multitudes spread their coats and tear palm branches from the trees and put them in the road before Jesus.

If you were a Jew at that time you would know to do this from Moses' instructions fifteen hundred years prior.[5] From in front and behind the people shout, "Hosanna"[6] meaning, *God save us.* They believed that this was the beginning of the Messianic Kingdom where God would rule rather than the Romans.

It appears that the multitudes are completely convinced that Jesus is the long-awaited Messiah. The Jewish leaders should be elated, but instead, they are scared and angry. They plot to get rid of Him. But are the crowds truly with Him? We'll see ...

---

[1]Matt. 20:17–19   [2]John 12:1   [3]John 11:57   [4]Zech. 9:9; Matt. 21:8
[5]Lev. 23:40   [6]Matt. 21:8

The Truth Behind the Adoring Crowd

"Seeing a fig tree by the road, He went up to it but found nothing on it but leaves. Then He said to it, 'May you never bear fruit again.' Immediately the tree withered." Matthew 21:18–19 (NIV)

We have all witnessed crowd mentality whether it was at a big sporting event, a political rally or some gathering that heightened everyone's emotions. We have seen the pandemonium of European soccer events where dozens of people are injured and even killed. Hitler was a master at whipping up a crowd. We have witnessed political rallies on television where angry mobs have resonated hateful chants for or against a political rival.

When Jesus rode through Jerusalem on a young donkey, local Jews, as well as pilgrims who came from other districts, knew from the Scripture and Rabbinic teaching that this is the way the Messiah would enter. They yell Hosanna (God save us) and it appears to be a genuine expression of excitement that the time had finally come.

That night, Jesus and the twelve apparently stay in Bethany at the home of Lazarus and his sisters. When Jesus and the twelve leave Bethany the next morning for the three-mile walk to Jerusalem, Jesus walks over to a fig tree with full green leaves. It looks healthy, but to the disciple's dismay, He curses the tree and when they return later that day, they are startled that it had withered and died. Puzzling to them was that it was six weeks prior to the time for figs to ripen. A healthy fig tree will produce small, *pea-sized* nodules that are edible, but Jesus saw that there were none there. Jesus is painting a graphic picture for the disciples that just as the tree was, by its green leaves, making a false proclamation about its health, the crowds were doing the same by their shouts of Hosanna." Though appearing to accept Jesus as Messiah, this is the same crowd will in four days shout, "Crucify Him" when Pilate beckons to the crowd after His trial.[1]

Have you ever become so caught up in the moment that you said something you weren't sure you really believed? All may have seemed right to the multitudes at the time, but the influence of the Pharisees was so great that they could not keep their footing. The Jewish leaders had been their *shepherd* and, as false a shepherd as they were, the people could not re-boot and accept Jesus as the Good Shepherd who would provide them with *Living Water.*

---

[1]Matt. 27:22

The Passover Lamb is Examined

Exodus 12:3–6

Though Jesus had only a few days to live He wanted to prepare the disciples for the deception and hatred that awaited them after His death. He will continue to teach these young men even as He hung on the cross. But the fig tree cursing was a visual picture of what they will face for the rest of their lives. People will say what they don't mean, they will disappoint and deceive. Jesus will teach them that faith can move mountains if they trust God and that they must forgive those who betray them along the way.[1]

For the next four days, until His arrest, Jesus will continue to teach as He undergoes intense scrutiny and examination by the Jewish leaders. On a human level, we wonder why they didn't just arrest Jesus at will. Fear of the crowds was the human reason. Rome would have stripped any authority they enjoyed if a riot started during Passover. From a spiritual standpoint, Jesus' safety during these days was strictly due to God's sovereignty.

The multitudes are still flocking to Jesus and the Pharisees want to somehow discredit Him in their presence. They ask a series of questions trying to trap Him. They first question Him as He teaches on the matter of authority, for according to Pharisaic theology no teaching was authoritative unless it had been sanctioned by the Rabbis.[2] They try to imply tax evasion by asking if it was right to pay taxes to Caesar.[3] The Sadducees ask Him to solve a long-running debate with the Pharisees about marriage in heaven and he leaves them speechless by saying, "they neither understand the Scriptures nor the power of God."[4] They ask him about his position on divorce hoping he will insight the crowd. One by one the questions fail to hit their mark. In Exodus, Moses required that the Passover lamb was to be put up on the tenth of the month and observed until the fourteenth to ensure that it was flawless for sacrifice.[5] Jesus enters Jerusalem on the tenth of Nisan and undergoes intense observation and questioning by the Jewish leaders as we have seen. From then on, "no one dared ask any more questions."[6] This means that Jesus was the flawless Lamb of God … but they will condemn Him to death anyway.

These leaders suffered from classic cognitive dissonance. They knew what he said was true but refused to believe it because it was uncomfortable and inconvenient to do so? All of this was also God's plan and they didn't know it.

---

[1]Mark 11:22–26   [2]Matt. 21:23–27   [3]Mark 12:13–14   [4]Mark 12:19–23
[5]Exod. 12:3–6   [6]Mark 12:34b

377

The Day Before Jesus' Arrest

Matthew 26: 6–16

In His last public address to the crowds, Jesus takes dead aim at the Pharisees, blasting their theology and attacking their incompetent and dangerous brand of leadership. He contrasts them with a true servant leader.[1] Jesus will then discuss with the disciples the destruction that is to come, referring to the fall of Jerusalem in 70 AD. They will ask Him questions about His return and what will happen in the last days in Matthew 24—25. He will again discuss His crucifixion with them and later in the home of Simon a pivotal circumstance occurs. Mary, the sister of Lazarus anoints Jesus with expensive oils. She is preparing Him for His burial. The disciples are incensed, especially Judas who considers it a waste of money.[2] I believe this is the straw that broke the camel's back for Judas because soon after this he cut a deal with the Jewish leaders.[3] He will turn on Jesus for thirty pieces of silver. In perspective, thirty pieces of silver was the value of a dead slave that had been gored by an ox.[4] According to Zechariah, this was the price of God's value to the people.[5] It was also a way of indicating a "trifling amount."

Why does Mary know what the disciples don't? She sat at His feet. Serving God is important, but it can't replace intimacy with Him. This is the source of wisdom. Jesus says what Mary did will always be her legacy, wherever and whenever this story is told. Think of that; it was this act of devotion on which Jesus shines a bright light, not the sins of her past! This is the way God thinks.

On Thursday afternoon Jesus sends Peter and John to prepare for the Passover meal. The Seder meal is very important to Jews. Every part of the meal and the ingredients used has great significance in the remembrance of their journey out of Egypt and the bonds of slavery. From the first cup of wine, *"the cup of blessing,"* to the eating of a green vegetable dipped in saltwater and *the breaking of the middle matzah*, every nuance of the meal holds significance. Even their reclining around the table speaks of freedom. Slaves in Egypt were made to stand while eating.

It was early in the meal that Jesus girded Himself with a towel and washed the disciple's feet. He knew that Satan had put it in the heart of Judas to betray Him, but he even washed his betrayer's feet. He was secure in who he was. Judas soon departs to prepare for his betrayal. Jesus tries to comfort the disciples telling them He would not leave them alone but will send the Holy Spirit.[6] This was their security and it is ours as well.

---

[1]Matt. 23:1–39 [2]Matt. 26:7–8 [3]Matt. 26:14–16 [4]Exod. 21:32
[5]Zech. 11:12–13 [6]John 14:1–7

The Walk to Gethsemane

John 15–17

Judas has left the Passover meal ostensibly to buy supplies, but he is meeting with the Jewish Leaders. They need an insider to identify Jesus as they seek to take him at night. They want to manipulate circumstances where He could be arrested in a private setting. They need Judas to bring an indictment against Him so that Pilate can order a cohort of Roman soldiers to apprehend Him. They also need him to be an official witness for Jesus' *civil trial*.[1]

Meanwhile, Jesus continues to teach the eleven as they leave the upper room and begin the walk down through the Kidron Valley to the Mount of Olives. John 15 and 16 are called the Olivet Discourse because He teaches as they walk there. The Hillside is ablaze with campfires dotting the landscape. Over 200,000 have come for Passover and will camp out wherever there is room.

It is Thursday night (Jewish Friday, in that each new day begins at sundown). Jesus has only a few hours before He will be arrested. What will be His final words to the disciples? What would be your final words to those you love the most? Notice in these chapters Jesus does not give a *How-to* sermon. He does not teach *Seven Ways to Win the World*. Everything He speaks of is about relationships … with God, each other and the world. He begins, "I am the vine and you are the branches." He teaches about abiding in the Vine.[2] Then He tells them that the bond between them must be unbreakable.[3] He tells them that the anger the world vented on Him would now be aimed at them but that the Truth will sustain them.[4] Finally, in John 16 Jesus reminds them of the sustaining power of the Holy Spirit. He will teach them all they need to know,[5] and in time their grief will turn to joy.[6]

Now Jesus needs time alone with His Father. He needs this time more than the air He breathes. He will pray for His disciples and for all believers. It is a time of great stress and the Father will send an angel to comfort Him.[7] He prays that this "Cup" might be taken away but submits His will to that of His Father. The disciples follow Jesus to the place where He will be betrayed. Gethsemane is where olives were pressed to make olive oil. Jesus is being pressed in a manner, not unlike the olives.

They can hear the cohort of soldiers and see the line of torches as they ascend to the Mount of Olives to make their arrest. Taking a deep breath, Jesus walks out to meet His accuser.

---

[1]Luke 22:3–6   [2]John 15:1–11   [3]John 15:12–17   [4]John 15:18–21
[5]John 16:13   [6]John 16:22   [7]Luke 22:43

The Betrayal and Arrest of Jesus

"Jesus, knowing all that was going to happen to Him, went out and asked them Who is it you want? Jesus of Nazareth, they replied. I am He, Jesus said."
Matthew 14:47–67 (NIV); see also John 18:2–12

After Judas was paid by Caiaphas, he was sent to Pilate to convince him, as an insider, that Jesus was not simply a religious radical, but was a threat to Rome. The Jews knew Pilate couldn't care less about His claim to be God's Son, but if He posed a threat to Roman sovereignty, He posed a threat to Pilate. Because of the enormous crowds, Pilate agreed to send a large contingent of soldiers to arrest Jesus in case there was mob violence. But Jesus had no intention of resisting.

Logistically, the Jewish leaders have a nightmare on their hands. They must get Jesus arrested, tried, executed and in the ground by sundown on Friday before the Sabbath and Passover begin. Impossible! What stands in their way are the Jewish Laws that require up to three days for these proceedings. The Pharisees were sworn to protect the Jewish Laws at all cost. It was their reason for being. What they will do is to break twenty-two laws in order to get Jesus on the cross by 9 am. This is how desperate they are to rid themselves of what they perceive as a great threat to their power and prestige. Jesus walks out to meet the soldiers and identifies Himself.[1] Chronologically, Judas' kiss of betrayal comes after Jesus had

already said, "I am He." This underlines the level of his hypocrisy. Jesus asks that His disciples be allowed to go free and the soldiers comply. Jesus is taken to Annas, the Father-in-law of Caiaphas.[2] Annas' hatred is obvious but after questioning Jesus he is unable to produce a legitimate crime He has committed. He sends Him to Caiaphas' Palace for His religious trail in front of the Sanhedrin.

Meanwhile, John, whose family knew the High Priest, gains entrance to the palace courtyard. Apparently, John was the reason Peter was able to get in as well. His three denials take place there, in the courtyard, amid a large group of people waiting for the trial to end.

Jesus is brought in for His religious trial[3] which is a sham. False witnesses are presented whose testimony is contradictory and Caiaphas breaks one Jewish Law after another to accomplish his goal. Finally, the Sanhedrin officially condemns Jesus for blasphemy in declaring Himself God's Son.[4] He will now be sent to Pilate for His civil trial.

Great was the Jewish Leader's respect for the Law, but greater still was their hatred of Jesus and obsession to kill Him.

---

[1] John 18:4–9   [2] John 18:12–14; 19–24   [3] Matt. 26:57–68   [4] Matt. 27:1

Jesus' Civil Trial Before Pilate

Mark 14:53–65

While a great drama is unfolding at Caiaphas' Palace, across the city, a tortured soul is learning that a guilty conscience never takes a holiday. Judas has tried to return the blood money to Caiaphas, but it is too late; his remorse was not true repentance and the guilt is more than he can live with. He hangs himself.[1] At dawn, the body is discovered, but a dead body by law cannot remain in the city limits during Passover. Judas' corpse is thrown down into the Hinnom Valley until after the festival.

Now, Jesus is taken to Pilate, where He will be judged according to Roman Civil Law. Pilate demands a formal charge by the accusing witness. This is a problem because their key witness is lying somewhere in the Hinnom Valley. Pilate tells the Jews to judge Jesus themselves. But they cannot enact the death penalty, so they make up their own charges saying that *he is "subverting our nation, He opposes paying taxes and claims to be a king."*[2] Pilate questions Jesus privately but is interested only in whether He has political aspirations. Jesus says that His kingdom is not of this world and Pilate finds no guilt in Him.[3]

Pilate had a hidden agenda. He was appointed Procurator by a man named Sejanus, the Chief Administrator of the Roman Empire. Sejanus hated the Jews and He appointed Pilate because he hated the Jews as well. Sejanus is caught in a plot to overthrow the Emperor Tiberius and is tried for treason. Rome is, therefore, watching Pilate closely because of their relationship. Pilate wants no part of what he considers a Jewish squabble.

The Procurator is amazed that Jesus will not defend Himself, but as he listens, one phrase from the Jewish accusers is music to His ears. "He stirs up the people all over Judea with His teaching starting in *Galilee.*"[4] The magic word ... *Galilee.* Who oversees Galilee? Herod Antipas! Pilate now thinks he can extricate himself from this whole mess by sending Jesus over to Herod's palace. It doesn't work,and Herod sends Jesus back to Pilate. He figures that if He scourges Jesus, it will satisfy the Jews. But they want Jesus on the cross and from God's point of view, it is an absolute necessity.

Remembering a Jewish tradition, Pilate goes before the crowd and offers a prisoner to be released on Passover. The crowd, prompted by the Jewish leaders asks for Barabbas, a prisoner charged with sedition against Rome.[5] Despite Pilate's wife warning him about a dream she had concerning Jesus being "a righteous man," Pilate sends Him to be scourged and crucified.

---

[1]Matt. 27:3–10   [2]Luke 23:2   [3]John 18:33–38   [4]Luke 23:5   [5]Mark 15:6–7

The Walk to the Cross

Jesus had to be on the cross by 9 am on Friday, the fifteenth of Nisan (April 7) 30 AD. He must be crucified; He must be executed and die and His death would be substitutionary (His righteousness for our sin). This and many other prophecies had to be fulfilled and God chose people like Caiaphas and Pilate to accomplish this. He knew their personalities, their weaknesses, and their proclivities and He used them to accomplish the greatest victory known to man.

Jesus is beaten unmercifully by a Roman lictor. He is mocked and humiliated as the soldiers put a robe on his bleeding back and a crown of thorns on His head. They replace the robe with his own seamless garment and march Him through the streets carrying his own cross to Golgotha. Women weep as He passes, and He falls under the weight of the cross. A man named Simon, from North Africa, is enlisted to help him. As they reach "Skull Hill" Jesus is laid on the cross and spikes are driven into his hands and feet. His body is lifted up and the cross dropped into a hole.

It is 9 am as the cross is set in place. At that exact moment, the Chagigah sacrifice takes place in the Temple. The Lamb is sacrificed for the sins of the world. Jesus will be on the cross for six hours. The first three will cause intense physical pain but during the second three hours, darkness will cover the earth and the excruciating pain will be overcome by a level of spiritual pain no human being will ever know. God eclipsed the sun so that He and *His* Son could privately endure separation from one another. When Jesus cries out, "My God, my God, why have you forsaken me?" God had to turn his back on His own Son as the sins of the world were poured into Him. Jesus died spiritually! He was no longer *one* with His Father. It is the only time He ever referred to His Father as "God." The intimacy was severed.

Even in His pain, Jesus had given the promise of eternal life to a thief on a cross beside Him.[1] He thought of His mother's need to be cared for and asked John to be a son to her.[2] He thought of his enemies and asked God to forgive them.[3]

At 3 pm, Jesus entrusts His soul into His Father's hands and says, "It is finished." His head dropped forward and it truly was finished ... everything needed for a human being to live a life of freedom and abundance was made available in these moments. "He made Him who knew no sin to be sin."[4] The victory was won, the mission was accomplished and the union of the Father and the Son was restored. That was just the beginning ...

---

[1]Luke 23:42–43   [2]John 19:26, 27   [3]Luke 23:34   [4]2 Cor. 5:21

Unprecedented Things that Happened

On the day that Jesus died, we know from all four gospel writers that a strange darkness covered the earth. This is documented historically. A scientist in Egypt, named Diogenes, wrote that he saw "solar darkness of such like that either the deity Himself suffered at that moment or sympathized with one that did." Another writer, Phlegon, of a place called Tralles, wrote that in the fourth year of the Two hundred and second Olympiad, which is roughly 30 AD: "there was a great and remarkable eclipse of the sun above any that had happened before."

In my study of Jewish history and culture and how it fits within the biblical narrative, I am aware of recorded facts in various texts that affirm the fact that something unique happened on the 7th of April, 30 AD. These events are not in the Scripture, but they were recorded by unredeemed Jews who would have no reason or desire to affirm what the gospel writers wrote, yet they do.

The doors of the Temple mysteriously opened by themselves

Josephus wrote, "*the eastern gate of the inner [court of the] temple, which was of brass, and vastly heavy, and had been with difficulty shut by twenty men, and rested upon a basis armed with iron, and had bolts fastened very deep into the firm floor, which was there made of one entire stone, was seen to be opened of its own accord about the sixth hour of the night.*"

The Middle Lamp of the Menorah Mysteriously Extinguished

In the Holy of Holies of the Temple, the Menorah or Golden Lampstand had 7 branches; each held a lamp. The center lamp was called the *Ner Elohim* and provided light for the holy place.

The Talmud says, *The "Ner Elohim" (I Sam. iii. 3), was left burning all day and was refilled in the evening. It served to light all the lamps. The Ner Elohim contained no more oil than the other lamps, a half-log measure enough to last during the longest winter night (Men. 89a); yet by a miracle that lamp regularly burned till the following evening (ib. 86b). This miracle, however, ceased after the death of Simeon the Righteous, who was high priest forty years before the destruction of the Temple (Yoma 39b)* The Jewish Encyclopedia affirms that "the miracle of the middle lamp" was never again able to be lit.

It is not coincidental that Jesus is seen standing in the middle of a golden Lamp Stand Rev.1:9-16. His eyes are like flames of fire. His face like the sun shining in its strength.

There were several other fascinating occurrences like this that attest to the fact that something happened on that Friday afternoon that is unprecedented in human history.

The Aftershock and the Burial

After taunting and gawking for an entire day, the multitudes slowly began to dissipate and make their way back to their dwelling to prepare for Passover. Under Jewish Law, a corpse was to be buried on the day of death so the land could remain undefiled.[1] It was late afternoon on Friday, the day of preparation for the Sabbath at sundown. The Jews approached Pilate to ask that the legs of the crucified be broken to speed up the death process. Pushing upward with the legs was the only way to open the lungs to breathe and to break them would cause a person to suffocate. The two thieves' legs were broken, but they found that Jesus was already dead fulfilling the Scripture[2].

A man named Joseph of Arimathea requests Jesus' Body for burial.[3] He was a prominent member of the Sanhedrin who was a secret disciple of Jesus; a good and righteous man who voted against condemning Jesus. He is joined by Nicodemus, also a Sanhedrin secret believer. They take Jesus' body to Joseph's family tomb for burial preparation.[4] Jesus' mother and Mary Magdalene watch from a distance and then leave to prepare spices before the Sabbath. They honor the commandments and wait until after the Sabbath to return to the tomb.

Remembering Jesus' words that He would rise in three days, the Jewish leaders fear that the disciples would try to steal the body. They request a guard unit to ensure against it. Pilate agrees and a Roman seal is placed over the entrance.[5] To break it was punishable by death.

The women had seen the two men prepare Jesus for burial but apparently felt their efforts were not adequate, (My wife would have done the same) and after Sabbath ends, they return with spices to do the job *correctly*. The women are on their way to the tomb before dawn on Sunday morning. While they are in route, an angel appears, rolls the stone away and the guards shake with fear and are catatonic, like dead men.[6]

The disciples are scattered and weeping because they cannot process their master's death. The unredeemed Jews, however, rejoice because they think they have rid themselves of a fraud. Their lack of wisdom illustrates, in King Solomon's words, "the end of joy may be grief."[7] This will surely be the case, for in forty years (70 AD) that generation of Jews and their children will be slaughtered in Jerusalem by the Roman army.

---

[1]Deut. 21:23   [2]John 19:31–33; Num. 9:12; Ps. 34:20   [3]Mark 15:43–45
[4]John 19:38–42; Luke 23:50–51   [5]Matt.27:64–66   [6]Matt. 28:2–4   [7]Prov. 14:13

He Has Risen!

John 20:2–18

It was just before dawn on Sunday morning. Mary Magdalene, Mary the mother of James and Salome brought spices to anoint Jesus.[1] Apparently, Mary Magdalene ran ahead of the others because John tells us that she arrived alone and is startled at what she sees.[2] The stone had been rolled away. She assumes the body had been stolen and hurries to tell Peter and John. They run to the tomb to see for themselves. Meanwhile, the other women arrive at the tomb after the sun had risen.[3] They see that the large stone had been rolled away and they look inside. There are two angels there. Mary Magdalene had apparently not looked inside and seen the angels. They tell the women that Jesus has risen and gone ahead of them to Galilee and will see them there.[4] The women are fearful, but with great joy, they hurry off to tell the other nine disciples.[5]

Consider for a moment the immensity of what is happening to these faithful friends. Their world had collapsed as Jesus was arrested and then executed. The fear and confusion of how to carry on without Him must have been devastating. Now the nine disciples, who are crouching in fear, do not believe the women who come to tell them that Jesus has risen.

In that culture, at that time, their skepticism was simply because *women* told them. Oral Laws (not the Scripture) put many restrictions on what women could say in a court of law. No one seeking to create a hoax would have made women the key witness, as their testimony would not be valid in a court of law.

Peter and John sprint toward the tomb. John runs faster, reaches the tomb and sees the linen wrappings but does not go in. Peter arrives, goes past John and enters the tomb. He sees the graveclothes and is stunned by what he sees.[6] Why? The grave-clothes had been hardened by the spices and forming a *plaster-like* cast. Jesus had resurrected through the wrappings. Luke says Peter "marveled" at what he saw, but apparently was still was in limbo.[7]

Peter and John return to their lodging and the women return to the tomb probably frustrated that the nine disciples did not believe them. Mary Magdalene enters and, in a very dramatic encounter, breaks into tears. A man whom she assumes is a gardener comforts her but she turns around and realizes she is speaking with Jesus.[8]

This is the first of ten appearances Jesus will make before He ascends to heaven.

---

[1]Mark 16:1 [2]John 20:1–2 [3]Mark 16:2 [4]Matt. 28:5–7;
Luke 24:5–6 [5]Matt. 28:8 [6]John. 20:6–8 [7]Luke 24:12 [8]John 20:11–17b

The Resurrected Christ: The Final Commission

The women, along with John, the youngest disciple, are convinced that Jesus has risen. Peter is almost there, and the remaining disciples are skeptical. The Roman guards, who witnessed the angels moving the stone, had gone to the Jewish leaders, not Pilate, and reported what had happened. The Chief Priest and elders concoct a lie and pay the soldiers to say that the disciples stole the body while they slept and that the Sanhedrin would cover for them if Pilate found out.[1] I'm not sure how they could know the disciples stole the body if they were asleep, but this notion is believed by many Jews today.

Jesus will appear before two men as they walk along to Emmaus and talk about all that has happened. They do not recognize Him until He begins to teach them about the Messiah and, suddenly, they knew and "their heart burned within them."[2] They return to Jerusalem and tell the eleven what had happened. At this point, the disciples thought He had only risen spiritually.[3] We know from Paul's letter to the Corinthians that Jesus appeared to Peter first, before the other disciples.[4] This shows the remarkable compassion and forgiveness of Jesus in the face of Peter's three glaring denials. Jesus had already intentionally forgotten them!

Jesus will appear to the ten disciples, minus Thomas, and they finally believe.[5] They tell Thomas, but he is a pragmatic young man and wants to see for Himself.[6] Notice that Thomas said, "Unless I see and touch the wounds in His hands and feet, I will not believe."

It's not that he couldn't believe, it was that he wouldn't. It was an issue of his will. It is not that people need more information; belief is a matter of your will. Jesus comes to him and holds out his pierced hands and offered Thomas the chance to satisfy his doubt. He never touches the wounds, but falls on his face and says, "My Lord and my God."[7]

The disciples had been told to meet Jesus in Galilee three different times and they had not yet gone. I love the reason we discover they did not go even after ten of them believed. They would not leave without their brother, Thomas. I have to believe that even though they had ignored His command the first two times, this last time I think He loved the fact that they would not move ahead with one of their companions not yet on board.

Jesus will make several more appearances including one to 500 people on a mountain in Galilee.[8] He will commission these men to take his *Name* to the entire world;[9] to *tell the story and present the Savior.* Only then does He ascend back to His Father.

---

[1] Matt. 28:11–15   [2] Luke 24:32   [3] Mark 16:13b   [4] 1 Cor. 15:5
[5] Luke 24:41–43   [6] John 20:24–25   [7] John 20:26–31   [8] Matt. 28:19   [9] 1 Cor. 15:6

Some Reflections on the First Easter

"If Christ has not been raised, your faith is worthless; you are still in your sins. Then those also who have fallen asleep in Christ have perished. If we have hope in Christ in this life only, we are of all men most to be pitied." 1 Corinthians 15:17–19

How did the multitudes conclude Jesus was guilty? Their leaders told them. They had shouted "Hosanna" during His Triumphal Entry, but they drew their conclusion because they had been persuaded by leaders who lacked any level of wisdom. The people then cried, "Let His blood be on us and on our children."[1]

It was only after I became a parent that the full force of this horrifying crowd hysteria leveled me. You will never hear anything more perverted than that! The multitudes had been so brainwashed by their leaders that they were willing to gamble, not only their lives but the lives of their children, on the words of self-absorbed, elitist religious leaders. *If we are wrong, let our kids pay the price … and they did in 70 AD when the Romans decimated Jerusalem and 1.1 million Jews died. Many were the sons and grandchildren of those in the crowd.*

Many have tried to disprove the resurrection, and all have failed. Scores of them have come to faith by looking at the facts that we know. There is *the swoon theory* where they try to say Jesus only fainted and did not die. But, consider the Roman punishment of scourging and crucifixion. When you also consider that Jesus had no food or water since Thursday at the Passover meal, no sleep for three nights, a spear thrust in His side and was laid in a tomb with approximately a hundred pounds of spices over him, it becomes more than absurd.

The idea that the disciples stole the body is just as fanciful; they were mostly teenage boys. They ran in all directions after Jesus was arrested and hid until the women came and told them Jesus had risen. For them to have snuck by the Roman guards, push a huge stone up an incline to enter the tomb and carry Jesus out without being seen is ridiculous.

On and on the theories go with one basic motive in mind … if it can be proven that Jesus was not God, they are free to live however they please without any fear of consequences. If there is no Moral Authority, then there is no right and wrong and you can follow the dictates of your own desires. Our lifestyle would then inform our morality because *I create my own standards and you create yours.* If they clash, it is simply survival of the fittest.

I believe the biblical story of Easter, not simply because I am compelled by the evidence, but because I want to believe it. The evidence is there, but faith is ultimately an act of your will.

---

[1] Matt. 27:25

We hope you have enjoyed this book!

Please visit

nebhayden.com

for the best price on additional copies of this book

to arrange for Neb to speak

or to contact him